The Social Novel in England 1830–1850

I/. Rich & Poor

II/- Not so sple (see §46's statem...

since = & Trafford

a Sy>. Second part & the

landowners & then enters rich circle

III/-

The Social Novel in England 1830-1850

Dickens Disraeli Mrs Gaskell Kingsley

Louis Cazamian

Translated, with a Foreword, by

Martin Fido

Department of English, University of Leeds

Routledge & Kegan Paul
London and Boston

Translated from Le Roman social en Angleterre (1903)
First published in Great Britain in 1973
by Routledge & Kegan Paul Ltd
Broadway House, 68–74 Carter Lane,
London EC4V 5EL and
9 Park Street,
Boston, Mass. 02108, U.S.A.
Printed in Great Britain by
W & J Mackay Limited, Chatham
© Routledge & Kegan Paul 1973

ISBN 0 7100 7282 1

Contents

Contents

Contents

Translator's foreword

Cazamian's *Le Roman social en Angleterre*, still after almost seventy years unrivalled in its field, has a double advantage of distance. It was written in France. And it is now as distant from us in time as the books it deals with were from Cazamian himself. We do not expect a foreigner from the turn of the century to have a declared interest in one side or the other of nineteenth-century English social life, and this is extremely useful when the subject dealt with is as sensitive as the rise of the labour movement, and the division between early radicals and idealists. Cazamian's occasional notes of personal bias – his belief that Disraeli was a cold and unpleasant person, for example, or his view that Victorian society would have been utterly detestable were it not for the presence in it of idealistic interventionists – can neither offend nor distract the reader today.

Its very foreignness provides the book's great strength. English critics tend to work empirically. We analyse a novel, and assume that what we discover within it tells us almost all we need to know about the writer's outlook. Arnold Kettle, Raymond Williams, and John Lucas are only three critics who have described and assessed individual social novels far more cogently than Cazamian ever did. But as a rule we are far less confident in grasping broad movements and sweeping intellectual trends. An English critic is likely to leave his reader enthusiastically determined to read a particular novel again and get the best out of it, but he is unlikely to go very far in relating it to a clear understanding of the thought of the society that produced it. Here Cazamian comes into his own. Although he devotes a good deal of space to analysing individual novels, his real subject is the intellectual movement linking one book to another. He forces us to perceive and understand a nationwide reaction against Benthamite utilitarianism, and to see how each novelist under consideration was influenced by it and influenced it.

Of course, this approach is sufficiently un-English to present us with some difficulties. The 'English nineteenth-century idealistic and interventionist reaction' is not a part of our mental furniture, and we may be daunted by such a broad vision of a group of writers. We are, as a matter of fact, much better at seeing trees than woods. But the woods can help us to understand how the trees grow, and once Cazamian has made clear the importance of idealism, reactionary conservatism, and interventionism in his key term, our understanding of Dickens, Disraeli, Mrs Gaskell and Kingsley is enhanced.

Cazamian paints his picture in bold strokes, and this creates stylistic problems. 'Idealism', for example, is a word he uses more colloquially than philosophically, and he allows 'reaction' to mean resistance to new impositions or a wish to impose bygone conditions as suits his purpose. 'Democratic' means egalitarian more often than not in his vocabulary, and 'socialist' is a term of infinite flexibility. He compensates for this confident imprecision by the use of repetition and dramatic phraseology, which have made his style notorious. As it seemed more important that his essential meaning should be conveyed readably than that a perfect impression of the original book should be re-created, I have fairly ruthlessly cut repetitions, rearranged sentences within paragraphs, and abandoned his phraseology whenever this seemed necessary.

Time has had a harsher effect on Cazamian's critical judgements. It does not much matter that he assumed there was no topical satire in *The Beggar's Opera* or *Jonathan Wilde*; nor does his overrating of Kingsley matter greatly; indeed, it might stimulate us to ask whether we do not slightly underrate a writer who is always vigorous and energetic. His view of Dickens's good characters as markedly superior creations to his comic villains is startling, but does not seriously affect his main thesis. But his Chestertonian belief that late Dickens is of little value is crucial. The 'Carol philosophy' as Dickens called it, which takes up Cazamian's fourth chapter, is essential to an understanding of his social and moral view of life, no matter how unfashionable his Christmas jollity may be today. But equally, we cannot disregard the sombre, pessimistic view of society presented in the late novels without misrepresenting Dickens. And this Cazamian does.

This oversight blinds him to one of the most curious features of the broad pattern of the social novel: the way in which Dickens worked against the trend, meeting his contemporaries on the same ground around 1850, and then stepping chiastically onto territory they had abandoned, while they moved into his earlier terrain. As Cazamian shows, early nineteenth-century social fiction attacked the whole structure of society, and condemned its injustice, even though it might do this with all the flippancy and superficiality of Bulwer's *Paul Clifford*, or the spurious claims to moral comment of 'Silver Fork' writers. But in his early days Dickens did not see the whole social organism as unhealthy: contrary to

Orwell's statement, he did indeed think that the spots (workhouses, Yorkshire schools) could be cured by cutting them off. And, as Cazamian shows again, he enjoyed some remarkable practical successes. By 1850 industrialism was beginning to appear as a 'spot' to be cut off, and in *Hard Times* Dickens showed his growing awareness that it would not respond to such simple treatment. It was 'all a muddle', and he was at one with his fellow novelists in fearing the revolutionary cure as much as, or more than, the evils that had invoked it. Yet when trade improved in the 1850s he did not join those writers of the younger generation whom he had influenced, and who faced society confidently while they attacked local abuses. Reade might protest about a prison here, an asylum there; Collins might query the legitimacy laws and the social treatment of prostitutes; Dickens had reverted to the nation's earlier view of society as terrifyingly corrupt, mismanaged, and neglectful of its duties. Individuals might more or less redeem themselves through love, but even they could hardly hope to escape all tarnish of the prisons and dust-heaps that symbolised the social organism. Of course he was profounder, more powerful, and less of a practical reformer than the early nineteenth-century forerunners of the Victorian social novelists. But it remains true that the novel began the century by dealing with a diseased society, and trailed off into attacking specific sectional disorders by the 1860s, while Dickens moved in the opposite direction.

This critical limitation of Cazamian's book does, to some extent, set it back in the period when it was written. It has therefore seemed reasonable to leave his documentation and bibliography more or less as they originally stood, as evidence of the material available to him, rather than to suggest more up-to-date sources. Error does not deserve the same respect, and I have silently corrected numerous mistranscriptions and misdirections in the footnotes. This does not mean that every reference has been checked; only those where obvious error or direct quotation necessitated examination may have been corrected. I have occasionally changed dates and places of publication so that correct references might be given to the editions available to me from which I transcribed. Similarly, ease of access encouraged me to give references to Bulwer Lytton's *Life* by his grandson rather than that by his son wherever the wording was unchanged. On the two occasions where passages quoted by Cazamian have proved impossible to trace, I have provided the English version given in his edition of 1903, together with his reference, and the added note that the passage will not in fact be found in the work he names. The evidence of Joseph Hebergam (not, as in all previous editions, Habergam) on p. 67 has been taken direct from the Sadler Report, as it does not occur on the pages of Cooke-Taylor cited by Cazamian, nor have I been able to trace it anywhere else in his writings. I have, to date, been unable to obtain a copy of *Judge Lynch of America: his Two Letters to Charles Dickens*, and so I have substituted a translation in reported speech for Cazamian's translation in direct speech from this work. I have silently absorbed into the text footnotes containing afterthoughts which fit into the flow of the argument, and omitted those which expound commonplace details of English life for the benefit of French readers. Some additional information (usually places or dates of publication) has been given in the bibliography, but no entries have been added or subtracted, and there has been no serious attempt to bring the apparatus into line with modern standards of detail and consistency. The division into two volumes bore no relation to any division in the text and has traditionally been swept aside by English bookbinding, and so I have ignored it and presented eight consecutive chapters without a break after chapter 4.

Cazamian's rather tentative Introduction shows how much of a pioneering work *Le Roman social en Angleterre* was in 1903, and as such it would have been well worth reprinting. In fact it remains a work of great importance, the standard study of its subject, and one whose view of Victorian fiction could well be allowed more influence than it has normally been granted in England.

I am indebted to Miss Alison Hodgson for her extremely thorough and helpful editorial reading of my manuscript. Routledge's editorial staff have also tried to bring greater accuracy and consistency to my work, as well as Cazamian's. But I am responsible for such error as remains. Mr and Mrs Arne Gordon and Mr and Mrs Hugh Fido kindly put me up when I had to consult libraries at a distance from Leeds, and Mrs Helga Hanks prepared the index. My wife, mother, and daughters helped me correct proofs.

Leeds   Martin Fido

Introduction

The subject

This study attempts to examine the psychological working of a section of social history. Its subject is an intellectual movement. It sets out to understand cause and effect in a group of literary works. Its starting point and justification is the relation between literary and social evolution, and in turn it may shed some light on that relationship. The history of England in the nineteenth century is taken as the working basis for the study, which then has to conform to the framework and chronological limits of this period.

Victoria's reign began in 1837, but in all respects that of William IV (1830–7) is inseparable from it. After 1830 the progress of liberal ideas and the aftermath of the July Revolution made the Reform Act of 1832 inevitable: the years 1830 and 1832 mark the birth of a new England.

The long and prosperous development which followed may be divided into three sections. Quite apart from historical research, popular opinion has recognised this division: we usually speak of the early-, middle-, and late-Victorian periods. And these concepts represent a more precise actuality than their superficial sense suggests. To define this actuality we must find points of reference fixing the boundaries of the periods.

Political history readily supplies the first. 1848 saw a decisive crisis in England, as on the continent. 10 April and the end of Chartism closed one era and opened another. National life was changed, and men were aware of this. By contrast, the extension of the franchise in 1867, even if it really did inaugurate English democracy, was very far from shaking society to its foundations, and did not trouble the surface of the reign. On the contrary, it increased and strengthened that social optimism which characterised the mid-Victorian period. It is later that the appearance of a new spirit must be noted; round about 1880 the signs of economic depression and the reawakening of socialism disclose the advent of the third period.[1] We are only concerned in this study with the first.

It is not possible to attribute anything but a symbolic value to these dates. The more or less rapid transitions that they represent envelop and overlap them. The first phase of the Victorian era certainly did not end abruptly in 1848. The economic or moral factors which produce a new age do not take effect immediately. The rebirth of national prosperity, the principal of these elements, made its effects felt by degrees from about 1846 onwards. If Chartism was finished as far back as the middle of 1848, the minds of the ruling classes were not at rest until 1850 or 1851. The Exhibition of 1851, which disclosed to England the spectacle of her wealth, was an important agent of social appeasement. And at length the Crimean War in 1854 and 1855 opened a phase of public life dominated by foreign affairs. So it was between 1846 and 1855 that the early-Victorian period ended. If a symbolic point must be selected, 1850, the mid-point of the century, might mark the boundary between the two periods.

1830 to 1850, the period under consideration, was distinguished from the years that followed by strikingly contrasted domestic affairs. It was the revolutionary phase of the young English democracy, and the heroic age of socialism. The political problem partly resolved in 1832 reappeared in the activities of the classes still disenfranchised, and the social questions which appeared alongside it contracted a partial and poorly-defined alliance with it. It was a time of riots, bloody strikes, and violent clashes between capital and labour. Poverty and industrial troubles reached an unbearable pitch, and revolution seemed imminent. Society, still tinged with many traces of ancient barbarism, had to make an immense effort to raise its conduct to the level of its thought. Politically, England was indecisive and unsure of herself for a time. The series of reforms which exhausted the victorious bourgeoisie's positive programme left the country confused, while the sharp shocks indicating the presence of a new malaise caused alarm. The political parties were transformed, allying and dividing in unrecognisable combinations. Meanwhile, under the pressure of social need, there appeared the ideas and sentiments which were to renew English life. This was the germinal and creative phase wherein those ideas and movements developed which were to flower in succeeding periods. Until the end of the century, England lived off the intellectual substance of this troubled time.

By contrast, the period which followed was tranquil and confident. It fell into simple, harmonious patterns, and saw the splendour of the Victorian era develop magnificently. Material prosperity, intellectual optimism, enthusiastic or resigned anticipation of inevitable democracy – in a word, peaceful progress – was the character of England between 1850 and about 1880.[2]

We all know how trouble and discord reappeared at the close of the great reign. Renewed social crisis was the significant feature of that period. Between 1880 and 1900 problems that were believed to have been solved arose again.

We are examining one aspect of the intellectual movement which accompanied and expressed the social agitation between 1830 and 1850: namely, the formation of a new emotional and intellectual response to the subject of social relations on the part of English society in general, and the middle class in particular. This new outlook, curious in itself, owes its historical interest to its consequences. It influenced the theory and practice of relations between men. Its long-term effects are not yet exhausted; but we shall make only passing allusion to this as we study the results which immediately obtained. The documents selected for consideration will enable us to understand the rise of a compassionate interventionist spirit between 1830 and 1850, when humane or religious feelings, allied with self-interest, gave rise to the concept of society's corporate responsibility to all its members. The philanthropic reform of English social life: the restraint of violence inflamed by abject poverty, and the preservation of a threatened public order: these, together with the overturn of those theories by which social quietism had been justified, were the work of the movement of opinion in which Dickens and Kingsley participated. And whatever their part in it may have been, their writings make them of outstanding importance.

From this point of view it is possible to categorise the confused aspirations underlying the disarrayed ideas and interests of the time. The movement which we are examining belongs, together with the social struggle and the moral crisis, to the second term of an antithesis. The first term brought into conflict the partisans and adversaries of individualism. The *laissez-faire* principles of classical economists and the liberal bourgeoisie were opposed by a demand for both state and individual intervention, stemming from the needs of the proletariat and the malice of the landed gentry. It seemed that the two opposite poles around which temperament and interest might group men were on the one hand untrammelled liberty, and on the other regulated social relationships. In the intellectual sphere, rationalist doctrines and logical preferences were ranged against idealistic theories and emotional sympathies. And the second opposition was directly related to the first. The dominant feature of the thought of the time was the affinity of clear and systematic ideas with individualism, and of vague, emotional ones with social responsibility. Interventionism, one of whose sources we are studying, was intimately associated with the renewal of English idealism.

From 1830 to 1850 there was a general awakening of practical and moral activity for which the only proper epithet is 'idealistic'. The

Oxford Movement revitalised Anglicanism. In aesthetics, the feeling and desire for beauty were reanimated. In Carlyle's hands philosophy became intuitive and mystical; social charity and philanthropy took on the force of a national impulse. Certain common psychological characteristics can be found in all these movements: they tend to make sensation and emotion dominate the logical and abstract operations of the mind. We may justifiably consider them under one head and attribute to them a profound interior unity. And as their moral effects and social consequences are inseparable we may see them all as one movement, which might be described as 'the idealist and interventionist reaction'.

To identify this movement we shall have to examine the ideas and activities opposed to it: that is, the rationalist movement and individualism. But the heart of our investigation will, necessarily, be elsewhere, in that complex mixture of economic and psychological facts, class interests, and ethical preferences from which were assembled the practical solutions that England brought to the social problems of the time. We are studying the social aspect of the idealist and interventionist reaction.

The very nature of this movement gives a primary importance to literary documents. They are numerous. Carlyle's social writings are the most profound expression of the interior reaction which produced English interventionism. Although there were few socialists or economists capable of contradicting the classical liberal analysis of society, and the influence of such as there were was small, nonetheless they did exist, and should not be overlooked. Popular poems and Chartist literature form another class of documents, as do the writings which affirm the aristocratic ideal of feudal socialism. Finally, the novels of Dickens, Disraeli, and Kingsley are richly significant, and it is these which we have chosen to study.

One distinct type of novel emerged around 1830, and survived until the end of the century. It maintained a close relationship with political agitation, and its development mirrored the phases, and to some extent took on the pattern, of the Victorian era. The social 'novel with a purpose' appeared with the early-Victorian period in 1830, and until about 1850 exhibited characteristics analogous with it. Impassioned, challenging novels took as their subject the grave problems which concerned the whole of society, discussed them in their entirety, and proposed precise formulas or vague aspirations for the total reform of human relations. The novel took on the emotional tone and generous idealism of the age in which dying Romanticism found a new lease of life in political and social aspirations.

By contrast, the *roman-à-thèse* in the mid-Victorian period became prudent and scientific. The great questions were removed from literature, as they were from political life. Novelists attacked specific abuses, or displayed in their treatment of fiction the historical and critical spirit through which evolutionism impregnated English thought.[3]

At last, about 1880, the social novel took on a new vigour with the return of economic depression and political pessimism. Gissing, William Morris, and Mrs Humphry Ward put forward theories tending towards the transformation of society.

If it is difficult to determine the precise opening and closing dates of the Victorian epoch, it is still more difficult to assign limits to the corresponding phases of the social novel. Certainly *Paul Clifford,* the first true *roman-à-thèse,* was published in 1830, the year of the July Revolution. But this was mere coincidence, as is shown by the fact that *Paul Clifford* does not touch on political questions. The liberal philanthropy which fills the book could have found expression some years sooner or later. Likewise, if intellectual pacification was far from instant in society in 1848, it took still longer to come in the novel. This is a normal phenomenon: literature more often than not comes in the wake of events. Two novels, Dickens's *Hard Times* (1854) and Mrs Gaskell's *North and South* (1855), prolonged for several years the artistic response to social agitation which had been stilled.[4]

It remains to justify our chosen topic and outline our method of approach.

Justification

In the first place, environmental conditions coupled with the nature of the form ensured that the *roman-à-thèse* was the outstandingly influential didactic literary genre of the period. Its appearance coincided with two important phenomena: the accession of the middle class to power, and the submission of Parliament to public opinion. The popularity of novels during the period is well documented.[5] One commercial innovation, publication in monthly parts, brought the novel within reach of all purses, so that a great diversity of intellects, superficial as well as thoughtful, confronted the novel. And the general climate of sensibility was influenced by this form which could instruct and divert, persuade and affect, at the same time.

Literary realism was the best weapon social idealists could have wielded against the attitude of mind they opposed. Utilitarianism and political economy were alike abstract. The idealist reaction was able to castigate individualism for its failure to appreciate the real and concrete; for its substitution of the single faculty of reason for all others; and for its replacement of complex human nature with one single type, economic man. The social novel implanted realism in English thinking. It exposed facts, and selected the most important of these for discussion. Its valuable philosophy of life was experimental and demonstrative: it showed the direct way from experience to principle. And under the writer's guidance the reader took an instructive walk through society which was not offered him by any economist.[6]

Individualism was as cold-blooded as it was abstract. A desiccating wind of self-centred analysis and argument seemed to have blown over England: the chief characteristics of bourgeois society seemed to be selfish business calculation and cool theoretical lucidity. By contrast, the idealist reaction appealed to the emotions. It entered all areas of life and letters: artistic feeling, religious enthusiasm, and social conscience. It was diffuse and powerful and it stimulated new ideas and practical activities. A whole new theory and practice of altruism sprang from it as men's emotions gave them an intuitive grasp of organic human relationships. The novel, being above all an emotional stimulant, with pathos frequently, if not invariably, at its centre, was easily involved in this movement. When Dickens and Kingsley revealed the extent of the social distress around them, and inspired compassion for the sufferers, they were providing their readers with actual experience, and informing their social consciousness with the feeling it had hitherto lacked.

On the other hand, certain novels (happily for us) exhibit the other prominent social doctrine informing English life between 1830 and 1850. Bulwer and Miss Martineau were inspired by utilitarianism and classical economics. We have only to pass chronologically from them to Dickens, Disraeli, Mrs Gaskell, and Kingsley – all leading interventionists – to observe human sensitivity opposing social rationalism. In addition, the literary merit of the works is in proportion to the special interest they have for us. The utilitarian novels are feeble, the interventionist novels, rich. And either by coincidence, or because of the whole climate of feeling, both the novel with a purpose and the historical idealist movement reach the same point in the end: both culminate naturally in Christian socialism.

The novelists themselves were usefully representative citizens. They were of average intelligence, lacking the exceptional ratiocinative powers of philosophers or sages. They were of middling birth and social standing: even Bulwer, whose family was noble, and Disraeli, whose habits were aristocratic, made strenuous efforts to bring themselves within the horizons of the bourgeois public. As for Miss Martineau, Dickens, Mrs

Gaskell, and Kingsley, they all belonged to different levels of the middle class. Disraeli was the only original thinker among them: the other novelists assimilated ideas, but tended not to devise new ones. The unusual imaginative powers which made them novelists did less to set them apart from the general public than philosophic intellects would have done.

The personalities of the novels' heroes are as representative as their authors. To be acceptable to public taste, they could not stray very far from life, or from that idealised half-life which comprised their existence. Their feelings and reflections as they encountered new areas of society were to be instructive to readers who might undergo similar experiences. And as most of the novels deal with conversions, describing the path from apathy to altruism, they offer a stereotyped and simplified version of the growth of feeling in average minds for us to inspect.

It would be quite impossible to use the socialist writings of Owen, Hodgskin, and Thompson as the focal point of this investigation: these writers never appreciably influenced the bourgeoisie. Similarly, popular poems and Chartist tracts, interesting as they are in the history of the working-class movement, are of secondary importance for the under-standing of 'social conscience'. And even Carlyle, the most profound thinker of the idealist reaction, lacked immediate influence and popular esteem commensurate with his genius. The bizarre qualities of his mind and the obscurity of his style cut him off from the wide public, and it was left to his disciples to make his ideas generally known. Then, in the second phase of the Victorian era, his stimulating force, compounded with that of Ruskin, became effective. But between 1830 and 1850 only a few men understood him and tried to make him understood. And the popularisers of his thought prove to be none other than the social novelists: Dickens, Disraeli, and Kingsley.

Thus the novel exerted a particularly extensive influence, and provides unusually suggestive information about the social aspect of the idealist reaction. The other documents cannot, however, be disregarded. They will be cited as much as is necessary for a proper understanding of the general movement wherein the novel and its influence are to be placed.

Method

One preliminary problem is the guiding principle by which we should select works for discussion. For in one sense, every novel dealing with human customs is a 'social novel'. But the term is used here in a more restricted sense: by social novel we mean 'novel with a social thesis': a novel which aims at directly influencing human relations, either in general, or with reference to one particular set of circumstances. Of course, private manners and public affairs are too closely connected for the former to be altered independently of the latter. Every moral critique has its social repercussions. Nevertheless, those works which only examine the private failings of individuals in society have been ignored, together with any which do not directly assert their reformatory intention. Our main purpose is to study the development of interventionism, and by definition interventionism involves a positive attempt by the individual or the community to improve social relations. If a novel is truly a part of the interventionist movement, then its author must expressly have demanded positive action, either from the State, or organised institutions, or private persons.

The problems of industrialism dominated the thought of the time, and posed in an acute form the choice between active charity and passive non-interference. Well-meaning literature inevitably had something to say about this. Central to our study, then, is the pro-interventionist novel in general, and any novel which suggested remedies for the ills of industrial anarchy in particular.

Setting boundaries in time, as has been observed, is more awkward. Between 1850 and 1860 some didactic novels are early-Victorian in spirit, and some mid-Victorian. In distinguishing these from each other we have accepted the internal evidence. Charles Reade, for example, began to write during this decade, but his works are obviously mid-Victorian in spirit.[7] On the other hand, *Hard Times* and *North and South* treat of industrial problems in what is palpably an early-Victorian tone. Dickens, indeed, was able to go on writing until 1870 without ever ceasing to be an early-Victorian commentator. Artistically, he never was a contemporary of George Eliot. The social elements in his novels after 1854 are exceptional, unimportant, and naturally blended with the other elements enriching the work of his maturity.[8]

This procedure leaves us with two unequal groups of novelists. Bulwer, with *Paul Clifford* (1830), and Miss Martineau, with her *Illustrations of Political Economy* (1832–4), represent the 'utilitarian novel'. *Pickwick Papers* (1837) and *Oliver Twist* (1838) mark Dickens's entrance on the scene; henceforth he was to use his imaginative fertility in the cause of compassionate interventionism. Disraeli, in *Coningsby* (1844), *Sybil* (1845), and *Tancred* (1847), served the same cause, though not without private ambition. With *Mary Barton* (1848) and *North and South* (1855) Mrs Gaskell achieved the success that had eluded Mrs Trollope in *Michael Armstrong* (1840) and Charlotte Elizabeth (Mrs Tonna) in *Helen Fleetwood*

(1841). Kingsley's Christian socialist novels *Yeast* (1848) and *Alton Locke* (1850) finally brought the social welfare movement to its natural conclusion.[9]

These novels are to be examined analytically, although this runs the risk of reducing them to a set of formulations, and missing their literary essence. In their case, the essence is the convincing demonstration of social conditions they offer; therefore the range of the analysis has been stretched as far as possible. The novelist's intentions are not exhibited in his explicit declarations alone; we must consider the thousands of details which reveal the writer's opinion of his characters and show the purport of the plot; the hints which expose the nature of the settings, and show how appropriate artistic modes have been found for the treatment of the different areas of society presented. Taken all together, these disclose social attitudes on the part of the author which are fully as important as his systematised theories. It is hoped that these have been brought out.

In a study of the reciprocal action and reaction of novels and life, two questions recur: what elements in the book gave it its influence? And what historical factors permitted the public to feel this influence? We have to know which books in a given period actively affected their audience, and we have to understand how that audience was peculiarly well adapted to be affected, so that, in one sense, it ultimately became the result of the novels. A novel has a dual historical interest. It has the *a priori* value of a historical fact: it contains a certain amount of documentary evidence related to its didactic purpose; and it has exerted some definite influence on the public. This study sets out to find the information on social problems and proposals for their solution with which social novels persuaded their readers. It is also hoped to measure, as accurately as possible, the extent of social novels' influence.

Novels also have a representative value. They reflect their authors, the public which accepted them, and literary taste. If we keep a novel in the foreground, and examine it in the context of that psychological responsiveness of which it is at once cause and effect, our understanding of the novel may lead us to a better understanding of the psychology, and thus to a grasp of the whole general mental climate. But for this final development it is not enough to examine novels alone; they must be compared with evidence from other sources. Four particular procedures are here employed to make use of these.

The psychological make-up of the novelist who, as has been said, was a normal member of society, offers us a key to the state of public feeling. Dickens and Kingsley may have had superior emotional and imaginative faculties, but they were not alone in sensing social misery. Others were led by their feelings to the same kind of conclusions.

Secondly, we may infer something about society's moral outlook when we examine fictional characters in the light of the fact that they were drawn from reality, and were accepted as realistic by the public. Any sympathetic or antipathetic touches in their portrayal may show us something of the author's whole outlook, though, of course, we must be careful not to overlook the private and personal relation of character to author.

A third object for study is the public who gave the book its success, appreciated it, resembled it, and even imitated it. And the novels themselves are as valuable as any external evidence in our assessment of these people.

Finally, without losing sight of the novels, it is possible to set them aside for a quick glance at writings which are 'social' in the same sense, and whose consequences were parallel and similar. All these procedures are followed without systematic logic or rigorous order: rigour in such matters is liable to be a matter of form only.

The definition of 'social novel' given above, and the mode of study outlined, carry certain negative implications. These works might be examined in other ways: for example, novels might be regarded as historical documents, and scrutinised for the material for a reconstruction of social life. Such research would aim at description rather than explanation. The novel of manners does, indeed, give us evidence on aspects of society concerning which other documents all too often leave us in ignorance. It shows us the dynamics of social exchange instead of a tableau; life and action are breathed into modes of conduct which we would otherwise only know as laws, regulations, and surface appearances. It would be possible to try and re-create a picture of early-Victorian life with the aid of Dickens, Mrs Gaskell, and Kingsley.[10] But this is not our intention. We hope, first and foremost, to explain a movement in public opinion, in so far as the novel allows us to grasp the causes and feelings involved. On the other hand, the social novel is a distinct subdivision of a literary genre, whose development, content, and form might be studied like any other branch of literature. Aesthetic criticism would find rich food for thought here in the great problem of the compatibility of didactic and artistic intentions. Such a purely literary study is dimissed also. But this is not to say that these two possible approaches are entirely neglected: as far as possible, they are brought together in our work.

As we compare the settings of the novels with their sources, their value as contemporary descriptions will be continually made evident.

Realism was a vital factor in their success, and cannot be ignored, so that the historical surface of social life will be displayed as part of our analysis: it is of particular importance as a source of plot-material. Aesthetic criticism will assume the position it holds, as of right, in any study of literature's influence. The 'condition of England' novel points to changes in the mood of the public, and from this point of view it is interesting to note the origins of social novels before 1830 and the reasons for Kingsley's emotionalism giving way to George Eliot's positivism. It hardly seems worth considering the question whether the social novel is a true art form: it existed in fact, and this seems a sufficient answer, although we shall point out places where this or that novel is weakened by excessive preaching.

One last problem of exposition remains: for reasons of space it is impossible to give a full descriptive account of every book examined. Yet mere plot synopses are thin, flat, and banal. Therefore detailed accounts of full plots have been left aside, and the works are examined through relevant extracts. But this procedure obviates one essential feature of importance to social history as well as literature: there can be no discussion of the general development of a work as a whole, with the organisation of scenes and characters for dramatic effect considered as the plot unfolds. We have tried to overcome this difficulty by thinking of each separate element under discussion as being in the context of a plot, and examining each section as part of a larger whole, so that the reader should carry away a reasonable impression of the total work at the end, although the action is not followed through from start to finish. It has not been possible to do this in the case of Dickens. His output is too copious and too densely packed with social observation to allow separate consideration for each novel. Perforce, his didactic moments have been extracted without being replaced in their narrative framework.[11] It is assumed that most of his novels are familiar: fortunately they are the best known of all the books under consideration.

Finally, it seemed sensible to adopt a systematic plan of presentation. Thus the analysis of each group of novels is preceded by an account of the views which they hold in common and by which they are to be understood. It is impossible to understand Miss Martineau without some knowledge of the individualist movement, or *Sybil* without an acquaintance with the growth of social romanticism. Certain details from the novels themselves, however, are used together with the general historical evidence in the descriptions of these attitudes. To this extent, the conclusion precedes the exposition.[12] It is some compensation that the link between the social novel and public opinion is thereby made clearer.[13]

Introduction

Premisses

From its inception, this work is involved with a philosophical debate extending beyond its chosen scope. The literary character of the novel lends it a moral influence; the point in time with which we are concerned is marked by the confrontation of two opposing forces: the economic phenomenon of the industrial revolution, and the psychological phenomenon of the idealist reaction. On the one hand the period seems dominated by the infrastructure of demand and supply, with historical determinism truly representing the nature of events. On the other hand, this is directly challenged by the superstructure of art and philosophy, wherein it seems that the power of man's mind is a reality, and the history of ideas shows what is actually happening. We have been compelled to bow to one or other of these readings of history, and on the whole have inclined towards idealism. Our study, therefore, attributes real influence to moral energy, and sees the idealist reaction as an important part of the historical environment. We discern an internal coherence and an independent psychological progression in the evolution of ideas which interact with economic progress in ways which are difficult to define. We shall indicate the particular data which lead us to this position when they arise.

We likewise believe that opposing opinions derive from psychological differences. When men of the same class hold different views of society this must be accounted for by differences of temperament. We find, in fact, the elementary opposition of intellect and sensibility underlying the divergence of idealists and men of action. Thus we note on the one hand social science, the remarkable outcome of an almost perverse alliance between manufacturing interests and mathematical abstractions. It offered an exceptionally clear and lucid exposition of society, and of the necessary principles and consequences of individualism. But its field of vision was narrow, and excluded the truths of sensitivity, organic social relations, human sympathy, charity, and moral or religious responsibilities. On the other hand we find social consciousness, the flowering of some of the central seeds of English philosophy whose potential had already been glimpsed in the great religious and cultural movements of the early nineteenth century. Here the perception of reality was clouded by compassion, yet for all its vagueness it was more complete, and marked by a sympathy for suffering which found an echo in the observer, and led to individual or collective relief work.

These two points of view which we have presented as opposites are not mere personifications of abstract tendencies. They represent the two poles around which individuals ranged themselves unmistakably, in accordance with the diversity of their temperaments. They have certain common features, and certain tangled local disputes. Yet when these are discounted, England between 1830 and 1850 reduces simply to this classic opposition, which has certain national qualities, and constitutes a decisive moment in the psychological history of the nation.

Throughout the period, the preoccupation with individual autonomy and the demand for private freedom was characteristic of the social analytical personality as well as the political representatives of bourgeois economic interests. And the socially aware personality shared with the political representatives of labour and the landed interest a preoccupation with charitable intervention, and a demand either for some sort of state socialism, or a more or less philanthropic paternalism.

Of course, reality is complex, and comprises various gradations between one pole and the other. The Chartists, whose programme was one of democratic social reorganisation, were in the main emotional and passionate enthusiasts. And Kingsley and his Christian socialist friends gave fervid support to certain similar democratic policies of social engineering. But such exceptions are more apparent than real: the individualism of radical philosophy had little in common with Chartist egalitarianism, and Kingsley returned to his temperamental stance as aristocrat and conservative.

The central opposition remains unchallenged. Different men urged two separate aspects of progress, each offering an incomplete programme. Utilitarian individualism was better reasoned; compassionate interventionism was truer to human nature. The latter was, perhaps, more needed at the time, yet its policies were inadequate and checked unfeeling indifference at the expense of individual enterprise.

All this does not mean that we believe social conscience to have been perfectly disinterested. In many of its most illustrious exemplars it was associated with utilitarian 'enlightened self-interest'. Indeed, its partial success could be explained in terms of a national instinct for self-preservation. Thus we must pose a very delicate question concerning the English idealists: how far did they recognise the compatibility between their selfish interests and their social opinions? We hope to suggest an answer to this question, and to note the difference between the utilitarianism of Bentham and that of Carlyle.

We adopt these hypotheses as basic assumptions in our study, justifying such use of them by their value in explaining events. They seem to accord with most of the evidence, and permit the clearest possible understanding of it.

One

The rise of individualism

The industrial revolution, a great economic movement, increased the power of the individual and extended his potential for consumption of goods and services. Utilitarian philosophy, an important intellectual movement, argued that such power and consumption was based on moral law. Around 1830 these movements combined to give massive support to self-interest in public affairs.

The industrial revolution and 1832

Individualism was the product of events. Between 1800 and 1830 the mighty industry engendered during the previous quarter of a century in England reached full growth.[1] Division of labour and the reorganisation of the work-force into units of mass production created factories; the application of technology to industry and the harnessing of steam and water power produced modern manufacturing.[2] At the same time, increased production evolved a new people who made their living from it.[3] The spinning and weaving of cotton and wool, metal-working, and its related industries, all grew with the same vigour. Coal and iron mines were desperately strained to meet their needs. In the North and Midlands there came into being a nation quite different from the traditional England:[4] there were weavers in Manchester, ironworkers in Birmingham, miners in Lancashire, and potters in Staffordshire. The great build-up of trade which had preceded the growth of industry was turned to its service: English products inundated Europe in spite of a continental attempt to impose an embargo. The docks of the great industrial ports, Liverpool, London, Glasgow, and Hull, teemed with windjammers at first, and steamers subsequently.[5] Only a fraction of the railway system was built by 1830, but Brindley's canals and McAdam's roads had opened up the country for commerce.[6] Finance and speculation throve alongside industry, and the great joint-stock companies floated adventures reminiscent of the South Sea Bubble: the crash of 1825–6 was but the first of the series of financial crises by which over-production periodically set industry back. The economic system of nineteenth-century England was fully formed by 1830.

As trade and production expanded, the nation grew richer. Between 1815 and 1830 the population rose by 25 per cent, but the incomes of the middle and upper classes rose by 50 per cent. While national prosperity concealed the wretched conditions of the poor, the numerically powerful ascendant bourgeoisie mounted a bold and vigorous assault on the citadels of power. Northern manufacturers, unchallenged by foreign competition, pressed on with day and night production, and accumulated massive fortunes. London and Liverpool merchants exported English iron and cottons all over the world, and their fleets fed the nation, which had already lost its agricultural self-sufficiency. The reduction of taxes and the removal of spice duties after the Napoleonic War increased the amount of money in circulation,[7] and more financiers came into being. They, like the merchants and manufacturers, became a power in the land. The farmers had grown enormously prosperous as a result of the Corn Laws and the continental embargo, but they must be seen as separate from and opposed to the agricultural labouring community, whose wages had fallen. The descendants of the 'yeomen' had been driven from their villages by the enclosure of common land, and went to the towns to swell industry's labour surplus.[8] More and more the youth of the land left agriculture, and the new industries were the beneficiaries. By 1831 agriculture employed only 28 per cent of the total population; in 1811 it had still employed 35 per cent.[9] The powerful men of the day came from factories and workshops where their fathers had been small employers, still capable of working with their hands when necessary. Over a few years their fortunes swelled until the cotton kings had grown into a race of grandees, outside the ranks of the traditional aristocracy. New men came from the Thames and the Mersey, where the wharves were laden with wealth; from the City and the Stock Exchange, where speculation set millions whirling on a fantastic merry-go-round. Their opinions and tastes were identical: they were all stamped by the economic conditions which had created them. They came together and united to form a single, homogeneous, powerful and energetic class: the great middle class of 1832 which rode rough-shod over all time-honoured forces of resistance, and wrenched political enfranchisement from the landed oligarchy.

A deep antagonism, indeed, divided this new and thriving class from the old order. The vehement aggression of these sons who rejected their heritage wounded the peaceful, patriarchal spirit of agricultural England, slumbering in self-satisfied torpor. In the old society everyone knew his place. The great families governed the country; the squires and justices of the peace administered their own localities. The state of affairs handed down from the past seemed unshakeable to eighteenth-century England.[10] The Poor Laws dealt with the relatively simple problem of agricultural poverty, without bitterness or strife. Personal ties, as of vassal and overlord, were maintained in the gentler relationship of squirearchical paternalism and tenant deference. But the demands of the new bourgeoisie and the pressure of the industrial revolution introduced ideals of liberty and enfranchisement to this society where, hitherto, material and moral ties had chained the individual to his ancestors' station in his own locality. For production to rise and prices to fall, it was vital that men should become interchangeable economic units who could be dispersed and reassembled into new temporary groupings by the pressure of wages and profits. Men would have to cut themselves off from their native society and become free and independent, relying on the strength of their intelligence or wealth, if they had any, and their muscular strength if they had not. Thus they would enter the merciless battle of each against all for life. The new bourgeoisie had a love of struggle bred in its bones; it saw the effort which attended its own achievements as an inevitable feature of health and progress. Contest was the framework of its thought as well as its economic actions, and the world seemed an arena in which weak and strong joined battle under the free light of commercial competition. The fallen were trodden underfoot: so much the worse for them. 'Each for himself and the law of England for all' was the motto of industrialism. These men were filled with pride when they contemplated the great wealth they had amassed from the products of their own energy. And they were enraged by the ridiculous impediments which still hindered individual freedom. Remainders of feudalism, relics of old institutions, Acts of Settlement, Statutes of Apprentices, and protectionist Corn Laws were all so many obstacles to be knocked down in the march of progress. Or the march to wealth.[11]

In the writings of Baines and Ure, two spokesmen for this spirited generation, one can see the contempt with which they regarded the landed aristocracy:[12]

> Grandees, as the spoiled children of the state, may be indulged in their learned play things, as in the ribbon and the star, to mark their exclusive caste, and they may be allowed freely to waste their early years in the pastime of scanning Greek and Roman metres, provided they do not fancy themselves thereby, albeit ignorant of the principles of Science, Art, and Trade, qualified to scan the measures and to regulate the affairs of empires at their will.

Ure preferred 'the bloodless but still formidable strife of trade'[13] to the feudal exploits which bolstered the pride of the aristocracy: 'To impair the resources of a rival at home by underselling his wares abroad, is the new belligerent system, in pursuance of which every nerve and sinew of the people are put upon the strain.'[14]

And he proclaimed the divine origin of middle-class achievements in a tone of religious conviction:[15]

> The great truth, that Providence has assigned to man the glorious function of vastly improving the productions of nature by judicious culture, and of working them up into objects of comfort and elegance with the least possible expenditure of human labour [is] an undeniable position which forms the basis of our Factory System.

The new men were conscious of their material prosperity and assured of the moral value of their gospel of competition. Through them, individualism emerged from the undergrowth of economics to become a force in society.

Utilitarianism

Individualism found expression in a corpus of philosophical thought. With one accord, the theoreticians of the period mounted a powerful assault on the moral and emotional foundations of the old England, and sought to replace it with a society meeting the wishes of the bourgeoisie. (We restrict ourselves here to a brief sketch of this united effort.)[16] Bentham and his disciples had faced the conservative reaction at the start of the nineteenth century without wavering in their enthusiasm for reform. As liberal ideas again came to the fore, around 1815, the Benthamites took over this revival, and a coalition was formed comprising all the forces seeking the overthrow of oligarchy. Jeffrey, Sydney Smith, and the *Edinburgh Review* Whigs; Cobbett and the radical democrats; the working-class leaders, who were already disturbing the peaceful surface of society – all accepted the intellectual leadership of the doctrinaire liberals, so that Place and his friends served to introduce utilitarian theory into political agitation. Meanwhile, individualist economics had solidified into a body of doctrine, based on Adam Smith, extended by Malthus, and codified by the clear mind of Ricardo. Between 1820 and 1830 philosophical radicalism became the social and political gospel of English democrats.[17] Bentham and the economists presented a ready-made Bill of Rights to the new bourgeoisie, as it felt for its place in society and demanded industrial freedom and a share in government.[18]

Utilitarianism was rationalism with a mathematical bias. The ideal of scientific exactitude permeated its massive attempt to synthesise and explain ethics, psychology, politics, and economics. In an effort to reduce the moral order to a set of laws, it applied concepts which had proved essential to recent research in the natural sciences: the mechanistic approach was accepted as the way which had cast the clearest and most definitive light on the material universe. Bentham's phraseology typifies the methods used in all areas of this philosophy: terms like the 'ontological calculus' or the 'arithmetic of pleasures' are a key to the Benthamite frame of mind. The moral, psychological, and political principles of utilitarianism postulated a division of reality into widespread unitary factors, such as individuals, their basic needs, or single concepts. These could combine arithmetically with like units to produce the more complex areas of experience – society, duty, or opinions. This approach was two-edged: it could be used in defence of the past and tradition, or it could justify egalitarianism and lay claim to the future. A common-sense preference for the natural, deriving from Hume, conflicted with Bentham's instinctive rationalism. On the whole the latter prevailed, and philosophic radicalism put forward the doctrine of political equality.[19] This rested on the simple mathematical principle that the aim of government should be the greatest good of the greatest number. Democracy was the best way of pursuing this goal. For all men tend to serve their own selfish interests: a king will do this as an individual; an aristocracy will act as a concerted body. These, in a favourite utilitarian phrase, are 'sinister interests' running counter to the good of the nation. Private interests can only be neutralised, or brought into some kind of generally beneficial accord, if all citizens are participating in government. Democracy goes as far as is possible towards the reconciliation of private and national interests by giving power to majorities.[20] Thus the internal groupings of citizens within the community will be related to the ends they pursue. This, in essence, was the doctrine of philosophic radicalism. Its formulaic precision explains the self-confidence of its proponents, and their rather supercilious attitude towards alternative arguments based on sentiment, habit, or prejudice.

After 1820 political economy was equally rigid in its approach to society. Ricardo had applied his intelligence to the analysis and simplification of experience: economic man, a mere atom endowed with the simple, single-minded energy of self-interest, came into play with his fellows, and thereby produced the harmonious totality of society.[21] This closed system of tiny antagonistic forces was contained within the limited environs of cultivable land, where it produced order out of chaos. The phenomenon of rent was an inevitable consequence; likewise all classes,

landowners, businessmen, and workers, would sort themselves out so that
they received economically proper returns on their property or labour.
The greater the freedom given to the separate units in society, the more
easily they would find ways of working together, and the nearer society
would approach to an ideal state. Ideal, here, could not mean perfect,
for harmony was unfortunately bound to be disturbed by the limited
quantity of resources. Providence had not set the human atomic system
in a vacuum, but had confined it to the cultivable parts of the world.
Ultimately, then, as population was increasing in proportion with
industrial production, it was mathematically bound to exceed the available resources. Thereupon wages would fall relatively; profits would
drop absolutely; and rent-rolls would grow endlessly larger. But this
vision of future calamity was not a matter to disturb the serenity of
theoreticians foreseeing it. The world still appeared far from unpleasant,
and any improvement to be made lay in the direction of greater freedom
for individuals. Indeed, the danger of world over-population might best
be met by ensuring that nothing by way of ignorance, sentiment, prejudice, or legal restraint hindered the free play of self-interest. Procreation
might have to be restrained, but in all other ways freedom should be
encouraged, that competitive self-interest might devise combinations of
greater use and ingenuity. This remarkable simplification of the new
industrial society was Ricardo's system. It rested on totally abstract principles, which reduced the rich complexity of human nature to the one
quality of self-interest.[22] This was the second element in the body of
doctrine which, unusually for England, gave rise to a rationalist ideological crisis in 1830.

Rationalism was central to individualism, but the aims of its supporters
were by no means theoretical. A sincere concern for the public good gave
them a reforming spirit, and they favoured reform by the practical application of ideas. These dry and abstract utilitarians were far from being
the soulless monsters that popular prejudice made of them. Adam Smith
and Bentham exhibited a simple and humane public spirit: this became
more pessimistic and doom-laden in Malthus and Ricardo, and burned as
a pure flame of logic in James Mill. But it was present in all of them,
running as a vein of sentiment throughout their lives and writings. Their
work did more than separate the old and the new Englands: they played
a large part in the process of social amelioration which continued
throughout the nineteenth century. They put down abuses by exposing
them in their analysis of society: they had their own philanthropy, and
were able to collaborate with other philanthropists.[23]

It is interesting to see how much their choice of social concerns was influenced by the essential nature of their philosophy. Their wish for social justice often found expression as part of a wish to tidy society up. The need for logic and clarity gave reason enough for launching an attack on the centuries-old mass of inchoate and contradictory law on the statute-books. The whole rationale of their proposals for law reform sprang from their wish to see things properly presented in a logically comprehensible order. Their aim was to codify English law, although their schematisation would at the same time have made it more humane: disproportionately heavy sentences and unnecessary use of the death penalty were among the illogicalities they would have swept away. Of course, the law had already been modified in practice: a long tradition of judicial clemency went a long way towards improving on statutory barbarism. But how absurdly irrational was this very division between prescription and practice![24] The prison system was another scandalous affront to humanity: Howard obeyed his philanthropic sentiment in working for its improvement. Bentham, too, turned his mind to the problem of penitentiaries, but only to conceive of the 'Panopticon', the geometrically designed prison which applied the laws governing the expenditure of energy to reduce the labour of surveillance to a minimum. Finally, it was abstract and mathematical benevolence that gave the utilitarians their faith in education and led to their campaigns for a free press, the popularisation of scientific knowledge, and the enlightenment of the populace. The best possible way to persuade the people to recognise and pursue their own class-interest would be to spread education throughout society. Then all the units of humanity would start equal in the most important respect in the competition of life. For, setting aside property as an uncertain asset, only one thing created inequalities between citizens, namely their greater or lesser ability to define their own interests. The suppression of educational inequality as far as possible was, then, an act of justice rendered necessary by the advance of industrial democracy.

These were the main lines of the doctrine which held such powerful sway over England. It was almost totally rationalist: an extension of the eighteenth century into the nineteenth, and a curious invasion of abstract ideology into the home of empirical thinking. The radical philosophers and economists were a minute, little-known faction, antipathetic to the general public where they were known. Yet as long as their voice was heard their influence was enormous. For they were in harmony with social and economic developments and, consciously or accidentally, forged alliances which put them at the centre of the great revolutionary force producing individualism. We have to see how far they were typical of this movement, and how far they were extraordinary; and we must try and discover the factors which on the one hand made them leaders of a great movement in English intellectual life, and on the other hand led them to arouse a passionate national reaction against themselves.

The Reform Act

Meanwhile the new bourgeoisie enjoyed its triumph. The Reform Act of 1832 was its decisive victory, and it was preceded by a series of partial successes that paved the way for it, and laid the foundations of the society which saw the rediscovery of the social novel.

Ricardo outlined his political economy in 1817.[25] Mrs Marcet produced a popular account of the theory in her *Conversations* (1818), and the Political Economy Club became the main platform for Ricardian propaganda. A petition in favour of Free Trade was presented by London tradesmen as early as 1820. When Huskisson entered the cabinet he initiated a series of commercial reforms which he intended to crown with the repeal of the Corn Laws. Radical agitation focused on administrative corruption and sinecures; 'Black Books' in 1820 and 1823 listed the recipients of government pensions. Joseph Hume conducted a parliamentary crusade for 'Retrenchment and Reform', which became the watchwords of the radical liberals. Some preliminary legislative and administrative reform cleared away the worst abuses in the 1820s. Mackintosh continued Romilly's noble exposure of the criminal code, and in 1823 Peel moderated the terrible severity of the penal laws. In 1828 Brougham spoke for six hours, giving an outline of the 'true crimes of the law'.[26] The most important reforms of the period were Catholic emancipation in 1828, and the abolition of the laws against workers' combinations in 1824. The latter was not quite so clear a victory of liberal reason over bourgeois class interest as it seemed. The radicals claimed to be following their principle of non-interference in allowing workers' societies freedom within certain limits. But in fact they sensed a spirit of collectivism in the nascent trade unions which threatened individualism, and they hoped that freedom to strike would bring about the final downfall of the unions.[27] In Catholic emancipation the utilitarians scored a partial victory over the Established Church. It is remarkable how utterly removed from the spirit of religion their ideas were. James Mill put forward a scheme of ecclesiastical reform in 1835 which amounted to the secularisation of the Church. The clergy would be employed to give 'lectures on morality, botany, political economy, and so on'.[28] With allies like this the Catholics and Nonconformists might have won more than civil rights for themselves: separation of Church and State was the dearest wish of Bentham and James Mill. But the Whigs, whose lukewarm piety found Catholic emancipation perfectly acceptable, clung to the Established Church for its social usefulness. They brought off a triumph of compromise in preserving establishment, and thereby demonstrated the difference between instinctive Whig utilitarianism and systematic philosophical utilitarianism.

After a furious struggle, a coalition of liberals and radicals of all shades carried the Reform Act. The Lords' resistance was overcome, after frequent upsets, in June 1832. It was high time. This period of constitutional political activity had taken on a revolutionary character, with public impatience and frustration building to pent up fury, and actual outbreaks of violence in places.[29] The prospect of social change had aroused the proletariat from its lethargy, and it is impossible to imagine what socialist dreams they expected reform to realise.[30] In the end, the Reform Act was far from totally democratic. The franchise was extended to freeholders to the value of £10; the constituencies were revised and the 'rotten boroughs' replaced by new towns; and that minute fraction of the community which enjoyed hereditary electoral rights lost this privilege. Essentially, this was all the measure achieved, and yet its effect on public morale was incalculable. It was the end of the old order and the opening of a new. The leaders of the bourgeoisie officially took their place among the governing classes, where their wealth and initiative promised them supremacy. Then did English democracy really begin in 1832? John Stuart Mill thought so: 'To most purposes, in the constitution of modern society, the government of a numerous middle class is democracy. Nay, it not merely is democracy, but the only democracy of which there is yet any example.'[31]

The new England was ripe for individualism. For the moment political thought was under the direction of theoreticians, and it seemed that the philosophic radicals were going to run the country. Yet in fact the power of doctrinaire partisans was to decline steadily after 1832. In 1841 the Tories were returned to power by a popular reaction of conservative prudence. Thereafter utilitarianism as an active revolutionary force was overwhelmed, although its influence continued to be felt in such measures as the codification of the criminal law (1833) and the attenuation of its more extreme penalties (1837). But the reformed Parliament hardly attended to anything but the immediate interests of the bourgeoisie. Thus it wished to destroy the social ties between men and classes which had characterised the old England; it was determined to do away with the paternalistic, personal approach to government, and chose to withdraw the Poor Law's official recognition of society's responsibility to its members. The Municipal Corporations Act of 1835 was the principal step towards the destruction of the old social forms: it replaced the unpaid administration of squires and magistrates with professional bureaucrats serving elected councils.[32] After a public inquiry, the Poor Law was revised in 1834. For a long time liberal economists had denounced the harmful effects of the right to public assistance, established under Elizabeth and confirmed by successive statutes.[33] The maintenance of paupers by parish rates was as offensive to the principles of theoretical economists as it was expensive to the pockets of bourgeois ratepayers. A premium paid to the unemployed was an encouragement to the endless multiplication of socially useless individuals and a long-standing grievance to the Malthusians. They argued from statistics that increasing unemployment and rising poor rates made reform necessary. But reform, when it came, was carried out in a spirit of ruthless schematisation. Public assistance was centralised: the central committee was empowered to join parishes together in 'unions' and to compel them to pool their resources and build workhouses. These were to be run on a strictly disciplined regimen. Under no circumstances were able-bodied men to be given relief outside the workhouses. Bastards were to be a charge on their mothers. The new system sharply replaced the old with the cruelty of a radical measure. The separation of the sexes and deliberate harshness of workhouse life were intended to discourage malingerers, but they also oppressed the truly needy. Opposition to this reform was significant: no single issue offered a clearer polarisation of utilitarians and men of feeling.

Similarly revealing was the great Free Trade campaign which engaged all radicals and economists from 1838 to 1846. Here a sincere and disinterested concern for the public good went hand in glove with class-interest. Cobden and Bright, the leaders of the campaign, were industrialists first and philanthropists second. The artificial maintenance of high bread prices for the benefit of the landed interest had been denounced repeatedly.[34] The Anti-Corn Law League then organised a brilliant propaganda campaign, with all the essentials for success. By 1842 the Government had been won over to the cause. Peel, as a Conservative minister, still hesitated, but his budget was already a partial victory for Free Trade. In 1846 a serious economic crisis and the prospect of famine finally broke down the resistance of agricultural Toryism.[35] An immediate improvement in the condition of the poor was felt, and the repeal of the Corn Laws was one of the primary causes of the return of national prosperity after 1850. And yet some radical democrats were suspicious of the Free Trade movement, and the Chartists, the spearhead of the workers' demand for political rights, were for the most part actually hostile. This was because the altruism of the Free Traders was, in their view, vitiated by class-interest. The industrialists of the League would be striking a mighty blow against the landed gentry, their class antagonists, if they carried the repeal of the Corn Laws. At the same time the cost of living would fall, which meant that conditions for trade would become easier, and wages could be lowered while profits were raised. Cobden admitted as much in 1843.[36] 'I am afraid,' he said at Manchester on 19 October, 'that most of us entered upon the struggle with the belief that we had some distinct class-interest in the question.' The Chartists' suspicions were right, even if class loyalty concealed the true interests of the masses from them.[37] Their attitude clarifies the true social conflict in this complex and uncertain period.

The political problem and the social problem

The confusion of English history between 1830 and 1850 arises from the fact that the same social forces were involved in two separate systems of confrontation. On the one hand there was the political and administrative battle of the middle class as they tried to force open the historical English social alignments, against the opposition of the conservative landowning aristocracy of the established order. The bourgeoisie wanted the assistance of the masses in this struggle, and succeeded in gaining their involvement by conjuring up the image of common middle- and working-class opposition to the holders of power, and vaguely promising a better future once the oligarchical base of government had been extended. This movement was analytical and individualist, and generally progressive. Cobbett supported it, and persuaded the first working-class movements that their place between 1815 and 1830 was with the bourgeoisie, whose cause was the cause of all the people. After 1832 the pressure built up over the years continued to provide the motive force for a number of separate social movements. Thus Chartism claimed to be continuing and completing the work of the Reform Act. And sporadic associations of the middle and working classes continued individualist social activity until the end of the century, through Free Trade agitation, successive electoral reforms, and the last stages of the struggle with the persistence of feudal attitudes. The first social confrontation, then, was between feudal traditions and the spirit of modernity, and although this was partially resolved by the Reform Act and became of less importance thereafter, it was protracted into the early twentieth century by the slow progress of democracy. As long as the demand for political equality was not met, a part of the populace was ready to continue the struggle. And it cannot be said that the electoral reforms of 1867 and 1884 met their demands: the English class structure is so tenacious that the radical aim of individual independence and equality could not be described as achieved until the twentieth century.

On the other hand, a second arrangement of the same social forces, with a different or even contrary orientation, came into being at the very moment of individualism's first political triumph.[38] The industrial revolution carried the seeds of a new antagonism which was to divide the classes along new party lines. In the light of industrialism, the middle and working classes could see themselves as quite separate, with different interests underlined by their economic conditions. The question of political power now became secondary: the battleground had changed, and different principles were invoked. As far as the victorious individualists were concerned, the needs of the proletariat and the dismay of the former ruling classes were alike obstacles to the reorganisation of society they proposed. Thus the bourgeoisie, hitherto the allies of the people, became an enemy, and their victory signalled even more cruel oppression. Now the old aristocracy seemed a possible ally against the bourgeoisie, and the weapons they had forged in the previous struggle could be taken up by the workers. This sequence of events took place in all the advanced nations of Europe, but it was far more rapid in England than anywhere else. The amazingly swift development of industrialism, coupled with stubborn resistance to social change, meant that the resolution of the political power struggle in 1832 coincided with the birth of the social class war. In France the struggle for socialism was half a century away from the struggle for democracy; in England they took place almost simultaneously.

It was difficult for men to make the mental adjustment from the first problem to the second, as they appeared to be flatly opposed. Hardly anyone saw socialism as an extension of democratic principles to the economic sphere. Among the Chartists, only the followers of Owen and Hodgskin wanted to attack the basis of property. Everybody else – the estate-holders who had survived from the old order in spite of the depredations of bourgeois radicalism; the factory hands who were denied legal protection against overwork; and the middle-class altruists whose consciences revolted at the competitive principle – upheld the ideal of intervention in opposition to the liberal economists' *laissez-faire*. The social changes they hoped for involved the maintenance of such social relations as offered safeguards to the participants, the replacement of industrial anarchy by a hierarchical structure guaranteeing more security to its members, and the creation of new social responsibilities by government action. State socialism and Guild socialism combined to polarise opposition to individualism. Men of all classes, allied by permanent or ephemeral sentiments, preferences, or interests, combined to produce various theories which were united in their opposition to the common enemy. When Christian socialism was added, the whole mass of anti-*laissez-faire* activity became the pivot around which the struggle for social change revolved after 1832.

Thus from 1830 to 1850 two quite separate philosophies of progress were thriving, side by side. Each had its own justification: the need for democratic individualism had not terminated in 1832. And although the other 'progressive' movement was less self-aware, it was nonetheless necessary. And this is why we find such confusion on the ideological plane throughout the period. Contemporary witnesses exhibit intellectual uncertainty, difficulty in the face of new questions which cannot be answered by old principles, and a diversity of opinion which, for example, created problems for politicians dealing with industrial legislation. Greville noted in his *Journal*:[39]

> I never remember such excitement as has been caused by Ashley's Ten Hours Bill, nor a more curious political state of things – such intermingling of parties, such a confusion of opposition. . . . Some voted, not knowing how they ought to vote, and following those they are accustomed to follow; many who voted against Government afterwards said they believed they were wrong. . . . The whole thing is difficult and unpleasant.

Nor is it surprising that even the most clear-sighted men of the time were unable to detect more than one of the forms of social conflict around them. Their viewpoint from within society concealed from them either the need for social justice, or the need for democracy. At that time, more than any other, individualism and socialism presented hostile faces to each other, and seemed implacably opposed; yet this, too, was the moment in English history when socialist sympathies were most likely to be found among reactionaries, and democratic tendencies circulated among the conservative *laissez-faire* bourgeoisie.

Most people were quite incapable of distinguishing between or reconciling the two problems, and they tended simply to adopt random principles and policies from both. The leaders of opinion who influenced the national conscience throughout the period exhibit a singular confusion of contradictory ideas. And habitual abstract thinkers were as confused as men of action. Furthermore, the classification of ideas around the separate poles became increasingly confused. Of course, for a long time there were many unwavering disciples of individualism: but their number fell steadily, and their theories were gradually adulterated with ideas borrowed from their opponents. At the other end of the scale, there were a considerable number of convinced socialists among the educated workers. But between these two extremes every possible shade of moderate opinion was to be found, divided into old and new progressivism. The word 'radical' – meaning a root and branch reformer – lacked any precise political definition.[40] It was applied indifferently to doctrinaire liberals, Free Trade industrialists, class-motivated Chartists, and socialistic philanthropists. At one extreme lay the bourgeois radicals like Bright, passionate individualists, and deeply opposed to industrial legislation. At the other extreme were Carlyle and his followers, the furious adversaries of individualism. Between the two lay philosophic radicals, decidedly democratic, but still adhering to classical economics. And there were the radical Chartists, filled with dreams of social change.[41] The use of the word 'radical' to describe individualists and socialists alike points out how powerfully the old liberal view of the political struggle outweighed the new economic alignments in the minds of the protagonists. This explains why a man like Dickens described himself as a radical: he was defining his stance as a middle-class opponent of aristocratic power, although the bulk of his opinions and sentiments place him in the forefront of the interventionist reaction.

The break between the middle class and the people

Great confusion was created by the coincident appearance of revolutionary political principles and the problems of industrialism. But the social aspirations aroused by the Reform Act were so powerful that their disappointment was a violent blow to the mood of the people. Mrs Bulwer, the novelist's mother, wrote to a friend in 1831:[42]

> The other evening, a ragged fellow who was crying out the King's speech, announced it with the following appendage: 'Good news for the poor! Great and glorious speech of His Most gracious Majesty William the Fourth! The Reform Bill will pass! Then you'll have your beef and mutton for a penny a pound. And then you'll all be as fine as peacocks for a mere trifle. To say nothing of ale at a penny a quart. In which you may drink His Majesty's health, and His Majesty's ministers' health, and the glorious Reform Bill's health, all without a ruining of yourselves!' . . . All the

common people are now persuaded that the Reform Bill will feed and clothe them for nothing. Poor geese!

The utter disillusionment of such naïve and passionate ambition produced inevitable rebelliousness. The alliance between the bourgeoisie and the people was dissolved immediately after 1832.

Once in power, the middle class became conservative. The philosophical radicals might have calculated that the Reform Act was a first step towards universal manhood suffrage; Cobbett's readers might have dreamed that a war on poverty would follow Reform, and be carried to a swift conclusion; but parliamentary activity took quite a different direction after 1832. Lord John Russell's celebrated declaration of finality in 1837, earning him the nickname of 'Finality Jack', confirmed the dashing of popular hopes.[43] The Whigs rallied to a Tory programme, accepting the *fait accompli* of Reform, but banning any further alteration to the constitution of the electorate. At the same time, the property-owning classes, noting the progress of trade unionism and the first co-operative movement, and remembering the Bristol riots, feared the advent of revolution. After 1830 Lord Melbourne favoured turning the clock back on 1824, and reviving the legislation against combinations of workers. Nassau Senior, the economist, wrote in the same spirit in 1838, 'There is scarcely any act performed by any workman as a member of a trade union, which is not an act of conspiracy and a misdemeanour', and he urged that certain actions, whose criminal character was still not clearly recognised, should be made punishable offences.[44] These feelings were not acted upon, but they cast a vivid light on the spirit of government after the Reform Act. The case of the Tolpuddle Martyrs is equally significant: these six Dorset labourers were swiftly transported to Australia for joining an agricultural workers' union, in spite of indignant radical protests at the sentence. *The Times* congratulated the judges on dealing with 'the criminal and fearful spirit of combination which had seized, like a pestilence, on the working classes of this country.'[45] Although they were reprieved the same year (1834), the victims were still held in Australia for a further three years. No incident did more to hasten the rupture between the bourgeoisie and the labour movement.

Economic individualism played its part here too. The question of industrial legislation was pushed to the fore by the urgency of industrial conditions. Public inquiries and a widely-reported debate led to the first of the Factory Acts in 1833, and throughout the following years the problem of government intervention in industry was discussed in Parliament, in the press, and in literature. A major philanthropic effort gradually forced through protection for women and children in factories, in the teeth of indifference and greed. And all this time representative middle-class spokesmen defended public inaction. Philosophical radicals, utilitarians, employers on large or small scales, tradesmen and financiers all found themselves resisting would-be interventionists.

The habitually reflective characters among them make a fascinating study, as one investigates the motives underlying their obstinate attitude. Setting aside class interest, one finds here dogmatism and arid intellectualism. Harriet Martineau delivered one of the fiercest attacks ever launched against Dickens in a virulent pamphlet. In it one can detect the indignant asperity of a logical mind convinced of its own rightness:[46]

> Here we are once again in the midst of confusion and actual danger to our liberties, from the same tendency in busy and shallow minds to recur to legislation for the carrying of their objects, encouraged as that tendency is by the ignorance and carelessness of our lawmakers and their constituents, as to the principles which should prescribe and limit the sphere of legislation.

In Ure, positivist thinking and an invincible hatred of sentiment is as powerful as self-interest:[47]

> The sentimental fever then excited by the craft of the Operatives' Union was inflamed into a delirious paroxysm by the partial, distorted, and fictitious evidence conjured up before the Committee of the House of Commons on factory employment of which Mr. Sadler was the chairman.

Francis Place added the systematic spirit to his own cramped and painstaking mental industry: he evinced the faith of a believer to whom Malthus had revealed absolute truth when he wrote, 'Every suggestion which does not tend to the reduction in number of working people is useless, to say the least of it. All legislative interference must be ruinous.'[48] He confessed, moreover, that he had no direct acquaintance with large-scale industry: 'I have never seen', he wrote in 1835, 'the interior of a cotton factory.'[49] And this, indeed, was the case with all these intellectuals. All it would have taken to challenge their rigorously abstract convictions would have been some direct experience of the things they were dealing with. Gaunt faces, crooked limbs, the smell of sweat, and suffocating cotton dust would have shaken their faith. Place actually did come to some awareness of this misery through his reading of parliamentary reports, though this experience only made him fear greater insight:[50]

I have read all the evidence taken by Committees of Parliament; I have read books and pamphlets; I have conversed with numbers of cottoners, masters as well as men. . . . But I cannot voluntarily submit to see the misery of working it before my eyes. I abhor such scenes of degradation as even the best of the cotton mills cannot be free from.

How important, then, was the social novel, which could reproduce the full misery of industrialism in its pages with telling emotional impact!

From the very beginning there was an instinctive hostility between the bourgeois liberals and the working-class radicals. The utilitarians and their friends mistrusted these turbulent allies, whose language was coarse, and among whom there were few philosophers, and none with any respect for the harmonious symmetries of classical economics. Place's composed mind was distressed by the demagogic violence of Hunt and Cobbett, and the vehement passion of their rhetoric. And this division was accentuated by events. Farm labourers regarded the 1834 Poor Law as an outright class attack on their well-being, and superstitious scare stories about the new workhouse régime circulated. Social crisis loomed again as the financial and industrial recession of 1836–7 revived economic hardship.[51] In 1838 Chartism was born. Rampant individualism had divided England into two hostile nations.[52]

Alongside the separate class interests determining this rupture one must place the equally decisive influence of a moral and temperamental division. For the future the middle class was to originate public opinion and dominate political life: yet this class was itself unequally divided between doctrines. For reasons that were, at bottom, unconscious, many of the bourgeoisie thought and worked in opposition to the general tendency of their class. A different perception of the same set of truths orientated their efforts in a different direction. Some unlikely allies were to be found in the confused movement which demanded some ill-defined social change and formed a party within the nation. On one side of the line separating philosophical radicals from Carlylean radicals we find systematic, abstract, dry, lucid minds of the utilitarian type; on the other, emotional, imaginative, and intuitive temperaments. When these co-existed with social and economic equality, it seems that tendencies deep within the personality urged men towards individualism or interventionism. The new antagonism which arose after 1832 might be explained psychologically as well as economically.

Individualism and the first stirrings of reaction

Writings dealing with social life between 1830 and 1850 seem, on examination, to proceed from two principal casts of mind. Certain personalities at the extremes exhibit one or the other unalloyed; average people share a little of each. It had long been accepted that there was opposition between hard-headed realists and men of imagination in England, but now the confrontation became explicit, and provided poles about which the whole gamut of individual types could cluster.

Outside England the realist is seen as the typical Englishman, practical and pragmatic. At first sight this was, indeed, the more striking type: it dominated the middle class, whose characteristics were increasingly to determine the popular image of the national character. It may be that pragmatic realism is the most striking feature in the genius of England, and accounts for much that is peculiar to English history. The huge achievements of practical materialism are everywhere apparent: political liberty, heavy industry, national prosperity, and social comfort.

The second, and rarer, English type is less familiar abroad. It may be met in all ranks of society, but is predominantly to be found among the artistic and intellectual *élite*. Its achievements are just as considerable as those of pragmatism, but are usually less tangible.[53] But it can be discerned in the literature, art, and religion of England: in the imaginative idealism of Shelley and Ruskin, or the ethical mysticism of Bunyan and Wesley. It has raised powerful hidden movements which have taken effect within the life of the nation. Puritanism and Methodism are the most famous of these: less well known, but comparable to the great soul-shaking historical movements, was the turmoil of social concern and philanthropic idealism which transformed England in the course of the nineteenth century, and which we are now investigating in the hope of finding out more about its origins and nature.

English individualism has been associated historically with the realistic materialist cast of mind. Towards the end of the seventeenth century such tendencies were crystallised in the social and political theory of Whiggism.[54] This doctrine proved itself in harmony with the spirit of England by winning a long period of power for those who professed it; and being, then, in the forefront of public discussion, it became more firmly rooted in the mind of England. The Whig faced politics in a practical, realistic spirit. His interest in immediate questions and material benefits gave him a constant determination to see political action produce results. His keen awareness of his own personal interest made him sensitive to any encroachment on it, so that he watched the Government closely and checked its tendency to interfere with the subject. He eschewed mysticism, and viewed social ties legalistically. Individualism and liberalism were the traditional characteristics of Whiggism, which dominated the eighteenth century, and only slowly lost ground in the nineteenth, for despite the stir created by philosophical radicalism, it was really the Whig spirit that ruled England after 1832. The continuity of its success and the adherence of successive generations to the same political attitude can be explained by its versatility and open-mindedness. It gained its essential viability from its appeal to one of the two basic English temperaments, but at the same time Whiggism did not openly affront the other. It was not a precise, inflexible doctrine with a systematic organisation that excluded alternative possibilities; it was more empirical than theoretical, and willingly accepted the collaboration of emotional idealism for practical ends. In fact, the principal exemplars of the Whig type in the nineteenth century were philanthropic men of affairs: witness Sydney Smith, or Macaulay, both of whom reconciled in themselves the dual psychology of the English character.[55]

Utilitarian philosophy was also a product of the realistic outlook. The definition of well-being on which it was based was of that concrete nature favoured by the English. The principle of utility did not originate with Bentham, but was handed down to him from traditional English philosophy.[56] For the rest, the utilitarians applied themselves to practical matters: 'His was an essentially practical mind,' said John Stuart Mill of Bentham; 'It was by practical abuses that his mind was first turned to speculation.'[57] Bentham offset this practical bias with an abstract analytical philosophic methodology: he reduced everything to logical minutiae, and then re-created his own systematic constructs. Mill described his 'sifting and anatomizing method'[58] as 'breaking every question into pieces before attempting to solve it.'[59] In this way his ideology fell prey to restrictive intellectualism, and became dry and rigid. It opposed imagination and feeling and accepted the dictates of common sense as the intuitive heart of reality and moral life.

At that point utilitarianism diverged from the mainstream of British thought. The popular stereotype of a Benthamite, by 1820, represented him as an alarming eccentric: Mill complained of 'that cold, mechanical and ungenial air which characterizes the popular idea of a Benthamite.'[60] The overriding demand for logic ruffled some very powerful national habits of thought, and the exclusion of emotion, imagination, and idealising vitality was unobtrusively wounding to at least half the genius of England. James Mill was the extreme exemplar of this type of utilitarian. His son has left an unforgettable picture of him in his *Autobio-*

graphy. In the elder Mill, contempt for poetry and feeling, the intellectual rationalisation of all emotion, and a concentration of the mind on the exclusive pursuit of truth were taken to an extreme. 'He, in a degree once common, but now very unusual, threw his feelings into his opinions.'[61] To a lesser extent these characteristics were to be found in all the members of the philosopher's circle. Ricardo the financier, whose dealings on the Stock Exchange had made him rich, had a passion for pure mathematics, as did the philosophical radical Molesworth.[62] It was the young John Stuart Mill who first succeeded in breaking out of this emotional desert. His upbringing had been a masterpiece of concentrated intellectualism, and at the same time, the ultimate condemnation of exclusively rational philosophy. The crisis which aroused living emotions in Mill might almost symbolise the return of thinking England to its natural pattern, so deep was its intensity, and so far-reaching its consequences.

The anomalous ideology of utilitarianism had, indeed, been aided by fortune in the early 1830s. The philosophers at the centre had formulated their ideas and broadcast them to the mass of the nation; those who were so inclined understood and appreciated them, while others imitated them, and echoed a passable imitation of intellectual utilitarianism. Thus the age took its character from this controlling force in the cultural ethos. It was curiously similar to the English Augustan age, when French values came to dominate English cultural life, and the pleasures of the understanding seemed more important than the pleasures of the feelings. In the 1830s, many Englishmen were challenging the time-honoured concepts underlying society and the law, and asking what logical arguments or rational demonstrations supported them.[63]

> To Bentham more than to any other source might be traced the questioning spirit, the disposition to demand the 'why' of everything, which had gained so much ground and was producing such important consequences in these times.

This 'disposition' spread from bookish men like the Mills to politicians like the philosophical radicals, and on to tradesmen like Place. Christianity offered no resistance to this critical analysis: the utilitarians dared not to believe, even if they did not dare to say so too loudly.[64] As if it supported their criticisms, the Established Church was itself coldly unenthusiastic, suffocating in an eighteenth-century torpor, with arid moralising predominating inside its doors as in the world outside. Religious idealism seemed quenched for ever. 'To English ears in the first half of the nineteenth century, "mysticism" was as ugly a word as "reserve".'[65] The utilitarians had enemies, but no worthy adversaries. The clergy approved and adopted Malthusian theory, and the Englishman's soul seemed to have lost all capacity for feeling.

What caused this phenomenon? It seems likely that the answer is to be found in the rise of the new bourgeoisie. The class which came to power in 1832 was instinctively utilitarian, unconsciously practising a debased form of enlightened self-interest. 'In highly civilized countries,' said Mill, 'and particularly among ourselves, the energies of the middle classes are almost confined to money-getting.'[66] Their moral vision was as narrow as that of the utilitarian philosophers, though they lacked the justifying system. Psychologically at least, English industrialism was the product of mechanical ingenuity and the practical materialistic temperament. This temperament was, in turn, reinforced by industrialism, and swelled to the point where it might be described as a national industrial obsession. A whole generation acquired an arithmetical outlook from their preoccupation with profits, accounts, and the growth and increasing complexity of business enterprises. Everything was evaluated quantitatively: figures sketched in the limits of experience to the businessman's imagination; material objects became the being and substance of experience; statistics replaced actual observations. Thus an attitude of materialist metaphysics, as it were, evolved, in which monetary value determined all questions. The proud, grasping bourgeoisie, whose virtues lay in the domain of energy, put forward a wretched code of moral standards: self-interest and materialism; the pursuit of profit, to the exclusion of other considerations; a strictly quantitative assessment of worth. The common yardstick of profit was applied to feeling, responsibility, and even religion: 'The Gospel truth, Godliness is great gain, is never', observed Ure, 'more applicable than in the case of the administration of an extensive factory.'[67]

This is what Carlyle exposed so effectively in his essay on the 'Signs of the Times' (1829):[68]

> Were we required to characterize this age of ours by any single epithet, we should be tempted to call it, not an Heroical, Devotional, Philosophical or Moral age, but, above all others, the Mechanical Age. It is the age of Machinery, in every outward and inward sense of that word. . . . Men are grown mechanical in head and in heart as well as in hand. . . . Their whole efforts, attachments, opinions, turn on mechanism, and are of a mechanical character. . . . We may trace this tendency, we think, very distinctly in all the great manifestations of our time; in its intellectual aspect, the studies it most favours and its manner of conducting them; in its practical

aspects, its politics, arts, religion, morals; in the whole sources, and throughout the whole currents, of its spiritual, no less than its material activity.

The words are exaggerated, but the profound impression mechanisation had made on men's minds is apparent. It may also be observed that there is a correlation between businessmen totting up accounts and philosophers analysing experience quantitatively. We noted a mathematical tendency in utilitarian philosophy: the parallel bourgeois outlook may help us to understand this.

Thus individualism, a traditional outlet for the realistic materialist temperament, came to full flower in ideas and manners around 1830. To the extent that an economic revolution had increased the number and social standing of men who lived by individualist principles, a dominant position in intellectual life was available to a philosophy which sought to present the entire moral order schematically. Yet individualism was distorted by its take-over of thought and action: it lapsed into sterile abstraction among the utilitarians, and grew into sheer commercial greed among businessmen. There were affinities between these parallel deviations: the narrow moral vision engendered by industrial attitudes, and elevated into a kind of abstract principle, was common to both. And each seemed alarming to those imaginative idealists who instinctively sought to redress the moral imbalance in the nation. Average men, who combined a modicum of practicality with a modicum of idealism, tended instinctively to support the reaction in favour of a fuller emotional life as it began. Exclusive rationalism and exclusive self-interest were not a part of normal life, which consisted of a steady attempt to adjust to things as they were. In the hands of the Benthamites and their bourgeois allies, the old Whig spirit of practical realism had become theoretical and inadequate: it had contradicted its original nature, and ceased to be practical.[69] This explains why the bulk of the people found themselves in sympathy with the idealistic reaction when it came: psychologically, as well as socially, it met their needs.

Two

The utilitarian novel

The conditions of the 1830s put new life into the social novel. The form had existed previously, but Bulwer and Miss Martineau, who were deeply indebted to Ricardo and James Mill, now revitalised it. We must consider briefly the origins of the social novel prior to 1830, bearing in mind the factors favouring its rise to prominence after the Reform Act.

Novels with a purpose before 1830

The social novel derived from two sources. The first was the late-eighteenth-century revolutionary novel, a form linked by outlook and feeling to *Paul Clifford* and *Illustrations of Political Economy*. The French Revolution had a powerful impact on England; there was a liberal *avant-garde* of philosophers and political writers in the country between 1790 and 1800 and, as revolutionary aspirations spread among progressive thinkers, it seemed that the nation might be won over to the cause of reform as early as 1792. The whole movement was halted by the Terror, the war with France, and the automatic conservative response they evoked, so that by 1800 the upsurge of radical fervour was over. Wordsworth recovered from his political fever; the radicals withered away, and were a forgotten species within fifteen years. Yet between 1798 and 1800 English public opinion was keyed up to receive challenging new ideas.[1] In this atmosphere the *roman-à-thèse* appeared and flourished. The leader of the school was William Godwin, and he and Thomas Holcroft, Elizabeth Inchbald, Amelia Opie, and Charlotte Smith pressed imaginative literature into the service of their revolutionary faith. Charlotte Smith explained their intention in the following words:[2]

> There is a chance that those who will read nothing if they do not read novels, may collect from them some few ideas, that are not either fallacious or absurd, to add to the very scanty stock which their insipidity of life has afforded them.

Thus the new form grew spontaneously out of the popular taste for novels acquired during the eighteenth century and the need for propaganda created by the agitation of the time.

The principal examples were Godwin's *Caleb Williams* and *St. Leon* (1794 and 1799) and Holcroft's *Anna St. Ives* (1792). This last novel contains the essence of the programme common to the whole school.[3] As the result of an implacable analysis of social conditions, anarchism and the theory of positive progress are put forward as combined ideals. Logical inquiry is applied to the institutions of civilisation, and the long accumulations of day-to-day experience crumble under its pressure. Condorcet's dream of humanity undismayed by the prospect of death (which shall itself have died, perhaps overwhelmed by life's splendid happiness) is to be realised through the abolition of marriage, the family, and property, and the practice of simple living, obedience to instinct, and a free expansion of human virtue. This intransigent doctrine appealed to those who favoured an artistic way of life. But mingled with the vaguely humanitarian effusions, it is interesting to discover Godwinian philosophy, that crabbed logic which Wordsworth was ultimately to lift himself out from.[4]

Like the utilitarians of 1830, this group of theoreticians found themselves faced with an anomalous situation created by their overwhelming passion for reason. Normal human nature rejected Godwin's philosophy, and only a handful of disciples could stomach it. After a short burst of prominence at the end of the century, the revolutionary novel, which depended on this philosophy, disappeared. Mrs Opie's *Adeline Mowbray* (1804) and Godwin's *Fleetwood* (1805) were the last representatives of the form, which seemed utterly spent.[5] From 1800 till 1820 the general public was in the grip of a Tory reaction which flatly rejected radicalism. The swing to conservatism meant that no-one wanted to read arguments favouring revolutionary change.

Thus the origins of the utilitarian novel were singular. It looked back to an isolated group of original works produced by the fusion of rationalism and imaginative literature at the end of the eighteenth century. By comparison the sort of social novel Dickens wrote belonged to a continuing, unbroken tradition, embedded in the instructive and moral quality apparent throughout English art, and reflecting the constant English preoccupation with the ethical goals which artists and common humanity alike may pursue. In painting as well as literature the English, from the Reformation onwards, had tried to describe and depict the soul of man: no English artist could consider the moral stance of art as a neutral, abstract, aesthetic question. And this outlook left its mark on the novel more than on any other genre. The novel borrowed its main features from life, and was naturally led towards passing judgement on what it described. It condemned inadequate reality by opposing to it idealism and duty. The more realistic the novel, the greater its preoccupation with moral assessment, and ethical questions only failed to engage English writers when they concerned themselves with works of pure fantasy. But as art eschewed this and approached closer to reality, it dedicated itself the more assiduously to moral instruction. If we examine the inspiration behind English realistic writing, we are more likely than not to discover that the work is animated by fiery passion. The creator's mind has usually been driven by a moral or religious fervour springing from emotion rather than intellect. The story of the novel, from Richardson to Dickens, is the story of that fervour: how it became social in its application; how evil came to appear under the guise of social injustice; how the love of virtue was replaced by pity for the wretched. Dickens's moral message differed from Richardson's because his century saw eternal evil in social terms.

The English novel was didactic from the first. Lyly's *Euphues* (1578) was far from being the mere stylistic squib that literary fashion read into Its tone was serious and its outlook religious, and in its description of a cultured man, the pursuit of Italian elegance was never allowed to obscure the importance of post-Reformation morality. The same instructive intention may be seen in the great imaginative works of the eighteenth century which founded modern English realism. Defoe, in *Robinson Crusoe*, gave a lesson in active fortitude. Richardson's intensely puritan conscience was the mainspring of his work: he was well aware of his moral purpose, and openly stated it. Fielding's greater experience and wider outlook did nothing to diminish his trust in human nature, honesty, and the calm acceptance of life. Sterne held up his characters' sensibility as a model for his readers, his pages radiating goodness of heart with infectious sympathy. Even Smollett, with his self-centred rancour against people and events, penetrated to the need for regret and the hope of improvement. Johnson's *Rasselas* was a treatise on the vanity of human wishes. Towards the end of the century, the educational theories expounded in Rousseau's *Émile* produced the pedagogic novel, typified by Thomas Day's *Sandford and Merton* (1783–9). Maria Edgeworth's stories for children enjoyed considerable literary success a little later (*Moral Tales*, 1801; *Popular Tales*, 1804).

Thus there was a long didactic tradition behind the novel by the 1830s, when the leading practitioners, struck by the vicious conduct of a society which Methodism had still failed to regenerate, turned their own reformative efforts in the direction of moral satire. When Dickens reached manhood social questions formed a part of the general intellectual ambience: this was certainly not the case in Richardson's day.

It is interesting to recall some of the books which had previously raised social questions. More's *Utopia* (1515–16) was a sixteenth-century communist novel. To the comparative detriment of English society, the author drew an ideal city. It was the dream of a sober and steadfast imagination, brought up on Plato, and then stimulated by the great Renaissance discoveries and enlargement of human understanding. Mrs Aphra Behn's *Oroonoko* might just be regarded as a humanitarian work exposing the horrors of slavery.[6] Defoe, in *Moll Flanders* (1722), lifted the veil from the seamy side of urban life, and exposed poverty and vice in London.[7] Smollett's bitter criticism of certain abuses he had encountered in experience made an appreciable impact on public opinion as it appeared in his work.[8] Finally three books, Henry Brooke's *Fool of Quality* (1766–70), Goldsmith's *Vicar of Wakefield* (1761), and Charles Lloyd's *Edmund Oliver* (1798), point to the invasion of the novel by Methodism and the philanthropic movement. John Wesley praised the first of these novels which, like *Euphues*, depicts the Christian ideal of an honest man. But Brooke's hero, instead of cultivating his wit and style, visits prisons and hospitals, helps the afflicted, and practises social welfare. Goldsmith introduced a dissertation on the penal code and the prison system into his ecclesiastical idyll, at a time when public attention was not in the least interested in these problems.[9] Finally Charles Lloyd, the son of a Quaker philanthropist, used his epistolary novel to attack Godwin's views on marriage. As a friend of Coleridge, Lloyd fits neatly into the anti-rationalist movement. With him, as with Goldsmith and Brooke, we are aware of the opposition existing between the philanthropic and the revolutionary novel.[10] These three works anticipate the social teachings of Dickens and Kingsley, just as Godwin and his circle herald the philosophical propaganda of Bulwer and Miss Martineau.[11]

There is, nevertheless, a break in continuity between these two rival groups of reformist novels and *Paul Clifford*, the work with which our study begins. Between 1815 and 1830 Sir Walter Scott's historical novels dominated English and continental fiction alike. His powerful personality and copious output gave him a unique control over popular taste. Romanticism learned from him a sense of history and a passion for things historical; artistic attention was directed to the past. A host of imitators followed in Scott's footsteps and ignored the fine analytic skills of Jane Austen. But the spirit of *Ivanhoe* and *Rob Roy*, antithetical as it was to the outlook of Godwin, had affinities with the spirit of Disraeli. Scott, heading the romantic reaction, was conservative in his tastes, and his work diametrically opposes *Caleb Williams* and *Paul Clifford* alike. But his work indirectly influenced and allied itself with that intellectual movement we are calling the idealist and interventionist reaction. It has been noted that the crowd – a new actor upon the literary stage – has a place in his novels.[12] But this is only one detail in the patriarchal appearance of the Middle Ages as described by Scott: his overall picture was intended to inspire the reader with regret for past times. He pointed out the charm and merit of the ancient hierarchical society which had been destroyed by the bourgeoisie's individualist energy. He described a simple human order where everyone knew his place as patron or dependant, and a united regional and national way of life where nobleman and beggar stood shoulder to shoulder in their opposition to strangers.[13] Scott was the predecessor of 'Young England' conservatism and of Guild socialism. Carlyle took his celebrated observation of the superiority of past over present from Scott.[14] A sense of the continuity of national life lies at the heart of the Romantic novel, and is later to be found in social Toryism and the Oxford Movement. Newman acknowledged Scott's influence; Disraeli exploited it.

Finally, the worldly novelists of the 'Silver Fork' school, contemporaneous with Scott, evoked by their utter insipidity a public reaction in favour of realism. 'Silver Fork' writing was called into being by the jealousy of the aristocracy for its privileged position when it seemed threatened, and the literary requirements of the new bourgeoisie with its admiring curiosity about refined life and vague aspiration after elegance, which produced snobbism.[15] But endless perfumed descriptions of drawing-room manners whetted a public appetite for 'rude, rough human nature'[16] which the social novel satisfied with its realistic content.

We still have to outline the conditions which favoured the reappearance of the *roman-à-thèse* after Scott's death. We are not now discussing the great economic and intellectual forces which gave matter and direction to the novels, but the changing circumstances which facilitated a literary approach to social questions. Of course, just as in 1790, political upheavals and industrial crises produced an intellectual and moral ferment in society from which problem novels arose. The questions were in the air; radical and philanthropic themes were taken up, and once again writers automatically responded to the preoccupations of the public.[17]

At this point the public which was to hail the success of the social novel came into being. When the middle class achieved political power it moved into the world of letters, and the first democratic extension of the franchise coincided with an enlargement of the literate public. For the radicals' crusade for popular education was starting to bear fruit: popular educational writings were on the increase, and some of the masses – artisans and skilled craftsmen – were learning in Mechanics' Institutes to read sufficiently to appreciate Dickens's works.[18] The press took a great stride forward as it shook off part of the burden of Stamp Duty.[19] New readers were steadily attracted by the great journals and reviews founded in the late-eighteenth and early-nineteenth centuries, and the constant discussion of social problems guaranteed a large audience for didactic novelists. Meanwhile the novel itself had broken into new markets. Dickens's novels were published in parts, and fragmented thus they were no longer so expensive as to exclude lower middle class and artisan readers. Sales of each number rose to unprecedented heights.[20]

At the same time public opinion became the strongest power in the land. The Reform Act altered the basis of politics: ultimate power no longer rested with the House of Commons, but was transferred to that nebulous force, the will of the people. Parliament was in contact with the people, and was sensitive to every move they made. But the daily press was the true ruler of this new source of power. And any instrument capable of communicating with the hearts and minds of people in the mass, and thereby determining the current of their opinion, could be sure of attracting immediate attention in government circles.[21] Social, religious, and political propaganda became the distinctive feature of the age. Pamphlets, books, and articles for and against all parties and public figures were published on all sides. Around 1830, then, the new social classes entering upon intellectual life extended the boundaries instruction could influence at the same time as public opinion's increased hold over the Government swelled the potential effectiveness of such influence. This explains the kingly popular success of a Dickens as well as the measurable success of social novels in changing society's laws and customs.

Bulwer: the utilitarian phase

The social novel was only a passing phase in Bulwer's career. But it is worth spending a little time on *Paul Clifford*, a book with a twofold historical interest: it marks the point when utilitarianism became genuinely influential in literature; and it had some influence on penal reform.

Edward Bulwer (1803–73) was the youngest son of General Bulwer and the rich heiress Miss Lytton.[22] Thus he was descended from two ancient families. He was brought up by his mother at her country house, Knebworth, and proved a precocious child with a lively, inquiring mind. In 1825 as an undergraduate he won the Chancellor's Medal at

Cambridge for his poem on sculpture. By the time he was twenty he had already published some poems in imitation of Byron. These were followed by a novel, *Falkland*. In 1828 *Pelham*, another novel, enjoyed a fashionable success. This, coupled with Bulwer's affected modishness and public ostentation, gave him the artificial appearance of a dandy of the period, distinguished only by his satirical mind and literary talent. Nothing about him suggested the serious philanthropist or dedicated social reformer. The young, brilliant novelist might glance at social ideas with his piercing intellect. But his versatile nature was, for a short time, to combine with an attitude acquired at the university, and make him a public crusader.

J. S. Mill has described the effect produced on his Cambridge contemporaries by Charles Austin. It was, said Mill, 'an historical event; for to it may in part be traced the tendency towards Liberalism in general, and the Benthamic and politico-economic form of it in particular, which showed itself in a portion of the more active-minded young men of the higher classes from this time to 1830.'[23] Austin was an effective speaker, never defeated in Students' Union debates. He twisted utilitarian ideas paradoxically, according to Mill, presenting them 'in the most startling form of which they were susceptible, exaggerating everything in them which tended to consequences offensive to any one's preconceived feelings.'[24] Naturally, young men were delighted by this pursuit of paradox, and one group followed Austin's example, and prided themselves on extracting the most outrageous conclusions from Benthamist argument. Although Mill does not mention Bulwer by name in this group, we know that he was at Cambridge at the time, and when, in 1825, Mill and his friends formed a discussion group in London to examine Ricardo and Bentham, they brought together, he says 'nearly all the most noted speakers of the Cambridge Union and of the Oxford United Debating Society. . . . Besides those already named, we had Macaulay, Thirlwall, Praed, Lord Howick, Samuel Wilberforce (afterwards Bishop of Oxford), Charles Poulett Thomson (afterwards Lord Sydenham), Edward and Henry Lytton Bulwer, Fonblanque, and many others.'[25] The novelist and the philosopher kept up personal contact until 1833, at which date Mill wrote a critical study of Bentham's philosophy for Bulwer's book *England and the English*. And Bulwer's own political writings are powerful proof of the impression Benthamism made on him.

The novel whose success made him famous, *Pelham, or the Adventures of a Young Gentleman*, contains valuable evidence about the nature of Bulwer's conversion to philosophy. The hero is Bulwer himself.[26] Cynical, witty, and brilliant, Pelham is not remotely like the typical traditional Benthamite. He is an aristocratic young dandy who comes to know the world in the course of adventures in London and Paris, and seeks nothing higher than the satisfaction of his own curiosity. But one day, while he is breakfasting in a country-house library, his uncle Glenmorris undertakes to re-educate him. 'You see this very small pamphlet,' he says; 'it is a paper by Mr. Mill upon government.'[27] And having praised its worth he opens it, and proves from it a dry, mathematical case which cannot be faulted or contradicted by logic. The effect on the hero is magical. He develops a taste for such work, reads all Mill's articles in the *Encyclopædia Britannica*, proceeds to the less abstruse writings of Bentham, and finally plunges headlong into the arcane mysteries of political economy. He finds it hard to tear himself away from this stimulating science, from which he gains a distinct moral advantage: he learns the principle governing right conduct. 'I no longer divorced the interests of other men from my own.'[28] A highly utilitarian concept, without which he would not know how to avoid doing evil, for 'nothing, perhaps, is less innate than virtue.'[29] Within a page, the dandy reappears: '"True, my dear mother," said I, with a most unequivocal yawn, and depositing on the table Mr. Bentham on "Popular Fallacies".'[30]

These passages, together with a whole host of others, exhibit Bulwer's enthusiasm for utilitarianism. As a young Cambridge student with an inquiring mind and a passion for novelty, he found outlets for his self-esteem and tastes in Charles Austin's paradoxes. He was persuaded to accept the doctrines of utilitarianism because there was still something daring and suspect about them which fed his appetite for striking originality and superiority over common minds and common sense. At the same time, like others of his contemporaries, he was excited by the absolutely systematic schematisation of the moral order.[31] Under his uncle's guidance, Pelham discovers 'how inseparably allied is this great science of public policy with that of private morality.'[32] But he is too much of a dilettante to put all his faith in Bentham, and as a man of the world sneers at the boring solemnity of the very works he venerates. In a word, Bulwer's conversion to utilitarianism was a passing intellectual fancy or mental frolic. Moreover, *Pelham* neither offers nor pretends to offer any serious message. Only a handful of brief asides anticipates the reforming ambitions of *Paul Clifford*.[33] Utilitarianism emerges as little more than a superior attitude of mind.

The novels immediately following *Pelham* were equally undidactic.[34] But a new influence was added to Benthamism which modified without contradicting Bulwer's utilitarianism, and completed his formal philosophical equipment. Shortly after the publication of *Pelham* he made the acquaintance of Godwin. The grand old man of English communism had lost none of his abstract convictions and philosophical austerity. But Bulwer, radical and dandy, interested him as a personality. Godwin wrote to him in 1830:[35]

> I have known you but a short time. I knew you as the author of *Pelham*, a man of eminent talents, and devoted, as it seemed to me, to the habits of high life. I heard from your lips occasionally high sentiments of philosophy and philanthropy. I was to determine as I could which of these two features formed the basis of your character.

Reassured by Bulwer's political stance and his participation in the liberal campaign for the Reform Bill, Godwin opened his heart to him. This very dissimilar pair exchanged ideas. One letter of Bulwer's shows him defending utilitarian ethics against Godwin's criticisms: the latter had objected that the principle of self-interest made virtue impossible; morality rested on benevolence, not self-interest. Bulwer replied that if he was at fault it was 'in words, not things'.[36] In the course of their conversations the themes of *Paul Clifford* must have been discussed. Half the social philosophy of that novel derives from Godwin and, as the Preface to the first edition shows, Bulwer was aware of his indebtedness.

This Preface is interesting. In it Bulwer shows that he is acutely conscious of a need to put his ideas into a novel. The form, he says, was imposed on him. What else might he have written? Poems? But the time is unfavourable: 'A tide of popular opinion has set against poetry.'[37] No, the novel is fashionable, and has the longest hold on public attention. 'Does the biography, or the essay, or the treatise, last even the year for which a novel endures?'[38] Moreover literature must be adapted to the decided tastes of the middle classes, who now demand instruction from novels. 'People will only expend their time for immediate returns of knowledge. . . . Readers now look into fiction for facts.'[39] Certainly Bulwer has mastered a new and exciting philosophy. So in writing a light novel he endeavours to hit upon 'some amusing, perhaps even some useful, truths'.[40]

In this way Bulwer combined originality with a bow to public taste. For the philosophical novel had become extremely rare. Godwin was its sole exponent, and his works were as crabbed as his mind. Bulwer, on the other hand, was trying to combine instruction with comedy. He intended a return to the spirit of Fielding. The original idea for the book may have come from Godwin:[41]

For the original idea of Paul Clifford, I am indebted to a gentleman of considerable distinction in literature, and whose kindness to me is one of my most gratifying remembrances. . . . I should add, first, that I feel I have given a very inadequate form to a conception that appears to me peculiarly felicitous; and secondly, that . . . I have made use of his idea rather as an adjunct to my story, than as the principal groundwork of the story itself.

But in the end, the book was written as much for fashionable acclaim as for its message, and Bulwer eschewed overtly serious discussion. He hinted his intentions instead of presenting them directly. And so the writer who revived the social novel was aware from the outset of the need for innovation and the dictates of public taste.

'Paul Clifford'

In writing *Paul Clifford*, Bulwer imitated Gay's *Beggar's Opera*, wherein a comic transposition makes petty criminals the heroes of the piece (or in Macheath's words, 'Through the whole piece you may observe such a similitude of manners in high and low life, that it is difficult to determine whether (in the fashionable vices) the fine gentlemen imitate the gentlemen of the road or the gentlemen of the road the fine gentlemen'), and Fielding's *Jonathan Wilde*, which uses a criminal career to illustrate the thesis that only social circumstances and our mental prejudices make any real difference between a great rogue and a great conqueror. For Gay and Fielding the message is purely literary and lacks topical application. But Bulwer's dramatic flair spotted the possibility of exploiting the device for social satire. And Godwin proffered a suggestive title – 'Masks and Faces'. The author of *Political Justice* had always been haunted by the Rousseauesque theory that society was responsible for crime, and this would be restated in a work which unveiled hypocrisy, re-examined human nature under the stifling forms of convention, and exposed the evil done by laws, customs, and established institutions.

Criminals, moreover, were inevitably involved with two of the dearest concerns of Benthamism – the penal code and the criminal law. And so Bulwer took a highwayman as his hero; contrasted the frank freedom of his life with the furtive vices of respectable folk like judges; made him the victim of social circumstances which made him take up crime, and prison which completed his corruption; and finally hinted at the absurdity of legislation which destroyed the guilty instead of reforming them. All this satisfied the public taste for instructive novels, outlined Godwin's critique of society in the structure of its plot, and served the cause of Benthamism in its denunciation of the law's barbarity.

Paul Clifford was dedicated to Albany Fonblanque, the brilliant young journalist whose name was long associated with law reform. He was a close friend of Bentham and Mill, and through him Bulwer came into contact with the chiefs of the reform movement, such as the utilitarians Romilly, Mackintosh, and Brougham, the philanthropists Elizabeth Fry, Wilberforce, and Buxton, and the editor of the *Morning Chronicle*, Black, who ran a fierce crusade against the evils of the penal code and the régime in prisons after 1823. By 1830 reform was in the air despite all such resistance as that personified by Eldon among the judiciary.[42] And at this point, Bulwer struck.

Paul Clifford, a foundling, grows up amid squalor and crime in London. He falls into bad company, is arrested for another's crime, and is sentenced to three months imprisonment.[43] An edifying spectacle confronts him in the Bridewell: a gang of hardened ruffians, living in the enforced intimacy of a single room, intensify each other's wickedness.[44] The child's natural virtue is not strong enough to withstand exposure to this: the sophistry of a philosophical sharper, Tomlinson, initiates him into the joys of a life of theft.[45] This is the beginning of a criminal career in which the hero is the world's most gallant highwayman, and never spills blood unless it is absolutely essential. His person and spirit are so elegant and charming that he can mingle, incognito, with the very best society, where his mysterious attractions are so distinguished that he wins the love of Squire Brandon's supposed daughter Lucy over the heads of a score of rivals.[46] Captured at last, he is charged with armed robbery, an offence, like many others, carrying the death penalty under English law.[47] A providential twist of fortune saves Clifford, and his penitence exposes the absurdity of a law which chooses to kill instead of rehabilitating. Bulwer ends on the true utilitarian note: 'The very worst use to which you can put a man is to hang him.'[48]

He was talking sense. The number of offences punishable by death had risen to 223. Between 1819 and 1825, 579 people were hung in England and Wales. Twenty years later, four-fifths of the crimes for which they suffered would no longer carry the death penalty.[49] On this list we find 21 executions for horse-stealing, 29 for sheep-stealing, 62 for forgery and uttering forged instruments, 5 for secreting and stealing letters containing bank-notes, 2 for sacrilege, 10 for arson and other wilful burning of property, 128 for burglary, etc.[50] Judges themselves were appalled by the law's barbarity and did not always exact its full penalties; in many cases

a measure of indulgence was traditional, if not strictly legal, and anticipated the introduction of greater humanity into the penal system.

The prisons were a similar offence to reason and humanity. Howard's
work did not survive him. Prisoners were still treated with astonishing
cruelty and neglect, and their minds and bodies degraded by the absence
of any moral or physical hygiene. Cynicism and habitual routine hindered
the reforms demanded by conditions. Prisoners were still herded together. When Bulwer visited Coldbath Fields Prison and the Bridewell
he saw the results of 'classification' – a regulation imposed by a law of
George IV which separated convicts according to age and sex.[51] Experience showed that it was totally inadequate.[52] Prison inspectors reported
officially that '*absolute impunity* would, in many cases, have been prefer-
able to the ruinous effects of commitment to a gaol.'[53] Thus, Paul
Clifford's words at his trial were justified by reality: 'Your laws are but
of two classes; the one makes criminals, the other punishes them. I have
suffered by the one – I am about to perish by the other.'[54] And Bulwer
observes wittily that 'young people are apt, erroneously, to believe that
it is a bad thing to be exceedingly wicked. The House of Correction is so
called, because it is a place where so ridiculous a notion is invariably
corrected.'[55]

Such is the obvious serious message of *Paul Clifford*. But there is
another, less precisely stated, to be extrapolated from its pages, wherein
Godwin's influence can be seen. This is a general criticism of the order of
society, in so far as it rests upon convention and delusion. Parallel with
the career of Paul Clifford, the life of the respectable lawyer, Brandon, is
slowly unfolded. In the eyes of the world the first stands for vice and the
second for virtue. Yet Paul would have been a good man had not society
done everything in its power to make him fall victim to temptation. And
Brandon is corrupt in spite of material circumstances which have shielded
him from any distress or calumny. Brandon turns out to be Paul Clifford's
father, and is ultimately called upon to sit in judgement on him. In a
dramatic confrontation the worthy citizen and the felon face each other
across the statute-book. Paul then forthrightly denounces the established
order which has condemned him:[56]

> Let those whom the law protects consider it a protector: when did
> it ever protect *me*? When did it ever protect the poor man? The
> government of a state, the institutions of law, profess to provide for
> all those who 'obey'. Mark! A man hungers – do you feed him?
> He is naked – do you clothe him? If not, you break your covenant, you
> drive him back to the first law of nature, and you hang him, not

because he is guilty, but because you have *left* him naked and starving.

Elsewhere in the novel, Bulwer's social criticism is blander. He does little more than parody well-ordered society in the operations of robbers taking their toll from the roads, and suggest that civilised manners and customs may be found among highwaymen.

Paul Clifford has its *roman-à-clef* element: prominent political personages including the King himself appear under the transparent guise of thieves assembled to divide up their booty.[57] Whigs and Tories are abused equally, each political party being no better than a gang of pickpockets, while the honesty of a minister is like that of a footpad. In the end Tomlinson, the underworld philosopher, holds forth amusingly on the beauties of a social order that hangs its Paul Cliffords and appoints its Brandons to the judiciary. And by way of an appendix he passes on to us the maxims he has learned from experience and set down for posterity. These *Tomlinsoniana* are a collection of paradoxes on social morality, expounding in a variety of ways the gap between appearance and actuality – 'Masks and Faces'.[58]

This facile irony tends to detract from the serious impact of the penological argument, and compromises the novel's message. Godwin's anarchism was profound and powerful when treated with his own sincerity. But in Bulwer's hands it became a *jeu d'esprit*, and his book's cool dandiacal tone contrasts singularly with the revolutionary audacity of its ideas. With a smile on his lips, Bulwer defends the lives of those wretches who have been corrupted or destroyed by the law. His wit is not underpinned by any firm foundation of passion: it is superficial and good-humoured. Which means, in this context, that it is wrong. The gallant outlaw Paul Clifford and his followers are sheer fantasy. They are characters created to a logical pattern which cuts them off from any contact with the urgency of real life. The character of Brandon is the only one endowed with a certain amount of vitality.

The whole book is marred by this artificiality. The accounts of the poor and the teeming populace of London's underworld are transparently false. The aristocratic author has given slums and tenements no closer inspection than a quick glimpse in passing.[59] The novel's irredeemable failure is apparent in the utter lack of any real sympathy for the poor or genuine compassion for the law's victims. Not one word of the book is written with absolute sincerity.[60]

Nevertheless it was very successful. The first impression was published on 4 May 1830, and a second was called for by 27 August.[61] Godwin hailed its publication enthusiastically, and wished he could consign all his own work 'in the province of fiction' to the fire.[62] Some readers were offended by the novel's cynicism: Paul Clifford succeeded too well in confusing the distinction between good and evil, and perhaps there is something irresponsible about upsetting the ordinary standards of right and wrong throughout the course of a long book. This, at any rate, was the central weakness that Thackeray pounced on in his witty parody of Bulwer's paradoxical dilettantism.[63] But contemporaries were more impressed by *Paul Clifford*'s one undoubted literary merit, the dramatic appeal of its narrative. Ebenezer Elliott, the 'Corn-law Rhymer', testified to its attraction in the following words:[64]

> You have ruined me by writing 'Paul Clifford'. I can think of nothing else. Adieu Jeremy Bentham! Adieu all my old teachers, more solemn, but not wiser, and less inspired! . . . The dramatic power of the book is wonderful.

It is not surprising that so enjoyable a book influenced public opinion. A translation into French provided arguments for continental opponents of capital punishment. Louis Blanc called it a 'beautiful and philosophical novel'.[65]

In England, according to R. H. Horne, it rendered 'the lowest characters. . .interesting to the imagination.'[66] Sure enough, a series of novels whose heroes were criminals followed *Paul Clifford*. Ainsworth's *Jack Sheppard* (1838) was the best known of these, but Dickens's *Oliver Twist* too owes something to Bulwer's work. Criminal slang appeared for the first time in *Paul Clifford*, and was to be exploited by novels in the future.[67] Finally, and plainly, 'The publication of "Paul Clifford" did much to stimulate public opinion in favour of carrying Criminal Law Reform far beyond the point at which it had been left by the labours of Romilly.'[68] The fact is that the exertions of the philanthropists (like those of the utilitarians) were to bear fruit after 1830. In 1835 a committee of the House of Lords pronounced itself in favour of separate cells for prisoners, and two prison inspectors condemned the way Newgate was run. The number of crimes carrying the death penalty was sharply reduced in 1832, and again in 1837.[69] The justice of its cause rather than the excellence of its writing made *Paul Clifford* one of those books which have an effect on historical events.

Yet the author did not repeat the experiment. His next novel, *Eugene Aram* (1832), made no comment on society. True, Bulwer still proved himself the disciple of Bentham and Godwin, preoccupied with abstract psychology, logical argument, and the search for 'vast and complicated theorems in the consideration of our nature, social and individual.'[70] But the immediate imperfections of contemporary society no longer interested him even in the abstract. He was drawn instead to the study of moral anomalies. *Eugene Aram* is a bridge between *Paul Clifford* and Bulwer's later works, where his inquiring mind was focused on distant ages, bizarre mentalities, and mysticism. His radicalism hardly survived his brief period as a Benthamite. He had always felt his position as one of the minority ruling class, and as his lulled aristocratic instinct revived, his opinions came to harmonise with his temperament.[71] Around 1850 he returned to politics, giving his support to conservative policies. In 1859 and 1860 he campaigned against electoral reform. When he became Lord Lytton he took his natural place among England's hereditary rulers. His supple and versatile talent was employed throughout his life in a wide variety of writings – plays, historical novels, psychological novels – almost all interesting, yet never quite good enough to sustain serious attention.[72] A certain lack of intellectual stamina vitiates his conscientious adoption of successive attitudes. One might almost say that philanthropic utilitarianism would have been better expounded by some other novelist. Yet Bulwer's faults as man and writer, his moral astringency and artificiality, certainly provide a perfect contrast to the impassioned convictions of Dickens and Kingsley. The literary mediocrity of *Paul Clifford* is closely akin to the psychological character we found to be prevalent in the weaker hangers-on of Bentham and the utilitarian temperament.

Harriet Martineau: 'Illustrations of Political Economy'

Apart from the anarchist theorising, which Bulwer himself did not really grasp, the argument of *Paul Clifford* is taken from the positive, generous side of individualism. The utilitarian attempt to rationalise society appears in the form of hostility to a cruel penal code, and the individual whom Bulwer defends turns out to be, predominantly, the socially weak individual: the ordinary victim of bad laws. Harriet Martineau's work, on the other hand, represents the negative aspect of individualism. The *Illustrations of Political Economy* (1832–4) are the sharp, chilling response of dogmatic learning to popular aspirations.

Economics had established itself by 1830. Universities had created chairs of economics,[73] and no alternative system of thought had appeared to contradict it. At first it was taken up by the industrial bourgeoisie; then politicians were converted, and at last even the nobility capitulated.[74] But the masses remained hostile to the new science which they opposed with instinctive repugnance. In spite of the clearly defined outlines,

Ricardian economics proved abstract and difficult. Some attempts were made to disseminate economic thinking more widely,[75] but by 1832 the work of popularisation still seemed urgently necessary. The agitation over the Reform Bill had frightened the victors themselves; the bourgeoisie sensed hidden dangers in the public anger it had stirred up. This was the beginning of the revolutionary period of trade unionism, when the dream of a general association of all workers seemed on the verge of realisation. The National Association for the Protection of Labour was founded in 1830 and joined by 150 unions. Its organ, *The Voice of the People*, appeared in January 1831.[76] The problem of the Poor Law seemed to grow thornier every day as complaints about the anomalies and injustice of the old régime poured in from all quarters. But the system could not be changed until the people's deep-rooted conviction that they were entitled to public assistance and paternalistic State care had been eradicated.

In the end a species of intellectual philanthropy came to the aid of political economy. When Miss Martineau's first stories were published in 1832, informed opinion stood thus: the masses suffer because they do not understand the laws regulating society; all their misery springs from these inexorable socio-economic laws, and if they really want to attack the social order they must first understand it. Therefore it would be a useful and noble work to show them where their mistakes lie.

The writer who undertook this ungrateful task of expounding political economy in fiction was an unusual person. Harriet Martineau was born at Norwich in 1802, the descendant of a Huguenot who had settled in England after the revocation of the Edict of Nantes. Harriet's background was bourgeois: her father manufactured cheap cloth, and her mother was the daughter of a Newcastle sugar-refiner. The family's Unitarianism had hardened into a puritanism which, on the evidence of Harriet's *Autobiography*, was harsh and joyless.[77] The Napoleonic Wars weakened her father's financial position, and he was bankrupted in the slump of 1825. He died the following year, leaving his eight children without any support. The family faced poverty and Harriet earned her living by needlework. She might have married in 1827, but her fiancé lost his reason and died. She herself suffered permanently from poor physical health and mental distress. As a nervous, sickly child she had been distressed by her brothers' thoughtless boisterousness: 'I was almost the youngest of a large family, and subject not only to the rule of severity to which all were liable, but also to the rough and contemptuous treatment of the elder children, who meant no harm but injured me irreparably.'[78] In 1813 she was sent to boarding school where she began to lose her hearing. By 1820 she was deaf. All her life she had no sense of smell and little of taste. Only once did she appreciate the flavour of a leg of mutton: she thought it delicious. And this deprivation of sensory pleasure in her life was matched by a lack of emotion. The family's austere discipline cut her off from affectionate happiness. As a child she was sulky and withdrawn; as a young girl she suffered from nervous irritability and her parents were compelled to send her away from home. 'I am sure', she wrote, 'that a little more of the cheerful tenderness which was in those days thought bad for children would have saved me from my worst faults, and from a world of suffering.'[79] When a stranger made a fuss of her on one occasion she cried hysterically. It was not until she was sixteen that she discovered in an aunt 'the first person I was ever not afraid of'.

In spite of this her intellect and determination had developed a precocious strength. She applied herself to a course of self-instruction with stubborn, concentrated energy. 'My mind...was desperately methodical', she noted; 'Everything must be made tabular that would at all admit of it.'[80] At the age of seven she read *Paradise Lost* and learned most of it by heart. She approached religion as an intellectual problem, and systematically reasoned out her faith. At eighteen she was fanatically following a Unitarian minister, and read the Bible as a source of argument. Religious controversy led her to philosophy. Hartley and Priestley, the predecessors of the utilitarians, appealed to her logical mind, and she thought the former's *Treatise on Man* 'next to the Bible, the most important book in the world'. It gave her a determinist satisfaction to accept the doctrine of philosophic necessity. When she began writing herself, in 1827, it was to offer some polemical articles to a religious journal. In the same year she sent some short stories, one of which, 'The Rioters', dealt with the question of wages, to a London publisher, and planned a theological novel. In 1830 and 1831 she was awarded the prize offered by the Unitarian Society for three essays to convert Catholics, Moslems and Jews. By now she was contemplating a series of stories to expound political economy: in Dublin she sounded her brother James on the project in 1831, and he approved. Harriet's reason showed her that the task was necessary, and her conscience made it a duty for her to undertake. She would set about the conversion of the masses to economic truth just as she had set about the conversion of Moslems to Protestant truth.

Her *Autobiography* tells us a lot about the way she worked. There can be few examples of such logical and deliberately-willed artistic creation. The fusion of utilitarian rationalism and literature took place under paradoxically appropriate conditions:[81]

The whole business was the strongest act of will that I ever committed myself to, and my will was always a pretty strong one. . . . I strengthened myself in certain resolutions, from which I promised myself that no power on earth should draw me away. I was resolved that, in the first place, the thing should be done. The people wanted the book; and they should have it. Next, I resolved to sustain my health under the suspense, if possible, by keeping up a mood of steady determination, and unfaltering hope. Next, I resolved never to lose my temper, in the whole course of the business. I knew I was right; and people who are aware that they are in the right need never lose temper.

She describes all sorts of difficulties she faced. Publishers let her down; James Mill, when consulted, disapproved of the plan and recommended a book of pure instruction. At last, on 10 February 1832, the first volume appeared. It was an immediate and dazzling success. For two years she worked on at a steady pace. 'I am confident', she wrote, 'that intellectual industry and intellectual punctuality are as practicable as industry and punctuality in any other direction.'[82]

Her method of composition was significant. 'When I began, I furnished myself with all the standard works on the subject.'[83] We know what they were: Ricardo for theory and Mrs Marcet for popular exposition. 'I had made a skeleton plan of the course, comprehending the four divisions: Production, Distribution, Exchange and Consumption.'[84] She would jot down her own ideas on each particular question, and check them against the standard authorities. Then she would outline the economic principles to be illustrated in each narrative. This, she said, was 'the most laborious part of the work, and that which I certainly considered the most valuable.'[85] By now the setting and characters for the story could easily be devised. It only remained to find a character to personify each economic principle; the 'mutual operation of these embodied principles'[86] would furnish a plot! If the protagonists and the setting were unfamiliar to her, Miss Martineau would brief herself from books of travel. Finally she divided her material into chapters, which were ended not merely where the actions of the characters might indicate, but when they had offered 'all the political economy which it was their business to convey, whether by exemplification or conversation.'[87] This part of her work was so fatiguing as to make her feel unwell at times, but from then on it was easy going:[88]

I paged my paper; and then the story went off like a letter. I never could decide whether I most enjoyed writing the descriptions, the

The utilitarian novel

narrative, or the argumentative or expository conversations. I liked each best while I was about it.

One last detail: 'On average I wrote twelve pages a day – on large letter paper (quarto, I believe it is called) the page containing thirty three lines.'[89]

In this methodical manner, three series of tales were written.[90] They are not, strictly, literature; they lack art, if not artifice. But they are immensely valuable psychological documents. They bring to life one whole aspect of their period, of which their author was representative. They lay before us the energetic, positive spirit of the industrial bourgeoisie: self-disciplined, and equally firm with others; materialistic and accurate to the core; limited and insensitive emotionally. The Preface to the first collection (1832) is instructive: the apologia is informed with a hatred of all that is irrational, unproductive, and feudal: 'If a stranger had entered the castle of a nobleman, eight hundred years ago, and, grieved at what he saw, had endeavoured to put matters on a better footing, how ought he to set about it, and in what temper should he be listened to?' And the author imagines him giving the noble family a lesson:[91]

> I have been among the abodes of those who hew your wood and draw your water, and till your fields, and weave your garments; and I find that they are not allowed to exchange the produce of their labour as they will, but that artificial prices are set upon it, and that gifts are added to the profits of some which are taken out of the earnings of others.... These things need not be. There are methods of governing a family which will secure the good of all.

This passage offers a perfect example of the enormous gulf dividing the industrial outlook of the early 1830s from the later attitudes of the movement headed by Carlyle, Disraeli, Newman, and Ruskin. Biblical phraseology like 'hewers of wood and drawers of water' has its place in the feudal world Carlyle describes in *Past and Present*; but his intention is to exalt patriarchal, organic society at the expense of modern materialism's brutal anarchy.

Like the stranger in her Preface, Miss Martineau wanted to teach people the facts of social economics. Then why did she not compile a textbook? Again, for a practical reason: 'The reason why we choose the form of narrative is, that we really think it the best in which Political Economy can be taught, as we should say of nearly every kind of moral science. Once more we must apply the old proverb, "Example is better than precept."'[92] The pages of the Preface are shot through with Miss Martineau's conviction that she is purveying absolute unshakeable truth;

54

her intellectual enthusiasm for economic doctrine is almost an aesthetic appreciation: 'when truth is once laid hold of, it is easy to discover and display its beauty; and this, the last and easiest process, is what remains to be done for Political Economy.'[93] And she claims that her work is important for all sections of society: 'If it concerns rulers that their measures should be wise, if it concerns the wealthy that their property should be secure, the middling classes that their industry should be rewarded, the poor that their hardships should be redressed, it concerns all that Political Economy should be understood.'[94] These large promises are reminiscent of the early economists' calm dogmatic self-assurance, the impassioned zeal of their disciples, and the vague, generalised benevolence with which they confronted rich and poor alike.

To read one of Miss Martineau's stories is to know them all. The same artistic inadequacy runs throughout the series. The style is prosy; the characters are pedantic assemblages of parts; the incidents are unconvincing; the whole effect is lifeless. These failings were inevitable, and Miss Martineau actually deserves respect for having kept them to a minimum. Her language is clear, her structure logical, and the abstract ideas she handles are deftly simplified. Indeed, in this last respect she worked miracles: Ricardo's entire theory of rent is expounded and summarised through two simple, ignorant inhabitants of the Orkneys.[95] And among all the poor writing there are some interesting passages which carry a universal message and explain the success of the series.

The first tale, 'Life in the Wilds', is designed to illustrate the theory that wealth is a product of labour. A small, isolated colony in South Africa is attacked by natives who carry off all the settlers' tools and possessions. Thus they are reduced to the hypothetical position in which physical strength is the only form of wealth. They all set to work bravely, and man's continuous energetic struggle to overcome nature is depicted. Something of *Robinson Crusoe's* austere grandeur ennobles the writing at this point, although the overriding intentions of the story have turned the protagonists into economic puppets. After their initial despair, the community rallies, and each individual sets aside his private concerns and works for the common good. This opening may have evoked a deep emotional response in the bourgeois public of 1832. Life in a strange environment, the quiet courage of pioneers, and the solidarity of labour could be read into the pages. The flat, dull story communicated a philosophy as relevant to England as it was to distant colonies: the religion of power and work which gave the soul the strength to face the struggle of daily life. Its tenets might be summarised as follows: neighbour must help neighbour in the hardest tasks, for the group may succeed where the individual would fail. The only personal qualities that matter are the manly characteristics of strength and tenacity; sensitivity is no more than a hindrance to positive action. Ethics should be a code of useful social conduct. Religion is a way of asking a supernatural source for the strength to continue productive work.

In all this Miss Martineau was at one with the industrialists whose profound unconscious beliefs she expounded. She had made herself accept unquestioningly the dogmas of classical economics, and had so internalised them that they determined her spontaneous views. She was a perfect example of her social kind, and we can watch a habit of thought develop in her personality until it has become a complete elevation of abstract theories and formulas.

The bourgeois mind's practical energy had a challenging vigour whose very strength made it beautiful. But it was also a mind containing pettiness and cruelty, and this too can be deduced from Miss Martineau's work. We might conclude from 'Life in the Wilds' that the following characteristics were typical of her class: a smug acquiescence in established conventions, including social inequality; a tacit admission that material values are the only ones that count; an utter lack of idealism. Stone, the chaplain to the colonists, thanks Providence for the fact that 'we know we have only to work...to provide ourselves and our child with all that is necessary now, and with comforts and luxuries by and by.'[96] A child dies of snakebite, and 'it was an affecting thing to observe how George was missed by everybody,' comments the author; 'a sure sign what a valuable member of society he had been.'[97] The little band's efforts are ultimately rewarded by material prosperity: their storehouses are filled and their possessions replaced, and Adams, their leader, sums up the moral:[98]

> Let us still be united, let us still be industrious....Let us be tolerant of mere folly, and honour wisdom and reverence virtue, and we shall be sure of enjoying all the happiness a benignant Providence thinks good for us. Let us try whether it be not true of societies as well as of individuals, that Providence places their best happiness within their own reach.

This happiness consists of security: a roof overhead, a reserve for the future. It constitutes a decent, orderly society, but has no place for purely spiritual values or the dedicated pursuit of social justice.

The problems of industrialism are treated in the same spirit. 'The Hill and the Valley', the second tale, is supposed to outline the relationship between capital and labour. Wallace, the manufacturer, is an economist's dream: sensible, hard-working, well-intentioned, and unsentimental. His fortune has been built up over three generations: his great-grand-father was a labourer, his grandfather a shop-assistant, and his father a shopkeeper; a thumbnail sketch of the rise of the new bourgeoisie. Wallace has a methodical mind, makes prompt, firm decisions, and never allows his heart to rule his head. His wife shares his outlook, even pre-ferring a workshop to a scene of natural beauty: 'I know nothing more beautiful than to see a number of people fully employed, and earning comforts for themselves and each other.'[99] But a fall in the market hits the ironworks; profits drop, and wages are cut accordingly:[100]

> The first reduction was taken quietly; the second excited murmurs among the ignorant, and fear and sorrow among the clear-sighted of the sufferers; the third occasioned threats of actual rebellion. Some of the men refused to work for such wages. Their masters explained to them the necessity of keeping the works going, and continuing to produce as much iron as possible, at however low a price, in order to retain their stand in the market as long as their capital could be returned entire.

To economise still further, they introduce new machines:[101]

> This created an outcry; but how could it be helped? There was no other way of preserving the capital of the concern, and on that capital every man belonging to it depended as much as the partners.

Some redundant workers are dismissed, it being 'hoped by their masters and neighbours that they would carry their labour where it was more wanted, and leave the place in peace.'[102] But instead of meekly obeying the law of supply and demand by making new lives elsewhere, the unemployed men stay and spread dissension among their companions. A strike leads to violence, and the works is burnt down.

Wallace knows his rights, and is inflexible in doing nothing that would exceed his duty. His own interest is his only motive for action: his logic in dismissing his redundant employees is pitiless. He sees himself as an economic abstraction, linked by the cash nexus to other economic ab-stractions. It seems to him inevitable that the workers should bear the brunt of economic depression: any attempt to revolt against the system rests on miscalculation and will result in disaster:[103]

> Of all the parties concerned in this outrage, your masters suffered the least – though their sufferings are not small – and yourselves the most.
> You may say that the county will repair our losses, and that we

may soon build up what is destroyed, and go on as before. It is true that the damages must be paid out of the public fund; but it is not so true that a remedy will thus be found for the distress which violence has brought upon you. The state of trade being what it is, and confidence being so completely destroyed between the two parties to the original contract, there is little encouragement to enter on a new one. My partner and his family will depart immediately. I shall remain with a very few men under me to assist in disposing of our stock, and to wind up the concern; and then this place, lately so busy, and so fruitful of the necessaries and comforts of life to so many hundred persons, will present a melancholy picture of desertion and ruin.

'A Manchester Strike'[104] has the same tone and significance. 'Weal and Woe in Garveloch'[105] preaches the same doctrine. If supply exceed demand, the price of labour must fall. There are just too many workers, which is their own fault. They should resign themselves to the fact, and practise family limitation to ensure a better future for their offspring. All the postulates of Ricardian economics – deliberate self-interest throughout society, mobility of labour, absolute freedom and flexibility in the economic machine – are implicitly accepted. And Miss Martineau has no beliefs to deflect her from resolutely thinking her economics through to a relentless conclusion. In this too she spoke directly to her generation.

All the evidence is that she was accepted instantly. Each monthly part of the *Illustrations* sold more than 10,000 copies. The author was unknown one day, and the celebrity of the moment the next. Polite society talked about her; politicians wanted to meet her. Hallam, Sydney Smith, Malthus, Bulwer, and the Mills, the leaders of the liberal coalition, became her friends. Lord Brougham supplied documents in support of her plans for stories on the Poor Law; Malthus paid a special visit to thank her for her work. Even Robert Owen tried hopefully to win the brilliant writer to his cause. The press resounded with her praises: 'I was overwhelmed with newspapers and letters containing every sort of flattery. ...Members of Parliament sent down blue books through the postoffice.'[106] Only the Tory *Quarterly Review* attacked her, with a lively outrage that almost degenerated to coarseness when it concentrated on her frank account of Malthusianism: 'A *woman* who thinks child-bearing a *crime against society*! An *unmarried woman* who declaims against *marriage*!!'[107] But the great Whig organ, the *Edinburgh Review*, was dithyrambic by contrast:[108]

> The next three stories, 'Ella of Garveloch', 'Weal and Woe in Garveloch', and the 'Manchester Strike' are so beautiful in their poetry

and their painting, and so important in their moral, that, were we to
begin to praise them, we should not know where to stop.

So she was widely read. But did she persuade any readers who were not
already convinced political economists? Charles Knight, the liberal
historian, wrote thirty years later that her literary skill 'excited the
admiration of thousands of readers, who rose from the perusal of her
monthly volumes without the "Principles" having taken the slightest
hold upon their minds.'[109] On the other hand, he conceded that the
Illustrations influenced the development of the social novel:[110]

> Nevertheless, we hold these remarkable little books to have, in a
> considerable degree, led the way in the growing tendency of all novel-
> writing to extend the area of its search for materials upon which to
> build a story, and to keep in view the characteristic relations of rich
> and poor, of educated and uneducated, of virtuous and vicious, in our
> complicated state of society.

Miss Martineau had unwittingly prepared the ground for Dickens and
Kingsley.

Be that as it may, she was compelled to abandon her dogmatic convictions as the years went by. Contact with real poverty and the suffering
of others softened the cold intellectual philanthropy evinced in the stories.
In 1834–5 she found another abstract cause for herself: the abolition of
slavery. And she aroused intense hostility in America when she visited
that country and made some lofty pronouncements about the evil of
slavery. But in Ambleside, where she passed her noble and philosophic
old age until her death in 1876, she was generous to the poor, helping
them with her purse as well as her sympathy, in spite of the precepts of
political economy. Her *Autobiography* proves that she was completely
changed. She was a willing hearer for the social critics of the 1850s who
overturned the prevailing orthodoxy. Many years later, writing of her
life in 1846, she described her 'orderly comprehension of what I then took
to be the science of Political Economy as elaborated by the Economists
of our time;' and added, 'but I believe I should not have been greatly
surprised or displeased to have perceived even then, that the pretended
science is no science at all, strictly speaking.'[111] Slender though her confidence in emotional life might be, it had proved sufficient to undermine
the elaborate intellectual edifice she had constructed in her youth, and
bring about its downfall.[112]

Conclusion

From the utilitarian novel we can see how widespread the dissemination of individualism was in 1832. It evinced two obvious features: contempt for the inherent abuses which persisted under the old order; and opposition to any movement which provided means of expression for the obscure ideal of social change. Individualism attacked the legalistic apparatus associated with the hereditary aristocracy, and at the same time resisted the demand for true justice which suffering and compassion were evoking in other sectors of society. Technically the utilitarian novels were poor: their interest is historical rather than literary. Bulwer expounded his paradoxical view of society without any profound conviction, and only assumed the tone of the learned social scientist to improve his attack on the criminal law. Miss Martineau, on the other hand, was completely overwhelmed by her vision of utilitarianism as absolute truth, and she did her utmost to demonstrate that it would work perfectly in practice. The reader is unhappily aware that neither writer is motivated by any feeling for human suffering, and the social consciousness of Bulwer and Miss Martineau has nothing to do with a longing for justice or charity. Instead they are inspired by the frigid clarity of rational conviction, which is incapable of growing into any kind of artistic creation with lasting value. Still, such writing was, in its time, easily accessible to the general public. The bulk of the middle classes had no hesitation in acknowledging its immediate appeal, for they recognised writing which reflected their own outlook accurately.

Three

Idealism and the interventionist reaction

Between 1835 and 1850 a new spirit revitalised the social novel. Alongside the old social alliance for individualism a new social grouping emerged, determined to correct the imbalances of individualist society. At the same time an emotional upheaval in the public mind developed into the concept of mutual social responsibility. The novels of Dickens and Kingsley were at the same time cause and effect of this process; they are inevitably linked with this second phase of English history from 1830 to 1850.

Classes injured by individualism

The new bourgeoisie expanded at the expense of the other sectors of society. Their triumph meant hardship for landed gentlemen, small shopkeepers, agricultural labourers, and industrial workers. The concerted pressure of these groups led to a re-examination of the facts of social life, and an interventionist opposition to *laissez-faire* economics.

Everything the middle classes gained was taken direct from the nobility of England. The Reform Act marked the collapse of the aristocratic principle in England. From the first rank in the state, the aristocracy slipped to the second. Henceforth they were not to be the rising power, and the external forms of respect they retained were empty. The national economy changed to their disadvantage: agriculture was no longer the basis of public wealth. England's centre of gravity shifted from south to north; the England of the squirearchy was replaced by an England of merchants and manufacturers. Political power passed to the victors. And the country gentlemen were as hard hit in their pockets as in their pride. The Free Trade movement was to take away the advantage they gained from protective duties on corn; rents would fall, and with them the incomes of the great proprietors. The bourgeoisie joined battle in a spirit of intense jealousy: they denounced the special privileges which the aristocrats hung on to as long as their wealth would allow, such as Game Laws, and other feudal rights which annoyed country folk.[1] The industrial upstarts made no secret of their contempt for ancient families:

they mocked their indolence, their conservatism, and their out-dated ostentation, already eclipsed by their own insolent, new splendour. Bourgeois radicalism harried the stupidity and inertia of Toryism. The iron railways with which the industrialists linked their cities to each other ran through time-honoured woodlands and knocked holes in parklands, from which frightened deer ran away. With the passing of their social and political power the gentry felt that peaceful rural life which had been the mainstay of their prestige was slipping away also. Of course, they were still a power in the land, morally if not economically. For a long time to come they would be assured of the semblance of power, if not the reality, as they received the deference of conservative instincts. But they were unhappy in the new England they could not understand, and loathed the bourgeoisie who had seized a place in the sun at their expense.[2]

The artisans and smallholders of the lower middle class suffered even more. Their inadequate capital resources and economic dependence on others left them at the mercy of the industrial revolution, and they offered no resistance to the destructive power of individualism. The yeoman class which had populated the old rural England was driven from the villages by the enclosure of common land. Great landowners formed huge estates which were profitable when worked by proletarian day-labour. The old independent peasantry went to the towns in search of work, or laboured for hire in the country.[3]

At the same time competition from the big manufacturers ruined cottage industry. Weavers who had supported their families independently fell under the domination of middlemen who exploited them; master craftsmen became proletarian workers. The idyllic pattern of rural social life, with the shuttles working cheerfully in the country cottages whose gardens linked agriculture with industry, was all passing. What was left of this historic section of the nation tumbled pell-mell into the working-class quarters of the cities where most of them swelled the ranks of the proletariat.

But in the big city centres a new lower middle class came into being, rootless and unstable. All those who were unable to keep up with the competition of economic life sank to the bottom level of the middle class, that ill-defined social region from which Dickens drew so many characters. New, unlooked-for people were for ever arriving at this unhappy social level where their former social standing was lost, but they could hide their bruises out of reach of the bracing air of industrial activity.

But it was the proletariat which seemed, in 1830, to be the principal victim of the industrial revolution which had brought it into being. It comprised some historic sections of society and some new industrial offshoots, and was hardly aware of its own existence. It counted for nothing politically. It was entitled by its numerical strength to considerable power, but its members were so ignorant and unconcerned with public life that its inevitable rise to power was a halting, secretive struggle of about half a century. The bulk of the workers passively accepted the consequences of every national crisis without ever finding the means to articulate their grievances. A number of factors contributed to the simultaneous disabling of labourers in town and country. English farmers had enjoyed a period of prosperity during the Napoleonic Wars; the peace of 1815 led to a sudden fall in the price of wheat which the Corn Laws strove in vain to remedy. Chronic stagnation settled over agriculture; labourers' wages fell, and were not to rise again until almost the middle of the century. And at the same time the farm-worker lost his traditional place in his master's household; as in industry, the old security of personal relations between master and man was replaced by casual, anonymous employment. A surplus population was created in the countryside by the introduction of machinery, the employment of women and children, and the rising number of paupers, whose survival was guaranteed by the Poor Law.[4] The new Poor Law tried to combat this evil, but its initial effects were cruel: it took from many their only means of existence – a deliberate refusal to provide for the poor could have done no worse. The average wage of a labourer at this time was between six and eight shillings a week, and large families would have to live on this.[5]

Contemporary observers drew a gloomy picture of this poverty. Cobbett's attention was drawn to the sort of men who had been the backbone of England, and he lamented the passing of patriarchal society.[6] The inquiry necessitated by the 1834 Poor Law revealed the extent of the malaise: in some villages the poor rate took up all the income of the well-to-do.[7] 'An English agricultural labourer and an English pauper, these words are synonymous,' said a Member of Parliament in 1831.[8] Landowners were alarmed by the rise in the number of paupers, and tore down cottages, refusing to build new ones for the inhabitants. Labourers huddled together in crowded, insanitary dwellings; fever was almost universally chronic. Decent food was unknown; a rasher of bacon constituted a special treat, and the workers were undernourished and fearfully ravaged by drink. They received no advice and no moral guidance. The representatives of the Established Church, finding their task overwhelming, neglected their duty more often than not. Parson and squire, the two props of paternalistic rule in the villages, failed their charges utterly when they were most needed.

Industrial poverty may have been no worse, but it was more striking.

It is the most important social feature of the period, and characterises it indelibly. It fascinated the most independent, clear-sighted thinkers of the time. Foreigners came to study this by-product of heavy industry in its country of origin. And so the phenomenon is incomparably well-documented.[9] It is difficult to summarise the contemporary accounts: the precise details and personal observations to be found in official reports of the time are irreplaceable.

Light industrial workers attracted more public concern than the hands in heavy industry. The economic revolution had drastic consequences for small productive industries which had no means of adapting to the new conditions. They suffered all the hardship of change and enjoyed none of the benefits. The hand-loom weavers became depressed workers, and provided the classic example of industrial poverty for the social literature of the time. One special parliamentary report was devoted to them alone.[10] For a long time their earnings had been falling in the face of mechanised competition, and at last they reached the level of the lowest-paid workers, unable to provide for themselves. If they remained self-employed their produce was usually passed to a middleman who took the profit. And precisely when economic conditions should have dictated the disappearance of the hand-loom weaving trade, their numbers were increasing steadily because Irish immigrants preferred this sedentary occupation, and most weavers were vaguely alarmed by the prospect of regimented factory work and clung to their traditional way of life. Among all the hordes in the poorest areas of the great cities, the hand-loom weavers fought the most desperate battle against starvation. In Spitalfields Market their average earnings, after they had paid for raw materials, ranged from five shillings to eighteen shillings per week.[11] One of the ablest among them made an average weekly profit of fifteen shillings over a period of 430 weeks. He was asked by the assistant commissioner whether he had any children, and the following dialogue took place:[12]

A. No; I had two, but they are both dead, thanks be to God!

Q. Do you express satisfaction at the death of your children?

A. I do; I thank God for it. I am relieved from the burden of maintaining them, and they, poor dear creatures, are relieved from the troubles of this mortal life.

Absenteeism was common, and the assistant commissioner found it impossible to believe the number of hours daily work expected of weavers; an average working day of twelve hours he could accept, but sixteen or seventeen hours seemed incredible: 'A poor man, ill-fed constantly living in close air, cannot perform miraculous labour, which the strongest man would be unable to accomplish.'[13] '"It grieves me," said one weaver, "after I leave my work, to hear the looms going as I pass along the street; but it grieves me much more still to hear them as I come home at 11 o'clock at night. . . . Some even work on Sundays. . . . It is a sad necessity which causes all this."'[14] Detailed evidence of physical and moral distress was collected: dilapidated housing, infected streets and degeneration of health and strength. Most of the victims of the cholera epidemic of 1832 were weavers. 'Yet', observed the commissioner, 'in their humble sphere they exercise virtues, the merit of which men more favoured may neither well understand nor appreciate.'[15] And the same note is sounded in the parts of the report dealing with the North and Midlands.[16]

Another light industry to become notorious was tailoring, in connection with which the expression 'sweating system' was coined around 1848. Ready-made clothes shops were increasing their share of the market more and more, and a large output of cheap clothes had to be organised to meet their demands. So employers gathered together workers who had been reduced almost to starvation by the economic situation, and herded them into insanitary workshops where they were effectively slaves, fed and clothed by a boss who paid them derisory wages. They were driven to work feverishly by piece-rate payments, and the sweated tailors of East London became the classic example of exploited workers, as the weavers were the representative depressed workers.[17]

The problems of modern society, however, developed most obviously in heavy industry. Vast numbers of men were employed in mining, metalworking and power-driven textile milling. Their production was of national importance, and the distress of an individual employee was likely to represent the sufferings of a whole class. Many general factors contributed to the depression of 1842. The Corn Laws kept the cost of living high. The rapid growth of the working population stimulated competitive bargaining in the labour market and led to a general lowering of wages. The first steamships brought over crowds of depressed immigrants from Ireland, ready to take work for any pay. Agricultural labourers, uprooted by the new Poor Law, arrived in the cities to aggravate the situation. The trade unions were legally unrecognised, and were not strong enough to restore a balance between capital and labour. And finally, over-production with consequent unemployment had become a periodic bane of working-class life. The depression of 1825–6 had been followed by a period of high productivity, reaching a peak around 1832. But in 1836–7 the market collapsed again and production was checked. And from 1839 until 1842 a series of bad harvests combined with business stagnation to intensify the depression and make its effects widespread.[18]

Other causes of working-class distress stemmed from flaws in industry, which had still not succumbed to state pressure to put its house in order. No doubt the worst excesses of industrial expansion as they had existed before the Napoleonic Wars were set right by public demand round about 1830.[19] But the first attempts at industrial legislation were inadequate. The law was evaded or flouted. It remained for the years to come to protect women and children, ban excessive hours of work, enforce insurance against industrial injury, and reform the wage structure.

Pauper children, handed over to northern manufacturers by public welfare authorities, were subjected to extreme overwork and cruel beating at the hands of overseers. Distress compelled parents to give way to the temptation of handing their children over to the factories. There they underwent the same work-loads as adults. After the Factory Act of 1833, the manufacturers of Oldham circulated a petition in which they claimed that it was 'absolutely necessary to the carrying on of the cotton trade with advantage, to allow the employment of children of eleven years of age for sixty-nine hours a week'[20] – that is to say, twelve hours daily Monday to Friday, and nine hours on Saturday. The inquiry of 1832 heard some revealing evidence.[21] From a little girl:[22]

> Many a time has been so fatigued that she could hardly take off her clothes at night, or put them on in the morning; . . . thinks they are in bondage; no much better than the Israelites in Egypt, and life no pleasure to them.

From a spinner:[23]

> I find it difficult to keep my piecers awake the last hours of a winter's evening; have seen them fall asleep, and go on performing their work with their hands while they were asleep.

Often, when their day's work was done, children would hide in the workshops and spend the night there, too tired to walk home. In 1834, 56,435 children under the age of thirteen were still working in factories. Joseph Hebergam, a seventeen-year-old worker, made a deposition to the effect that he commenced working as a worsted-spinner at Bradley Mill, near Huddersfield, at the age of seven. The hours of labour were from five in the morning until eight at night, with thirty minutes interval at noon for refreshment and rest. They had no time for breakfast or refreshment in the afternoon, 'not one minute; we had to eat our meals as we could; standing or otherwise.' At seven years of age he had fourteen and a half hours of actual labour daily, and wages of two shillings and six-pence a week. There were about fifty children of about the same age as he was in the mill. 'They were often sick and poorly; there were always, perhaps, half a dozen regularly that were ill.' The children were beaten with a strap to keep them at their excessive labour; strapping children was the main business of one of the three overlookers. 'I had at that time a brother and a sister; they called him John, and my sister Charlotte. I cannot say how old my sister Charlotte was [when she began working at the mill] but my brother John was seven. . . .they were often sick.' John had died three years previously, aged sixteen years and eight months. His mother and the medical attendants attributed his death to 'working such long hours, and said that it had been brought on by the factory.'[24]

Chronic illness was indeed one result of exploitation. Other visible consequences were malformations and a physically stunted populace. Gaskell summarised as follows an examination of 2,000 children taken at random from several large establishments:[25]

> The children were stunted, pale, flesh soft and flabby; many with limbs bent, in most the arch of the foot flattened; several pigeon-chested, and with curvatures in the spinal column; one hundred and forty had tender eyes, in a great majority the bowels were said to be irregular, diarrhoea often existing, and ninety shewed decided marks of having survived severe rachitic affections.

Adults had the same sickly appearance. Their life-expectancy was diminished by overheated workshops, unduly long working hours, sometimes extending partway through the night, nervous tension, and cotton waste breathed into the lungs. Only 143 out of 22,094 operatives in various Stockport and Manchester factories were over 45 years old.[26] The great majority of diseases recorded as causing the deaths of workers in the mortality tables for Manchester were 'compatible with a very extended life; few being fatal of themselves'.[27] Industrial accidents were common as no precautions were taken. Owners often left machinery unguarded in the middle of the shop floor, and an injured worker could expect dismissal without proper compensation. In 1843 the Manchester Infirmary was caring for 962 injured and mutilated victims of industrial accidents.[28] Young girls, pregnant women, and women who should have been lying-in were employed, and contributed to the further lowering of general standards of physique.[29] The 'truck' system was widespread; wages were paid in kind by storekeepers who recouped in higher prices the commission they had to pay the employers. The system had been prohibited by statute in 1831, but this was hardly applied with any severity until almost the middle of the century.[30] Tied cottages looked more harmless. Employers would build houses at rock-bottom prices and let them to their workers. Housing was a good, sound investment, yielding thirteen to fourteen per cent on capital, yet the workers were still compelled, under threat of dismissal, to pay rents above the market rates.

Conditions in the mines were even worse, as was shown in the Report of 1842.[31] Children between the ages of four and seven were made to wait in the darkness on their own beside doors which they had to open to let wagons through. Half-naked women and children crawled on their hands and knees along low, narrow galleries, dragging wheelless buckets of coal with harnesses and chains between their legs. Even the healthiest miner's strength would be broken in a few years by dampness, foul air, and coal-dust. Miners aged prematurely and died young. The mines were poorly maintained, so that accidents, explosions of fire-damp, and roof-falls were common occurrences: the *Manchester Guardian* used to report at least two or three a week in Lancashire alone. The mining districts were still fairly barbaric, and the peculiarly brutal industrial oppression to be found there was related to local uncouthness.

The physical state of working-class housing was a constant source of misery. In London and the great midland and northern cities, modern slums had already been built. The unexpected masses who gathered round the factories had to be housed somewhere, so developers promptly threw up whole streets of identical jerry-built houses resting on poorly-drained marshland. This was a profitable speculation, as there was no municipal control of standards. The average life of these houses was fourteen years. Two or three families might be found living together in cramped, ill-ventilated rooms, without a bed or a table between them; all furniture was often in the hands of the pawnbrokers who flourished in working-class districts. Adshead reported that 2,000 families in Manchester held 22,417 pawntickets between them at one time.[32] Manchester was the second city in England, and the classic example of an industrial city. It was the perfect location for field research into working-class life. And researchers came – not always in the disinterested pursuit of knowledge: the epidemics which ravaged the poor districts had been known to spread to the better side of the town. The cholera epidemic of 1832 left the new middle class vaguely aware that it shared a common interest in hygiene with the proletariat. Bureaux of health were established, and Manchester was divided into fourteen districts which were visited by inspectors. Kay recorded the results of that inspection.[33] Of 687 streets visited, 248 were unpaved; 53 were only partly paved; 112 were badly aired; 352 contained dungheaps, deep potholes, and pools of stagnant water. Of 6,951 houses, 6,565 needed to have their interiors whitewashed; 960 needed structural repairs; 939 were badly drained; 1,435 were damp; 452 were poorly ventilated; 2,221 lacked sanitation. In 1840, 12,000 of the poorest families were examined on the initiative of a group of citizens.[34] 2,040 of these families, a total of 9,179 souls, were living in cellars, usually without proper flooring. Damp ran down the cellar walls, and when the river rose they were flooded. There was no ventilation, as the air-shafts ended below street level. In one of these cellars a visitor found:[35]

> R. Cann, five in family, three children; all out of work, man sick, and one child sick. The child was laying [sic] down on a few shavings of wood in the corner of a damp cellar, without a rag to cover it. Nothing whatever in the cellar. The man said he had been out of work for sixteen weeks.

According to Gaskell, there were 20,000 people in all living under similar conditions in Manchester.[36]

But nothing can compare with Engels's description of the heart of the old town, a sewer where all the physical effluvia of industrial poverty gathered. He found that the poorest of the poor lived in a row of covered passages beside the River Irk, far from the prosperous residential areas, and out of the eye of official concern. Civilised society had abandoned these people. Furthermore, even in the new town he found places like the district known as Little Ireland, beside the industrially polluted river Medlock.[37]

> In a rather deep hole, in a curve of the Medlock and surrounded on all four sides by tall factories and high embankments, covered with buildings, stand two groups of about two hundred cottages, built chiefly back to back, in which live about four thousand human beings, most of them Irish. The cottages are old, dirty, and of the smallest sort, the streets uneven, fallen into ruts and in part without drains or pavement; masses of refuse, offal and sickening filth lie among the standing pools in all directions; the atmosphere is poisoned by the effluvia from these, and laden and darkened by the smoke from a dozen tall factory chimneys. A horde of ragged women and children swarm about here, as filthy as the swine that thrive upon the garbage heaps and in the puddles. . . . The race that lives in these ruinous cottages, behind broken windows, mended with oilskin, sprung doors, and rotten doorposts,

or in dark, wet cellars, in measureless filth and stench, in this atmosphere penned in as if with a purpose, this race must really have reached the lowest stage of humanity.

350,000 people lived like this in Manchester and its environs. And similar sights could be found in Edinburgh, Liverpool, Nottingham, and Bradford. London, according to Buret, was 'more disgusting than the filthiest villages in France'. He had found houses there 'built in the midst of veritable sewers, and surrounded by heaps of pig-dung instead of gardens'.[38]

The harm done by these material conditions went further than the breakdown of physical health; moral standards, family ties, and consideration for others perished also. Cramped rooms where whole families were packed together without a moment's privacy quickly snuffed out delicate-mindedness. Brutal experience coarsened the mind; a gross way of life was commensurate with the physical setting. Contemporary observers insisted that the workers were being degraded from the moment they were born, and that factory life intensified the process. The prostitution of working-class girls was taken for granted. Unstable families left children at the mercy of dangerous influences. They received no education, for both parents would be out all day at work in the factories. The family bond became purely financial; fathers claimed their children's wages, which they often refused to hand over. At fifteen or earlier the child would leave home to set up on his own account.

Inevitably, poverty led to some peculiarly depressing forms of drunkenness. Scenes of gross brutality took place in cellar wineshops. The consumption of alcohol trebled in fifteen years: in 1823 duty was paid on 1,976,000 gallons of spirits in England and Wales. By 1837 this had risen to 7,875,000 gallons.[39] One house in ten in Glasgow was a public house in 1840.

Crime rose twice as fast as the population between 1824 and 1842. In 1823, 12,268 people were brought to trial, and 8,204 convicted. In 1842 the figures were 31,309 and 22,733 respectively. By 1836 there were 52,000 transported convicts in Australia.[40] The proportion of juvenile criminals rose steadily. Such schools as there were for working-class children were few and bad, and the teachers were unbelievably ignorant. The radicals' campaign for popular education made no impression whatever on the lowest class of society. Clauses in the Factory Acts making the education of children obligatory were openly violated. Inquiries showed over and over again that working-class children lacked the most elementary knowledge. 'To the question who Christ was R. H. Horne received the following answers among others: "He was Adam," "He was an Apostle," "He was the Saviour's Lord's Son," and from a youth of sixteen, "He was a king of London long ago."'[41] It should be borne in mind that religious instruction was the basic education offered in these schools. 'A boy, seventeen years old, did not know that twice two are four, nor how many farthings in two pence even when the money was placed in his hand.'[42]

Yet amid all this ignorance and squalor, some robust, decent moral attitudes survived. Impartial observers praised the workers' good sense, energy, and fundamental honesty. Although atheism made some headway among the Chartists, bourgeois writers admitted that they were men of high moral worth. Above all, the workers' care for each other was admirable. They made thousands of tiny sacrifices daily in automatic response to the promptings of common humanity. 'The poor give one another more than the rich give the poor,' said Dr Parkinson, Canon of Manchester.[43] The social canker which had ravaged the lower classes for fifty years had still only done superficial damage to their moral nature. But the situation was worsening daily, and everyone clear-sighted enough to understand the nature of the depression had reason to fear the future.

Around 1842 poverty reached the proportions of a national affliction. At that date the public assistance registers of England and Wales recorded the existence of 1,429,000 paupers – one in eleven of the entire population.[44] This was the time of the second Chartist petition and major industrial troubles. Revolution seemed imminent. The two nations, the rich and the poor, stood face to face, and it looked as though nothing could prevent their collision. Two attempts were made on the Queen's life in the space of three months. Buret ended his study of poverty in 1840 by describing England heading down a dead end 'which can only lead to unavoidable ruin, or the most radical, and perhaps the most terrible of revolutions'.[45] Engels's book is dominated by his vision of impending carnage: 'The vengeance of the people will come down with a wrath of which the rage of 1793 gives no true idea. The war of the poor against the rich will be the bloodiest ever waged.'[46] Cooke Taylor, in his letters to the Archbishop of Dublin, described the bitterness of the Lancashire working men: 'Teeth were set, hands were clenched, and curses of fearful bitterness pronounced with harrowing energy. "We wait but for the word to begin," was stated broadly and openly.' And they told him, 'We used to think that something better would turn up, but we have waited so long that hope itself is worn out: we must do something for ourselves, for those above us will never do anything for us.'[47] Dr Arnold expressed his fears: 'We are engulfed, I believe, and must inevitably go down the cataract.' And Ebenezer Elliott, the Corn-law Rhymer, declared that he would have fled to France, if only he knew French, to avoid the coming revolution for the sake of his children.[48] Even Disraeli voiced the general opinion, giving Sidonia, the fantasy-self of his novels, the following words: 'I am inclined to believe that the social system of England is in infinitely greater danger than that of France.'[49]

Yet the theoretical and practical exponents of individualism, the professors of political economy and the manufacturers, produced nothing but negative, pessimistic palliatives for the depression. Nassau Senior, in the final Report on the hand-loom weavers, barely disguises his belief that a salutary thinning of the ranks of the poor by hunger, disease, and death offers the only possibility of relief for the survivors. He abides by his scientific principles, and preserves a serene patience as he observes that supply 'does not appear...to have a tendency to adapt itself to the irregularities of demand'.[50] This was the last word of economic ortho-doxy! It confessed that it was impotent to check natural anarchy in the market. Revolution was now stirring among those who resented in-justice or suffered physical deprivation, and soon it would find expression in ideas and actions.

The revolt against individualism; Chartism

The reactions of the other classes to bourgeois supremacy varied accor-ding to the injury they had suffered as the bourgeoisie rose. The actual existence of the aristocracy had never been seriously threatened, and the gentlemen of England had no enthusiasm for a protracted struggle which they could not hope to win. So they restricted their socio-political activity to the preservation of their own privileges. They contested the Reform Bill to the bitter end, and never reconciled themselves to the rise of democracy. Yet once the Bill was law, they accepted the *fait accompli*, and regrouped around protective tariffs. The general interests of great landowners were threatened by the Anti-Corn Law League, and the gentry argued simply that it was they who had paid for the Napoleonic Wars, and they were entitled to some compensation from the State. Furthermore, English agriculture would never survive foreign com-petition: Free Trade would be its ruin. The landed interest answered Cobden's cosmopolitan vision with their own dream of a self-supporting England. It took seven years, a general depression, and a degree of co-operation between bourgeois propagandists and the working-class movement before the Corn Laws could be overthrown.

The new Poor Law, on the other hand, was quite acceptable to the nobility. The abuses of the old system had hit them harder than anyone else; it was in the country that poor rates had reached exceptional heights. But all the odium for the new measure fell upon the new bourgeoisie, for the gentry's paternalistic traditions inhibited them from giving much open support to official denunciations of the right to public assistance. Indeed some of their number were among the fiercest opponents of the new law. Greville complained in 1837:[51]

> The Tories behaved exceedingly ill in one respect during the late contest, and that was in availing themselves as much as possible of the cry that had been raised against the Poor Law. Inasmuch as the Tories are the largest landed proprietors they are the greatest gainers by the new system.

Finally, the aristocracy took the offensive in one respect. They used Factory Acts to return blow for blow with their opponents as the Corn Laws were attacked. Whenever Cobden and his friends denounced the selfishness of the great landowners, they retorted with the cruel evils of industry. An alliance of convenience between the Tory party and the radical workers came into being. According to Samuel Kydd, 'the *Quarterly Review, Blackwood's Magazine*...distinguished themselves by an unreserved condemnation of factory cruelties, and a defence of the necessity for regulation by law,' and the tone of several articles fully justified his words.[52] The conservative press was playing its part in the fight against the cotton kings.

As for the lower middle classes, they were a disunited, heterogeneous mass. Neither in town nor country were they sufficiently well organised to act as a class. Among the social protests of the time their voice was unheard. But they were indirectly important. The idyllic memory of their former way of life as contrasted with their present degradation was taken up by many writers as material for the indictment of modern society. Nostalgia for the old pre-industrial forms of production sustained a backward-looking element in the interventionist alliance. A comparison of the social aspirations of Dickens with those of Sismondi shows that the former takes his outlook from the new lower middle class, the transient city populace with whom he lived and suffered as a boy.

The proletarian reaction against individualism was vigorous, but disorganised. It was the response of a strong class which still lacked real awareness of its own nature. All its efforts failed to the extent that they were revolutionary; only those which restricted themselves to reformist goals enjoyed success. The most primitive workers, the agricultural labourers, rose in short outbursts of violence, venting their despair in barbaric activity. Their usual procedure was nocturnal incendiarism, burning down barns and haystacks, and sometimes pillaging farms. From 1839 to 1846 not a winter elapsed without some such actions being reported. On dark, moonless nights, little bands of masked men would assemble, carry out their revenge, and disappear. They nearly always evaded capture, and the fabulous 'Captain Swing' was popularly believed to be the hero of these mysterious exploits.

The first industrial protest also took the form of blind, destructive violence. Machines were perpetually creating unemployment and hunger by making men redundant when they were introduced. And so the installation of new machinery led to furious riots in which looms and spinning-frames were torn to pieces. This form of strife was particularly strong at the beginning of the century, when steam-power was revolutionising the textile industry. The Luddite riots took place in 1812. But hatred of machinery lasted until 1830, and a number of Chartists saw mechanisation as nothing but an instrument of capitalist oppression.

After 1824 the strike was a legal weapon in disputes. The bourgeois press tried assiduously to present it as an adjunct of social revolution, and indeed striking had its revolutionary features. The great strikes of 1842 were, in effect, genuine uprisings. In August of that year, the workers of Staffordshire and Lancashire laid down their tools, and marched across the neighbouring countryside in armed bands, closing down factories by force, and living off the land. Strikers frequently used violence to deal with dissidents, and the vitriol with which they punished blacklegs came to play a major part in the hostile mythology surrounding combination. This was the revolutionary phase in the history of strikes; unionism, too, underwent a revolutionary period.

From 1829 to 1834 the trade unions really hoped to become an instrument of class war. The Grand National Consolidated Trade Union of 1834 was almost a class association. In a matter of a few weeks Owen and his followers recruited half a million members and openly prepared for a general strike. From January to July the property-owning classes had reason to fear that the moment of violent expropriation was upon them. When it came to the point, the threat collapsed in a few days, but the unions were still a prey to communist aspirations, and their rapid decline after 1834 did nothing to exorcise the dreadful memory of the fears they had once aroused. At that time the trade union movement had copied the proceedings of secret societies, adopting masonic rituals of initiation and oath-taking to make conspirators of their new members. It was for binding themselves by oath to a secret society that the Tolpuddle Martyrs were arrested and convicted in 1834. Torchlight meetings on the moors at midnight were a tradition of trade unionism, as of Chartism.

This last was the most deliberate proletarian move against the bourgeoisie. It had its roots in several sources: radical workers' dissatisfaction with the Reform Act was one; bitterness and hatred evoked by the new Poor Law – 'The Poor Man Robbery Bill' as Cobbett nicknamed it – was another. The failings of the old Poor Law were less apparent in the industrial North than in the agricultural South, and the workers of Lancashire protested vehemently against a reform as pointless as it was harsh. The House of Commons was deluged with petitions against the new Law from 1837 to 1839. The press published accounts of the hardship of life in the workhouses, and popular opinion throughout the country had it that the intention of the Law was to punish poverty. At the general election of 1841 the cry was raised in Leicester, 'Let us end the power of the Whigs. Vote for the Tories in preference to the Whigs, the authors of the accursed Poor-law.'[53] The bitter radical campaign against Stamp Duty also went towards the making of Chartism, although it partially succeeded in winning freedom for the press in 1836. And finally, socialist propaganda played its part. Owen had made some progress among the educated workers, and the overwhelming majority of his followers threw in their lot with the Chartists.

Thus, in the first instance, the movement came into being in answer to demands for social justice and an extension of democracy. On the surface, the clauses of the People's Charter drawn up by the London Working Men's Association in 1837 were purely constitutional, and were no more than the demands formulated by the radicals in the 1780s: equal electoral constituencies; annual parliamentary elections; payment for M.P.s; secret balloting; and, above all, universal franchise with the property qualification abolished. But the workers of 1837 hoped to use genuine democracy to change the economic system. Chartism was shot through with socialist ideals, though they were not always made obvious.

The history of the movement is familiar. The Charter was published in 1838, and in 1839 the workers' National Convention met outside the bourgeoisie's Parliament, to which the Chartist petition was presented. The rejection of the petition split the movement between moderates, advocating 'moral force', and activitists, advocating 'physical force'. O'Connor's popularity brought the extremists to the fore; the second petition in 1842 was as badly received as the first had been; and the final act in the drama of Chartism was played out on 10 April 1848 as the movement, weakened by quarrels among its leaders and damaged by

O'Connor's revolutionary rhetoric, collapsed amid ridicule, its widely advertised demonstration a miserable flop, and its monster petition greeted with laughter when a cab took it to Parliament. The momentary reanimation of Chartism by the European struggles of 1848 did not survive the general reaction which followed.

Agricultural riots, revolutionary strikes, and bellicose trade union agitation all faded out in the same way after 1842. By 1850 the people had given up the idea of class warfare, and the workers' organisations prepared for a peaceful struggle: with what success, we know today.

It seemed in 1850 that the workers' reaction against individualism had proved completely abortive. But this was not so. The disorganised movements through which the workers drew attention to their suffering made an impression in the minds of onlookers. A revulsion against economic facts and the activities they dictated arose, and ultimately influenced the realm of ideas and public sentiment and brought about a correction of the worst excesses of do-nothing laws and conduct. But before this could happen, pre-existing moral principles of a different kind had to be assimilated.

Intellectual opposition

The opposition to individualism took a contrasting form to the systematic, rational social philosophy which individualists propounded in formulaic propositions. The many people who opposed this philosophy rarely expressed their ideas through logic, and evolved no overall system. They comprised a great movement of idealists with a wealth of varied elements, but their alliance was tenuous, and the movement's outlines were not clearly defined. Spiritual, emotional, and atavistic motives brought people together in moral opposition to individualism. By 1830 the native English form of emotional life, which had undergone a wonderful renaissance since the turn of the century, answered the deepest needs of an altered society. To understand the economic troubles of the Victorian period, it is necessary to go back and consider the thinking behind the industrial revolution: it is likewise necessary to examine the psychological origins of interventionism.

The nineteenth century reacted against the eighteenth: this is a cliché of political and literary history. Events in Europe between 1800 and 1848 are clarified in the brilliant image of flux and reflux, so that we find a climactic turning point in 1820, before which reaction holds sway, and after which it loses power. But this general pattern does not apply in detail to England, where three stages can be discerned, and the intellectual tide did not flow simply in one direction. Nor was complete victory gained by any one current of thought; both ancient and modern tendencies were always more or less present, and the period can only be understood in the light of both.

From 1800 until 1820 England, like the rest of Europe, passed through a reactionary phase of social and political life. The revival of liberal ideas between 1820 and 1830 was like a return to eighteenth-century rationalism; but from 1832 until 1850 the spirit of the nineteenth century took over, and corrected the doctrinaire excesses of the liberals. Utilitarian rationalism, however, had not been quiescent throughout the Napoleonic Wars; nor did reactionary religion and social conservatism disappear while the liberals put their ideas into practice. And both remained forces to be reckoned with in the years after the Reform Act. This should be borne in mind whenever the simple antithesis of nineteenth century with eighteenth, Romanticism with Augustanism, is made.

Between 1800 and 1815, while Wordsworth was composing much of his greatest poetry, a large number of people held a wide range of differing opinions which all shared the common feature of hostility to the eighteenth century as they understood it. By a process of simplification they managed to find a homogeneous similarity in all the variety of English life from 1688 to 1760, and dismissed it all as a period of unfeeling, rational morality. The sceptical and dissolute social life of the reigns of Queen Anne and the early Hanoverians, the cool, analytic philosophy of Locke and Hume, the wordly politics of Walpole, the closely-reasoned theology of Butler, and the polished poems and essays of Pope and Addison were thrown together into an harmonious compendium which pointed out the effect of certain dominant psychological tendencies of the time. For Augustan England had broken with past tradition, and given to ratiocination primacy over feeling and sentiment in intellectual life, thought, and art. The demand for clear, disciplined thinking and a more restricted imaginative life had been stimulated by various conditions in the late seventeenth century, among which were the influence of French culture, a reaction against Puritanism, and the exhaustion of the great age of lyric and tragic writing from Marlowe to Milton. When Shaftesbury felt it necessary to write an apology for enthusiasm in 1708, the native tradition of religious idealism and passion had reached its nadir. A slow transition led from this point to nineteenth-century Romanticism, but the whole eighteenth century was sufficiently imprinted with rationalism that the French Revolution seemed its natural product, and from the point of view of the succeeding age, cast a sinister light on the whole rational ideal. Wordsworth and Southey believed that rationalist impiety had, from its nature, led to the collapse of society and morality. And so the revival of sentiment became the hall-mark of anti-Augustanism. A quick recapitulation of the successive victories of feeling and sentiment in late-eighteenth-century English life will indicate the background and strength of this revival.

The first stirring of sentiment came in religion. Methodism was a call to spiritual upheaval and a reawakening of conscience. Wesley's public preaching began around 1740, and from then on a hidden current of religious enthusiasm quietly undermined the dominion of reason in thought, art, theology, and conduct. But this was a long, slow revolution; it was fifty years before the Wesleyan impetus made a serious impression inside the Church of England, when the Evangelicals, after 1800, adopted Methodist ideals. The most distant and unlikely heirs of Wesley's emotional Christianity were the Oxford Movement, after the Reform Act. It had taken a century for the moderate, rational faith of Paley and Butler to suffer rout; English Christianity was not completely rejuvenated until about 1850. But Methodism was the real source of romantic religion.

'Sensibility' and its attendant activity, philanthropy, brought emotion into daily life. Richardson, like Rousseau, moved his readers to tears: facile pity was characteristic of England and France alike in the late eighteenth century. For practical people philanthropy was the natural outcome of sensibility. Towards 1790 Howard and Wilberforce set rolling most of the great campaigns which were to attract the altruism of the next generation. Prison reform, criminal law reform, and the abolition of slavery and the slave trade were the principal public outlets of philanthropy. The philanthropists were people of the highest moral character – Wright, Mrs Fry, Buxton, William Allen – and with the religious support of the Methodist conscience, they made up the second strand of the reaction against the eighteenth century. In one respect they found themselves working alongside the utilitarians, and although their fundamental differences would mean opposition in the future, they willingly supported the utilitarian critique of society out of compassion for that society's victims. The journal *The Philanthropist* was founded in 1811, and run by a group of Evangelicals, among whom was William Allen, the Quaker. But the reformist views of anti-religious utilitarians were given a sympathetic hearing in its pages: James Mill wrote for it, and Bentham was accepted as an authority.[54] The two movements found common ground in the struggle against legal and penological abuses. But their deep-seated antagonism remained, nonetheless, and became increasingly apparent as it became more and more evident that economic orthodoxy was an integral part of utilitarianism.

Spiritual tension was restored to literature in the mid-eighteenth-century revival of impassioned poetry under Thomson, Young, Gray, and Collins. A multitude of national and continental influences expanded the current to an irresistible tide, until it grew to the great period of English Romanticism, with Coleridge, Wordsworth, Byron, Keats, Shelley, and Scott. Here, more than in any other area of life, individual temperament led to divergence from the mainstream. English Romantic literature cannot be summed up under one definite heading. Certain features – Godwinian social philosophy in Shelley, for example, or pessimistic individualism and satire in Byron – prohibit the over-simple definition of Romanticism as a reaction against all things eighteenth-century as they were then understood. Undoubtedly the Tory reaction which was at its height when the second generation of Romantic poets emerged, towards 1810, provoked them into social satire. The hypocrisy of established laws and conduct was an offence to their wish for strong, free passions. And so two strands in Romanticism are discernible: anti-authoritarian libertarianism on the one hand, and a revaluation of poetic aesthetics on the other, which, as in France, led to the new concept of the artist as a superior personality. But this individualist aspect of Romanticism was never primary. The literary independence of the individual, like his social liberation, was less important than his emotional freedom and moral improvement. England was not France: there could be no triumph of the ego over the secular shackles of traditional classicism, for in England it was classicism itself which broke the tradition. Romanticism was an easy, natural return to native patterns of feeling, and there was nothing violently revolutionary in the artist's assertion of his right to express his own feelings. The dry, prosaic, rationalist outlook against which art rebelled was only a transient phenomenon.

Herein lay the essence of the revival of sentiment. And it follows, from its national character, that the sensitivity of the new poets was not solely, or even principally, a matter of personal joys and griefs. In Wordsworth, Coleridge, and Shelley it took the form of the most elevated altruism, and the profoundest links with other men. Byron's individualism and Shelley's radicalism are explicable in terms of their lives and temperaments; but the pathetic intensity of the former and the emotional idealism of the latter are the most characteristic aspects of their genius and, of course, relate directly to the mainstream of Romantic poetry.

The new spirit also played its part in the realm of pure thought. Intuitive and mystical philosophy appeared towards 1800. Coleridge and Southey carried on Burke's resistance to French ideas. Romanticism substituted understanding for reason as the faculty of apprehension in English philosophy, and gave greater esteem to pure feelings than to intellectual analyses. German philosophy played an important part here: Coleridge introduced Kant's ethics and Herder's mysticism to England. In 1840, when John Stuart Mill described the opposed philosophies of the eighteenth and nineteenth centuries, he called the latter 'Germano-Coleridgean'.

As early as 1815, then, there existed a powerful amalgam of forces opposing every manifestation of rationalism. Religion, daily life, literature, and philosophy had all been penetrated by a new mentality. But in the area of political economy, rationalism was still unchallenged. We have seen how and why the industrial revolution carried the individualism of Bentham and Ricardo to the heart of the nineteenth century. From 1815 to 1832 the liberal revival was accompanied by a falling-away in the revival of sentiment. Utilitarian philosophy held the stage from 1820 to 1830, and Coleridge and Southey were uninfluential. The new England needed reason and analysis to disentangle itself from the past; cool clear thought destroyed the premises supporting the old order, and economists encouraged competition as an aid to industrial expansion. Slowly but surely the face of Romanticism changed. In literature, religion, and philanthropy only isolated individuals concerned themselves, like Byron, with questions of social justice. This was the position when the new bourgeoisie achieved power in 1832: one group of intellectuals sought to make intuition and feeling the main guides to human conduct, and another thought that logic and reason should be supreme. And the bourgeoisie evoked so powerful a reaction that the party of sentiment broke into the area which had seemed finally closed to them and, in Carlyle, brought to its ultimate development the 'social Romanticism' which had been implicit in Burke, Wordsworth, Coleridge, and Southey.

It must be confessed that these spiritual parties are only identified by abstract generalisation after the event. To all appearances at the time, the successive forms of Romanticism were interdependent and overlapping. Mid-Victorian social Romanticism, called into being by industrial anarchy, had already existed in essence in earlier Romantic manifestations. Methodism was not merely a salvationist revival; it was a living fount of good works and public charity. Many of the finest examples of devotion to the common good come from Methodism, whose practitioners were numerically strong among the heroes of Chartism. Wesley's evangelical revival fermented like yeast in private and public life from 1750 to 1830. Religious convictions imposed personal duties, and at the same time illuminated and reinforced the notion that men were bound to each other by moral obligations. Thus the moral reawakening which Methodism brought about led to a strengthened social conscience.

Philanthropy was, by definition, social duty. It cannot be separated from Methodism, and was equally bound up with the interventionist reaction. It did not confine itself to attacking specific public scandals like the prison system, but took prompt action on behalf of any victims of economic competition. The everlasting proximity of poverty and a close knowledge of social evils gave philanthropists a desire for a better social structure. Buxton visited the poor districts of London at the beginning of the nineteenth century, and lived among the wretched Spitalfields weavers, thereby inaugurating individual social work which would be copied by others throughout the nineteenth century, down to and including the Salvation Army. Owen was in the first place a philanthropist. Idealistic pilgrims made their way to New Lanark to see the factory where he put his paternalistic theory of employment into practice. In spite of his hostility to established Christianity and his hatred of Toryism, Owen was a social Romantic. Cobbett was another such man of spontaneous passions and natural sympathy. The first stirrings of English socialism seem to be tied to emotional protest against the cruelty of individualism.

The growth of philanthropy was encouraged by the coincidence that anti-slavery agitation took place at the same time as the inquiries into workers' welfare. The suppression of the slave trade (1807) and the abolition of slavery in British colonies (1834) did much, indirectly, to improve social conditions in England. For just when the public imagination had been aroused by the lot of slaves, industrial oppression was exposed, like a new form of slavery. Over and over again white victims of the factory system were compared with black plantation slaves. When it comes to comparisons between the overseer's lash and the foreman's leather strap, it is apparent that abolitionist themes loomed large in the formation of interventionism.[55] The philanthropists made up an important group among the supporters of industrial legislation.

Finally, Romantic literature too was full of social comment. Perhaps one should isolate its permanent value as literature, and say that by its translation of certain passing social and psychological phenomena into artistic forms, it ensured that conscious human brotherhood became an inevitable part of the revival of sentiment. In this respect Wordsworth, Coleridge, and Southey were the first perfect representatives of the reaction against the eighteenth century. Between 1800 and 1830 they had outlined every possible idealistic, intuitive reaction to the rational fragmentation society was undergoing at the hands of economists and utilitarians. Although the liberal revival caused a break in continuity, a direct connection between the early Romantics' sketches and the finished social Romanticism of Carlyle may be traced. In Wordsworth's *Excursion*,[56] Coleridge's *Lay Sermons*,[57] and Southey's *Colloquies on Society*[58] we find the seeds of interventionism which came to full growth after the Reform Act.

Thus when, around 1830, it became clear that classical economics and the industrial society were the theoretical and practical faces of individualism, a great many people shared a cluster of ideas which would tend to propel their political activities towards the expression of sympathy for their fellow beings. Those classes who had suffered at the hands of the new bourgeoisie brought their demands for reform to this group and, after slight changes, a predictable pattern of social thought emerged. It was reactionary inasmuch as it was historically backward-looking. Methodism and philanthropy looked to great ages of faith, like the Puritan era, for a spirit to oppose eighteenth-century doubt and laxity. Romantic writers revered relics of the Middle Ages, and drew much of their subject-matter from England's past after the publication of Percy's *Reliques* and Ossian. After Chatterton, poets like Wordsworth, Southey, and Keats, and novelists of the 'Gothic' school, as well as Scott, the historical novelist, all found imaginative inspiration in nostalgia for distant times. The political and philosophical reaction associated with Burke was not merely a rejection of revolutionary ideas: it was a revival of instinctive conservatism, and an impassioned attempt to link the present with the spirit of the past, putting a high value on the continuity of national life, and preferring the positive grandeur of what once was to the dangerous uncertainty of what might be.

Thus genuine historicism lay at the heart of English Romanticism. Its general inspiration and tenor was not unlike German historicism. But whereas German speculative thinkers produced abstract theories about political and social rights, and were 'logicians in spite of themselves',[59] English historicism remained a tenuous matter of emotion, and drifted through the Romantic atmosphere as a vague reactionary predilection. Its influence was, nonetheless, considerable. It suggested an ideal and a possible remedy to anyone who found industrialism an affront to the sensitivity. Just as the ruin of the contented, stable lower middle classes had evoked a wish for a return to the old order in those who wrote about them, so now poetic idealisation of the Middle Ages went a step further, and gave ammunition to opponents of the new order. It looked as though present conditions would have to be changed for the better, and this could only be done by a return to the past.

Carlyle's social writings

Carlyle's social thought is central to the interventionist reaction. No Englishman gave such powerful expression to the ideas which perturbed people between 1830 and 1850. Carlyle's writings are the boldest and most complete account of idealism available; in them the spiritual renaissance can be seen expanding until it has enveloped social relations.

The story of his youth is important. It embraces two of the factors which produced state interventionism: economic poverty and the moral reaction against the eighteenth century. Born in 1795, Carlyle came of a family of small farmers in Scotland,[60] where agriculture was as depressed as it was in England. Carlyle's entry into the great world was difficult: he was an Edinburgh student, a schoolmaster, a tutor, and a writer, always uncertain of his living until the belated day when his *French Revolution* brought him celebrity. He married in 1826, and earned his living by writing, but want and hardship haunted his domestic life. Thus from an early stage harsh personal experience combined with his recollection of the poverty he had seen in the slums of Edinburgh and Glasgow, so that he was prepared to accept intuitively the hidden element of justice concealed within the incoherence of popular demands. At the same time he renounced a ministerial career, although his profoundly religious temperament drove him puritanically to seek a freer and more sincere apostolate as a literary preacher. He was tormented by a tragic sense of human mortality and his own inadequacy, until the day when a spiritual crisis replaced this negative suffering in his mind with an affirmative endorsement of life. From then on the Nonconformist conscience, with its inspection of personal conduct and anxiety about salvation, appalled Carlyle. His own puritanism developed into a positive and reverent confidence in the justice of the universe, and the fitness of healthy work for plain, honest men. This optimistic expansion and intensification of the old faith which had become impoverished in the hands of Wesley's evangelical successors was to a considerable extent the result of German influences. Like Coleridge, Carlyle was led back to Germany by his rejection of French ideas.

Kant's categoric imperative agreed with puritan notions of moral obligation, and dignified duty with the prestige of transcendental revelation. Goethe's pantheistic naturalism was immediately comprehensible and attractive to a conscience nurtured on Kant. The soul of the universe, it stated, was apparent in nature, and consisted of pure justice and righteousness. This was obscured by the various symbolic forms under which it was manifested, yet it alone had real existence, and it surrounded humanity with mysterious infinity. Material structures and organisations of life, such as societies, civilisations, or religions, were the changing garments which the divine spirit wove for itself in time. These vestments emerged and decayed, and it was the perpetual task of humanity to replenish the web as dogmas and hypotheses rose and fell. Thus religion, morality, and metaphysical idealism all converged. Feeling became the source of understanding and the principle of right conduct. An intuitive understanding of the supreme mystery whereby man's existence hangs between two chasms should guide all thought and action. Only the inner life was true; things only existed under their spiritual aspect. And society itself revealed to a philosopher's gaze the hidden spirit of justice by which it was sustained. Social evil was the outcome of spiritual sickness: all social reform had to be moral reform.

This was the loudest and most sustained response to the problem of poverty. In his earliest writings Carlyle declared himself to be the prophet of a vehement reaction against the predominant modes of feeling and thought. His essay 'Signs of the Times' (1829)[61] proposed the substitution of 'Dynamics', based on moral intuition and faith, for the 'Mechanics' which governed life and thought:[62]

> There is a science of Dynamics in Man's fortunes and nature, as well as of Mechanics. There is a science which treats of, and practically addresses, the primary, unmodified forces and energies of man, the mysterious springs of Love, and Fear, and Wonder, of Enthusiasm, Poetry, Religion, all of which have a truly vital and infinite character.

It was time that the fallacious, impious materialism of the eighteenth century should be seen for what it was: a negation of those spiritual activities which alone gave meaning to social life. It was time to recognise the great, forgotten dynamic truth that poets and thinkers had formerly indicated, and that other sages must proclaim today. In 1839, after the failure of the first Chartist petition, Carlyle set down his own philosophical interpretation of society in a curious pamphlet.[63] The main outlines had already been settled in his mind by contemplation of his own direct observations. Now the gravity of the situation rang in his ears like a cry for help.[64] Politicians were blind to the peril threatening England. Chartism was beaten but its spirit lived on. And however heroic or brutal popular violence might be, it was maintained by the spirit of justice. It had been grinding poverty and the grievances of a downtrodden populace which led to Chartism in the first place. In 1841 the lectures on *Heroes and Hero-Worship* defined the function of the great man in the preservation of social health. And in 1843 Carlyle published a book bringing together all of his social thought. *Past and Present* was the most effective manifesto of the interventionist reaction. It may be seen as an immediate response to the great depression of 1842, the most dangerous moment, perhaps, in the history of Victorian England.

By chance, Carlyle came across an obscure monk's chronicle written in the twelfth century[65] which crystallised the ideas at the back of his mind. This negligible origin evoked the definitive fusion of historicism with social idealism. The title of the book demonstrates the starting-point clearly enough. A critique of the present finds its natural complement in an appraisal of the past. Carlyle's intensely powerful imagination re-captures the simple, straightforward organisation of feudal life in im-passioned pages. In spite of the dark corners of the medieval mind and the enormous mistakes of the time, it was still a noble and beautiful epoch, for it had faith. Leaders were selected for the confidence they inspired in their peers, or by the divine right of natural superiority, and they regarded government as a serious, difficult task. Labour and rewards were distri-buted in the spirit of Christian justice. Reciprocated social obligations saved men from the individual isolation which lay at the root of modern unhappiness. Of course the past was confused, and gross superstitions existed alongside admirable virtues. But neither were to be found in the nineteenth-century struggle of self-interest. And so the simple story of Abbot Samson, as told by Carlyle, became the symbol of that strong, just, paternal government to which the feudal system owed its existence and its long survival.[66]

The present cut a sorry figure beside the past. Society was disorgan-ised: anarchy replaced benevolent despotism. Poverty held the masses, and their complaints were unheard by the well-to-do. Thousands of able-bodied men sat with their heads bowed in workhouses, per-manently cut off from the free and healthy dignity of work. A Stockport couple were charged with having poisoned three of their children for the burial society money. In the countryside ricks blazed, while in Ireland one third of the population spent thirty weeks of the year without even rotten potatoes to eat.[67]

The malaise had two causes: no contracts were permanent; and the only social ties between men were monetary. Instability was inimical to civilisation: nothing insecure could survive, and time was essential in the field of human activity if there were to be any increase, whether for good or ill: 'I am for permanence in all things, at the earliest possible moment, and to the latest possible. Blessed is he that continueth where he is.'[68]

But if human contacts were to harmonise into stable relations, it was essential that the brittle web of economic ties should be reinforced by duty, affection, morality, and religion. A society in which the payment of wages was the sole recognition of services rendered was contrary to the laws of God and man.[69]

> 'My starving workers?' answers the rich mill-owner: 'Did I not hire them fairly in the market? Did I not pay them, to the last sixpence, the sum covenanted for? What have I to do with them more?'

Over and over again, Carlyle returned to his famous formulation: 'cash payment, the sole nexus between man and man.' Slaves were better treated: domestic animals were better treated:[70]

> The master of horses, when the summer labour is done, has to feed his horses through the winter. If he said to his horses: 'Quadrupeds, I have no longer work for you; but work exists abundantly over the world: are you ignorant (or must I read you Political-Economy lectures) that the Steamengine always in the long-run creates additional work? Railways are forming in one quarter of this earth, canals in another, much cartage is wanted; somewhere in Europe, Asia, Africa or America, doubt it not, ye will find cartage: go and seek cartage, and good go with you!' They, with protrusive upper lip, snort dubious; signifying that Europe, Asia, Africa and America lie somewhat out of their beat; that what cartage may be wanted there is not too well known to them. *They* can find no cartage. They gallop distracted along highways, all fenced in to the right and to the left: finally, under pains of hunger, they take to leaping fences; eating foreign property, and – we know the rest.

Masters of men had done no less. The upper classes had failed in their task of governing with foresight. The aristocracy was arrogantly indolent and inert: it was afflicted with Dilettantism. What did the nobility do when the hungry besought their protection? They carefully preserved the Game Laws; they proclaimed their faith in the justice of the Corn Laws; they rigged themselves out in effeminate dandy's clothing; and they murmured the futile phrases of fashionable conversation. The spirit of justice which had been the essence of feudal nobility was gone. Nobility was now a mere phantom, whose corruption pointed to a cancer which must end in destruction.

The bourgeoisie on the other hand was vigorous and effective, yet its greed for profit was a weakness. Mammonism – the pursuit of wealth – was opposed to Dilettantism, yet under the surface they were both heartless and unnecessarily cruel. The businessman cared nothing for the soul, imaginative life, or metaphysics: the fear of hell was, for him, no

more than 'The terror of "Not succeeding;" of not making money, fame,
or some other figure in the world, – chiefly of not making money.'[71] He
was responsible for the dissolution of the organic ties of English society:
industrial anarchy was his achievement:[72]

> We call it a Society; and go about professing openly the totalest
> separation, isolation. Our life is not a mutual helpfulness; but rather,
> cloaked under due laws-of-war, named 'fair competition' and so
> forth, it is a mutual hostility.

And this general field-day of selfishness was justified by the dominant
philosophy. The great legacy of the eighteenth century was an impious
negation of moral, human, and religious duty. Atheism, enlightened
self-interest, and erroneous moral standards were allied, and from them
sprang French Revolutionism, Radicalism, and Chartism. England was
morally sick. 'There is no religion; there is no God; man has lost his soul,
and vainly seeks antiseptic salt.'[73] *Laissez-faire* economics was a form of
that[74]

> brutish godforgetting Profit-and-Loss Philosophy and Life-Theory,
> which we hear jangled on all hands of us, in senate-houses, spouting-
> clubs, leading-articles, pulpits and platforms, everywhere as the
> Ultimate Gospel and candid Plain-English of Man's Life, from the
> throats and pens and thoughts of all-but all men!

By contrast, work was doubly ordained by religion and morality. Work
was the essence of life and worship. 'Blessed is he who has found his work;
let him ask no other blessedness....The latest Gospel in this world is,
Know thy work and do it.'[75] A profound belief in man's vital spiritual
need for employment led Carlyle to respond to the spectacle of utter
poverty with a demand for social intervention, a doctrine he upheld.

How was it to be done? What were the principles for reforming
society? It would be unjust to say that Carlyle recommended a return to
the feudal system. His sense of history was acute, and he could see the
absurdity of such a proposal. Feudalism moreover was not faultless, and
for all its anarchy, the modern age contained the seeds of a potentially
richer, greater social order. Carlyle bluntly accepted that the future
belonged to heavy industry. It offered the possibility of exploiting the
blind forces of power, and opened up to man a new vista of justice and
welfare.[76]

> Manchester, with its cotton-fuzz, its smoke and dust, its tumult and
> contentious squalor, is hideous to thee? Think not so: a precious sub-
> stance, beautiful as magic dreams, and yet no dream but a reality, lies

hidden in the noisome wrapping. . . . Hast thou heard, with sound ears, the awakening of a Manchester, on Monday morning, at half-past five by the clock; the rushing off of its thousand mills, like the boom of an Atlantic tide, ten-thousand times ten-thousand spools and spindles all set humming there, – it is perhaps, if thou know it well, sublime as a Niagara, or more so.

For Manchester worked, and work was life. Mammonism was more promising than Dilettantism. It was a misplaced excess of that valuable old Saxon industriousness harnessed to the conquest of nature. This secular toil had hardened and shrivelled the hearts of the bourgeoisie: somehow they must grow spiritually without losing their practical energy. Social health would come from a regeneration of the employing classes, not their overthrow. Labour would have to be organised: a task for the next century, in which the army might be taken as a model. Its perfect adaptation of the art of destruction to modern conditions was the only clear success of modern society. A strong, paternal discipline, attentive to everyone's needs, would have to replace the harsh impersonality of industrial slavery. The factories would have to start running on the model of regiments: 'captains of industry', with their absolute power, must safeguard the physical and moral well-being of their men.

What of freedom and democracy? 'Liberty, I am told, is a divine thing. Liberty when it becomes the "Liberty to die by starvation" is not so divine.'[77] Democracy was merely negative: it put paid to the power of tyrannous minorities, but unless this led to its becoming a basis for the power of heroic leaders it was nothing but atheism and anarchy. Parliamentary government was a caricature of liberty: it gave a man a 'twenty-thousandth part of a Talker in our National Palaver'.[78] Liberty must find its true course for itself, and take it by main force. The factory owner was like a nation's hero: he ruled because he was the strongest. Power was divine, and could never be separated for long from rule. Yet it was far from being the only form of aristocratic distinction. The ownership of land was the basis of all nobility, and carried the weightiest privileges and responsibilities. It was essential for Dilettantism to change its nature if it could. The natural leaders of society would have to make their rank a reality by fulfilling their duties. The country-house oligarchy must teach, govern, and protect its tenantry in the same spirit of paternal authority as the factory oligarchy. Did they but know it, no one had a more gracious role in society. And this was not all, for the state would still need spiritual guides and philosophers, prophetic heroes of the modern age who would listen in the stillness of their hearts to the dim, quiet voice of nature, through which Providence reveals duty and destiny to man.

Such was to be the division of social roles. Authority, based on justice, would rule, and translate the divine will into human terms. Every man would have work, food, and a place in society. Poverty and degrading idleness would disappear, and so would the arrogance which refused obedience to natural superiors.

How was the ideal to be realised, and the present evil which threatened the existence of society to be overcome? Only one institution remained standing amid the conflict of interests which effectively neutralised all the others: that one was the State. A pitiful State the parliamentary system made of it, too! It was as anarchic as everything else, and incapable of really vigorous, purposeful action. But it could still be brought back to life if there could be found a single minister who perceived the needs of the age, and spoke like a hero to the great, silent spirit of England. And even before such a man emerged, a government of 'seven to eight hundred Parliamentary Talkers'[79] such as existed might tackle the worst abuses. Was it not clear that the law would have to intervene between Capital and Labour?[80]

> Nay interference has begun: there are already Factory Inspectors, – who seem to have no *lack of work*. Perhaps there might be Mine-Inspectors too: – might there not be Furrowfield Inspectors withal, and ascertain for us how on seven and sixpence a week a human family does live!

Equally, there was nothing to prevent sanitary legislation. 'Baths, free air, a wholesome temperature, ceilings twenty feet high, might be ordained, by Act of Parliament, in all establishments licensed as Mills.'[81] Why not enforce the cleansing of urban sewers? Why not open parks where the children of the poor might breathe fresh air in working-class districts? Above all, the State would have to make itself responsible for education. Some light must be let into the dim minds of the Chartists, and Satan should give way before the advancing threshold of learning. An efficient central administration must organise education as a public service. And why should not the State control emigration? It was a necessary blood-letting which relieved industrial overcrowding and, moreover, established a new England overseas. Let the navy, which was rotting in port, carry the surplus working population to the new territories which were available to anyone.[82]

> Our little Isle is grown too narrow for us; but the world is wide enough yet for another Six Thousand Years. England's sure markets

will be among new Colonies of Englishmen in all quarters of the Globe.

And thus the great dream of imperialism took shape in Carlyle's mind, bringing hope to relieve the spectacle of contemporary social evils. His faith in his race's energy is persistent; his pages are coloured by a mystical belief in the destiny of the English as he compares the modern warriors of the workbench and counter with their Teutonic ancestors, and urges them on to renewed conquest with the assurance of victory. The struggle was to be absolutely moral; man must triumph over his own selfishness, sensuality, and sloth in order to survive and strengthen society. Carlyle looked forward to the arrival of a spiritual renaissance, for without such regeneration all reform would be in vain; social evils were not to be healed with medicinal pills:[83]

> O brother, we must if possible resuscitate some soul and conscience in us, exchange our dilettantisms for sincerities, our dead hearts of stone for living hearts of flesh.

Emerson had revived idealism in America: there were some indications that old England might expect a similar revival:[84]

> Yes, here as there, light is coming into the world; men love not darkness, they do love light. A deep feeling of the eternal nature of Justice looks out among us everywhere; . . . an unspeakable religiousness struggles, in the most helpless manner, to speak itself, in Puseyisms and the like.

This was Carlyle's social prescription: a sort of aristocratic, Christian, State socialism. It was reactionary in that it proposed the return of despotism on a divinely approved basis. It was progressive in accepting the fact of industrial change, and endeavouring to extract the cure for the new social ills from the industrialism which had created them. It was a vigorous and impassioned critique of society, and it was well timed. No thinker of the time was more implacably hostile to individualism. There was desperate turmoil in the mind of the nation, and Carlyle's seminal teaching acted powerfully upon it. In time it would produce subtle effects, though at the time when he wrote, Carlyle's influence was limited. Only an *élite* read him, and were affected by his ideas. Among these interpreters of Carlylean doctrine we find the greatest of the social novelists: Dickens, Disraeli, and Kingsley.

Religious, aesthetic and literary idealism after 1830

Spiritual regeneration did, indeed, emerge on all sides around Carlyle.

The idealist reaction was a matter of the heart, and appeared utterly remote from economic considerations. The connection between class-interests and the Oxford Movement is barely perceptible, and the same is true of the poetic innovations of Tennyson and his contemporaries. Nevertheless these phenomena exerted some influence on social thought, and brought together demands for reform which had been stimulated by the observation of reality.

For the first third of the nineteenth century, Methodism silently went on with its work. A spirit of puritanism slowly spread from the lowest classes of society to the highest, and became a matter of public importance around the time of the Reform Act, with the rise of the industrial bourgeoisie. Private life, public life, and politics all seemed to be transformed and purified, while a narrower code of morals introduced new restrictions. In future, public opinion was to impose rigorous morality – or a convincing imitation of it – upon society. There were various indications of this alteration in public feeling, such as the religious panic which seized England during the cholera epidemic of 1832, when Parliament decreed a national day of prayer and fasting in March. Again, there was the new tone of fashionable life set by the Court with the accession of Queen Victoria, which led Greville to remark that 'There is a strong Puritanical spirit at work and vast talk about religious observances.'[85] The robust, outspoken tradition of English caricature was transformed into the decorous cartooning of *Punch*.[86]

Religion was refurbished, as well as morality. The evangelical party and orthodox rigorists had ensured that the Church of England had some share in the revival of faith between 1800 and 1830. But their sectarianism and inadequate theology detracted from their influence, and for all their zeal and philanthropy they were unable to arouse the mass of the clergy from lethargy. A more vital and poetic mysticism was required for that, such as the universities soon supplied. At Cambridge, around 1830, an important group of distinguished men carried on the new spiritual crusade against rationalism. Frederick Denison Maurice, and his friends Hare, Thirlwall, Whewell, and Sedgwick, continued in the spiritual direction laid down by Coleridge. Like him they defended the insights of imagination and intuition, and denounced arid eighteenth-century logic and utilitarian atheism. Faith expanded among them, and was enriched by lofty emotions. Once again art, poetry, and passion were accepted as ways of reaching the divine.

The Oxford Movement began at almost the same time. It came into being as a reaction against the rise of liberalism. The utilitarians, as has been observed, carried on a vigorous campaign against the Established

Church, whose structural weakness and spiritual exhaustion seemed to assure them of victory. When the Whig administration set about reforming the Church of Ireland in 1833, and dissolved ten of its twenty-two bishoprics, the more zealous adherents of the Church of England took fright, and on 14 July 1833 John Keble preached his sermon on National Apostasy. This was the beginning of the Movement. But Newman and his followers did not restrict their opposition to the encroachment of civil powers on Church territory: they repudiated liberalism in all its forms. In their view, the same sterile, negative, eighteenth-century outlook ran through the rationalism that struck at dogmatic beliefs, the utilitarian philosophy that blurred moral certainty, and the radical politics that attacked the established order. The Oxford Movement opposed all this and expressed a spiritual longing for mysticism and feeling. All its manifestations were inspired by the same interior exaltation. It was a psychological upheaval which aroused certain dormant tendencies. Religious life which had been drab and prosaic was brought to life again. It overflowed with lyrical joy in Keble's poetry; with heartfelt devotion in Pusey's and Ward's sermons; and with impassioned argument in Newman's polemical writings. Powerful inner feelings evoked aesthetically splendid ritual, and lent every kind of value and beauty to the causes of clerical dignity and Church power. Religion was to be as lovely, rich, and poetical as the believer's soul.

Inevitably this growth of idealism had its social manifestation. Contemporary poverty stimulated the Christian ardour of the Church's apologists, and the ideal of holy charity was renewed as they urged the Church to take up its role in relieving distress. This was quickly translated into a clerical crusade in the big city parishes. In *The Ideal of a Christian Church*, Ward gave a concise outline of the Oxford Movement's social message. After describing the sufferings of the working classes, he described the enthusiasm with which an ideal church would dedicate itself to their relief:[87]

> What a scene presents itself to the imagination! How careful at once her inquiry, what may be those branches of labour in which, whether from the kind or the amount of toil, the leading of a Christian life would be impossible; and how stern the prohibition, enforced by all spiritual sanctions, against any of her children engaging in those branches! In less extreme cases, how loving and considerate her tenderness to the poor sufferers!

Of course the demand for social intervention was in no sense the starting-point of the Movement. It emerged slowly as a part of the whole idealistic religious reaction against rationalism, with charitable action as one of its objective expressions, like the renewal of ritual. Spiritual exaltation had been part of the experience of Methodism and Evangelicalism, but these had felt no need to express their feelings through aesthetic symbolism. There was a new element in the Oxford Movement, compared with its predecessors: sensibility, as well as passion, was aroused and opposed contemporary society. For industrial society was not only aridly intellectual: it was overwhelmingly ugly. Modern life offended the bodily senses as well as the spirit. The crushing toil of rich and poor alike alienated them from art and nature as the fever of production eliminated critical values from life.

The Oxford Movement was closely associated with an aesthetic revival. Religious devotion did not content itself with increased fervour, as had been the case with Methodism and Evangelicalism: rather it expanded outwards to embrace the whole mind and all the senses, which had alike suffered from the constricting, suffocating spirit of the times. In the previous generation Romantic poetry and novels had drawn attention to external appearances. Wordsworth had given his readers the capacity to respond to beauty by idealising the poor and the simple externals of nature. Maurice and his Cambridge friends now insisted on the physical aspect of divine revelation. Their imaginative Platonism gave spiritual value to beauty. In Oxford an Architectural Society was founded in 1838, and a Motet Society for the study of sacred music in 1841. And the Camden Society was founded in Cambridge in 1839 for the advancement and study of Christian arts and antiquities, particularly those relating to church building and decoration. Ritualism had already become the hall-mark of the Oxford Movement as the growth of aesthetic demands made itself felt on all sides. Philanthropists demonstrated the ugliness of working-class life, and Victoria Park was laid out in north-east London shortly after the Queen's accession to give the poor somewhere pleasant, as well as healthy, for recreation. The National Gallery was established in 1832. Westminster Abbey was opened to the public in 1845. And so Ruskin's masterpieces met with a favourable climate of public opinion. The first volume of *Modern Painters* appeared in 1843, the second in 1846. *The Seven Lamps of Architecture* came out in 1849, and *The Stones of Venice* in 1851 to 1853. Aestheticism became a serious question of conscience in England.

As is well known, it ventured into the social domain and exercised a considerable influence there. No other form of idealism lent itself so immediately to the theory and practice of human relations. It must be observed, however, that the social message of aestheticism did not emerge until after 1850. At that date Ruskin was still an isolated, misunderstood sage with a new way of feeling. In 1853 William Morris was a student at Oxford, and had barely embarked on his intellectual life. The writings in which Ruskin first expounded his economic ideas fall neatly into the mid-Victorian period: *The Political Economy of Art* in 1857; *Unto This Last* in 1860; and *Munera Pulveris* in 1862. Between 1830 and 1850 the crisis of social conscience owed to aestheticism little but a vague feeling of sensitive idealism. On the other hand it is impossible to overlook the debt Ruskin and his followers owed their predecessors. The idealist reaction which Carlyle had inspired made their work easier. Readers of Dickens and Kingsley were prepared for Ruskin's reforming strictures, and *Past and Present* even contained the essence of his social thinking. It was a book which came on Morris as a revelation while he was at Oxford.[88] Of course, a line of continuity can be traced in the idealist movement; none the less, it was affected by those general factors which altered the appearance of English life after 1850. The age of Carlyle was different from that of Morris, and was more truly creative and productive. The latter only reaped what the former had sown.

Finally poetry became idealistic once more. Under Byron's influence, Romanticism had made an extraordinary deviation into cynical pessimism. The literary current through which Wordsworth and Coleridge had expressed their moral and emotional reaction against the eighteenth century had been turned upon itself by their successor. In 1820 Byron's mocking individualism appeared as part of the liberal revival. Byronism became fashionable among artists and men of the world, although official England and the middle classes repudiated it. It was a state of mind in which Romantic feeling took the form of a tragic view of human destiny, accompanied by a negative, critical attitude to social conventions and traditional duties.[89] Byronism was restricted to a small section of the British public,[90] but for them it answered the problems of an unstable period, with upheaval in the affairs of Europe, and an exaggeratedly strong conservative reaction in England. Hypocrisy and a façade of morality had become an aristocratic habit, and yet one about which an uneasy defensiveness clung. Byronism met this uncertainty with sharp sincerity or, alternatively, an affected alienation from society.

Idealistic poetry took shape in opposition to this affectation. The first factor in this process that must be acknowledged is the influence of Carlyle. No one did more than this writer of prose to ensure that English poetry should undergo a moral resurgence. From the first, his writings had denounced the dangerous absurdities of Byronism. *Sartor Resartus* is an account of a mind passing from cynicism to transcendental affirmation. 'Close your Byron, open your Goethe,' the hero says. Work was to replace the pursuit of pleasure. Private despair might remain, but it was to be kept in check by the energy which uncovered new hope in the performance of one's duty. Little by little Carlyle drove egotistical emotions out of the minds of the young, and the way was then clear for outgoing feelings. His active, religious pessimism led others to a position where they could accept a poetry of optimism.

The new poets who emerged between 1830 and 1850 contrasted strongly with the school of Byron. Tennyson was democratic and humanitarian, and clothed idealistic creative emotion in perfect technique. 'Locksley Hall' was inspired by the belief in universal progress, with mankind marching towards greater justice and happiness. Some of Tennyson's celebrated verses even went s far as to contrast noble descent with nobility of spirit, and to outline the responsibilities of the rich:

> Clara, Clara Vere de Vere,
>   If time be heavy on your hands,
> Are there no beggars at your gate,
>   Nor any poor about your lands?
> Oh! teach the orphan-boy to read,
>   Or teach the orphan-girl to sew. . . .

Robert Browning created a poetry of serious, deeply-felt, psychological analysis, shot through with religious and moral philosophy. But his heart was in the past, and he did not touch on the burning questions dividing his contemporaries. Mrs Browning, on the other hand, stirred public opinion deeply with 'The Cry of the Children', her moving poem on the lot of children in factories:

> Do you hear the children weeping, o my brothers,
>   Ere the sorrow comes with years. . . .

Other minor poets were led to write strikingly successful expressions of their sincere response to social conditions. Hood's 'Song of the Shirt', first published in the Christmas number of *Punch* for 1843, is still remembered in connection with the worst years of the depression. Elliott's poems had already given voice to the distress caused by the Corn Laws.[91] Lively, ribald songs expressed the masses' enthusiasm for their cause. And poets abounded among the Chartists.[92] *The Purgatory of Suicides*, which Thomas Cooper wrote while in prison in 1845, created a notable public impression. While Carlyle published his social writings, English poetry at every level was penetrated by the spirit of philosophical idealism.

These revivals in religion, aesthetics, and poetry were linked by more than their superficial similarities. Ornate ritualism, glorifying the church, the impassioned quest for beauty in life and art, and the evocation of noble sentiments in poetry were all intimately connected. Keble, Ward, and Newman himself, among the founders of the Oxford Movement, were poets. Ruskin's aestheticism drew heavily on scriptural inspiration. Tennyson's idealism found its chosen expression in the quest for the beautiful, so that the *Idylls of the King* is almost a Pre-Raphaelite work. The three movements were inevitably intertwined, for they all gave expression to the same lofty spirituality which had been called into being by changed social conditions and the pendulum-swing of psychological evolution.

The convergence of the movements

Between 1830 and 1850 various factors assembled and arranged themselves within patterns of class-interest to produce the intellectual movement we have designated the 'idealist and interventionist reaction'. Over all, this movement embraced the reaction against eighteenth-century attitudes which, as we have seen, had come to the top in the England of 1815. And some people remained unaffected by the intervening triumph of liberalism, and found their old opinions strengthened by the political, social, and psychological state of the nation in 1832.

The movement was inherently reactionary, and this aspect was intensified by the triumph of the new bourgeoisie, the destruction of the lower middle classes, and the reduction of aristocratic power. A return to antiquated social structures, it was hoped, might remedy the new ills of society. Feudal life seemed better than the new order: servants who knew their place, masters who behaved benevolently, and small agricultural and industrial units of production all seemed appealing. The industrial revolution, by contrast, was inseparably associated with democracy. Although the Chartists had tried to achieve social justice indirectly through democracy, the non-proletarian victims of industrialism had special interests, and varying political ideals which the demand for social reform channelled into reactionary directions. It seemed that handing over power to a privileged class or a single individual would produce better results than egalitarian competition.

The element of 'idealism' was a social psychological change which had started well before 1830, as full emotional life began to regain that place in men's minds which it had yielded to the demands of logic. The Romantics had revived sentiment in all areas of life, and this revival was given fresh impetus once the new bourgeoisie acquired power in 1832. For whereas their utilitarian rationalism, vulgarised into mere commercialism, purported to have routed lofty spiritual idealism, in fact the realisation of commercial aims only made manifest their ugliness and sterility. This meant that Romantics and idealists found that their opposition to positivism and rational analysis gained increasing support from people who found themselves to be adversely affected by the new order.

Interventionism, in the last analysis, was a combination of reactionary and emotional attitudes. Nostalgia for the past and sympathy for the poor alike counselled the authorities to take firm measures for the relief of distress. The ideal of feudalism demanded that society encroach upon the liberty of the subject, and held that it was noble to do so. And the idealised recollection of the class of small, independent cottage industrialists justified the imposition of controls and restrictions on the growth of private industries. From the other party to the alliance came an impulsive demand for relief work evoked by sympathetic and imaginative observation of the sufferings of the poor. Grass-roots interventionism, like the industrial statutes it provoked, was intimately bound up with a deep, sensitive understanding of distress. The great psychological event which led to industrial legislation was the softening of John Bull's heart.

Idealism, interventionism, and reaction are not three arbitrarily associated terms, then. They are the response to that other trinity which dominated England in 1832: rationalism, individualism, and radicalism. These three survivals of eighteenth-century philosophy had come to full flower in the nineteenth, and all the interests they injured reacted against them. By 1840 there were two opposite poles of thought and action around which men clustered as circumstance, and perhaps temperament, dictated. Exceptions may be found, but on the whole it was the men gathered around the pole of idealism who did most to check the worst excesses of industrial anarchy during the first third of Victoria's reign.

As a matter of history, though, was this a united movement? Or have we made up an artificial synthesis of social and moral preoccupations, wherein the participants were completely unaware of any hidden bonds? Certainly few contemporaries noticed more than any one given aspect of the idealist reaction. Public attention would be held by social concern at one moment, and reactionary aspirations the next; and then the aesthetic or mystical revival would hold the field. John Stuart Mill, however, was aware of the movement in its totality. We shall examine those writings in which he drew attention to the general opposition between the speculative system and the practical system in 1840 and 1845.[93] And a foreigner who was in a good position to sense the opposition also perceived the full complexity of the phenomenon he was observing. Phila-rette Chasles wrote in 1850:[94]

> Between 1830 and 1845, the English were almost insensibly growing aware of that covert, unavowed, yet noteworthy, spirit which was to spread quietly over literature, the arts, manners, science, religion, and politics.

The general outlines of this great moral transformation are even more apparent with hindsight, but it is still worth while to note that they were visible to some contemporary thinkers.

Young England; the new philanthropy; industrial legislation

Reactionary tendencies and the aristocratic point of view were pre-dominant in Young England and Social Toryism. Around 1840 a number of young aristocrats who held certain philanthropic ideals in common undertook to regenerate the life of the nation. As Young Italy and Young Germany then held the attention of Europe, the name Young England was naturally applied to them. But far from being revolutionary, like their continental counterparts, the Young England group opposed liberalism forthrightly. They proposed a return to feudal life, with solicitously benevolent landlords whose tenants were completely depen-dent upon them, as a corrective for modern anarchy. There was a natural affinity between Young England and the Oxford Movement which led to some ties between the two. The party also contributed to the aesthetic revival, and its members were among the most vehement opponents of mechanisation and industrial progress. Of course, their reactionary feudalism excited the mockery of liberals and radicals, and *Punch* fre-quently made them its butt.[95] Disraeli was at the centre of the movement, and around him were gathered Henry Hope, Baillie Cochrane, George Smythe, and Lord John Manners. Tennyson might be regarded as a sympathiser. But it was Lord John who published a volume of poems in 1841 which naïvely set out the party's aims.[96] The poet falls into a reverie before St Albans Abbey. Reflecting on episodes from the early days of Christianity in England, he regrets the passing of the ancient Church, whose monasteries prove it to have been a contemplative institution, while its congregations comprised the whole of society. He sees rational-ism as a spiritual sickness of modern times, and laments Henry VIII's seizure of ecclesiastical property. The royal martyr Charles I, on the other hand, inspires lyrical enthusiasm as the poet recalls that true values and contentment flourished in the good old days under the shadow of Church and king.[97]

> Each knew his place – king, peasant, peer, or priest –
> The greatest owned connexion with the least;
> From rank to rank the generous feeling ran,
> And linked society as man to man.

What could be done to bring back the golden age and revive feudalism? Sedulous preservation of surviving customs and traditions was of primary importance. And a careful and respectful observance of proper ceremony might lead to the revival of some obsolete practices. Christmas ought to be celebrated in the old way in country houses, and landlords should participate in their tenants' recreations so as to regain an authority based on personal respect.[98]

> Oh! but it was a goodly sight,
>   The rough-built hall to see,
> Glancing with high-born dames and men,
>   And hinds of low degree.
>
> To holy Church's dearest sons,
>   The humble and the poor,
> To all who came, the seneschal
>   Threw open wide the door....
>
> And now, of all our customs rare,
>   And good old English ways,
> This one, of keeping Christmas-time,
>   Alone, has reached our days.

In spite of their archaic fantasies, these were influential men who were able to render some service to the people's cause. In 1844 their parliamentary associates helped the radicals defeat a bill which would have strengthened the powers of magistrates dealing with labour disputes.[99] But social Toryism went beyond Young England sentiment. It was a form of conservatism which saw constitutional tradition and the authority of the Crown as adequate safeguards against industrial trouble. Church and throne were to be regenerated and restored to their former power, and then they would establish sound and satisfactory control over society, triumphing over bourgeois radicalism. Stephen, Oastler, and Sadler, who enthusiastically promoted industrial legislation, were the popular representatives of social Toryism. Disraeli had shown them a perfect way of assessing social needs, as we shall see when his novels are examined.

At the same time a new philanthropy emerged. Here, aristocratic influence was less important, and the movement's principal members were recruited from the bourgeoisie. Lord Ashley was its chief: his noble figure dominated the period's social activities. His political ideas were in harmony with the Young England party's: like them, he was inflexibly opposed to democracy, and the three principal articles of his faith were the Crown, the hereditary aristocracy, and the Established Church. But whereas Disraeli and Lord John Manners leaned towards the Oxford Movement, Ashley adhered to Evangelicalism, the most austere section of Anglicanism. He initiated and carried out most of the crusades which achieved improvements in English social life. From the moment he accepted the heavy burden of upholding industrial legislation in Parliament he was indefatigable, and devoted time and energy unsparingly to the people's cause.[100] His speeches laid down the principles of the new philanthropy. Whereas charity had been seen in the past as a free gift voluntarily offered by one man to another, Ashley described it as a duty to be performed, or a debt to be repaid:[101]

> We owe to the poor of our land a weighty debt. We call them improvident and immoral, and many of them are so; but that improvidence and immorality are the results, in a great measure, of our neglect, and, in not a little, of our example.

Gradually the concept of class obligations began to appear in general thinking about charity, and it brought with it some recognition of the possibility, or even necessity, of legislative action.[102]

> Let your laws, we say to the Parliament, assume the proper functions of law, protect those for whom neither wealth, nor station, nor age, have raised a bulwark against tyranny.

Ultimately even more widespread feelings of 'social compunction'[103] troubled the consciences of the ascendant bourgeoisie. We have discussed general factors which might have predisposed society to acknowledge the claims of sentiment; to those must now be added the immediate concerns which aroused action. Principal among these were the sensational revelations made by public and private investigations into the wretched living conditions of the people. The complacent social optimism of England between 1830 and 1850 was disturbed by reiterated shocks. Carlyle put the disquieting but suggestive phrase 'the Condition-of-England question' into general use.[104] The expression was coined in 1839, but it spread swiftly until, as we shall see, it was used by novelists. Government Blue books were inaccessible to the wide public, but the press published their conclusions, and cheap extracts brought their substance within the reach of anyone interested.[105] As early as 1828 considerable indignation had been aroused by the sufferings of an apprentice named Robert Blincoe in the most brutal period of industrial oppression towards the beginning of the century.[106] The public was further disturbed by the Report of 1832 on children in factories, and again by the preliminary inquiry into the working of the new Poor Law (1834), and yet again by the commission set up in 1840 to examine mines and factories. This body's report had more impact on public opinion than any of its predecessors. The nation was appalled by the moral outrages which had been concealed in the darkness of the mines.[107] An anonymous work which attracted a good deal of attention when it was published in 1843 gives us some insight into the unease felt by ordinary people.[108] The author denounces the failings of bourgeois society. He notes that landowners and industrialists try to blame each other for the distress of the poor, and he agrees that the charges they lay against each other are just. But the root cause of the evil is more general:[109]

> It has happened, *because we have been labouring that it should happen.* The wealth of the wealthy has accumulated; because all legislation has made this its chief object. CAPITAL has increased; because statesmen and legislators and public writers have all imagined that the increase of capital was the *summum bonum* of human existence. The poor have not advanced, along with the rich, because no one has thought it desirable that they should. . . . But the prevalent doctrine has been, that CAPITAL was the object to be chiefly desiderated; and that the wiser course with 'POPULATION', (meaning thereby, the labouring poor,) was to employ 'the *Preventive* check'. Encouragement for 'Capital'; prevention for 'Population', these have been the two leading ideas with statesmen and legislators for the last thirty years. They have now succeeded in their object. They have immensely increased the growth of Capital; and *pari passu*, the growth of misery and distress also.

In this mood, the author dares to attack the tenets of political economy and unhesitatingly affirms that intervention has become necessary:[110]

> In a variety of ways, then, legislation may, and ought to interfere. It ought to say to the factory-owner, You shall not work little children fourteen or fifteen hours per day. It ought to say to the coal-owner,

You shall not send girls and boys of five years old into the coal-pit. It ought, and it *has* said this. But in a multitude of other departments, capital requires to be followed, and watched, and threatened with penal consequences.

It was in this way that most people came to accept the idea of legislative intervention. It was not the outcome of logical thought, culminating in a legal conclusion; rather it was an irresistible spontaneous impulse to see some corporate gesture of charity made, as it was perceived that collective endeavour would be more effective than individual action. Obstinate prejudice and self-interested resistance were overcome by strenuous exertions of moral and religious sensibility. The serious decision taken went to the heart of the problem society found itself faced with, yet abstract logic was not called into play. The contest took place in the region of sentiment. Both the outlook and the consequences of official economics were condemned: they were contrary to altruism; they would have stayed the hand of a Good Samaritan; they sanctioned the deplorable destiny which made the rich richer and the poor poorer; they did nothing to abate the evils they had themselves given rise to. By all classes of English society these arguments were turned against Malthus and Ricardo. And the novelists of the time used the same material to enflame their readers.

An unstated belief that the ruling classes and the State were in duty bound to protect the poor grew up. It was never formulated as a doctrine by its adherents, and was most accurately described by one of its adversaries. John Stuart Mill was deeply affected by the sufferings of the poor, yet he repudiated the authoritarian element in interventionism, and was thus well placed to define its doctrines:[111]

> Considered in its moral and social aspect, the state of the labouring people has latterly been a subject of much more speculation and discussion than formerly; and the opinion that it is not now what it ought to be, has become very general. The suggestions which have been promulgated, and the controversies which have been excited, on detached points rather than on the foundations of the subject, have put in evidence the existence of two conflicting theories, respecting the social position desirable for manual labourers. The one may be called the theory of dependence and protection, the other that of self-dependence.
>
> According to the former theory, the lot of the poor, in all things which affect them collectively, should be regulated *for* them, not *by* them. . . . The relation between rich and poor, according to this

theory... should be only partially authoritative; it should be amiable, moral, and sentimental: affectionate tutelage on the one side, respectful and grateful deference on the other. The rich should be *in loco parentis* to the poor, guiding and restraining them like children. . . .

This is the ideal of the future, in the minds of those whose dissatisfaction with the Present assumes the form of affection and regret towards the Past. Like other ideals, it exercises an unconscious influence on the opinions and sentiments of numbers who never consciously guide themselves by any ideal.

The movement should certainly be characterised as one of hidden influences and particular causes in which pure logic and judicial presentation of a case played no part. Its direct theoretical outcome was minimal; its practical consequences, huge. By its very nature it prompted direct action, and by 1845 Mill had noted the multiplicity of activities it promoted:[112]

> The stream at present flows in a multitude of small channels. Societies for the protection of needlewomen, of governesses – associations to improve the buildings of the labouring classes, to provide them with baths, with parks and promenades, have started into existence.

Gradually by insensible degrees Young England, with its aristocratic leanings, the new philanthropy, with its acceptance of communal responsibilities, and the theory of social interdependence, resting on instinctive patriarchalism, all became established. And equally gradually they converged and clarified their positions in united opposition to bourgeois society. It is at this point that they engage our interest.

The decade 1840–50 was of critical importance in the history of English public welfare. Among many evidences of this, industrial legislation was of primary importance. The Factory Act of 1833 had failed utterly to produce the intended effects. Employers had devised a shift system which made the clauses on the employment of children inoperable, and discontent had revived within a year. In 1840 a public inquiry into conditions of employment in coal and iron mines led to the immediate passage of an Act to suppress the worst abuses of that backward industry. In 1844 Peel's conservative administration passed a law which was intended to improve the Act of 1833 and bring it up to date. For the first time women were brought under the law's protection in addition to children. In 1845 special legislation controlling textile print works was introduced, and so began the process whereby legal intervention would spread across the whole of industrial life. Chartists and philanthropists alike had dreamed of a Ten Hours Bill, and in 1847, after the tenacious parliamentary work of Ashley and Fielden, it was carried, to take full effect from 1850. It provided that women and children were not to work more than ten hours a day in the specific industries it listed, and it implied that men should not work longer hours either.

At the beginning of the century lunatics were treated like criminals. In 1828 Ashley had a law passed to ease their lot. In 1844 he returned to the charge. An official inquiry exposed barbarous cruelty and negligence, and so a law was passed in 1845 giving control over asylums to the State and forbidding inhumane practices.

The condition of boy chimney-sweeps was a subject for indignant comment among philanthropists by the end of the eighteenth century. In 1785 Hanway denounced their work as hazardous, pointing to the number of fatal accidents, and accused the master-sweeps of cruelty. Mechanical sweeping was not invented until 1834, and in 1840 a law drafted by Ashley made it illegal to send children up chimneys. It was Ashley again who organised 'Ragged Schools' for the street urchins from the poorest districts of London early in 1843.

His work was made easier by active public support. Sanitary reform and the improvement of working-class housing was the order of the day. After the cholera epidemic of 1838 a commission of inquiry investigated the housing conditions of workers in town and country. In 1842 a society was formed to campaign against insanitary dwellings, and the Prince Consort himself became its president.[113] Model cottages were being built all over the place, and some attempt to improve the slums was being made. The Public Health Act of 1848 set up a permanent Board of Health, and the Common Lodging House Act of 1851 was praised by Dickens as the best Parliament had ever passed.

Popular education was supported by philanthropists as it had been by radicals. Between 1834 and 1839 the public education grant was insignificant, but thereafter it increased. Ashley had submitted an address to the Queen in 1834 demanding moral and religious education for the workers.

The press-gang was abolished in 1835, and soon afterwards the rigours of military discipline were somewhat relaxed. Around 1840 middle-class opinion set its face against duelling, and officers were legally forbidden to duel after 1844. Changing moral standards were reflected also in the statutory suppression of wilful cruelty to animals. After a long campaign led by Richard Martin, an Act was passed in 1833 which prohibited ox- and cattle-driving, bull-, bear- and badger-baiting, and cock-fighting within five miles of Temple Bar. By 1835 the law was extended to cover the whole country. The criminal law had been reformed in 1837, and after 1838 no one had been executed for any crime other than murder. But prison conditions still attracted public notice. It was at this time that cells were introduced, and Pentonville was built as a model prison.

The crusade against drink began after 1830, as swarms of volunteers preached total abstinence. Father Mathew, an Irish priest, made mass conversions to the pledge, and the consumption of tea doubled between 1833 and 1836. After 1842 the general improvement in the standard of living combined with heavy duties on spirits to reduce the problem of popular alcoholism.

Nor was philanthropical activity confined to Britain. The treatment suffered by negroes at the hands of foreigners was condemned, and the cruelty of West Indian planters to their slaves, who would have been free on British soil, aroused great indignation. Evangelical missionaries also redoubled their efforts to convert the heathen.

Thus philanthropy had become a mania. In 1842, during the worst of the depression, public opinion was scarcely reasonable, and fantastic, self-contradictory schemes for reform were proposed:[114]

> The repeal of the Poor Laws, their arbitrary enforcement, increased protection, free trade, wars having extended commerce as their object, treaties of reciprocity, the prohibition of child labour, the allowing children to work, gold as a standard of value, silver as a standard of value, paper as a standard of value – these were some of the suggestions which were made by responsible legislators for alleviating a vast load of misery.

Social sympathy had its foolish side. One contemporary account gives an illustration of the imaginative excesses poured out in the protest against industrial evils:[115]

> The burst of sentimental sympathy for the condition of the factory-operatives which, a few years ago, frightened the isle from its propriety, appealed largely to the number of accidents which happened from machinery, and I was myself for a time fool enough to believe that mills were places in which young children were, by some inexplicable process, ground – bones, flesh, and blood together – into yarn and printed calicoes. I remember very well when first I visited a cotton-mill feeling something like disappointment at not discovering the hoppers into which the infants were thrown. I have since found that such absurdity is only credited by those who, like myself at that period, could not tell the difference between a cotton mill and a treadmill.

And by 1848 a further reaction against such excess had set in. Carlyle and Dickens protested against the philanthropic tendency to inflate trivia. According to the former:[116]

> At present, and for a long while past, whatsoever young soul awoke in England with some disposition towards generosity and social heroism, or at lowest with some intimation of the beauty of such a disposition, – he, in whom the poor world might have looked for a Reformer, and valiant mender of its foul ways, was almost sure to become a Philanthropist, reforming merely by this rose-water method.

But this only represented the fringes of the movement. Essentially it was characterised by its seriousness and passionate sincerity. Its achievements point to its strength. Public attitudes changed, and the law followed suit. Thus there were two sets of consequences: from the practical point of view, a combination of statutory measures and private action which temporarily eased distress at its gravest and warded off revolution. From the intellectual standpoint the interventionist reaction had more indirect consequences. Little by little it induced modes of feeling which opposed the prevailing climate of ideas. By directly confronting rigidly dogmatic thinking, it prepared the rising generation to face new challenges. Mathematical abstraction was held in check, and in its place day-to-day experience, transmitted by social literature and journalism, was greeted with an emotional response. Economic theories would, from now on, be evaluated pragmatically. It would be their ethical validity and the amount of relief they could offer in cases of material distress which would prove their worth. And as the public had already withdrawn its faith in Ricardian doctrines, the way was open for critical attacks upon their intransigence to succeed.

It is unnecessary to insist upon the gap between this form of inter-ventionism and socialism proper. Owen, Hodgskin, and Thomson were far removed from the middle-class crisis of conscience. Of the three, only the first was known to the middle classes, and even he drew his followers from the ranks of the Chartists. The novel word 'socialism' began to be used between 1830 and 1840, but in the minds of the philanthropists it evoked images of violent revolution and the tumbrils of Paris. Charlotte Elizabeth (Mrs Tonna) became quite apocalyptic on the subject in a novel which, nonetheless, made an urgent plea for legislative intervention in industry:[117]

> It will suffice to say that some half dozen of the young men in that mill had become Socialists. Beyond this it was impossible to go –

Socialism is the *ne plus ultra* of six thousand years' experience on the part of the great enemy of man – it is the moral Gorgon upon which whomsoever can be compelled to look must wither away: it is the doubly denounced woe upon the inhabiters of earth – the last effort of Satanic venom wrought to the madness of rage by the consciousness of his shortened time.

And the Tory *Quarterly Review*, in an article favouring industrial legislation, condemned socialism and Chartism alike as the inevitable, but extreme, outcome of heterodoxy:[118]

> They are the natural and necessary development: Chartism of Whig principles, Socialism of Dissent. They are in fact nothing but Whiggism and Dissent pushed to their legitimate consequences.

These writers were evidently principally concerned with the irreligious aspect of socialism, but its purely social aspect always aroused the same nervous antagonism.

Carlyle never challenged middle-class proprieties; still less did Lord Ashley. Only Kingsley and his friends, at one stage, dreamed of a co-operative way of life to replace wage-earning. But the normal demand for intervention was limited to public benevolence; the goal was the relief of poverty rather than its elimination. According to Mill, the aim of the new philanthropy was 'to extinguish, not indeed poverty – that hardly seems to be thought desirable – but the most abject forms of vice, destitution, and physical wretchedness'.[119] The general public may have given tacit support to philanthropic work, but its innate conviction that national stability was of the first importance remained unchanged.

John Stuart Mill

In 1840 John Stuart Mill gave the following account of the general state of mind:[120]

> Every Englishman of the present day is by implication either a Benthamite or a Coleridgian; holds views of human affairs which can only be proved true on the principles either of Bentham or of Coleridge.

Likewise, two apparently irreconcilable schools of thought dominated philosophy:[121]

> Conservative thinkers and liberals, transcendentalists and admirers of Hobbes and Locke, regard each other as out of the pale of philosophical

intercourse; look upon each other's speculations as vitiated by an original taint.

This had to be recognised as the outcome of one of those periodic changes in national opinion whereby the excesses of a preceding generation are corrected:[122]

> Now the Germano-Coleridgian doctrine is, in one view of the matter, the result of such a reaction. It expresses the revolt of the human mind against the philosophy of the eighteenth century. It is ontological, because that was experimental; conservative, because that was innovative; religious because so much of that was infidel; concrete and historical, because that was abstract and metaphysical; poetical, because that was matter-of-fact and prosaic.

Thus the new philosophy was the product of an automatic psychological reaction, and its guiding principle was a search for balance between conflicting opinions. If the intellectual and moral life of the nation were governed by a consistent rhythmic or cyclical pattern, this would account for it.

Now the philosophy of sentiment had its social overtones, which combined with certain class interests and economic factors to produce interventionism. But what brought about the combination, and linked concrete social needs with the spontaneous liberation of the emotions? What part did historical determinism play in this? Should we not see the reaction against the eighteenth century as becoming preoccupied with material questions as soon as it perceived the social problems it had uncovered? If economic factors provide as clear an explanation of psychological movements as the progress of ideas, should we still speak of a restoration of moral balance? Is not the simplest explanation of any coincidence between society's needs and the climate of opinion the most attractive?

We have already noted in the Introduction that the nature of our subject leads us to postulate an important psychological component in social history. And concrete evidence justifies this. In 1840 there were two conflicting nations as well as two modes of thought. For all their internal divisions and dissensions, the ruling classes presented a united front to the proletariat in town and country. An obvious line of demarcation separated the rich from the poor, and contemporaries were well aware of this, as Disraeli's famous sub-title, *Sybil, or The Two Nations*, demonstrated. But the psychological divide did not coincide with political divisions. On the whole it is true that Benthamism prevailed among the bourgeoisie: it expounded their views and served their interests. And it is equally true that social sentiment was common among the victims of economic competition. But these classifications were completely over-ridden by individuals with strongly differentiated temperaments. In fact, as we have seen, the majority of adherents of the philanthropic move-ment were drawn from the ranks of the bourgeoisie. There is a prima facie case for saying that men tended towards charitable action or en-lightened self-interest according to the dictates of their own natures.

Of course, philanthropy itself might be regarded as basically self-interested. Ashley's reforms and Dickens's satire need not be seen as any-thing but instinctive class-preservation. But it would still be necessary to explain why these men were aware that their own best class-interests were served by working for the common good. And such insight, or its crass opposite, was not distributed along distinguishable class or monetary lines. We are still thrown back upon differences of temperament creating automatic moral opponents.

Thus Mill's theory remains plausible. Taking the idealist and inter-ventionist reaction as a whole, it might be seen as first and foremost a swing of the pendulum in favour of temperamental emotion and imaginativeness. In an average mind the characteristic English practicality and imagination would both be found, and if one of them became dan-gerously predominant in the nation as a whole, the other might be aroused defensively among ordinary people. It might be expected that individuals who found themselves accused of accepting the dominant trait to excess would give a perfect demonstration of the need for spiritual change in their public actions.

Now in the light of this we must reassess the psychological history of the interventionist reaction, and the evidence will be found to support the theory. In all the different movements which combined to produce inter-ventionism, we find a large number of sensitive, imaginative types. Well-balanced personalities displaying both sets of characteristics also participated in the movement, at the behest of their sentiments and idealistic tendencies. It was as though one half of the spirit of England reappeared after temporary submersion beneath the contrary attitude.

The spirit which was reviving had appeared throughout the nation's history. At times of crisis, a mode of interpreting social and political problems in the light of strong moral and religious sentiments had always emerged.[123] There had been the Lollards and fourteenth-century peasants' revolts, based on Wyclifian doctrines. The fellow-sufferers of Piers Plowman had launched their direct attack upon a corrupt nobility and scapegrace clergy from motives of moral outrage as much as physical hardship. Puritanism had put forward a secular doctrine as well as a religion, as it sought to use Holy Writ as a basis for government as well as private conduct. We have already looked at the social implications of Methodism. And so it can be seen that a long tradition lay behind the revolt against individualism in 1840. Economic orthodoxy ran headlong into powerful opposition from the widespread English tendency to place enormous faith in the Bible and the assimilation of Christian morality into mundane life. It was quite inevitable that Malthus should come into conflict with the Bible: at the heart of all the polemics against classical economics lay a barely-conscious perception of this opposition. Newman put it well, from the Roman Catholic point of view: he quoted some words of Nassau Senior from an official lecture delivered at Oxford University: 'The pursuit of wealth, that is, the endeavour to accumulate the means of future subsistence and enjoyment, is to the mass of mankind, the great source of moral improvement.' And Newman commented, 'I really should on every account be sorry, Gentlemen, to exaggerate, but indeed one is taken by surprise, one is startled, on meeting with so categorical a contradiction of our Lord, Saint Paul, Saint Chrysostom, Saint Leo, and all Saints.'[124]

Sensitivity and religious thought in England led inevitably to Christian socialism – or rather, Christian interventionism – whereby moderate means should lead to somewhat conservative ends. It can be seen running through all the social movements of the period, and was the basis of Young England, the new philanthropy, and social compunction. It always looked indecisive and tentative, and went in for a great deal of soul-searching. Only exceptional men were able to push it to logical conclusions, and when Kingsley and Maurice did so, this proved critical for the movement. But well before 1848 the direction interventionism would have to take if it were not checked by an alliance of utilitarians and positivists was plain. There were forerunners of the Christian socialists, like Minter Morgan, described by one of Kingsley's friends in the following curious recollection. Morgan was a friend of Owen who dedicated his life to the dream of Christianising Owenism. 'His scheme was a very simple one. He adopted Mr Owen's views as to the formation of village communities, only he would put a Church and a clergyman into each, and then call it a "Church of England self-supporting village".'[125] James P. Greaves, 'the Sacred Socialist', was another. He was a mystic and ascetic who gathered a group of disciples around him. In 1845 his papers were published posthumously, and proved to contain some strikingly original ideas.

These two were distinctive characters; others had less definite views.

When the long-suffering populace began to rise, 'fifth monarchism', the old social and religious dream of Puritanism, was revived. In 1838 a demagogue called John Thom led a rising of the peasantry near Canterbury. He announced himself as a Messiah come to relieve poverty, and promised his followers miracles, which won their obedient devotion until he died in a skirmish with an armed band. Earlier, in 1832, the 'Benbow case' had shown that scripturally-based socialism was endemic in the hungry masses, and could provide a mystical motive for revolution. Benbow, a fanatic, had taken advantage of the Reform Act agitation to preach the idea of a general strike: a 'Sacred Month', which would frighten the ruling classes and lead to a general division of property. He published a pamphlet, which[126]

> was embellished by the quotation of many texts of Scripture in justification of this step – 'The cattle upon a thousand hills are mine' being cited as proof that all oxen might be appropriated by the needy. Eager hopes and fears were aroused by the pamphlet – some operatives believing that the Sacred Month began when the pamphlet appeared.

Within the Chartist movement, the predominance of sentiment and moral idealism was in no way disguised by the diffusion of Owen's ideas, and his followers' hostility to organised religion. The tone adopted by Chartists made them instantly distinguishable from philosophical radicals: they were enthusiastic, given to impassioned rhetorical eloquence and deeply-felt diatribe. Among the masses this emotional tone may have been merely superficial and a cover for violence, but among the leaders it represented an intense degree of moral concentration. Lovett, Vincent, and Hetherington contrast sharply with a radical utilitarian like Francis Place: only differences of temperament can explain the totally different ways in which they set about the reform of society.[127] Thomas Cooper was a proselytising agnostic, but at the same time clearly a dedicated idealist.[128] 'Christian Chartism' made a place for itself alongside Vincent's 'abstinent Chartism', which proposed the union of the temperance movement with the struggle against political oppression, and Lovett's 'educational Chartism', which looked to an intellectual regeneration of the masses as a means to victory.[129]

> The Chartists of Scotland had in numerous places established Christian Chartist Churches, in which every Sabbath were preached political sermons, and these were to some extent established in England. At Birmingham, Arthur O'Neil was the pastor of a church of that description.

These beginnings were aborted as O'Connor's extremism became the most powerful force in Chartism. None the less they are evidence of the existence and achievements of considerable moral and mystical leavening.

Even more significant were those who led the attack on the industrial bourgeoisie and its self-interest. Oastler and Stephens, two allies of Chartism, had extraordinary prestige. They were quite extraordinary representatives of Social Toryism. Oastler was a Yorkshire landowner's factor:[130]

> 'The Altar, the throne, and the cottage' was his favourite motto, and no man ever more warmly denounced the rich for their intense selfishness, and their cold neglect of the suffering class, than did the tory Oastler. But it was against the water gruel philosophy of the liberal school that his efforts were mainly directed, and these he lashed most unsparingly. . . . 'Arm, arm, arm,' was the oft repeated exhortation with which he finished his speeches. He was styled the 'king of the factory children' from his long and earnest advocacy of their cause.

The Reverend Joseph Rayner Stephens of Lancashire was even more gifted as a rabble-rouser. He began as a Wesleyan minister, but was dismissed by his colleagues for his political beliefs. Popular subscription then raised three churches for him at Ashton, and here he preached 'freedom from the chains of despotism'. He was a convinced Tory, but his social diatribes went far beyond the most extreme radicals. His oratory had a stirring effect on Chartist gatherings, as echoes from the Bible and revolutionary ideas were strangely mixed together:[131]

> If they will not learn to act as law prescribes and God ordains, so that every man shall by his labour find comfortable food and clothing – not for himself only, but for his wife, and babes, – then we swear by the love of our brothers – by our God who made us for all happiness – by the earth He gave for our support – by the heaven He designs for those who love each other here, and by the hell which is the portion of those who, violating His book, have consigned their fellow men, the image of their God, to hunger, nakedness, and death; we have sworn by our God, by heaven, earth, and hell, that from the East, the West, the North, and the South, we shall warp in one awful sheet of devouring flame, which no arm can resist, the manufactories of the cotton tyrants, and the places of those who raised them by rapine and murder, and founded them upon the wretchedness of the millions whom God, our God, Scotland's God created to be happy.

Apart from the demagoguery and violence, this anticipates the arguments of Kingsley and Ruskin.

The social mission of John Frost was rooted in the same psychological soil. This businessman and magistrate was one of the most popular men of his time, idolised by the poor as[132]

> a sort of Moses who was to lead them into the promised land of liberty and plenty. . . . Of a deeply religious, though not a fanatical turn of mind, he looked upon God as the universal father, and mankind as brothers, whose rights should be equally respected and secured from invasion. In short, John Frost really and truly loved the people, and they loved him in return.

He was a man who never shrank from acting on his beliefs. Although he had been mayor of Newport, in 1839 he led the attack on the town which was one of the most violent episodes in the history of Chartism. He was only saved with difficulty from being executed, and spent fifteen years in the hulks.

Joseph Sturge, leader of the movement for 'complete suffrage', spoke in the same tone. He was the scion of an old Quaker family, and already well known for his philanthropic opposition to slavery. After 1832 the pitiful spectacle of abject poverty led him to demand a complete reform of the electoral system. The movement he founded in 1842 was exclusively middle class but, like Chartism, it was shot through with idealism. Sturge asserted that[133]

> patriotism and Christianity alike required men to strive by all peaceable and legitimate means to remove 'the enormous evil of class legislation'. As he had striven for the emancipation of black slaves. . .so now his heart went out to the white slaves who were at the mercy of industrial conditions and economic laws that seemed to be inexorable. But could not the power of the collective will mitigate those conditions and deflect those laws? Above all, did not religious principle require the effort?

This idealistic temperament was most commonly found among supporters of industrial legislation. Sadler and the clergyman Bull attacked proprietorial self-interest with crusading zeal.[134] Lord Ashley's life and work were a constant example of the noble endeavour to reconcile social life with Christian principles.

The bourgeois mentality exhibited a conflict between economics and morality, as may be seen in the writings of Kay, Gaskell, and Fielden.[135] Kay, who as Sir James Kay-Shuttleworth was in later life well known as a liberal philanthropist and public servant, was an influential doctor in 1840. He associated himself with the interests of the industrial bourgeoisie,

and held that scientific principles were incontrovertible. But as his attention veered towards the relief of poverty, so his explicitly-stated beliefs
seemed to become tainted by an unstated leaning to philanthropy and
idealism. Gaskell likewise accepted orthodox economic views. Yet these
were neutralised in his case by an even stronger disposition to social
consciousness. The tone of his writing was polemical, with a religious,
puritanical note. He even went so far as to challenge the officially-held
view of the proper goal of scientific economics: it was not, he said,
wealth, but 'the happiness, comfort and content of each individual
family'.[136] Fielden made no such attempt to refute economic thinking,
but his powerful moral integrity compelled him to oppose the practical
consequences of *laissez-faire*.

If this account of the interventionist movement is accurate, then its
widespread growth was evidently a result of deeply-held national attitudes. Economics may have determined the precise direction of these
attitudes, but the movement was not exclusively the outcome of economic change. Social conscience, both as a frame of mind and as certain
kinds of activity, derived from deep-seated latent national characteristics.
And although industrialisation had provoked religious and moral temperaments into a specific response, the law of intellectual cycles by which
an era of arid morality might be expected to be succeeded by an era of
passionate feeling, and the historically demonstrated affinity between the
religious temperament and Christian interventionism, were of equal
importance. Revolution was probably avoided in 1840 only because
independent-minded men noticed and denounced popular distress, and
the majority of the public followed their lead. Thus two factors – psychologically, the evocation of compassionate observation, and economically,
the condition of the workers – resulted in the social product, interventionism. The most obvious effect of industrialisation upon the minds of
those engaged in industry around 1830 had been the promotion of hard
abstract thinking, a rejection of intuitive understanding, and a moral
grasp of the nature of things. And yet, as we have seen, a completely
separate development with antecedents stretching back well before the
industrial revolution was working to restore the intuitive faculty to
many of these people. The industrial revolution may have had its origins
before 1750, but up to that date it had no serious effect upon society, and
was a potential rather than an active force. But before 1750 the first
stirrings of the psychological renewal of sensitivity had definitely made
themselves felt.[137] The rapid success of Methodist preaching among the
Cornish miners signifies a great deal more than the mere fact that
Methodism answered the needs of the industrial population. So it can be

seen that the meeting of social needs and religious sensitivity represented the genuine coincidence of two quite separate forces. And merely totting up the elements in each of these will not give a true picture of the outcome; rather we should look for a common cause outside either to find out what had happened.

A parallel with the transformed national conscience may be found in John Stuart Mill's mental life. A single crisis altered his whole philosophy, changed the direction of his life, and developed powers which had hitherto lain dormant in him. There was absolutely no outside stimulus in his case: his *Autobiography* states categorically that it was a purely mental upheaval. Mill was a young prodigy, and had a precocious understanding of himself. By 1826 this led him to recognise that he had achieved all his intellectual ambitions, as he had drawn up a systematic scheme of the moral order along utilitarian principles. Thereafter he found himself completely dissatisfied by all that had formerly pleased him. His vision of existence was dimmed by his mental aridity, and the intellectual ties which bound him to life seemed too brittle to survive serious examination. For a long time he endured this nervous breakdown in secrecy, until there came a day in 1827 when he was overwhelmed by the need to weep over a scene from Marmontel. Now superficially the whole experience might seem physiological, weeping triggering a restoration of an organic function. But can a precise boundary be drawn between physical and spiritual life? At any rate, according to Mill, 'From this moment my burden grew lighter. The oppression of the thought that all feeling was dead within me, was gone. I was no longer hopeless: I was not a stock or a stone.'[138] In this way the capacity for feeling was awakened within him, and with it came a sympathetic recognition of the sufferings of others. And as ripples spread out from this moral regeneration, it came to affect the most remote and abstract areas of his life. It was because of his collapse that Mill read Wordsworth's poetry, enjoyed it, and came to terms with himself through his response to the beauties of nature. It was over Wordsworth that he broke with the intransigent radical philosopher, Roebuck, who continued to see 'little good in any cultivation of the feelings, and none at all in cultivating them through the imagination'.[139] Conversely, the cult of Wordsworth served to unite him with the Coleridgeans, Maurice and his friends, and under their influence he came to understand the philosophical reaction against the eighteenth century. And this in turn led inevitably to developments in his economic thinking, until he gradually approximated to a socialist position.

As is well known, Mill himself ascribed the greatest importance to the personal influence of Mrs Taylor in bringing about these changes. She was the companion of his affections who inspired the famous chapter on 'The Probable Future of the Labouring Classes' in his *Political Economy*. 'She pointed out the need of such a chapter,' wrote Mill, 'and the extreme imperfection of the book without it: she was the cause of my writing it.'[140] What was this woman, who apparently played so important a part in shaping economic thought in England, really like? According to Mill, she was 'a woman of deep and strong feeling, of penetrating and intuitive intelligence, and of an eminently meditative and poetic nature.'[141] He went further, and compared her to the poet Shelley. But the essential point that emerges yet again is the influence of feeling upon ratiocination.

Moreover, when Mill summarised the new ideas he had gained from his reading of reactionary philosophers and the Germano-Coleridgean school, he reduced them to historical concepts of organic and internal growth. Yet he would not have been able to understand these concepts at all, had he not been writing from personal experience. So a vital connection between the man's psychological growth and the philosopher's changing ideas can be seen. Indeed, this is the only way in which we can understand how Mill's closed, all-embracing, inflexible intellectual scheme came to be broken down, enriched, and given flexibility.

Mill's breakdown and intellectual change came between 1826 and 1830. Carlyle wrote 'Signs of the Times', outlining his social thought, in 1829. The Cambridge manifesto of religious revival was delivered in Hare's two sermons against rationalism and utilitarianism, preached in 1828 and 1829. Keble's volume of poems, *The Christian Year*, appeared as a prelude to the Oxford Movement in 1828. Southey expressed his conservative interventionist views in a book published in 1829. The first of these events might symbolise all of them: around 1830 the spirit of England began to stir, and from this grew the idealistic interventionist reaction, the social and psychological extension of the reaction against the eighteenth century.

Four

Dickens: the philosophy of Christmas

The novel was the most important literary form involved in changing mental attitudes to arouse social conscience. The previous chapters have given some account of the intellectual crisis, but a detailed study of the novel will offer a closer insight into its nature, as well as showing the part played by the genre. Dickens, Disraeli, Mrs Gaskell, and Kingsley differed widely in their approach to didactic fiction: they wrote for the same reasons, but treated their material differently according to their different backgrounds, personalities, and varying comprehension of political problems. Idealism, interventionism, and reaction were evident in varying proportions in their works. Yet all their writings had their source in the same moral current of opinion which, in turn, they illuminate for us. We have seen something of the participants in the social drama, and know its outcome: the novel, from *Oliver Twist* in 1837 to *Alton Locke* in 1850, offers a continuous illustration of it.

Social conscience

Dickens's writings are overwhelmingly personal. His views are inseparable from his character and experience. His social opinions are complex and full of contradictions; like his class attitudes, they can only be understood in the light of his life, wherein a personality giving emotional resolution to the contradictions emerges.

His childhood was spent in lower-middle-class surroundings. His father was a clerk in the Navy Pay Office, earning £80 per annum at the time when he married. This later rose to £200, but he had eight children, and was improvident with his limited resources, so that the family was perpetually short of money. Life was difficult, first in Chatham, then in London, and the future never seemed secure. The political ideals partially realised in the Reform Act dominated the circles of clerks, shopkeepers, and small businessmen that the Dickenses moved in. When Charles (born in 1812) reached manhood, the alliance of the lower and middle classes against the aristocracy was the principal social ideal from his background to leave a permanent impression on him. He also carried irrevocable memories of his intimate association with the displaced lower middle classes and white-collar workers who swarmed over London, although he knew nothing of the rural proletariat, whose wretched condition was not displayed in the peaceful old towns of Kent, and the industrial proletariat which was concentrated in the big cities of the North. The family lived at Camden Town, and according to Forster, Bayham Street, where they had their home, 'was about the poorest part of the London suburbs then, and the house was a mean small tenement, with a wretched little back-garden abutting on a squalid court.'[1] From here the boy remembered aspects of a life which his mature genius was to associate with the special unhappiness of big-city life. The direction his interests were taking is shown by the passion he soon developed for wandering through depressed areas like St Giles's, Bethnal Green, and Whitechapel.[2]

> If he could only induce whomsoever took him out to take him to Seven-dials, he was supremely happy. 'Good Heaven!' he would exclaim, 'what wild visions of prodigies of wickedness, want, and beggary arose in my mind out of that place.'

The straitened circumstances of his childhood were humiliating to the boy's proud spirit, as he suffered from some neglect, and inadequate education. But between 1822 and 1824 he suffered the traumatic experience which marked him to the end of his days. His father was imprisoned for debt, and the family floundered in difficulties: the young Dickens was too much for his parents to support. He ran errands, and slipped out to the only-too-well-known pawnshop to turn chattels into food. And then, in spite of his advanced mental development, he was placed as an apprentice in a blacking factory:[3]

> It was a crazy, tumble-down old house, abutting of course on the river, and literally overrun with rats. . . . My work was to cover the pots of paste-blacking; first with a piece of oil-paper, and then with a piece of blue paper; to tie them round with string; and then to clip the paper close and neat, all round, until it looked as smart as a pot of ointment from an apothecary's shop. When a certain number of grosses of pots had attained this pitch of perfection, I was to paste on each a printed label; and then go on again with more pots.

The boy's sensitivity and youthful ambition were offended by his crude surroundings and companions, and he passed hours of hopeless dejection in the back of the squalid workshop amid the city's feverish activity.

He came from a higher class, and had anticipated a better career, and he deplored his fall in status, which wounded him deeply. 'No words', he wrote, 'can express the secret agony of my soul as I sunk into this companionship...and felt my early hopes of growing up to be a learned and distinguished man, crushed in my breast.'[4] The morbid recollection of this humiliating trial was to haunt him for the rest of his life. Although he never spoke of it to anyone, he never forgot it. It combined disrupted education and neglected childhood in his experience, and became a symbol of the injustice of many people's fortunes. There are signs that he tried to efface the past in later life, when he became over-particular about his clothes, and paid scrupulous attention to details of personal etiquette. And the peculiarly personal note informing those touching passages in his novels which deal with childhood's loneliness and frustrations may be traced back to the same origin.[5] He felt disgraced by the experience of manual labour, and this can be seen under his alternations of modest and overbearing conduct. He was still young when he arrived at fame, prosperity, and an expansive cultivated life, and he detected and enjoyed the way in which these things protected his dignity. He was driven to cling on to the most obvious signs of his social success. This too is why his pursuit of literary success could seem calculating, as he scrutinised his sales figures and haggled over royalties. The legacy of his youth was an anxious fear of poverty, and once he had a family to support his fears were not entirely selfish.

His childhood and formative years, then, induced certain attitudes. On the other hand, he had joined in lower-middle-class life. Henceforth his liveliest, most sympathetic and unforced insights would be reserved for clerks, small traders, and the *déclassé*. Middle-class politics too were encouraged by his family background, his injured youthful pride, and his subsequent success. At the time of the Reform Act Dickens, like the rest of the middle class, saw himself as an enraged victim chafing under aristocratic oppression. At this period aristocratic selfishness seemed to him the major cause of social evils. His radicalism was perfectly genuine; all his life he held the progressive ideals of 1832. He was one of the newly-arrived men, and he hated stupid Toryism, and damned the feudal past as an age of tyranny and superstition. This was the element in his thinking of which he was himself most fully aware. His intellectual background had formulated it satisfactorily for him.

On the other hand, his private experience prevented him from sharing the middle classes' buoyant individualism. Dickens knew the hardship of lower-middle-class life from direct experience, and he had rubbed shoulders with the urban proletariat. During the long afternoons he had spent in St Giles's he had taken in the external appearance of human degradation. While earning his own living he had come to know the life led by the children of the poor. He knew all about hunger, gazing into shop-windows at meal-times, snatching meals in the open air, slicing and sharing pies, and balancing an inadequate budget with difficulty, so that orgies of pastry-eating were followed by long periods of fasting. As a young man he had toured the London underworld while working as a newspaper reporter. He had watched the police investigate thefts, murders, and suicides, and accompanied detectives about their business. He had noted the withered look of everything in once-fashionable suburbs on the way down: yellowing curtains in the windows, shabby clothes on the people, and the look of care and anxiety on their faces. He took poignant note of the successive stages by which shops fall from grandeur to bankruptcy, and the external signs of their prosperity or ruin.[6]

All this experience lived within Dickens's mind, and it was impossible for him to tear himself away from the spectacle of poverty in his imagination. He always regarded charitable social work as an essential duty. The goal he automatically set himself was to free men and women and their families from the distress which had overwhelmed him and his parents. And so he repudiated such essential tenets of bourgeois radicalism as economic individualism, *laissez-faire*, self-interest, and the theory of competition. His recognition of the extent of unseen poverty compelled him to favour public intervention.

When it came to particular forms of intervention, Dickens's experience appeared as a limiting factor. He approved of private or public assistance for the most grievous suffering, and felt that closer personal contacts between fellow-citizens should be encouraged. He paid no attention to the enormous set of antagonisms heavy industry had created, the impersonal relations between capital and labour, and the local and national problems posed by the new industrial conurbations. His background had given him *petit-bourgeois* habits of mind, and his social ideals fell naturally into simple patterns: a better, physically and mentally fitter police force, with a more paternalistic outlook; higher wages for white- and blue-collar workers; employers, masters, and wealthy patrons showing more goodwill to employees, apprentices, and humble shop-keepers. The public and private practice of charity would re-establish a just social order as alms-giving and kindness relieved distress, and the sewer of vices cloaked by decent officialdom was cleansed.

These two tendencies continued to develop throughout his youth and into maturity, as unreconciled parallel growths. Dickens achieved distinction and influence with the success of *Pickwick* in 1837, when he was twenty-five. In his new circumstances he exhibited the self-made man's ambitions, and his personal success attached him inseparably to the ideal of progress. He carried to extreme lengths the reforming zeal with which the rising middle class attacked aristocratic inertia, and remained a radical, inexorably opposed to conservatism. 'By Jove! how radical I am getting,' he once wrote to Forster.[7] And yet a covert influence was directing his social preferences unconsciously towards the past. In childhood Dickens had known and loved the old-fashioned provincial life of Rochester and Chatham. In London he had lived in a lower-middle-class setting, and it had not been the terrors of industrialism that he suffered. In the unique metropolitan situation, where the oldest customs survived cheek-by-jowl with the most up-to-date, chance and temperament had cast Dickens on the side of the former. It was not the factories in working-class districts that he came to know, but the small industries housed in old buildings, and the wretched businesses from which small shopkeepers and street-traders scraped a living. He saw the relics of the old economic order, with corporations and apprentices and outdated officials. He loved the monuments to the past which survived in picturesque corners of the City and the Strand. Like Charles Lamb, he appreciated the drowsy charm of the Temple. As a solicitor's clerk in Gray's Inn when he was fifteen, and later as a reporter in Doctors' Commons from 1828 until 1830, he explored the dusty corridors where legal tradition slumbered. During the next few years, he travelled over the Home Counties and the South as a journalist, and engraved the physical appearance and life-style of old England on his memory. Twenty years later, his artistic imagination had received the stamp of the changed world-order, but at the time of the Reform Act it was still being shaped by the past. And although there were unmistakable signs of the shape of things to come – industrial expansion, the first railways, the fret of competitive modern life, agricultural distress, the flight to the towns, and industrial disasters – none of these attracted the young Dickens's attention. Instead he took in things which were about to disappear, and lovingly delineated them in his novels: long coach journeys, with lazy halts to change horses at the staging-houses; smoky old inns, full of appetising smells; innkeepers' conversation; sleepy little towns; and the whole familiar peaceful way of life which had scarcely changed since the eighteenth century. And Dickens enjoyed the appealing charm of the old world as a man as much as he appreciated its potential as an artist. It set him free in body and soul, and showed him an expansive, generous way of life in which patriarchal authority kept families together, and men were on terms of hearty goodwill with their fellows. In short, he found everything that modern life lacked, and thus was unconsciously drawn away from his progressive theoretical notions of an ideal society, and back towards old ways of life. In the most charming areas of rural England, as among the London masses, he believed that cheerful goodwill in human relations was the sufficient condition of social well-being. Thus his message contained a reactionary element, and his novels portray an outdated England.[8]

At the same time, little by little, circumstances were easing Dickens away from democratic ideas. Between 1831 and 1836, when he was not travelling the countryside he attended sittings in the House of Commons and made shorthand reports of the debates. This introduction to parliamentary manners did nothing to give him any respect for representative government. Throughout his works politicians, elections, and party intrigue are all matter for more or less serious satire – a habit already perceptible in 'The House' and 'Bellamy's' in the *Sketches by Boz*. In 1842 his radical convictions were shaken by his visit to America. He was shocked by the unattractive appearance of republican manners, and came to think that there was some association between democratic institutions and selfish brutality: 'I do fear that the heaviest blow ever dealt at liberty will be dealt by this country in the failure of its example to the earth.'[9]

About the same time he began to fall under Carlyle's influence.[10] This could not be reconciled with principles of parliamentary government; in fact the stringent criticism of public authorities which appears in the novels after 1848 is palpably inspired by Carlyle. The sage's diatribes against administrative red-tape and bureaucratic lassitude went well beyond the novelist's. The appalling maladministration exposed at the time of the Crimean War excited public indignation, and Dickens joined with Carlyle in denouncing the anonymous, irresponsible officialdom. These attacks somewhat tarnished the ideal of democracy. And all these influences quietly cut Dickens off from the radical bourgeoisie's individualism, and steered him towards the opposite pole of interventionism.

There was no question of mutually compatible concepts coming together in all this. The opposition of State socialism to *laissez-faire* liberalism was, as we have noted, far from self-evident to contemporaries, and Dickens was not the sort of man to recognise it, let alone resolve it intellectually. He never believed that being a radical made him an ally of the economists; nor did he see that his socialist leanings allied him with the conservatives. He launched equally powerful attacks on received economic opinion and the conservative party at the same time, and often in the same books. For all its social aspirations, Young England found no favour with him: in 1841 he wrote a parody of '"The Fine Old English Gentleman" to be said or sung at all Conservative dinners', burlesquing the fine old practices of the 'good old days'. For Dickens appreciated problems through his feelings, and not his reason; and it was through feelings that he sought resolutions. However provisional or relative such solutions might be, Dickens was satisfied if they worked. His feelings revolted against undue weight being given to a class or individual, as they did against industrial anarchy. The possible contradiction in the two sets of responses could only have become apparent if they had been logically formulated and pressed home to their conclusions. But Dickens was a classic example of the heart ruling the head. It should, none the less, be stressed that the democratic ideal as such was never put across very strongly in his works, and over the years it gradually dropped out altogether.[11] By retreating from democracy he escaped the reflection of economic individualism.

Having considered his background, let us now examine the man himself. For neither the experience of hardship nor education at Carlyle's hands could have made a reformer of Dickens without the concurrence of his temperament. He is one of the most perfect examples of the sensitive, imaginative type in the whole of English letters. He could create scene upon scene in endlessly varied combinations, all enriched beyond mere observation by his personal touch. To this was added a capacity for sensitive idealisation: the resonant sensitivity of Dickens's own heart could be harnessed effectively to the whole gamut of human emotion, objectively described. No artist was better at capturing the concrete appearance of things, and none was more liable to reveal his feelings of approval or disapproval about anything. Dickens described life in scenes packed with feeling. The whole problem of Dickensian realism – that extraordinary amalgam of objectivity and romanticism – might be resolved by examining the connection between his sensibility and his imagination.

The characteristic Dickensian note is one of compassionate or humorous response to a given situation.[12] Injustice, crime, and depravity outraged his sensibility, and he could not refrain from taking a strident tone in condemning them. But more frequently his indulgent mockery, gentle reproach, and laughter mingled with tears would be evoked by men's pardonable foibles, moral failings in their daily lives, and absurd physiques. And this cheerfully compassionate interpretation of life was tinged with idealism by an ever-present moral and religious conscience, which added force to the spontaneous judgements Dickens's sensitivity arrived at. Some men might be reproved, and others excused, but always at the top of his voice. Christianity seemed to Dickens to accord with his own nature, being composed of love, cheerfulness, and compassion. And so he felt human unhappiness keenly, and suffered with his fellows. He would soothe moderate unhappiness, and surround it with sympathetic banter. But given the extreme cases of suffering and death which might have been avoided but for someone's disregard of Christian duty and the moral law, Dickens denounced and grieved, and turned his fiery eloquence to the pursuit of the guilty party. Thus two sides of the same disposition made him appear now compassionate, now vengeful, turn and turn about. But whatever his emotional tone, it was always wholehearted, and buoyed up by the optimistic vitality which was apparent in his private life. He had no doubt that good would overcome evil. His temperament, his religion, and his sensibility all meant that his mind took the experience of suffering – whether his own or other people's – and extracted from it bold, cheerful reassurance of a better future. He might recognise tragedy at times, but he always had confidence in the morrow.

Dickens's social conscience was innate. No doubt *Oliver Twist*, the first novel in which he felt entirely free to try and arouse public opinion, owed something to *Paul Clifford*. The approach may be different, but the similarity in subject matter is too close for coincidence, and we know that *Paul Clifford* made criminal novels fashionable.[13] The subject, if not the spirit of the narrative, was suggested to Dickens by Bulwer's work. But his true masters were the eighteenth-century novelists, Smollett, Sterne, and especially Goldsmith, for whose gentle spirit he felt a deep affinity.[14] Like them, Dickens drew no sharp line between realism and moralisation.

Once he was his own master and assured of his public, he naturally turned to championing the poor. In the *Sketches by Boz* his attention had focused significantly on the lives of the poor and humble, and among these little cameos of London life which served as a testing-ground for his humour, there were some topics which anticipated the great reformer.[15] In *Pickwick*, although he was only commissioned as a hack writer with an order to amuse the public, a serious note had found its way into the book, and he had forthrightly denounced some abuses in the legal system.

But it was with *Oliver Twist* that Dickens began his career as a social commentator. He was to push social comment to the limit in his novels, and was sincere, principled, and irreproachable in the spirit in which he undertook this task, although his detailed presentation of facts might be found wanting. He was more interested in practical results than literary effects: he wrote of the praises showered on him for *Oliver Twist*, 'None

that has been lavished upon me have I felt half so much as that appreciation of my intent and meaning.'[16]

As a writer and as a private citizen he was intimately involved with the
philanthropic movement. Between 1840 and 1860 he tirelessly gave time
and energy to charitable works, presiding at dinners, and helping Lord
Ashley in his crusade against poverty and vice.[17] The journals Dickens
conducted were platforms for interventionist propaganda.[18] Furthermore
Dickens's unique position in the literature of his time gave him a personal
influence over innumerable readers who had found solace or amusement
in his writings, and felt that they loved the author. Humble folk used to
cry 'God bless him!' when they heard Dickens's name mentioned. At
Christmas he received quantities of simple gifts – fruit, vegetables, and
the like – showing the direct contact that existed between his heart and
the great public that thrilled to his voice. Whatever may have been the
limitations of his achievements and the flaws of his social teaching, the
sway he won over his readers' hearts and minds by the appeal and vigour
of his artistic sincerity and lofty inspiration can only be admired.[19]

The Christmas books; 'The Chimes'

Social teaching is scattered throughout Dickens's works. The recollection
of hardship and recognition of inequalities are never absent. Neither good
humour nor facetiousness provides a distraction from the class struggle
for any great length of time for, disguised though it may be, the basic
moral and dramatic structure in Dickens is the opposition of rich and
poor. Some narrative and descriptive matter, however, points to themes
which might be distinguished from this general didactic position. To
assess these it may be necessary to disregard Dickens's declared intentions,
and look instead at the many implications of narrative details, the feeling
with which they are recounted, and the fates reserved for the characters
the author has chosen to depict. Thus, without doing violence to the
whole corpus of Dickens's work, we may examine it systematically.

But Dickens's output imposes an initial division on us. He was at the
height of his powers between 1837 and 1850, and delivered the essence
of his social message in the masterpieces written in those years. If *Bleak
House* (1853) and *Little Dorrit* (1857) are still of some interest, the novels
following them are negligible. Dickens's major works belong to the
early-Victorian period both chronologically and spiritually.

Thus, taking his output as a whole, we propose to examine its declared
message first and then, in another chapter, its unstated implications. And
within the declared message we can distinguish between his general

philosophy of society, and particular attacks upon specific abuses.

The whole of Dickens's social message is contained in the Christmas books. And because they are short, deliberately didactic, and written with Christmas in mind, Dickens's thought is presented with unusual economy and precision. *The Chimes* makes a good starting-point; nor is this a random choice. It was written in 1844, and has all the marks of Dickens's mature genius. It focuses attention on the period, and the depression which had reached its worst point in 1842. Moreover, Dickens wanted to publish some sort of manifesto: as he told Forster, 'I like more and more my notion of making, in this little book, a great blow for the poor. Something powerful, I think I can do, but I want to be tender too, and cheerful; as like the *Carol* in that respect as may be, and as unlike it it as such a thing can be.'[20] He gave the book a lot of thought, and put his whole heart into it, as he told Douglas Jerrold and Lady Blessington. 'All my affections and passions got twined and knotted up in it, and I became as haggard as a murderer long before I wrote "the End".'[21] He travelled from Italy to England to present the manuscript to his friends. The reading, which was a great success, took place on 30 November 1844 before an intimate audience which included Carlyle – striking testimony to the tie which had grown up between the two. The reading affected its hearers deeply: 'Anybody who has heard it', Dickens wrote to his wife, 'has been moved in the most extraordinary manner. . . . If you had seen Macready last night undisguisedly sobbing and crying on the sofa as I read, you would have felt, as I did, what a thing it is to have power.'[22]

Toby Veck, the old ticket porter, nicknamed Trotty because of his gait, waits at his corner outside the church door, where clients can find him. All the year round, on cold or rainy days, the church bells keep him company.[23]

> They were so mysterious, often heard and never seen; so high up, so far off, so full of such a deep strong melody, that he regarded them with a species of awe; and sometimes, when he looked up at the dark arched windows in the tower, he half expected to be beckoned to by something which was not a Bell, and yet was what he heard so often sounding in the Chimes.

On the last day of December, Toby is unusually unhappy. His poor brain runs over all manner of dismal ideas: the weekly paper is full of bad news.[24]

> 'I don't know what we poor people are coming to. Lord send we may be coming to something better in the New Year nigh upon us!. . . I can't make out whether we have any business on the face of the earth,

or not. Sometimes I think we must have – a little; and sometimes I think we must be intruding. I get so puzzled sometimes that I am not even able to make up my mind whether there is any good at all in us, or whether we are born bad. We seem to do dreadful things; we seem to give a deal of trouble; we are always being complained of and guarded against. One way and another, we fill the papers.'

His daughter Meg brings him his dinner; it is quite a feast day, for she has brought tripe, covered up in her basket, and she merrily makes him smell it. Meg is a dressmaker, and her sweetheart, Richard, is a blacksmith; they have been in love three years, and have decided to get married the next day.[25]

'He says, then, father,' Meg continued, lifting up her eyes at last, and speaking in a tremble, but quite plainly, 'another year is nearly gone, and where is the use of waiting on from year to year, when it is so unlikely we shall ever be better off than we are now? He says we are poor now, father, and we shall be poor then; but we are young now, and years will make us old before we know it. He says that if we wait – people in our condition – until we see our way quite clearly, the way will be a narrow one indeed – the common way – the Grave, father.'

At this point Richard, a robust youth with bright eyes, arrives. But just when Toby has settled himself at a doorstep, his usual dining place, and given Richard a cheery greeting, the door opens, and a servant rudely turns the little group off into the roadway.

Three gentlemen come out of the house. The first seems to be a man of consequence; he has 'creaking boots, a watch-chain, and clean linen'.[26] This is the famous Alderman Cute, a smart fellow, and a good chap. The second is 'a low-spirited gentleman of middle age...who kept his hands continually in the pockets of his scanty pepper-and-salt trousers...and was not particularly well brushed or washed.'[27] He is Mr Filer, the economist, one of McCulloch's many disciples. The third is a red-faced, 'full-sized, sleek, well-conditioned gentleman, in a blue coat with bright buttons, and a white cravat. This gentleman had a very red face, as if an undue proportion of the blood in his body were squeezed up into his head; which perhaps accounted for his having also the appearance of being rather cold about the heart.'[28] Clearly, he is a typical Tory, the hearty old English gentleman, raised on beef and ale, and devoted to the good old customs. These three have evidently come from the dinner-table, and are very jolly. But the plate of tripe attracts their attention. They pick it up, inspect it, and shake their heads, wondering whether it can be the food of the poor. The economist is the first to realise the full gravity of the situation:[29]

> 'But who eats tripe?' said Mr. Filer, looking round. 'Tripe is, without an exception, the least economical and the most wasteful article of consumption that the markets of this country can by possibility produce. The loss upon a pound of tripe has been found to be, in the boiling, seven-eights of a fifth more than the loss upon a pound of any other animal substance whatever. Tripe is more expensive, properly understood, than the hothouse pine-apple.'

Toby makes a miserable bow:[30]

> 'You do, do you?' said Mr. Filer. 'Then I'll tell you something. You snatch your tripe, my friend, out of the mouths of widows and orphans.'
> 'I hope not, Sir,' said Trotty faintly. 'I'd sooner die of want!'
> 'Divide the amount of tripe before-mentioned, Alderman,' said Mr. Filer, 'by the estimated number of existing widows and orphans, and the result will be one pennyweight of tripe to each. Not a grain is left for that man. Consequently, he's a robber.'

The apoplectic gentleman with the shiny buttons, however, draws another conclusion from the encounter:[31]

> 'What's it possible to say?' returned the gentleman. 'What *is* to be said? Who can take any interest in a fellow like this,' meaning Trotty, 'in such degenerate times as these? Look at him! What an object! The good old times, the grand old times, the great old times! *Those* were the times for a bold peasantry, and all that sort of thing. Those were the times for every sort of thing, in fact. There's nothing nowadays. Ah!' sighed the red-faced gentleman. 'The good old times, the good old times!'

The Alderman still has not had his say: he has been too busy finishing off the tripe. He's a philosopher, is Alderman Cute; a practical philosopher – oh, very practical![32] He will come straight to the point:[33]

> 'Now, you Porter! Don't you ever tell me, or anybody else, my friend, that you haven't always enough to eat, and of the best; because I know better. I have tasted your tripe, you know, and you can't "chaff" me. You understand what "chaff" means, eh? That's the right word, isn't it? Ha, ha, ha! Lord bless you,' said the Alderman, turning to his

friends again, 'it's the easiest thing on earth to deal with this sort of people, if you only understand 'em!'

Famous man for the common people, Alderman Cute! Never out of temper with them! Easy, affable, joking, knowing gentleman!

'You see, my friend,' pursued the Alderman, 'there's a great deal of nonsense talked about Want – "hard up", you know: that's the phrase, isn't it? ha! ha! ha! – and I intend to Put it Down. There's a certain amount of cant in vogue about Starvation, and I mean to Put it Down. That's all! Lord bless you,' said the Alderman, turning to his friends again, 'you may Put Down anything among this sort of people, if you only know the way to set about it!'

And the jolly Alderman chucks Meg under the chin as a fine figure of a girl. Is that her sweetheart with her? Richard says sharply that he is, and that they are to be married on New Year's Day. Thoughtless words![34]

'Ah!' cried Filer, with a groan. 'Put *that* down indeed, Alderman, and you'll do something. Married! Married!! The ignorance of the first principles of political economy on the part of these people, their improvidence, their wickedness, is, by Heavens! enough to – Now look at that couple, will you?'...

'A man may live to be as old as Methuselah,' said Mr. Filer, 'and may labour all his life for the benefit of such people as those, and may heap up facts on figures, facts on figures, facts on figures, mountains high and dry, and he can no more hope to persuade 'em that they have no earthly right or business to be married than he can hope to persuade 'em that they have no earthly right or business to be born. And *that* we know they haven't. We reduced it to a mathematical certainty long ago.'

And Cute, as a Justice of the Peace, gives the young people some advice. Meg wants to marry, does she? To what end? To quarrel with her husband, become a distressed wife, and have crying children on her hands? And Richard is a fool to get married while his sturdy figure turns girls' heads in the street. And their instructor goes on his way, leaving the girl in tears, and the young man sullen and downcast, while the Chimes ring out, and seem to say, 'Put 'em down, Put 'em down! Good old Times! Good old Times! Facts and figures, Facts and figures!'[35]

Before going, the Alderman has given Trotty a letter to deliver to Sir Joseph Bowley, the great landowner and Member of Parliament. He is a philanthropist – the Friend and Father of the people. In his well-appointed library, where Lady Bowley tots up her annual accounts with the help of a secretary, he utters pearls of benevolence to Trotty. So long as a poor man is frugal and temperate, respectful, self-denying, prompt with his rents, capable of bringing up his family on next to nothing, and is imbued with a feeling of the Dignity of Labour, so long will Sir Joseph be a Friend and a Father to him:[36]

> 'Every New Year's Day myself and friends will drink his health. Once every year myself and friends will address him with the deepest feeling. Once in his life he may even perhaps receive, in public, in the presence of the gentry, a Trifle from a Friend. And when, upheld no more by these stimulants, and the Dignity of Labour, he sinks into his comfortable grave, then, my lady' – here Sir Joseph blew his nose – 'I will be a Friend and Father – on the same terms – to his children.'

Deeply moved, Toby trots off on his journey home, deep in thought. He runs into a poor countryman, with his little girl in his arms, who seems lost in the London streets. This is Will Fern, one of Sir Joseph's labourers, who is in rebellion against the Father of the people's charity. He has left his hovel, where he was starving to death, and come to the city to look for work. He tells Trotty of his poverty, and the rage against society it has bred in him:[37]

> 'I only want to live like one of the Almighty's creeturs. I can't – I don't – and so there's a pit dug between me and them that can and do. There's others like me. You might tell 'em off by hundreds and by thousands, sooner than by ones.'

Trotty is touched, and takes his new friend home with him to share his meal, while Meg rubs some warmth back into little Lilian's feet. When his guests have settled down Trotty opens the paper, where he finds yet again endless descriptions of the people's criminality and violence. A desperate mother has just killed her baby:[38]

> 'Unnatural and cruel!' Toby cried. 'Unnatural and cruel! None but people who were bad at heart, born bad, who had no business on the earth, could do such deeds. It's too true all I've heard today; too just, too full of proof. We're Bad!'

But suddenly the Chimes ring out, and their angry voices seem to convey a command:[39]

> 'Toby Veck, Toby Veck, waiting for you, Toby! Toby Veck, Toby Veck, waiting for you, Toby! Come and see us, come and see us, Drag him to us, drag him to us, Haunt and hunt him, haunt and hunt him!'

Toby is incredulous at first, and then fascinated. He feels drawn out by a mysterious power, and finds the church-tower door open, whereupon he climbs to the top, and falls down in a swoon among the bells.

When he comes to his senses, he finds strange, majestic figures gazing at him. These goblin spirits of the Chimes talk to him, and point out his weaknesses: he has mistrusted himself, and despaired of the future. He has lent his ear to the men of lies who oppose social progress, and long for a dead past; and to those who deny human brotherhood, and coldly calculate the worth of a soul by the cost of feeding a body:[40]

> 'Lastly, and most of all,' pursued the Bell. 'Who turns his back upon the fallen and disfigured of his kind; abandons them as Vile; and does not trace and track with pitying eyes the unfenced precipice by which they fell from Good – grasping in their fall some tufts and shreds of that lost soil, and clinging to them still when bruised and dying in the gulf below – does wrong to Heaven and Man, to Time and to Eternity. And you have done that wrong!'

For his punishment, Toby is to watch the future unfold, and see his fears come true. He is to learn from the fate of his own daughter:[41]

> 'Learn from the creature dearest to your heart how bad the Bad are born. See every bud and leaf plucked one by one from off the fairest stem, and know how bare and wretched it may be. Follow her! To Desperation!'

And the helpless father has to watch his daughter across the barriers of time and space.

He sees his own death that very night, the solemn tolling that sounds being his own passing bell. The scene changes. In a shabby room, Meg and Fern's daughter Lilian are wearing their eyes out sewing. Richard has deserted his sweetheart, his mind cleared of folly by the Alderman's practical sagacity. The two girls live together, one broken-hearted and ill, the other withdrawn and resigned:[42]

> 'So many hours, so many days, so many long, long nights of hopeless, cheerless, never-ending work – not to heap up riches, not to live grandly or gaily, not to live upon enough, however coarse, but to earn bare bread; to scrape together just enough to toil upon, and want upon, and keep alive in us the consciousness of our hard fate! Oh, Meg, Meg!' – she raised her voice and twined her arms about her as she spoke, like one in pain – 'how can the cruel world go round, and bear to look upon such lives!'

Hunger and poverty force Lilian onto the streets; she returns to die near her friend, and Toby sees delirious fever in his daughter's face.

Another scene shows him the country. We are in the midst of one of the celebrations Sir Joseph Bowley gives at his estate in honour of Lady Bowley's birthday. The grand ladies and gentlemen take their places for a great dinner; some food has been distributed to the poor, and Sir Joseph himself plays skittles with his tenants. Now who could feel the slightest anxiety for the future? But all eyes turn when Will Fern rushes into the crowd, grim and haggard, like a spectre of poverty. He has just come out of prison, for there is very little a poor man can do that is not punishable by law:[43]

> 'I goes a-nutting in your woods, and breaks – who don't? – a limber branch or two. To gaol with him! One of your keepers sees me in the broad day, near my own patch of garden, with a gun. To gaol with him! I has a nat'ral angry word with that man when I'm free again. To gaol with him! I cuts a stick. To gaol with him! I eats a rotten apple or a turnip. To gaol with him! It's twenty mile away; and coming back I begs a trifle on the road. To gaol with him! At last, the constable, the keeper – anybody – finds me anywhere, a doing anything. To gaol with him, for he's a vagrant, and a gaol-bird known; and gaol's the only home he's got.'

The poor are urged to show a scrupulous respect for property, but who can be honest in hovels where people die of starvation? Begin charity at the right end; give the poor houses and food; make the law more humane, and don't write up 'Gaol' at every turn:[44]

> 'There ain't a condescension you can show the Labourer then that he won't take as ready and as grateful as a man can be; for he has a patient, peaceful, willing heart. But you must put his rightful spirit in him first; for whether he's a wreck and ruin such as me, or is like one of them that stand here now, his spirit is divided from you at this time. Bring it back, gentlefolks, bring it back! Bring it back, afore the day comes when even his Bible changes in his altered mind, and the words seem to him to read, as they have sometimes read in my own eyes – in Gaol: "Whither thou goest, I can Not go; where thou lodgest, I do Not lodge; thy people are Not my people; nor thy God my God!"'

Servants drive the intruder away; but he appears later, gliding furtively into the garret where Meg still works. He has come to bid her a last farewell, as he declares war on society:[45]

'There'll be Fires this winter-time to light the dark nights, East, West, North, and South. When you see the distant sky red, they'll be blazing. When you see the distant sky red, think of me no more; or if you do, remember what a Hell was lighted up inside of me, and think you see its flames reflected in the clouds. Good night. Good-bye!'

The end is approaching, as Trotty realises, with an anguished heart. Meg has no work; she wanders into the frozen mud one winter's night, begging. At her breast she carries her baby. But she is rejected everywhere, and evicted from her room, and at last her steps turn towards the river.[46]

To the rolling River, swift and dim, where Winter Night sat brooding like the last dark thoughts of many who had sought a refuge there before her. Where scattered lights upon the banks gleamed sullen, red, and dull, as torches that were burning there, to show the way to Death. Where no abode of living people cast its shadow, on the deep, impenetrable, melancholy shade.

Then Toby clings distractedly to her, and feeling her slip out of his grasp' cries out his penitence to the bells:[47]

'I have learnt it!' cried the old man. 'Oh, have mercy on me in this hour, if, in my love for her, so young and good, I slandered Nature in the breasts of mothers rendered desperate! Pity my presumption, wickedness, and ignorance, and save her!'

And when he sees that the bells forgive him, and finds a new, giant strength, his joy bursts out in inspired phrases:[48]

'I know that our Inheritance is held in store for us by Time. I know there is a Sea of Time to rise one day, before which all who wrong us or oppress us will be swept away like leaves. I see it, on the flow! I know that we must trust and hope, and neither doubt ourselves, nor doubt the Good in one another. I have learnt it from the creature dearest to my heart. I clasp her in my arms again. O Spirits, merciful and good, I take your lesson to my breast along with her! O Spirits, merciful and good, I am grateful!'

And to the cheerful note of the Chimes, he wakes up in the armchair where he fell asleep, for it was all a dream. At his side Meg has finished sewing her wedding-dress; midnight is sounding, and a new year is beginning. And with matchless buoyancy, and the unrestrained optimism of Dickensian endings, his heart leaps up as the nightmare dissolves in cheerfulness and good humour:[49]

Had Trotty dreamed? Or are his joys and sorrows, and the actors in them, but a dream; himself a dream; the teller of this tale a dreamer, waking but now? If it be so, O Listener, dear to him in all his visions, try to bear in mind the stern realities from which these shadows come; and in your sphere – none is too wide, and none too limited for such an end – endeavour to correct, improve, and soften them. So may the New Year be a Happy one to You, Happy to many more whose Happiness depends on You! So may each Year be happier than the last, and not the meanest of our brethren or sisterhood debarred their rightful share in what our Great Creator formed them to enjoy.

Such is the book, with its powerful pathos and emotional overtones.[50] It exhibits all Dickens's artistic idiosyncrasies: his extraordinary mixture of verisimilitude and fantasy, compassionate humour and savage irony, comic verve and tragic power. Characters are sketched in bold, simple strokes, with a single trait – Toby's trotting, for example, or the Alderman's little laugh – which lays bare the basis of each personality. There is caricature and polemical exaggeration, and yet the picturesque details are true to life. The work as a whole is idealistic, and displays profound insight into truths of great sadness.

When one thinks of the other Christmas books, and relevant passages to be found across the whole corpus of Dickens's works, it is easy to perceive the 'Christmas philosophy' in isolation. It was a vague and sentimental form of Christian socialism. Its positive proposals were very tentative, though its criticism of the existing order was stronger, and it preached interventionism in the name of religious idealism. From a historical point of view it was responding to the needs of a society that had already half disappeared. It was adapted to the familial relations of small businesses and cottage industries. In this respect, and in this respect alone, it might be described as reactionary; otherwise it was progressive. Dickens flatly condemned the public features of reaction in society. He saw a need for benevolent authority, but was far from letting this sweep him into demanding that the people should be politically submissive.

The Christian element diffused through his writings is made explicit in the books dealing with the festival of Christmas. In *A Christmas Carol* the Nativity itself becomes a symbol for moral and social regeneration. In *The Chimes* it is the bells, the voice of institutionalised religious worship, which preach hope and duty to the poor. The New Year is substituted for Christmas as a symbol of the end of a wicked past and the start of a better future. In each book Dickens instinctively tried to link his message with the seasonal renewal of good will. He loved the self-examination prompted by Christmas, understood it, and responded to it as warmly as he did to the extravagant merry-making of the great week. Nothing could have brought him closer to the traditional feelings of the nation, and this concurrence with a nation-wide sentiment reinforced Dickens's determination to enlarge the feeling, and use it to find a solution to society's problems. Christmas was already the major family and Church festival; on Christmas Day men were open-hearted; old, dead affections were revived, and general sympathy prevailed. Families which had become separated were reunited under the paternal roof. And why should not the hostile members of the national family unite likewise in heart and soul? If the day's delights suggested good will, why not let it shine out beyond the domestic hearth, and take in all the humble, poor, and destitute? If groaning tables, trees hung with toys, the excitement of kissing girls under the mistletoe, and even outright drunkenness were all good and healthy things, promoting a renewed appetite for life, then, for heaven's sake, might not some thought be spared for those who were actually cold and hungry?[51] Thus the Christian festival which occasioned moral transformation might become the centre for launching a great increase in charitable activities. The Christmas books give solid evidence of the connection between Dickens's Christianity and his social thought.

The positive aspect of this was simple. Christianity inescapably ordained solidarity among men, which ought to find expression in the active solicitude of society's members for one another. Rich and poor alike had duties, though the latter already possessed unsuspected virtues: dedication and self-sacrifice were common among them and, contrary to expectation, they were morally superior to the rich.[52] But they still had to make the hardest effort of all, and hold on to faith and hope in addition to their charity. They must reject despair and class warfare; Dickens denounced revolutionary violence wherever he recognised it. Will Fern is a Dorset man, like the Tolpuddle Martyrs,[53] and Dickens uses him to expound and attack agricultural poverty. But there is no suggestion of Chartism about him or anything else in *The Chimes*, or indeed anything in Dickens's works. Toby Veck undergoes severe punishment for doubting human nature and, albeit unwillingly, playing the game ordained by oppressors and agitators. Just recompense is promised to the downtrodden in the future, only so long as they await it with sturdy courage and high hopes.

But the poor were not expected to bring about their own future by themselves; it lay with the rich and powerful to do all they could to right social wrongs. How were they to set about it? Dickens was no advocate of equal wealth; the socialist ideal seems scarcely to have impinged on him, and in so far as he was aware of it, he dismissed it as a chimeric revolutionary fantasy. Yet the plea of the poor to the rich was, in his eyes, a legitimate demand for recompense. Like the leading new philanthropists, Dickens saw assistance for the needy as their right. The ruling classes were responsible for the ills of society, and they had a natural, paternalistic authority over the weak and ignorant. There had to be public and private intervention in the lives of the lower classes: patient, dedicated, charitable action was needed in welfare and relief work. The first of the Christmas books lays down the duty of the rich with particular clarity; it is not just a matter of remote charity or useless good intentions. Anyone in any position of authority, from the greatest to the humblest, is responsible for the souls of his underlings. Scrooge, the businessman, would be making a contribution to the peace of society if he increased the salary of Bob Cratchit, his clerk. If all bosses were like Old Fezziwig, and treated their employees as friends, there would be less social friction. Within the limits of possibility, given the existing order, all injuries to body and soul that society tolerated were going to have to be stamped out. Otherwise the gulf between the classes would yawn wider every day, and revolution, which already seemed imminent, would overwhelm rich and poor alike. And Dickens created an unforgettable picture of revolution as the ultimate social catastrophe in his artistic realisation of Carlyle's epic history of the French Revolution.[54]

The negative side of Dickens's message was more direct. It attacked two enemies. One was stupid conservatism – Macaulay had called the Tories 'the stupid party' – the party of unthinking habit and pigheaded reaction. Here Dickens's radicalism found expression in his hostility to showy and self-important charity. He rated aristocratic socialism among the useless and humbugging forms of charity: Sir Joseph Bowley's relation to Young England is obvious.[55] But this was not an area where Dickens could make his greatest effects. The insulting tone of feudal benevolence offended him, but at bottom he did not really think that the people need govern themselves. Like Carlyle, he thought that reform would have to come from above, as is apparent in Will Fern's furious words to the assembled gentry at Sir Joseph's. When Dickens's friendship with Lord Ashley is taken into consideration, and it is noted that his novels never mention the Anti-Corn Law League's campaign, which was the radical bourgeois agitation *par excellence*, then it becomes clear that Dickens's bitterest hatred was reserved for radical individualism and all its works.[56] He was for ever attacking economic dogmatism, utilitarian theory, and business practices. He detested them instinctively, as the social expressions of a heartlessness which was anathema to one of his emotional make-up. In so far as he employed reason, he thought the doctrine of enlightened self-interest was unsound: his instinct told him it was contrary to Christian charity and the moral law. In Filer's Malthusian intransigence and misplaced application of mathematics to life we see Dickens divining, rather than understanding, that the use of theory is being extravagantly abused. The Alderman's practical good sense, with its cold and pitiless view of material interests, seems to him morally impoverished in just the same way, and with the same consequential dangers. He grasped intuitively the link between the business world's philistinism, and the constricting tyranny of abstract economic thought. He was not equipped to refute the latter, so he attacked the former.[57] Dickens's work as a whole represented a massive attempt to uproot the psychological offshoots of detached rationalism in the mind of the public, and to substitute compassion and interventionism. But this aspect of his writing is only apparent after close investigation. Dickens was only half aware of some of his most effective strokes, and we shall come to his conflict with individualism when we examine the implicit social message of his novels.

Reforming themes and their effect

The philosophy of Christmas is a powerful, if confused, encouragement of social altruism. It exhibits the best qualities of Dickens's heart, and all the limitations of his head. But although he had no real knowledge of economics and, in his biographer's words, 'He had not made politics at any time a study, and they were always an instinct with him rather than a science,'[58] he had the compensating gift of artistic vision, and an imaginative sensitivity which saw the whole human condition in any individual example of distress. He could comprehend some social evils and portray them so vividly that no one could fail to recognise them thereafter. Indeed, Dickens's vigorous criticism of certain abuses played a large part in the philanthropic improvement of social life in England.

The more precisely defined were the attacks he launched on specific targets, of course, the more obvious were his tangible results. *Nicholas Nickleby* put an end to the worst abuses of the State's lack of concern with education.[59] The Yorkshire schools had a detestable reputation; Dickens had heard tell of them in his childhood, and had never forgotten it: 'I was always curious about Yorkshire schools – fell, long afterwards and at sundry times, into the way of hearing more about them – at last, having an audience, resolved to write about them.'[60] Thus, in this instance, the didactic element was the starting-point of the novel.

Dickens took a trip to Yorkshire to collect material, and searched the newspapers for reports of civil actions brought against the Yorkshire schoolmasters. He devoted the first few chapters of the book to the theme, and the public was magically affected by his forceful, moving account of the life of 'the young gentlemen' at Dotheboys Hall, Squeers's ruffianly brutality, and the assistant master's misfortunes. Dickens's inimitable humour cast additional charm over all this, and the whole nation's attention was caught, with the result that the worst schools had to close down.[61] It was at this point that the State began to take a hand in public education, and increased the miserly grants it had previously made.[62] Circumstances favoured the movement, which was not to be halted. 'There were then, a good many cheap Yorkshire schools in existence. There are very few now,' wrote Dickens in 1867.[63]

Similarly, Mrs Sarah Gamp and Mrs Betsy Prig, the unforgettable sick-nurses in *Martin Chuzzlewit*, were national figures as soon as they were created. They were coarse, bibulous, unconscientious, and utterly cynical in their exploitation of sickness and death: public opinion accepted this as just criticism of nursing, whose failings had been disregarded for too long. Thenceforth, private initiative and public administration were united in their efforts to correct the abuses of nursing, and by 1900 the nursing force was one of the country's outstanding welfare institutions.

Mention must be made here of Dickens's influence on education in the widest sense. The emotional current of his writings, with their stress on family affection, their charming treatment of children as characters, and the realisation of the unhappiness of ill-treated children, helped to introduce a gentler spirit into educational practices. This is brought out, and perhaps exaggerated, in J. L. Hughes's book, *Dickens as an Educator*:[64]

> It will be admitted that he has done more than any one else to secure for the child a considerate treatment of his tender age. 'It is a crime against a child to rob it of its childhood.' This principle was announced by Dickens, and it has come to be generally recognised and adopted.

Dickens's agitation was most successful in the legal sphere. Prisons and the penal system were a perpetual preoccupation of his, experience having given him an intimate knowledge of the subject. As we have seen, ideas for reform were in the air. Dickens's merit was not that of a pioneer or original thinker; he lent his incomparable literary support to reforms which had already been started, and there can be no doubt that he expedited their completion. He often denounced the cruelty of the penal code, as he does, for example, in Dennis the hangman's story in *Barnaby Rudge*:[65]

> Mary Jones, a young woman of nineteen who come up to Tyburn with a infant at her breast, and was worked off for taking a piece of cloth off the counter of a shop in Ludgate-Hill, and putting it down again when the shopman see her, and who had never done any harm before, and only tried to do that, in consequence of her husband having been pressed three weeks previous, and she being left to beg, with two young children – as was proved upon the trial.

Still more, he attacked the unequal treatment of rich and poor at the hands of the law.[66] We have seen Fern's outburst in *The Chimes: Hard Times* faces the problem of divorce squarely, and asks whether it is right that this should be the prerogative of the rich.[67] *Oliver Twist* is a protracted complaint about the law's pointless severity with the downtrodden. Dickens played a large part in the suppression of public executions. In one episode in *Dombey and Son* he evokes pity for the lot of the infanticide mother, who has been lightly seduced and abandoned.[68] Themes like these recur insistently while, as we know, the law's severities underwent parallel curtailment.

No one did more to reform debtors' prisons. Unlike bankrupts, insolvents had their persons seized and their future income attached by their creditors. The state of their prisons was unbelievable: the law made no provision for minimal material, hygienic, or moral conditions to be maintained for the unfortunate prisoners. The public was indignant about the situation: the Court established by the Act of 1813 had released 50,000 debtors over thirteen years, one of its beneficiaries being Dickens's father at the end of his spell in the Marshalsea, where Dickens saw the conditions on occasional visits. But there were still very many prisoners under lock and key: in 1827, 6,000 people were arrested for debt in London alone. The law commissioners declared in 1830 that the widespread objections to the insolvency laws were justified. It was at this point that Dickens stepped in, and painted a convincing picture of the corrupting boredom of a pointless existence, the demoralising spectacle of rich debtors buying privileges, and all the cruelty of a system of debilitating, impoverished inactivity. Mr Pickwick's incarceration in the Fleet Prison served as a pretext for a lively tragi-comic description of this particular world:[69]

> We still leave unblotted in the leaves of our statute-book, for the reverence and admiration of succeeding ages, the just and wholesome

law which declares that the sturdy felon shall be fed and clothed, and that the penniless debtor shall be left to die of starvation and nakedness.

Later, in *Little Dorrit*, Dickens returned to the theme and exhibited the moral anguish of Marshalsea prisoners to thousands of readers. But by that time he was describing the past; reform had come swiftly after the publication of *Pickwick* in 1837. A measure to soften the law's rigour was put forward in 1838, but was thrown out. In 1844, after repeated efforts, Cottenham succeeded in bringing the penalities for debt closer to those for bankruptcy.

Dickens satirised the failings of lawyers and the law without mercy, and by now his criticisms are seen to have been correct.[70] After the publication of *Pickwick*, the devious figures of Dodson and Fogg and the immortal case of *Bardell* v. *Pickwick* suggested that the author had a distinctly limited respect for legal cunning and its practitioners. In *Oliver Twist* we are shown Mr Fang, the police court magistrate, whose brutal method of dispensing summary justice is made an eloquent protest, as Dickens portrays it. *The Old Curiosity Shop* introduces the characteristic figures of the attorney, Sampson Brass, and his sister Sally: a delightful pair who turn his slipperiness and her tartness against the letter and spirit of the law. *David Copperfield* takes us into Doctors' Commons and the old legal firms which cynically exploit their clients. *Bleak House*, in the last analysis, is a formidable attack upon the spirit, conduct, and very existence of the Court of Chancery. Here again the writer's strictures were amply justified: public attention had been focused on the weaknesses of Chancery for a long time.[71] Its endless delays, enormous costs, incessantly renewable appeals and countersuits, and exhaustingly complicated procedures were proverbial. We know from the author's Preface and Forster's research that the case of Gridley, 'the man from Shropshire', was based on an actual suit. 'What a mockery of justice this is,' wrote the author of the pamphlet on which Dickens drew:[72]

> The facts speak for themselves, and I can personally vouch for their accuracy. The costs already incurred in reference to this £300 legacy are not less than from £800 to £900, and the parties are no forwarder. Already near five years have passed by, and the plaintiff would be glad to give up his chance of the legacy if he could escape from his liability to costs, while the defendants who own the little farm left by the testator, have scarce any other prospect before them than ruin.

Two public letters addressed to Dickens in 1859 show the extent to which public opinion was behind him: the anonymous author asserted that he, like many others, was not only warmly attached to Dickens for the deep impression his books had made on him, but also for the implacable hatred he had always shown for the Court of Chancery as it existed then – a monster of iniquity.[73] The book may not have had an immediate effect, but for a long time legal practitioners were sensitive to its criticism of their ways, and it played its part in the reorganisation of the High Courts in 1873.

Elsewhere, when he was attacking less clear-cut targets, and describing complex evils, it is harder to demonstrate any direct Dickensian influence. His personal achievement here was merged with that of contemporaries working in the same sphere. But certainly it was an element in the moral evolution of interventionism, although we are reduced to conjecture when we try to deduce its precise importance. The popularity of Dickens's books, and his undoubted hold over his readers' hearts and minds, are evidence that such importance existed.

Dickens was acutely conscious of the direct link between poverty and social sickness. He knew that an honest, happy life was impossible in squalid, insanitary, unlit, waterless, fetid slum areas. The memorable sections of *Oliver Twist* describing slum conditions marked a new epoch in British letters. The author described[74]

> Jacob's Island, surrounded by a muddy ditch, six or eight feet deep and fifteen or twenty wide when the tide is in, once called Mile Pond, but known in the days of this story as Folly Ditch. . . . Crazy wooden galleries common to the backs of half-a-dozen houses, with holes from which to look upon the slime beneath; windows, broken and patched, with poles thrust out, on which to dry the linen that is never there; rooms so small, so filthy, so confined, that the air would seem too tainted even for the dirt and squalor which they shelter; wooden chambers thrusting themselves out above the mud, and threatening to fall into it – as some have done; dirt-besmeared walls and decaying foundations; every repulsive lineament of poverty.

No theme is commoner in Dickens,[75] and no social need aroused such vehement hatred of indifferent selfishness and half-hearted charity in him:[76]

> Look round upon the world of odious sights – millions of immortal creatures have no other world on earth – at the lightest mention of which humanity revolts, and dainty delicacy, living in the next street, stops her ears, and lisps, 'I don't believe it!' Breathe the polluted air, foul with every impurity that is poisonous to health and life; and have every sense, conferred upon our race for its delight and happiness, offended, sickened, and disgusted, and made a channel by which

misery and death alone can enter. Vainly attempt to think of any simple plant, or flower, or wholesome weed that, set in this fetid bed, could have its natural growth, or put its little leaves forth to the sun as GOD designed it. And then, calling up some ghastly child, with stunted form and wicked face, hold forth on its unnatural sinfulness, and lament its being, so early, far away from Heaven – but think a little of its having been conceived, and born and bred in Hell!

Inevitably, Dickens reacted by urging an escape to nature. Fresh air, country life, and the tranquillity of the English countryside open up vistas of refreshment in the novels, as he sketches in the theme that Ruskin was to perfect:[77]

The freshness of the day, the singing of the birds, the beauty of the waving grass, the deep green leaves, the wild flowers, and the thousand exquisite scents and sounds that floated in the air, – deep joys to most of us, but most of all to those whose life is in a crowd, or who live solitarily in great cities as in the bucket of a human well, – sunk into their breasts and made them very glad.

Thus Dickens, the literary pioneer of the great modern city, created it as a desert of bricks and mud, searing the mind in its horror.[78]

There is little consideration of industrial legislation in the novels. Dickens knew little about the industries around which the demand for legislation was centred: brief statements reveal his support for the Factory Acts as a part of his general hostility to the doctrines of *laissez-faire*.[79] But his feelings were aroused by one aspect of the question with which he was better acquainted. The employment or exploitation of children by their families or factory-owners, and their premature introduction to unhappiness, evoked furious protests from Dickens. Here personal feelings were mingled with altruism: he could see his own childhood in the unhappiness of others, and strove to ease a burden he recognised. The story of *Oliver Twist* was representative: it outlined imaginatively the sufferings of parish apprentice boys, like Robert Blincoe; paupers' children, born in workhouses, and hired out to manufacturers or journeymen.[80] The thought of rich children, healthy and happy with their toys, often called to Dickens's mind the contrasting picture of the poor, and he would interrupt his narrative for a renewed denunciation of the cruel indifference of public authorities.[81] He understood the danger threatening the nation, and poured out warnings on the fools who did not want to see it. The situation is put over most dramatically in *A Christmas Carol*, when Scrooge is confronted by the Ghost of Christmas Present:[82]

'Forgive me if I am not justified in what I ask,' said Scrooge, looking intently at the Spirit's robe, 'but I see something strange, and not belonging to yourself, protruding from your skirts. Is it a foot or a claw?'

'It might be a claw, for the flesh there is upon it,' was the Spirit's sorrowful reply. 'Look here.'

From the foldings of its robe it brought two children; wretched, abject, frightful, hideous, miserable. They knelt down at its feet, and clung upon the outside of its garment.

'Oh, Man! look here! Look, look, down here!' exclaimed the Ghost.

They were a boy and a girl. Yellow, meagre, ragged, scowling, wolfish; but prostrate, too, in their humility. Where graceful youth should have filled their features out, and touched them with its freshest tints, a stale and shrivelled hand, like that of age, had pinched, and twisted them, and pulled them into shreds. Where angels might have sat enthroned, devils lurked, and glared out menacing. No change, no degradation, no perversion of humanity, in any grade, through all the mysteries of wonderful creation, has monsters half so horrible and dread.

Scrooge started back, appalled. . . .

'Spirit! are they yours?' Scrooge could say no more.

'They are Man's,' said the Spirit, looking down upon them. 'And they cling to me, appealing from their fathers. This boy is Ignorance. This girl is Want. Beware of them both, and all of their degree, but most of all beware this boy, for on his brow I see that written which is Doom, unless the writing be erased. Deny it!' cried the Spirit, stretching out its hand towards the city. 'Slander those who tell it ye! Admit it for your factious purposes, and make it worse! And bide the end!'

On behalf of the social outcasts, the rejected, the vicious, the *déclassé*, criminals and vagabonds, Dickens launched a highly effective appeal to the public. None of these groups could rescue themselves from crime, poverty and death, unless superior social forces came to their aid. *Oliver Twist* took the reading public into a world known only to the police, and gave a better picture of it than *Paul Clifford*, by virtue of its greater accuracy.[83] Jo, in *Bleak House*, was an example of London's disturbing secret citizenry: dangerous, dehumanised, innocent victims of a society that did nothing for them.[84] And Dickens demanded that the State intervene to put an end to this evil before all others. When in America, he reported his enthusiastic admiration for that country's public charities, hospitals, asylums, and prisons:[85]

> It is a great and pleasant feature of all such institutions in America, that they are either supported by the State or assisted by the State.... I cannot but think, with a view to the principle and its tendency to elevate or depress the character of the industrious classes, that a Public Charity is immeasurably better than a Private Foundation, no matter how munificently the latter may be endowed.

His fierce campaign against red tape was prompted by the need for a more efficient social organisation. At the time of the Crimean War, when over-excited patriotism was the dominant public feeling, Dickens and Carlyle thought they saw a close connection between good order in the State, philanthropy, and the national interest. Dickens's ideas about national efficiency at this time showed traces of social imperialism. Thus he was quite willing to turn his fire on false charity, the dangerous exaggeration of his own natural outlook. He had previously attacked moral and religious hypocrisy in his caricatures of Stiggins and Chadband, and the more fully-rounded portrait of Pecksniff; and his hatred of the vice was strong enough to elicit a fair amount of mockery of Nonconformist sects from him. The quality of this hatred remained unchanged when its objects changed, becoming the humbugging companies floated by Ralph Nickleby, or Sir Joseph Bowley's parade of benevolence, or Mrs Jellyby's mania for civilising heathen countries. Her fabulous mission to Africa – 'We hope by this time next year to have from a hundred and fifty to two hundred healthy families cultivating coffee and educating the natives of Borrioboola-Gha, on the left bank of the Niger'[86] – is, as far as Dickens is concerned, a useless dissipation of her energies, and an utter waste of an organisation which might do useful and necessary work at home instead of being poured away abroad.

There was no lack of enemies to hurl similar reproaches back at Dickens. Rancorous opposition was stirred up by his pretensions as a teacher of social morals, his inadequately-prepared ventures into specialist territory, and the occasionally hasty and superficial nature of his judgements. Over and above those with a vested interest in individualism, he was attacked by people of refined sensitivity, who thought that art was incompatible with didactic ends.

From time to time the ideas Dickens put forward stirred up lively controversy. With hindsight we have to give Dickens credit for being morally in the right, though he was often wrong about details. For example, from the outset Dickens poured his most vehement abuse on the mentality he saw behind the new Poor Law of 1834. *Oliver Twist* (1838) introduces us to the cruelties of workhouse life, and explains that the intention of the Law was 'that all poor people should have the alternative ...of being starved by a gradual process in the house, or by a quick one out of it.'[87] The whole nation recognised Bumble's pompous bullying, and the board of guardians' utilitarian effrontery,[88] but the question remained, was the picture fair? Miss Martineau's energy distinguished her among defenders of the new Poor Law who insisted that Dickens had deliberately blamed the new Act for the very abuses of the old law it had set out to correct.[89] And in fact there is fundamental confusion of the two in *Oliver Twist*, so that it is never clear whether the old or the new régime is being described. Dickens seems to have had very little idea about the the exact differences between the two, and no understanding of the need for a reform of the old system, and the dangers of the methods of relief in use before 1834. But he did understand that the action taken, however necessary, was a miserable confession of impotence; he saw the misery caused by lodging paupers in prisons like an accursed race to be separated from the rest of the population, and he knew that such a measure could never be morally justified until all the resources of warmhearted charity had been utterly exhausted. From the Christian point of view, he was quite right to castigate the new Poor Law; it was, as he perceived, a striking, concrete example of the conflict between human politics and gospel teaching. And from the humanitarian point of view, he was quite right to condemn its all-too-rigorous application.[90] 'The newspapers of the time, the debates in Parliament, even the literature of the period, teem with stories of unnecessary harshness to paupers.'[91] Old people were suddenly cut off from their friends; nursing mothers were separated from their children. The sick had to walk a long way for help, and often fainted and died before help came. 'In many workhouses the diet was insufficient for the bare sustenance of life; the medical men complained that they could not obtain adequate food for their patients.'[92]

In 1846, an account of the cruelties practised in Andover Workhouse was published. It made a considerable impression on the public, and confirmed Dickens's charges. Little by little the new Law was forced to be less severe, as an unflagging philanthropic campaign backed by private initiative compelled those applying it to act less stringently. Louisa Twining, the woman whose public service did most to improve upon the cold, faceless work of local authorities, unintentionally left valuable evidence of Dickens's accuracy when she quoted the note made by Dr Roger, the medical officer at the Strand Union Workhouse in London:

'The master of the workhouse was a man who might have been the original of "Bumble" in *Oliver Twist*.'[93]

Dickens was an equally inexact, emotional partisan, with an intuitive penetration to the heart of suffering and injustice, in his campaign against the separate cellular prison system. The recently-established Pennsylvania system of solitary confinement was rigorously applied in Philadelphia. Dickens visited the prison in the course of his travels, and his imaginative sympathy was aroused by the sight of the unhappy prisoners. It is fascinating to examine the pages in which he deals with them: he saw despair and madness in their vacant faces, whether they were silent or talking listlessly. The *American Notes* proclaim his horror at this systematic legal barbarism; they speak of man's need for company, human faces and voices, and the physical and moral dangers of prolonged isolation. The book was a success, and won over public opinion. Yet as we have seen, English reformers had hoped, reasonably enough, that separation would stop prisoners from corrupting one another. And enthusiastic supporters of the cellular system felt that the more rigorously it was applied, the greater would be the dividends. In a violent pamphlet the philanthropist Adshead accused Dickens of barefaced lying, or half-intended misreporting, not to mention stupid sentimentality and the shameless pursuit of literary effects at the expense of truth.[94] He was substantially correct: by the time Adshead had finished with them there was not much left of the 'facts' adduced in the *American Notes*. But it is revealing to compare Dickens's imaginative vision with Adshead's rational interpretation of the same scenes. For example, Dickens observed[95]

> three young women in adjoining cells, all convicted at the same time of a conspiracy to rob their prosecutor. In the silence and solitude of their lives they had grown to be quite beautiful. Their looks were very sad, and might have moved the sternest visitor to tears.

Adshead checked the facts of the case from the Philadelphia press, and found that the young women were[96]

> engaged in seducing young men into their houses and company, and plundering them; and the last 'conspiracy' was for having decoyed an indiscreet southern gentleman, and robbed him of a large sum of money. . . . Two of them were mulattoes, and one a negress.

In the end, experience showed that Dickens was absolutely right about solitary confinement: experience showed that it was 'conducive to consumption, hebetude, madness, and suicide. Even in Philadelphia, in the end, it was found necessary to replace solitary confinement with a gentler system of separation.'[97]

Dickens's philanthropy characteristically exhibits a profound and just perception of social ills, based on his intuition and sympathy. But it also shows carelessness about the factual details of the tangled web of existing abuses and possible reforms, and Dickens tended to exaggerate the emotional aspects of trends he perceived, and to write imaginatively heightened descriptions of them. This was closely bound up with his habits as a writer: in each sphere, he took idealisation to the absolute limit permissible to the artist or the man of affairs, but he did not overstep the mark.

Five

Implicit social comment in
Dickens's novels

Dickens's strongest impression on his readers was not made by either his general theories or his criticisms of specific abuses. Rather his characters, by their words, deeds, and fortunes, combined to act as a subtle and indirect persuasive force. He was, after all, a powerful writer followed by a huge and enthusiastic public who took emotional cues from him, and laughed or cried as they loved or hated according to his whim.[1] Inevitably every word he wrote had some influence on his readers' tastes and feelings. But when, in these same novels, 'black' and 'white' villains and heroes with flat, rigid personalities were morally opposed to each other, and this moral and psychological opposition was made to correspond with a division between classes in society, the writer was employing the most effective form of fiction possible for didactic purposes, as his readers were swayed by their response to the characters, and through them, the principles they held.

At the outset of his literary career, while he was still drawing on his juvenile experience, Dickens had already developed just such a division of moral principles expressed through the vehicle of contrasted characters. The didactic form of the later novels can be discerned in the *Sketches by Boz*, an anthology of short pieces which roughs out the material which was to be used in the mature works. The *Sketches* deal with two social classes: the first ascendant but odious; the second depressed but attractive. The first is the vain, selfish, wealthy new bourgeoisie, preoccupied with superficial appearances, and obsessed with the attempt to conceal their humble origins and the novelty of their wealth.[2] The second is the lower middle class, merging imperceptibly with the non-industrial working class. These people have their foibles and failings, but they also evince some significant virtues. Hardship has taught them to support each other, and whenever the author describes this in comic or pathetic scenes, the laughter is gentle, and a lovable charm emerges.[3] Of course, Dickens's spontaneous social bias appears uncertainly in the *Sketches* as the merest outline. But the maturity of his genius was to confirm and develop the tendency. Certain attitudes – sympathy for humble folk, a love of generosity, hatred of wealth and selfishness – are to be found in all his novels.

It should be possible, then, to examine heroes and villains in his later books, note whether any of them are of working-class origins, and find out what place industrial problems are given in the novels.

Villains

One distinct social group with a common outlook on life dominates the villains – big businessmen: those merchants and financiers who live by a vulgarised utilitarian philosophy and consciously or unconsciously ally themselves with orthodox political economy. This group was immensely important in real life in the nineteenth century, and is given prominence in Dickens's novels accordingly. Ralph Nickleby, Scrooge, Jonas Chuzzlewit, Mr Dombey, Gradgrind, and Bounderby are the outstanding examples. Behind them lies a crowd of lesser characters, including such memorable creations as Filer and Alderman Cute.

These men have certain common characteristics. Their minds and their business practices alike are vitiated by the absence of a proper scale of values. Money-grubbing obsesses most of them, though a few find an alternative pleasure in ostentation. All of them have disciplined their minds with ruthless egoism until their feelings have been stifled. In particular, no altruistic emotions survive. Ralph Nickleby is perhaps the most heavy-handedly drawn character in this group; he has all the marks of a stereotyped caricature. Yet for all the exaggeration of his features and stagy heightening of his manner, Ralph obviously exhibits the mind of a bourgeois individualist. And it is important that he should do so, for he is one of these characters whom Dickens hates for their social role rather than their personal failings: in these men Dickens sees the ultimate enemies of human brotherhood.

Like the cotton merchants and financial wizards of his day, Ralph Nickleby is a self-made man. When he first went into business he took a penny loaf and a ha'p'orth of milk for breakfast as he walked to the City every morning. In his youth he deduced two maxims from experience: 'That riches are the only true source of happiness and power, and that it is lawful and just to compass their acquisition by all means short of felony.'[4] Since then he was worked patiently and tirelessly towards the shifting mirage that dominates his life. His ultimate goal, a sufficiency of wealth, continues to lure him on to acquire ever-larger sums. He has forgotten his friends and his parents, 'for gold conjures up a mist about a man, more destructive of all his old senses and lulling to his feelings than fumes of charcoal.'[5] His occupation is hard to define: 'Mr. Ralph Nickleby was not, strictly speaking, what you would call a merchant, neither was he a banker, nor an attorney, nor a special pleader, nor a notary. He was certainly not a tradesman, and still less could he lay any claim to the title of a professional gentleman.'[6] This characteristic is significant; he is a perfect example of the kind of dubious shady businessman to be found lurking at the remote corners of respectable affairs. Already by 1840 such men were an important feature of bourgeois finance: speculation was their way of life, and the joint-stock company a tool to their hand. It has been observed that Stock Exchange activity had increased between 1815 and 1830, with the first slumps occurring in 1826 and 1837. From 1845 to 1850 the speculative fever raged around railway construction.[7] The whole period was marked by intense financial activity. Ralph Nickleby sits on the board of the 'United Metropolitan Improved Hot Muffin and Crumpet Baking and Punctual Delivery Company, capital five millions, in five hundred thousand shares of ten pounds each'.[8] The ludicrous name should not disguise the fact that serious criticism of frauds practised on the public is being made. The three-guinea fee, for example, claimed by every director whenever he deigns to lunch with the board, is only too plausible.[9]

In one respect Ralph's character is unusual: he is capable of fierce hatred as well as avarice.[10] By the end of the book he has become a personified spirit of evil carrying out a Mephistophelian rebellion against all human and divine laws.[11] The pursuit of wealth has destroyed all feeling in him, and he is no longer a member of the family of mankind. His moral corruption, with its dreadful consequences, originates in his utilitarian suffocation of his imaginative life: this at any rate is how Dickens chooses to present him. We see the stern and hard-featured man of business walk doggedly on, elbowing passers-by aside.[12] We see him use his young, defenceless niece as bait for a rich debauchee.[13] Although the girl's tears arouse a fleeting instant of feeling in him, he is essentially dead to pity, love, or normal human sympathies. And it is this which makes him a representative type. Scrooge, in *A Christmas Carol*, has the same heartlessness: 'Hard and sharp as flint, from which no steel had ever struck out generous fire; secret, and self-contained, and solitary as an oyster.'[14] Jonas Chuzzlewit, worthy son of old Anthony, and heir to the firm of Chuzzlewit and Son, has exactly the same temperament, with added brutality and cynicism. His education has been rigorously utilitarian: the first word he learnt was 'gain' and the next 'money'. The pupil does his masters more than credit: he comports himself like a bulldog, and bites the hand that fed him. He regards his father as 'a certain amount of personal estate, which had no right to be going at large, but ought to be secured in that particular description of iron safe which is commonly called a coffin, and banked in the grave.'[15] Dombey, an unforgettable figure of bourgeois pride, has the same frozen spirit. He is a great merchant, enjoying a silent and gloomy intoxication with his firm's unassailable wealth: 'The earth was made for Dombey and Son to trade in, and the sun and moon were made to give them light.'[16] This is the finest of all depictions of the severe Englishman who is determined to hide or repress his emotions. The businessman's professional inflexibility has become second nature to him. Not a muscle of his impassive frame flickers at his wife's death or his motherless child's first cries; he has not a word of kindness to offer the little daughter who is growing up, starved of love, in his vast dreary house. 'Dombey and Son had often dealt in hides, but never in hearts. They left that fancy ware to boys and girls, and boarding-schools and books.'[17]

Bounderby and Gradgrind, the manufacturer and businessman in *Hard Times*, are of the same stock. In the former even family pride, the last resort of feeling, has disappeared:[18]

'I was born in a ditch, and my mother ran away from me. Do I excuse her for it? No. Have I ever excused her for it? Not I. What do I call her for it? I call her probably the very worst woman that ever lived in the world, except my drunken grandmother. There's no family pride about me, there's no imaginative sentimental humbug about me.'

And his colleague is introduced to us in the following terms:[19]

Thomas Gradgrind, sir. A man of realities. A man of facts and calculations. A man who proceeds upon the principle that two and two are four, and nothing over, and who is not to be talked into allowing for anything over. Thomas Gradgrind, sir – peremptorily Thomas – Thomas Gradgrind. With a rule and a pair of scales, and the multiplication table always in his pocket, sir, ready to weigh and measure any parcel of human nature, and tell you exactly what it comes to.

The great brotherhood of financiers, tradesmen, and professional advisers exposes an area of Dickens's thinking. They are dry and scathing in their speech, underhand and dishonest in their dealings, implacably hostile to the pointless expenditure of feeling, and present a solid front to any dangerous compassion or similar emotion that might undermine utilitarian power. Taken all together they comprise one aspect of his art. Pecksniff, the architect, is a first-class creation – perhaps the most elaborately developed character in all Dickens's works. He too is a middle-class egoist, but spurred on by circumstances, he applies his devious energies to stealing a fortune by hypocrisy and deceit, rather than conquering it by force of personality. There are many others: Tackleton, the toy merchant in *The Cricket on the Hearth*; the squalid moneylender Gride in *Nicholas Nickleby*; Murdstone of Murdstone and Grinby in *David Copperfield*; the Chancery lawyer Tulkinghorne in *Bleak House*; Merdle, the plutocrat of *Little Dorrit*. And because Dickens attacks these men with merciless hatred, while at the same time his optimism demands that his books be given happy endings, all these degenerate and bigoted disciples of Ricardo and Bentham suffer defeat or conversion at the hands of experience. Ralph Nickleby, overwhelmed by his nephew's success and triumphant innocence, kills himself. Jonas Chuzzlewit poisons himself to cheat the hangman. Pecksniff is unmasked, and sinks to the impotent rage of Tartuffe. Dombey is bankrupted and learns wisdom, returning to the arms of the daughter whose love he has disregarded. Misfortune proves to Gradgrind that his moral and social arithmetic is inaccurate. One obvious Dickensian conviction runs through all these histories: only through disaster and conversion can the bourgeois egoist find salvation from himself: 'Self; grasping, eager, narrow-ranging, over-reaching self; with its long train of suspicions, lusts, deceits, and all their growing consequences; was the root of the vile tree.'[20]

In addition to these characters, whose crudity leads to their overthrow, there are others, less driven by avarice, and less blackened by their author, who exhibit the minor defects of bourgeois individualism. These characters are not necessarily involved in the workaday world, though they all belong to the middle class. They are stiffnecked – they display a sovereign contempt for their inferiors. Yet they are base – they adore the nobility, to whom they are crawlingly servile, and they adhere meticulously to fashionable conventions and social form. Dickens was more pitiless, if less penetrating, than Thackeray in his hatred of snobbery. The Wititter-lys, desperately chasing after the latest fashions and the grandest connections, are snobs, and incorrigibly vulgar snobs at that![21] Miss Monflathers, the exclusive girls' school headmistress, behaves with loathsome moral cowardice when she abuses her humbly-born assistant, whose presence offends a baronet's daughter.[22] The great dinner-party at Dombey's house brings together a veritable gallery of bourgeois affectations and pretensions, thrown into sharp relief by the accompanying presence of aristocrats.[23] Mrs Sparsit of *Hard Times* belongs to this company. She is withered and cold-hearted, but obsessed with an impossible self-importance which is for ever suffering humiliation until she exchanges her silent grudge against fate for a positive hatred of the innocent and happy.[24] Henry Gowan is another; a cynical dilettante whose life disfigures what capabilities he originally possessed.[25] All his life Dickens was fascinated by the implicit denial of Christian brotherhood contained in his sick society. *Our Mutual Friend*, one of his last works, contains one of his most vivid satirical portraits: the *nouveau riche* Veneerings entertaining the vulgar and pretentious Lammles and Podsnaps in their brand-new house.[26] They form a fitting conclusion to the list.

Of course it is not only middle-class characters who are unsympathetic. The aristocracy never appears to advantage in Dickens's novels, and many of his most horrible villains are drawn from the dregs of society. But no group is as consistent and as prominent as the bourgeoisie, for whom the author feels an exceptionally powerful hatred which is transmitted to the reader. On the other hand, all the villains, no matter what their social standing may be, display remarkable affinities with Ralph Nickleby and Dombey. All are totally without generosity. Their feelings are frozen, and their lives are dominated by the drive for personal gain. It has often been said that Dickens's aristocratic characters are unconvincing: a fact adequately explained by his upbringing and interests. But it is as important to note the basic similarity between the weaknesses he observes in the aristocracy and the bourgeoisie. Sir Mulberry Hawk is cautious and calculating in his dissipation, with selfish joys, selfish pains, selfish sorrows, and selfish pleasures. If Cousin Feenix is treated less severely it is because there is some trace of honour and delicacy left in his cynical and worldly-wise old roué's heart. Lady Dedlock is another victim of world-weariness: 'So long accustomed to suppress emotion and keep down reality; so long schooled for her own purposes in that destructive school which shuts up the natural feelings of the heart, like flies in amber, and spreads one dreary gloss over the good and bad, the feeling and unfeeling, the sensible and senseless.'[27] Her husband, Sir Leicester, by contrast retains our sympathy by virtue of having loved her: 'It is she who, at the core of all the constrained formalities and conventionalities of his life, has been a stock of living tenderness and love, susceptible as nothing else is of being struck with the agony he feels.'[28]

The grotesque and picturesque monsters and rogues who haunt the bottom of society in Dickens's world-picture are similarly united by a common lack of feeling. Their hall-mark is their capacity to inflict pain without suffering a tremor of sympathy or remorse. Dickens presents them as essentially wicked men who have learnt from hardship to pursue evil rather than to co-operate with their fellow men. Fagin and Squeers are of this type, as are Quilp and Uriah Heep, two characters whose physiques effectively symbolise the depraved and writhing natures they conceal. Charley Hexam, the cold, fiercely ambitious child of the masses, is clearly the work of the same hand.

How much are these characters worth artistically? They have often been attacked. And no doubt these villains are marked by exaggerated features, oversimplification and stereotyping. Dickens was imperfectly acquainted with the groups he detested. Nonetheless Ralph Nickleby and Dombey provide highly significant pointers to the direction of Dickens's thought. Their very simplicity indicates plainly enough Dickens's attitude towards them and the standpoint from which he viewed them, and from this we can deduce the social philosophy which called them into being. Once they are seen in this light they cannot be denied the stature and dramatic energy which gives strength and distinction to caricatures.

One conclusion is inescapable. Dickens drew his utterly detestable characters from the rising classes, especially those connected with trade. Yet they permeate the whole of society around them, and from this we may conclude that Dickens's detestation was motivated by psychological rather than social factors. It was a temperament, not a class, that Dickens lashed, and if the upper middle class most frequently appears to be the object of his satire, this is only because it offers a perfect environment for such natures to flourish in. The hated personality is easily described: it is the dry egotistical individualist, the man whose determined and realistic outlook has been distorted by industrial and commercial practices. Hardheaded 'realism' is the soil from which *laissez-faire* opposition to State interference grows. Dickens's own nature was the reverse: he was a passionate and imaginative man. His spontaneous wish was to establish or restore moral harmony wherever he went, and a profound intuition showed him that the improvement of human relations was linked to the improvement of human nature. His own experience had shown him the cruelty of social evils; he never doubted that they were encouraged by the selfish outlook which opposed the application of the gospels to society. Like Carlyle and, indeed, all the idealists of his time, Dickens perceived moral questions at the heart of social questions.

Good characters

Good characters outnumber bad in Dickens. Leaving aside complex characters about whom the author offers no simply-felt judgement, there remains a rich and varied group of characters whose features have evidently been modelled with Dickens's compassion. His natural outlook was indulgent, and his art is alive with sympathy for his subjects. The pleasing or comforting aspect of life attracts him automatically, and the idealism of the works corresponds to the optimism of the man. Moreover, the charm of the good characters is more successfully conveyed than the repulsiveness of the villains. Dickens is better at encouraging us to love ordinary people than he is at teaching hatred for social egotism.

But if Dickens could make his poor characters live, and give them a striking realism even while he romanticised them, precisely who were these representatives of the poor? Most of the attractive characters are in fact drawn from the lower middle class, just as the upper middle class furnished the army of rogues. Strict categorisation would list a number of Dickens's virtuous figures as proletarian, but almost always it is the non-industrial working class which interests him: the milling urban masses among whom the failures of the old society and the flotsam of the new wash up.

Just as each villain was an individual variant of one central personality, so certain common features recur among the figures dear to Dickens. Goodness, compassion, family affection, generosity, and charity were the tendencies which sufficed to make a human being attractive in Dickens's eyes. When he put a lot of himself into characters he created almost perfect idealisations of imagination and feeling – Oliver Twist, Nicholas Nickleby, and David Copperfield. But such a temperament is associated with a certain delicacy and cultivation, and it could not be convincingly ascribed to the poor. Dickens knew life too well to repeat the audacity of *Oliver Twist*, where a street-orphan is endowed with imaginative delicacy of feeling. Rather he combined his natural exuberance with observation of life to create common people who were popular copies of the type of literary figure whose common sense, jollity, unimaginativeness, and generally picturesque characteristics give a powerful impression of solidity and reality. Indeed, only their capacity to feel deeply – to love and to mourn – suggests their descent from the kind of apostolic poet that Dickens was at heart.

It is actually a matter worthy of note that the common people should have been represented at all in literature, whatever the psychologica treatment they were given. There were profound social implications in Dickens's elevation of a whole social class to the dignity of artistic representation. For although it would not be true to assert that 'the people' had never before appeared in novels, yet this was the first depiction of the urban lower middle class. And when one considers Dickens in the context of his time, there is no doubt that he shifted the social frontiers of art. The most realistic of eighteenth-century novels had not transferred the centre of interest from the upper class to the lower orders. No novel had deliberately focused its attention below the line dividing opulent living, ample leisure, and cultivated manners from the steady pursuit of wages and a means of living. Wordsworth and Crabbe had brought about just such a change of subject in poetry in turning their attention to peasant life. But at the outset of Dickens's career the novel was not yet so democratic. It seemed impossible for a novel to have a hero who was not a gentleman unless it dealt with the fantastic figures of the Newgate school, like *Paul Clifford*. To partisan conservatives it seemed that Dickens's immediate success was an ominous sign of the times: a literary parallel to the Reform Act.[29] The *Quarterly Review* punned about *Oliver Twist* as a pie whose '"upper crust" was undoubtedly kneaded by reformers who now rule the roast.'[30] The tone of the article suggests that this has offended the critic's dainty palate:[31]

> The lower we descend in the social scale ... the nearer we approach to the brute, devoid of any thought beyond sensual necessities and gratifications, destruction and reproduction....
>
> It is perfectly natural that *Oliver Twist*, which is made up of de-lineating these propensities, should be the joy of the ten-pounders.

This was the characteristic of Dickens's writing that had already made an ineradicable impression on the public: to the end of his career he would be seen as the literary explorer of unknown class territory, and no one doubted the democratic bias of his works.

There was also a more explicitly social interest in his writing, though its influence was more subtle. Dickens did not restrict himself to taking heroes of humble birth, drawing attention to their merits, and ennobling them with the dignity of artistry: he went further. He loved them himself; he made his readers love them, and he put them forward as models of the way people ought to behave to one another. This didacticism was the more effective for being a barely conscious process. As a contemporary justly observed, Dickens's novels[32]

> tend to bring the poor into the fairest position for obtaining the sympathy of the rich and powerful, by displaying the goodness and fortitude often found amidst want and wretchedness, together with the intervals of joyousness and comic humour.

Indeed the sympathetic portrayal of the poor was the best means of kindling and fanning sparks of human charity. But sympathy goes further, tending to harmonise the sympathiser's whole being with the sympathetic object, and infectiously carrying the actor's emotions over into the spectator. And without question the humble characters on whom Dickens lavished love and devotion radiate irresistible family affection and social warmth. They are sources from which the demand for greater human selflessness can be recharged. And it seems that this is the basic message emerging from Dickens's entire contribution to literature. His novels encourage us to replace the cold life of selfishness with a life of sentiment, bent towards the recognition of human solidarity.

The poor practised the 'philosophy of Christmas'. We have seen the place of family love in that ideal of social order: the hearth was symbolic of people's moral and religious union. Now the families which Dickens had observed to be closely united, and which he depicts for us were, as a rule, members of the poorer classes. Whether or not reality justified this rosy picture, it was the outcome of Dickens's own experience. All the factors in labouring or factory life that broke up families and militated against bodily and spiritual health – poverty, insanitary housing, overwork – were to be found, to a lesser extent, among the lower middle classes. And yet these malign forces had completely failed to take their full adverse effect among them. Suffering had proved ennobling, and had taught tolerance and reciprocal charity, as it re-established the ties between men.

Could the Cratchit family be anything but poor and needy? They live in a very small way in one of the smoky brick four-roomed houses in the packed streets of Camden Town. Bob earns fifteen shillings a week; his eldest daughter, Martha, is apprenticed to a milliner, and between them they supply the family income. There are eight mouths to feed, but privations are born gaily, and humiliation or pain is forgotten as soon as a ray of sunshine gleams. After Dickens's description of Christmas itself as a day when all the shops and offices are closed, and all is holiday and happiness, we see every member of the poor Cratchit family set to the private and collective task of merry-making.[33] Mrs Cratchit wears a gown that has been turned twice, but she has bedecked it with ribbons. Bob has put on his threadbare Sunday suit, and carried Tiny Tim, his crippled youngest son, to church. Young Peter, the eldest boy, with one of his father's collars coming up to his ears, looks after the saucepan, while two other Cratchits, a boy and a girl, rush through the street past the bakery, smelling their family's delicious goose which is cooking there. Then we see this bird, brought in in triumph:[34]

Such a bustle ensued that you might have thought a goose the rarest of all birds; a feathered phenomenon, to which a black swan was a matter of course – and in truth it was something very like it in that house. Mrs. Cratchit made the gravy (ready beforehand in a little saucepan) hissing hot; Master Peter mashed the potatoes with incredible vigour; Miss Belinda sweetened up the apple-sauce; Martha dusted the hot plates; Bob took Tiny Tim beside him in a tiny corner at the table; the two young Cratchits set chairs for everybody, not forgetting themselves, and mounting guard upon their posts, crammed spoons into their mouths, lest they should shriek for goose before their turn came to be helped. At last the dishes were set on, and grace was said. It was succeeded by a breathless pause, as Mrs. Cratchit, looking slowly all along the carving-knife, prepared to plunge it into the breast; but when she did, and when the long expected gush of stuffing issued forth, one murmur of delight arose all round the board, and even Tiny Tim, excited by the two young Cratchits, beat on the table with the handle of his knife, and feebly cried Hurrah!

With evident satisfaction, Dickens puts the details of the familiar feast before us: happiness purchased by small sacrifices and domestic heroism, and then shared like this, is healthy. And this coarsely materialistic good cheer conceals bold and energetic idealism and beauty. The pudding arouses no less enthusiasm than the goose:[35]

Everybody had something to say about it, but nobody said or thought it was at all a small pudding for a large family. It would have been flat heresy to do so. Any Cratchit would have blushed to hint at such a thing.

We can understand the author's enthusiasm even more when the table has been cleared, and the family is gathered round the fire to think, sadly or cheerfully, about absent friends. Bob, in spite of Mrs Cratchit's quickly stilled remonstrances, makes everyone drink the health of his miserly old employer, Scrooge. Martha describes her day's work at the milliner's, and recalls the visit of a lord who looked like Peter. Tiny Tim sings a plaintive song about a child lost in the snow:[36]

There was nothing of high mark in this. They were not a handsome family; they were not well dressed; their shoes were far from being water-proof; their clothes were scanty; and Peter might have known, and very likely did, the inside of a pawnbroker's. But they were happy, grateful, pleased with one another, and contented with the time;

and that is why Dickens loves them, and earnestly advises all other families to be like them.

If the Cratchits know how to enjoy themselves together, they are equally good at bearing grief. We see them again on a day of trial; Tiny Tim has just died, and each of them thrusts aside his own pain, to try and assuage that of the others.[37] With perfect delicacy and accuracy, the author touches in convincing little scenes of consolation: the downcast father comes home from work, and is affectionately greeted by his children; there is a conspiracy of silence about the death, but their grief is too strong, and must break out. The tableau of family life is animated with the colouring of reality, and proves irresistibly touching.

A similar charm is to be found in all the similar groups of characters who bear life's burdens together, united in joy or sorrow: little Nell and the old curiosity dealer, her grandfather, hand in hand at the edge of the wide world; the Nubbles family, whose poor, but spotless, house we are taken into several times, to find Mrs Nubbles working from morning to night near the cradle where a three-year-old scamp with a wideawake expression rocks himself while Kit, the older boy, recounts the events of his day good-naturedly. But comes an evening out and they all go to Astley's circus with little Barbara; and the wonders of the show light up the stolid dullness of their lives for some time. Then there are the Pegottys, the fishing family, living in their upturned boat on the beach, with old Mrs Gummidge sunk in her memories of the past. And the Toodles, whose sanity and affection contrast with the unhealthy chill which wealth and pride cast over the Dombey family. And the Slearys, the fairground riders who stand for the truth of simple feelings in *Hard Times*, as opposed to Gradgrind's cultivated bourgeois dryness. We must even include Charley, the little girl of thirteen who is amusingly set before us in a delightful episode in *Bleak House*, comically acting the little mother for her neglected brothers, and rendered heroic by the utter dedication of her life. All these, and many others, fill Dickens's novels, as small inseparable groups, united by their common hardship or need, by their absurdity or foibles, and by their fundamental good nature and brave acceptance of misfortune.

There are other, isolated individuals, who are yet never self-sufficient, but allow their lives to expand outwards in automatic ripples of self-sacrifice and affection. Could John Browdy, Nicholas Nickleby's jovial friend, be imagined without his frank and free Yorkshire heartiness, happy to be alive, happy to help others in their lives, and rejoicing above all in the unforeseen outcome of mischievous kindness, though always aware that he has not plotted its results? Or Newman Noggs, Ralph Nickleby's clerk, without his awkward gait, hiding the delicacy of his feelings and the gentlemanly spirit which is all that has survived his financial ruin, ready to love and assist all the helpless creatures put in his way by fortune? Would Tim Linkinwater have the same charm, and the very special place he holds in our memories, without his touching, almost filial, devotion to his employers? What reader has ever begrudged Tom Pinch his blind, naïve confidence in Pecksniff's hypocritical virtue, through which he displays at the same time all his ingenuous honesty, his disposition to push himself into the background, and his spontaneous generosity? Among the humble characters to whom Dickens grants nobility of heart, none is more vivid than Joe Gargery, the blacksmith in *Great Expectations*. His spirit is gentle and homely, unschooled and delicate; he lacks words to express the simplest ideas, and untangle his uncertain flashes of sense; yet in his conduct towards little Pip, his adopted son, when his fortune changes, he evinces the finest generosity of feeling. For selflessness is the salutary virtue which compensates for all absurdity and weakness. With it, no one can be grotesque or unpleasant; without it, no one can be really pleasant. What but the ready kindness which suddenly springs up in his paradoxical personality makes us like the cheerful ne'er-do-well Dick Swiveller? And Traddles, David Copperfield's none-too-clever friend, will always be one of life's victims. Yet what a good fellow he is! Who has not felt the appeal of his universal good will? Even Miss Mowcher, the strange, sharp, self-mocking dwarf, betrays the reason for Dickens's evident predilection for her when her hidden compassion at long last bursts out, and she revolts against evil.[38]

All these characters are humble and poor. But there are some good rich characters. Here again, psychological distinctions matter more than sociological ones: Dickens favoured a given temperament, not a class. He did feel that the simple outlook on life was usually to be found among those with limited resources. But exceptions could be found, in life and in fiction, and Dickens collected them eagerly. He took the opportunity to preach directly, from their example, the duties of the ruling class. Such characters outline the paternalistic element in his thinking: the good rich man is generous, benevolent, and friendly; he is liberal with his overflowing heart and purse. He uses his wits to do good tactfully and delicately, although his greatest pleasure lies in surprising people with his unexpected generosity. In *Pickwick Papers* the type of the stout old gentleman with a beaming face, a twinkling eye, and pockets filled with loose change to be given away to children in the streets was beginning to emerge in the hero himself, and in his friend Wardle. The latter is a true squire, brimming with cordiality and animal spirits. The Christmas celebrations at Dingley Dell, with the lavish hospitality and dear old English customs, perhaps show Dickens closer to Young England than he ever came again. But the delightful figures of the Cheeryble brothers appear in *Nicholas Nickleby*: businessmen after Dickens's own heart. Here is the description of one of them:[39]

He was a sturdy old fellow in a broad-skirted blue coat, made pretty large, to fit easily, and with no particular waist; his bulky legs clothed in drab breeches and high gaiters, and his head protected by a low-crowned broad-brimmed white hat, such as a wealthy grazier might wear. He wore his coat buttoned; and his dimpled double-chin rested in the folds of a white neckerchief – not one of your stiff-starched apoplectic cravats, but a good, easy, old-fashioned white neck-cloth that a man might go to bed in and be none the worse for. But what principally attracted the attention of Nicholas, was the old gentleman's eye – never was such a clear, twinkling, honest, merry, happy eye, as that. And there he stood, looking a little upward, with one hand thrust in the breast of his coat, and the other playing with his old-fashioned gold watch-chain: his head thrown a little on one side, and his hat a little more on one side than his head (but that was evidently accidental, not his ordinary way of wearing it), with such a pleasant smile playing about his mouth, and such a comical expression of mingled slyness, simplicity, kind-heartedness, and good-humour, lighting up his jolly old face, that Nicholas would have been content to have stood there, and looked at him until evening, and to have forgotten, mean-while, that there was such a thing as a soured mind or a crabbed countenance to be met with in the whole wide world.

There is not a word of anything but genial tolerance, frankness, open friendliness, and above all goodwill, so much as hinted at in that delight-ful description. The Cheeryble brothers are, indeed, excellent fellows, as Nicholas and all who meet them are well aware. And this patriarchal ideal, with business conducted through personal or familial relations, as it used to be in the good old days of small workshops, can be found again, to the life, in the scene of wild gaiety on Christmas Eve, when old Fezziwig makes his apprentices dance with his daughters. In the twinkling of an eye Fezziwig's warehouse is swept, sprinkled, and cleared; the fiddler arrives; Mrs Fezziwig and her girls arrive, followed by the girls' suitors:[40]

In came all the young men and women employed in the business. In came the housemaid, with her cousin, the baker. In came the cook, with her brother's particular friend, the milkman. In came the boy from over the way, who was suspected of not having board enough from his master; trying to hide himself behind the girl from next door but one, who was proved to have had her ears pulled by her mistress.

Old Fezziwig opens the ball, and in the friendly equality of the Christmas holiday all social strife and unhappiness is forgotten.

Dickens has the same affection for the Garlands, young Kit's well-meaning, open, honest protectors in *The Old Curiosity Shop*; and for Jarndyce, the philanthropist of *Bleak House*, who spends his time and money in trying to bring happiness to those around him without showing his hand.

Thus an essential bond between the 'sentimental' temperament and altruism was established in Dickens's mind. He made no distinction between the faculty of loving and grieving, and the disposition to help one's neighbour. Therefore his writings are a vast, multifarious recipe for increased sensibility. Taine noted this essential quality when he observed, 'At bottom, Dickens's novels may be reduced to a single phrase, namely, "Be kind and loving". The only true happiness lies in the heart's affections: feeling is the whole man.'[41] Whatever might be the absolute worth of this message, and however grave its dangers in practice, we shall only be able to do it justice by seeing it in the context of contemporary intellectual currents. Dickens was an artistic ally of Carlyle and Lord Ashley. His attempt to soften the nation's heart and give emotion its due place in the moral make-up of Victorian man was provoked by the utilitarian aridity of moral life, and the egotistical severity of social life. His instincts and his compassion revolted against these twin dangers. By virtue of his own temperament, which provided him with an image of psychological health, and in the name of Christian ethics, which prescribed a rule of conduct, he demanded that everyone should practise the benevolence which was an inseparable part of charity.

The industrial problem; 'Hard Times'

Industry and the proletariat are by no means omitted from Dickens's works, but they play a remarkably limited part there, in the light of their importance among the social preoccupations of the period. This is because Dickens, as we have seen, was shaped by other influences, and saw the relations of rich and poor from another point of view.

In the long run he could not avoid turning his attention to the industrial crisis. His keen perception of physical change was inevitably struck by the general upset going on all round him. And so, little by little, the new life-style began to emerge in the novels until, in 1854,

Dickens devoted an entire novel to the industrial question. But his artistic vision was shaped by a different environment, and he was ill at ease in this new territory: *Hard Times* is far from being one of his best books, and as an experiment in industrial fiction it was not repeated. For the remainder of his career Dickens instinctively returned to the period of his youth, and the familiar customs of the years of his apprenticeship. None the less his detailed attempts to come to terms with the changing times are on the printed page, and by examining them we may arrive at a more precise knowledge of his outlook and the limits of his social philosophy.

For choice, Dickens preferred to write about the poorer members of the lower middle class, especially clerks like Bob Cratchit or Tom Pinch, or skilled craftsmen like the blacksmiths Gargery and Richard, Meg's sweetheart. Among such people the greatest sufferings are mental: the pride of a displaced class is more often in question than economic servitude. Governesses and female companions appear as the feminine victims of overweening bourgeois pride, a harsh experience suffered by Kate Nickleby and Ruth Pinch.

But there was one section of the working class that Dickens knew well: those whose occupations brought them inevitably, but unremarkably, into contact with the upper classes. The workers appearing in the novels are all intimately involved with middle-class life: they are self-employed, or have not reached the stage of being brought together in factories. For this was the sort of labour that Dickens would have seen in the old City districts. Toby Veck, the hero of *The Chimes*, is a ticket-porter. Yet how extraordinary it is that two years after the great disputes of 1842, with Chartism in full swing, so unrepresentative a worker should have been taken as a symbol of his class. By and large, working-class suffering is shown through the experiences of servants and dressmakers. Dickens's heart was wrung by the long hours, unhealthy conditions, and inadequate wages of milliners and apprentices, and this becomes a reiterated topic, as the moving lot of Kate Nickleby, Martha Cratchit, Meg and Lilian, and Amy Dorrit are movingly described. Servant girls, too, are given a place in Dickens's readers' sympathies. The 'Marchioness', with her domestic prejudices, indifference to rules, and lack of social standing, is a picturesque and touching example of these poor creatures, who bore a peculiarly harsh oppression that was not easy to describe.[42]

When we add up some shadowy City workers, dockers, stevedores, and street-porters,[43] the plasterer, Plornish, in *Little Dorrit*, inn-waiters and coachmen – there is hardly a novel without one or the other – among whom Sam Weller's unforgettable father stands out,[44] we have almost run through the list of working-class occupations Dickens knew well enough to write about freely. Agricultural labour was an absolute mystery to him; Will Fern stands as its sole representative in his entire output. A few bargees with rough voices, heavy movements, and fiery tempers appear for a moment, only to vanish again, in the wonderfully poetic journey of Little Nell and her grandfather across the Midlands.[45] An episode in *Bleak House* sketches, with brisk, lively strokes, an encampment of brickmakers, whose hurriedly glimpsed degradation and brutishness are fully justified by the evidence of contemporary documents.[46]

The countryside is consistently described in idyllic terms: it is the oasis of refreshment lying between the muddy brick towns. From the windows of his slow-moving coaches Dickens saw nothing but the rustic charm of woods and fields.[47] And finally, he never mentioned the troubles of Ireland in his books. Unlike Carlyle, he did not compound the social offences of England's ruling class with their national crimes.

Philanthropic work pitched Dickens into the campaign for industrial legislation. Moreover he tried himself to bring his books up to date, and move with the times. Otherwise his novels would probably always have put forward the same picture of English society. Toby Veck, Richard, and Meg might always have seemed typical Dickensian working-class characters. But like all generous-hearted men of the time, he was forced to turn his gaze north.

There is no concern with industry in the *Sketches, Pickwick,* or *Oliver Twist*; no factory chimney casts a shadow over them. But the success of *Oliver Twist* confirmed Dickens's determination to write on social topics, and the inception of Chartism meant that the burning social issue of the day was the problem of the working class. And so there is a reference to industry in *Nicholas Nickleby* (1839). Dickens had come out as a supporter of industrial legislation in 1838.[48] He travelled to Manchester to look at a factory, and it is worth noting that there, for the first time, he saw the reality behind the many parliamentary reports he had read.[49] He was appalled by what he saw:[50]

> I went, some weeks ago, to Manchester, and saw the *worst* cotton mill. And then I saw the *best. Ex uno disce omnes.* There was no great difference between them. . . .
>
> I mean to strike the heaviest blow in my power for these unfortunate creatures, but whether I shall do so in the 'Nickleby', or wait some other opportunity, I have not yet determined.

It could not be fitted into *Nickleby*: Dickens's feelings after this visit are only dragged in through a short, outraged passage alluding to the lives of factory-children at the end of the book. But his next novel, *The Old Curiosity Shop* (1840), devoted a substantial section to the question.

It is an important passage; it shows us why Dickens could not become the great, sombre poet of industrialism. The whole thing was too great a shock to his sensibility, and left him with impressions that were too hasty and superficial. Factories were infernos of smoke, flames, and noise to Dickens. Inside them, machinery monotonously ran through its cycle of movements, like a lot of demented monsters. The workers led lives that were identifiable with the metals they worked, and founded on furnaces: they were sunk in wearisome gloom, and a nightmare of tragic horror hung over their cities. The surrounding countryside was sooty; the hovels lining the roads were filled with dead and dying people; at night, armed bands laid the country waste by torchlight:[51]

> On mounds of ashes by the wayside, sheltered only by a few rough boards, or rotten pent-house roofs, strange engines spun and writhed liked tortured creatures; clanking their iron chains, shrieking in their rapid whirl from time to time as though in torment unendurable, and making the ground tremble with their agonies. . . . But, night-time in this dreadful spot! – night, when the smoke was changed to fire; when every chimney spirted up its flame; and places, that had been dark vaults all day, now shone red-hot, with figures moving to and fro within their blazing jaws, and calling to one another with hoarse cries. . . . when maddened men, armed with sword and firebrand, spurning the tears and prayers of women who would restrain them, rushed forth on errands of terror and destruction, to work no ruin half so surely as their own.

This sinister vision is too obsessively intense and unrelievedly cruel to be brought to life by Dickens's sensitivity. As a writer, he needed light and joy; the griefs he loved to describe were always close to wry smiles. And in the story of Nell and her grandfather he quickly draws away to a peaceful green landscape, and the slow jolting of a travelling caravan.[52]

The impression of industrialism is not only overstated; it is quite external. Dickens leads us through the industrial landscape like tourists, and comments on everything from an outsider's point of view. His glance falls on objects, but the people are cut off from him. The only worker he allows any dialogue is a shadow, lacking the characteristic realism of Dickens's other protagonists.[53] In fact he could not get to the heart of industrial life because he had no intimate contact with it. He had not discovered the gaiety and picturesque details lighting up the corners of that dismal environment. His sensitivity was unaccustomed to machinery, and his outlook was quite remote from those who tended it. He knew nothing of their joys and sorrows; he only seized upon a rapid, powerful vision of the dismal appearance of the world of industry, and his art enabled him to convey this to his readers. But he could not go any further. That unknown world was not to be opened up for the reading public until the coming of a novelist who had spent the best part of a lifetime there: Mrs Gaskell was fated to bring off what was beyond Dickens's powers. His own work suggests an observation made in *Fraser's Magazine*:[54]

> We know how difficult it is to convey an accurate idea of the manufacturing poor to the mind of a person who has never resided among them. The descriptions of them by casual visitors are mostly in extremes; the pictures are much larger than life.

The next few novels return to the older England, though light touches here and there show that Dickens was conscious of the changes being wrought in his favourite setting by industrialism. His journey to America in 1842 introduced him to a more up-to-date and feverish way of life than that of the Black Country. He visited model factories at Lowell, and admired the clean shop-floors and healthy workers, with their rewarding lives: in a poignant paragraph, he contrasted them with what he had seen at home.[55] The chapters of *Martin Chuzzlewit* drawing on his impressions of America contain the first account of a train journey in his novels. And at last, in *Dombey and Son*, trains, stations, and material relevant to them make an appearance, eighteen years after the building of the first railways. Toodle is an engine-driver, and the treacherous Carker is run over by a train. Some passages recall the temporarily disembowelled look of districts which had been dug up by the railways' penetration into the heart of London, and also the bustle of activity brought by the railway. We find here a completely fresh view of the period of 'railway mania'. And throughout the rest of the book runs the melancholy note of social change. Old Solomon Gills, the ships' instrument maker whose outdated business in the sleepy shop, deep in the City, stands for the things of the past, gently laments the passing of the old way of life, which has left him behind:[56]

> 'As I said just now, the world has gone past me. I don't blame it, but I no longer understand it. Tradesmen are not the same as they used to be, apprentices are not the same, business is not the same, business commodities are not the same. ... I am an old-fashioned man in an old-fashioned shop, in a street that is not the same as I remember it. I have fallen behind the time, and am too old to catch it again.'

Dickens has a very soft spot for him.

Electric telegraphy appears in *Bleak House*.[57] And the character of Rouncewell – an earlier and contrasting peer of Bounderby – shows that Dickens could do justice to the ingenuity, probity, hard work, and other good qualities of the industrial bourgeoisie. Here, confronted with Sir Leicester Deadlock's stupid Toryism, Rouncewell is a spokesman for Dickens's radicalism. The shadowy figure of an engineering inventor, Daniel Doyce, appears in *Little Dorrit*. Some of the Christmas stories published in *Household Words* and *All the Year Round* are set in trains and stations, playing on the comic and pathetic aspects of railway life.[58] Finally, the penultimate novel, *Our Mutual Friend*, is deliberately set in the post-industrial world. Here, at the end of his life, Dickens resigned himself to a world from which the stage-coaches had vanished for ever. But in the meantime he had tried to confront the industrial question squarely: *Hard Times* is the ultimate evidence of the attempt.

It is easy to trace the genesis of the novel. Disraeli's *Sybil* (1845), Mrs Gaskell's *Mary Barton* (1848), and Kingsley's *Alton Locke* (1850) fired Dickens with an ambition to emulate these successful working-class novels. The great engineering strike of 1852 had just drawn public attention to industrial disputes once more; according to Sidney Webb the strike, which lasted from January until March, 'interested the general public more than any previous conflict. The details were described, and the action of the employers and the policy of the Union was discussed in every paper.'[59]

Dickens had not yet risked placing the main action of a novel in the North. These factors decided him to do so. But he was badly caught out by his lack of first-hand knowledge; he had never seen a strike in an industrial city. According to Forster, he went to see one in Preston at the end of January, and wrote back that he was somewhat disappointed:[60]

'I am afraid I shall not be able to get much here. Except the crowds at the street-corners reading the placards pro and con; and the cold absence of smoke from the mill-chimneys; there is very little in the streets to make the town remarkable.'

The appearance and manners of north-country workers were different from those Dickens had known in London. He could not fathom their inmost thoughts and feelings, which Mrs Gaskell interpreted so ably: the passing scene did not speak directly to him. And so *Hard Times* is the imperfect work of an artist who tried to bring traditional modes of thought and feeling to a new subject. It is a repeat version of *The Chimes*, adapted to industrial conditions.

The novel puts forward two linked arguments: one social and one moral. The first is a transposition of the 'philosophy of Christmas' into industrial terms. Its place in the novel is limited: Dickens drags in a plea for the liberalisation of the divorce laws, as though he lacks the material to conduct a sustained argument in purely economic terms. Stephen Blackpool, the hero, seems to be more of a victim of conjugal slavery than industrial oppression. And when this fortuitous theme is removed there turns out to be very little left of the industrial drama.

We are in Coketown. That is to say, Manchester, or some such regional centre. The atmosphere of a manufacturing town is powerfully described through its external features: its raw, brutal ugliness; the complete extinction of nature, except for a few sooty blades of grass; all this is dealt with far more accurately, and with far more control, than was the case in *The Old Curiosity Shop*. We follow Dickens through the lighted streets at twilight, past the high factory windows, where light and noise stream out with the vibration of power looms at work. We see the mill-hands concentrating on their work, and count the weary hours with them, and come to feel the to-and-fro of the shuttles take over our minds as the very rhythm of life itself. But the details of factory workers' lives come as brief interludes; the whole picture is drawn in bold strokes, creating a general impression.

In Bounderby, Dickens presents the mill-owner as he ought not to be. He is a fierce scoundrel whose conversation, when we first hear it, is hollow and heartless. He is the crudest sort of upstart egoist; the exemplar of industrial materialism, impervious to delicacy or feeling. By contrast, Stephen Blackpool's common, working-class exterior conceals severe moral probity and deep affections. His melancholy fate is an instance of the just man being crushed between two hostile classes, whose equal implacability does not mean that they are equally blameworthy. Stephen refuses to join a strike, as he has promised that he will not. He is ostracised by his comrades, driven out of the town, falsely accused of theft, and fatally injured in an accident when he returns to establish his innocence. There is a sort of verisimilitude about his slow honest character, but he seems more like any ordinary English workman than a Lancashire cotton operative. It is noteworthy that Dickens eschews his normal practice of giving a long introductory description of him: 'He was a good powerloom weaver, and a man of perfect integrity. What more he was, or what else he had in him, if anything, let him show for himself.'[61] There is none of the local colour attaching to him that is to be found in Dickens's Londoners. His dialogue is moral, and often sermonising: English readers have never been able to see him as anything but an abstraction or, as Ruskin put it, 'a dramatic perfection, instead of a characteristic example of an honest workman.'[62]

Bounderby and his workers meet head-on in a strike, of which we see no more than one public meeting. Dickens certainly had not found out very much on his visit to Preston.[63] Whatever arguments the hands put forward, Bounderby offers the same rejection in reply. Their work is[64]

> the pleasantest work there is, and it's the lightest work there is, and it's the best paid work there is. More than that, we couldn't improve the mills themselves, unless we laid down Turkey-carpets on the floors.... There's not a hand in this town... but has one ultimate object in life. That object is, to be fed on turtle soup and venison with a gold spoon.

As for unions, they are scandalous criminal conspiracies, threatening social revolution. And furthermore, what does the well-being or hardship of the workers really matter? The only reality is clear profit; the only truth is figures. In opposing this sort of managerial philosophy Dickens is heart and soul with the workers. If their object is just, striking is just. Their open union is legitimate and just in view of the mill-owners' secret association: '"It is much to be regretted," said Mrs. Sparsit, "that the united masters allow of any such class-combinations."'[65] And they are justified in protesting to their rulers against the depressing, joyless lives of unrelieved toil they lead, however alarming the urgency of their demands may seem. But violence is to be rejected. The agitator Slackbridge stands for the worst sort of demagogy. His inflammatory speeches and defence of union tyranny show that Dickens saw a huge gap between peaceful proletarian demands and revolutionary activity.

But in the same cause of social tranquillity, their primary demands would have to be met. Public or private welfare would have to relieve the worst hardship; class legislation would have to be repealed, and the work of public authorities would have to let a little light and comfort into the workers' lives. State intervention was necessary, and the mill-owners' implacable resistance to it was indefensible.[66]

> Surely there never was such fragile china-ware as that of which the millers of Coketown were made. Handle them never so lightly, and they fell to pieces with such ease that you might suspect them of having been flawed before. They were ruined, when they were required to send labouring children to school; they were ruined, when inspectors were appointed to look into their works; they were ruined, when such inspectors considered it doubtful whether they were quite justified in chopping people up with their machinery; they were

utterly undone, when it was hinted that perhaps they need not always make quite so much smoke.

The reforms Dickens wanted would necessitate a change of heart on the part of the ruling classes, who would have to renounce their policy of enlightened self-interest, and disregard mathematics as the measure of human life. In a word, sentiment would have to triumph over utilitarianism.

The second argument, concerning moral values, follows directly from the first. The more extensive main plot deals with the family life of Thomas Gradgrind, a wealthy merchant who has retired from business life. He is a symbolic ally of Bounderby, and applies to his children's education the same principles that his friend employs in labour management. Like Filer, the economist in *The Chimes*, Gradgrind recognises no value but practical reality – facts and figures. Here he is, instructing the schoolmaster he has appointed to teach positivist principles:[67]

'Now, what I want is, Facts. Teach these boys and girls nothing but Facts. Facts alone are wanted in life. Plant nothing else, and root out everything else. . . . This is the principle on which I bring up my own children, and this is the principle on which I bring up these children. Stick to Facts, sir!'

He has indeed followed this principle. Louisa and Tom Gradgrind have never known childhood; they have never laughed or cried; never known the wonder of fairy tales, or the sweet dreams of childish imagination. The first thing in the world they ever became aware of 'was a large black board with a dry Ogre chalking ghastly white figures on it.'[68] There has been no affection surrounding them; only the stern, withdrawn solicitude of their father, and the self-pitying fussing of their crushed, valetudinarian mother. As they grow up the boy retreats further and further into himself, a sullen hypocrite, ready to take any kind of revenge on detested authority. The girl is more resigned. She is cold and wilful, but her eyes sometimes flash with a strange light from the hidden fire that finds no satisfaction in her life. Her father marries her off to Bounderby, in spite of the difference in their ages, and heedless of the open indifference to love shown in the cynical business alliance. But positivist education bears its fruits, and Nemesis comes. Tom caps a sequence of petty crimes with a theft for which he allows an innocent man to be blamed. A fashionable dandy with fashionable opinions makes advances to Louisa, who finds her long-suppressed appetite for love making her respond to him. At the last moment she runs to her father for shelter, confessing before him that she is overcome, helpless and powerless. And in this agonising situation Gradgrind sees the proud public façade of his life, and the certainty of his beliefs, crumbling together.

This is not our final view of the family. Dickens has no wish to demand the transgressor's head. But if the Gradgrinds are providentially saved from public scandal, the more logical and pessimistic reader can observe cause and effect in their story and deduce the author's message.

Hard Times is yet another exposition of the idealists' indictment of moral and social mathematics. Its considerable literary faults do little to weaken its energy. It is dedicated to Carlyle, and shows his influence throughout, even the style showing Carlylean traces, as brisk, mono-syllabic invocations in the second person singular recall one of the sage's favourite mannerisms:[69]

> Say, good M'Choakumchild. When from thy boiling store, thou shalt fill each jar brim full by-and-by, dost thou think that thou wilt always kill outright the robber Fancy lurking within – or sometimes only maim and distort him!

As for ideas, Bounderby stands for 'Mammonism', as Harthouse, the dandy, does for 'Dilettantism'. On 30 January 1854 Dickens wrote to Charles Knight, 'My satire is against those who see figures and averages, and nothing else – the representatives of the wickedest and most enormous vice of this time.'[70] The thought, and almost the phraseology, comes from Carlyle's essay 'Signs of the Times'. Dickens follows him in accusing mechanisation of destroying individual and social well-being, and like Carlyle he looks to spiritual regeneration for a solution. The false theory of human relations will lose its hold when the false structure of intellectual concepts has been overthrown. Bounderbys are the out-come of Malthus and *laissez-faire*; Gradgrind's 'facts and figures' are the system of classical economics. To make this quite clear, Dickens has Gradgrind call his youngest sons Adam Smith and Malthus. But Grad-grind's system omits the soul from its calculations, and so misses the essential.[71]

> So many hundred Hands in this Mill; so many hundred horse Steam Power. It is known, to the force of a single pound weight, what the engine will do; but, not all the calculators of the National Debt can tell me the capacity for good or evil, for love or hatred, for patriotism or discontent, for the decomposition of virtue into vice, or the reverse, at any single moment in the soul of one of these its quiet servants, with the composed faces and the regulated actions. There is no mystery

in it; there is an unfathomable mystery in the meanest of them, for ever. – Supposing we were to reserve our arithmetic for material objects, and to govern these awful unknown quantities by other means!

And when a little girl looks into her heart to consider the human question, she discovers the inadequacy of the science her instructors have pumped into her. It is not enough for a nation to be rich if most of its citizens are poor; the first principle of economics is 'To do unto others as I would that they should do unto me.'[72]

The life of feelings produced more than a new theory of society: it became translated into active solidarity with others to try and bring about the new society. To tell the truth, the theory itself was little more than a piece of practical advice. It was enough to obey the promptings of the heart; the rest would follow. Active selflessness would be drawn to the relief of distress. But distress was not exclusively material: the poor, like the rich, could suffer even more from mental torment. Prolonged, mechanical, unsatisfying labour destroyed sensitivity and spontaneous, healthy happiness, as did horribly ugly surroundings, a dismal atmosphere, and a life led in opposition to nature. True charity consisted of revitalising physical and moral sensitivity in the factory drudges.[73]

Utilitarian economists, skeletons of schoolmasters, Commissioners of Fact, genteel and used-up infidels, gabblers of many little dog's-eared creeds, the poor you will have always with you. Cultivate in them, while there is yet time, the utmost graces of the fancies and affections, to adorn their lives, so much in need of ornament; or, in the day of your triumph, when romance is utterly driven out of their souls, and they and a bare existence stand face to face, Reality will take a wolfish turn, and make an end of you.

The practical conclusion of such teaching would be the reforms recommended by Ruskin: re-establishing human contact with nature, and thereby restoring the inner health that mechanistic labour had destroyed. And Ruskin himself acknowledged the importance of Dickens:[74]

He is entirely right in his main drift and purpose in every book he has written; and all of them, but especially *Hard Times*, should be studied with close and earnest care by persons interested in social questions. They will find much that is partial, and, because partial, apparently unjust; but if they examine all the evidence on the other side, which Dickens seems to overlook, it will appear, after all their trouble, that his view was finally the right one, grossly and sharply told.

Thus we may see Dickens in *Hard Times* as an intermediary link between the social thought of Carlyle and that of Ruskin.

The book then has historical interest as well as intrinsic interest. Its artistic faults are those of Dickens's later style, aggravated by the lack of any close acquaintance between author and subject. Like Stephen Black-pool, Bounderby is a representative type rather than a real character. Industry is not really at the centre of the book, and Dickens gives no more than a rapid external sketch of it. The social teaching that emerges is as vague as that of *The Chimes*, and not so well adapted to its subject. The presence of a strike and the atmosphere of an industrial town under-line the distance between the 'philosophy of Christmas' and the economic needs of modern society. But Dickens did intuitively spot one of the essential aspects of the social *malaise* of his time, and even if his attack on mechanisation was inspired by Carlyle, he made it his own by the power and sincerity of his conviction. The propaganda on behalf of the feelings which runs through all his writings, and attacks selfishness at the roots, is strengthened in this book by a perfect demonstration of the universal need for sentiment. The merit of *Hard Times* lies in the strength with which Dickens has dramatically bound up his criticism of orthodox economic practice with an attack upon abstract intellectualism.

Psychological validity

It seems, then, that the social importance of Dickens's novels was psychological, lying in the emotions he felt himself, and aroused in others, as he saw and described general human inequality. The novels proffer no direct answers to the specific social questions posed by indus-trial society between 1830 and 1850. Dickens really was influential, but it was people's feelings that he influenced. He contributed to the deep-seated reaction in the national psyche, at the same time as he was affected by it. He strengthened the revolt of Christian sentiment against utilitarian aridity, and thereby drew upon one of the strongest and most ancient aspects of the national outlook. Thus Dickens's unique place among the great writers of his century, and the remarkable language in which his admirers tried to explain the nature of his genius, become explicable. He was, they said, above all a national writer: the true voice of England:[76]

> He has entered into our everyday life in a manner which no other living author has done. Much of his phraseology has become common property, and allusions to his works and quotations from them are made by everybody, and in all places.

The emotional tone of his writings contributed even more to his popularity than his literary genius.[76]

And as it was national, his writing was conservative. Public and private charity might be the means Dickens urged, but social peace was the goal. Following Carlyle's example, he prophetically offered a choice between immediate action and revolution. He himself worked to draw the classes nearer to one another, and there is abundant evidence that he made a contribution in this direction.[77] But if his clear-sighted and deeply-felt writing expounds the overall nature of the interventionist reaction, his personal experience of poverty and the nature of his class-consciousness kept him a long way from feudal or aristocratic thinking. The remnant of radicalism was peculiar to him among the movement's leaders. By contrast, Disraeli's social thought was based on the reactionary element.

Six

Disraeli: social Toryism

Disraeli's social novels have a distinctive representative value. The subject matter of the books gives them historical interest, as does their influence, which appears in their association with a powerful intellectual movement. In keeping with their author's personality, they are highly individual. The mental process which led him to social Toryism offers no illustration of the ordinary Englishman's crisis of conscience. With that reservation, it is legitimate to look at the books as representative examples of reactionary interventionism. From our point of view, Disraeli's tremendous political subtlety is less important than the assimilative skills by which he discovered and revived some of the public's deepest convictions, and the intuitive intelligence which enabled him to comprehend and formulate the new needs of the age.

Were his convictions sincerely held? And was his sympathy for the poor genuine? These questions are difficult, and may be unanswerable. One thing seems clear: unlike Bulwer, whose utilitarianism was a passing phase, Disraeli's whole being was bound up with social Toryism. His conception of the grandiose ideas which were to bring him personal success and his country civil peace and foreign greatness owed as much to the natural bent of his temperament as to any calculation of his own interests. He put his own spontaneous leanings into his imaginative theory of government: his profound belief in the weakness of ideas and the power of instincts to shape a nation's overseas power and domestic tranquillity.

Biographical content of the novels

Disraeli's youth is familiar today, and there is no need to go over any but the outstanding facts and major formative influences. The importance of race in his intellectual development is generally appreciated: at times he has been seen as the archetypal Jew, and at others as an exception to the laws of ethnology. The fact remains that Disraeli himself always had a strong sense of the importance of his Jewish origins, and that this increased the obstacles in his way to success. His family had been settled in England for two generations: his grandfather immigrated from Venice in 1748. His father, Isaac D'Israeli, was an intellectual after the eighteenth-century pattern: a bibliophile and man of letters who combined radical ideas with a taste for the monarchical splendours of the past. Benjamin was born on 21 December 1804, although he always claimed to have been born in 1805. In 1817, when Isaac withdrew himself and his family from the Jewish faith, he was baptised. The boy received an unusual and haphazard education. Although his father was a cultured man with a social position on the fringes of good society as a friend of many leading writers, Benjamin was not sent to public school or university. Instead, after going to two junior schools at Blackheath and Walthamstow, he continued his studies in his father's library, and under his direction. This was favourable to his literary development and his lively, quick-witted temperament, but it left one irremediable gap: he completely lacked scientific understanding. From 1821 until 1824 he worked in an attorney's office, serving his apprenticeship in the world of affairs, and displaying some remarkable talents. He was precocious, ambitious, and brilliant, with flexible, but tenacious, determination. His father intended him for the law, but he was destined to follow literature first, and then politics. A first novel, *Aylmer Papillon*, was never published. Then he came into contact with John Murray, the publisher, and projected a new national newspaper, the *Representative*, which he undertook to establish with all his varied and fertile resources. At last the brilliant success of *Vivian Grey* in 1827 – the first part had been published in 1826 – led him to the public stage he longed to dominate and control.

The biographical interest of *Vivian Grey* cannot be over-estimated. Just as *Pelham* showed the true nature of Bulwer's utilitarianism, so *Vivian Grey* provides a key to Disraeli without which his life and career would be incomprehensible. This youthful confession put forward implicitly certain intentions which scholarship has been able to uncover. The hero is charming, clever, and brilliantly gifted, but fate has placed him in humble circumstances. He sets out to repair this injustice with his genius. In the dedicated pursuit of success he proves himself indefatigably energetic and completely unscrupulous. Ambition, intrigue, the joys of contest, victory, revenge, and bitter defeat have never been set in motion with more dash and cynicism:[1]

> 'Power! Oh! What sleepless nights, what days of hot anxiety! what exertions of mind and body! what travel! what hatred! what fierce encounters! what dangers of all possible kinds, would I not endure with a joyous spirit to gain it!'

The book is full of witty dialogue, piquant satire, and portraits of real people. Alongside these runs the portrait of Vivian's will, bent on conquest, and capable of the deftest subtlety coupled with the utmost fixity of purpose. All that is known about Disraeli's youth justifies identifying him with Vivian Grey. Allowance must be made, of course, for literary exaggeration and a certain amount of Byronism, and it must be borne in mind that Disraeli was in every way the perfect dandy at this time, ready to create a stir by his amorality as much as by his elegant costume. Thus we are given a definition of the paramount duties of man as being 'to love, to hate, to slander, and to slay'.[2] Vivian, however, is an unfeeling monster, incapable of any sincere emotion, whereas Disraeli's correspondence at the time shows that he was capable of genuine affection.

All the same, *Vivian Grey* reveals a passionately ambitious, self-confident spirit, unscrupulous and ready for anything, and perfectly fitted for intrigue and the manipulation of other people:[3]

> 'Yes! We must mix with the herd; we must enter into their feelings; we must humour their weaknesses; we must sympathise with the sorrows that we do not feel; and share the merriment of fools.'

Just as Vivian seems to have attained all his ends, a sudden twist of fortune upsets him. Disraeli's early days seem to have proved equally delusive. He wanted to equal the scions of great aristocratic families, yet his birth and lack of a university education marked him as an inferior. He wanted to live a dazzlingly opulent life, but his slender resources meant that he had to get into debt to cut a dash. He tried to get into Parliament, and was rejected by the electorate four times. When he was finally elected he expected a great oratorical success, but his maiden speech, on 7 December 1837, was greeted with derision. Disraeli was admirably patient, and returned to the fray each time; he believed in his star, and had decided that he was going to become Prime Minister. One by one the obstacles fell away before him. His good looks and charming wit and the irresistible authority of his superior intelligence permitted him to impose himself upon an unwilling, exclusive society. In Lady Blessington's *salon* he schooled himself under Count D'Orsay to perfect his address and acquire an easy manner, while he cultivated the faculty of worldly mockery as he watched the vanity and foibles of those around him. After the success of *Vivian Grey* he travelled in the East from 1828 until 1831, and fed his imagination with the exotic scenes and modes of behaviour which instinctively appealed to him. In 1837 he married a rich widow, who made him a perfect wife, and secured him from immediate financial anxiety. He entered politics on the Liberal side, and frequented radical circles as a friend of Bulwer: O'Connell had supported him at his election. But radicalism could not hold him, and there were early signs of that reactionary temperament which would bring Disraeli to power in the Tory party. Thereafter he altered his policies, and in 1837 he was elected with Tory support. The change took place at the end of 1835, when Disraeli was elected for Maidstone. In 1840 he became Member for the rural constituency of Shrewsbury. He was unfortunate in his early speeches, but after a while he gained a hearing, and his speech on the Chartist petition in 1839 brought him into prominence. Peel paid no attention to his flattery, and remained hostile, refusing him a place in his ministry of 1841. Thereupon Disraeli prepared to revolt, organised a party and drew up a programme and, in 1846, harrassed his chief with savage attacks. As the leader of the Young England group, however, he was not to escape hostile mockery himself.[4] But when the repeal of the Corn Laws brought the ministry down, Disraeli stood at the centre of the opposition as the spokesman of the landed gentry. From then on his rise was assured. He became leader of the opposition in 1847, a minister in 1852 and, after several changes of fortune, Prime Minister in 1868. In 1876 he accepted the title of Lord Beaconsfield. But his later career need not concern us; we are only interested in the years of conflict when Disraeli's pen came to the aid of his political ambitions, and he preached the gospel of Young England in three novels.

He was in fact the moving spirit of Young England. He was personally friendly with George S. Smythe and Lord John Manners, and exerted the authority of his age and intelligence among his young partisans. We have tried to show the economic and moral origins of this eminently aristocratic form of interventionist reaction in 1840.[5] There were three principal aspects of Young England: the landed gentry were outraged by the encroachments of industrial radicalism; romantic young men were filled with imaginative enthusiasm for the majestic monarchy and beautiful religion of the past; and there was a feeling of simple, humane sympathy for the poor in town and country. The party's members earned respect for their seriousness, although their programme was almost absurdly childish. But they were well-intentioned, and carried out some effective social work. When one examines Young England in the intellectual context of its time, it takes on fresh interest from its association with the general crisis of conscience. But what led Disraeli to take up this cause? What was the link between the poorly-assimilated Jew,[6] born outside the aristocracy, with something of a liberal outlook about him still, and a confirmed habit of scepticism, and an instinctive conservative reaction, deriving from the same basis of birth and feudal tradition that had frozen the nation's greatest families into a posture of exclusive pride?

Here, in an acute form, we find the question of Disraeli's sincerity cropping up. Appearances are all against his having held sincere political convictions.[7] And in the normal sense of the word, we must admit that Disraeli was not sincere. He did not submit his beliefs to the impartial judgement of conscience or reason, dismissing self-interest, irrelevant feelings, and prior determination. All the evidence suggests that ambition and self-interest were the guiding lights when Disraeli took decisions. In 1841 he needed a programme; he was opposed to Peel, and that liberal-impregnated conservatism which had accepted Free Trade; his political past ruled out a return to radicalism; and Young England conveniently provided the idea of a revived Toryism. His natural intelligence, more-over, must have shown him the extent and intensity of the general feeling of which Young England was a symptom. The Victorian reaction, in politics, religion, and social thought, seemed to him a huge amalgamation of forces which was bound to sweep all before it in the future, and which might carry along his fortunes with it, and perhaps bring him to power. This was the nature of his conviction, which was always more a matter of social Toryism than Young England, in any case. His fine sense of the absurd could never have overlooked the ludicrous aspects of the group's reactionary programme; he must have had some mental reservations about Lord John Manners's naïve dreams. Yet these fantasies of feudal socialism find a place in his novels alongside his own profound views, and the sustained earnestness with which he purports to take the one as seriously as the other must be regarded with some suspicion. Finally, an emotional sympathy with the poor was an inseparable component of mid-Victorian interventionism as exemplified, for instance, in Ashley's philanthropy. But there is little evidence of sentiment in Disraeli's life or his writings, in which the tone is usually cool and detached. The psycho-logical evidence is all against Disraeli's having, like Dickens, followed his sensitivity and conscience without question in the direction of ben-evolent interventionist theories. Social Toryism served his interests too well for his sincere acceptance of it to pass unchallenged, and at least one part of his nature could never have been reconciled easily with its tenets.

And yet he brought much of himself to the movement. If Disraeli was never a man of feeling he was, first and foremost, a man of lively imagina-tion. He compensated for his lack of scientific understanding with in-tuitive insight into the present, and foresight into the future. He thought in symbols, and was acutely alive to the power of images over human thought and conduct, for he recognised it in himself. Guided by these habits of mind, he looked at social forces and institutions poetically, and dwelt on their externals. And, judging by his own experience, he saw people as creatures of instinct rather than reflection, who would be governed by striking appearances and large simple visions rather than by the cold and difficult light of logic. The new Toryism appealed to his hidden taste for the grandiose and sensuously beautiful when it insisted on the majesty of the throne and the splendour of the Established Church. It appealed to national tradition and a sense of the distant past. And it tried to bind all classes in society more closely together by reviving feudal solidarity, and basing charity on men's organic social interdependence. Although Disraeli had few tender feelings, and was capable of all kinds of cruelty in the political battle, yet his visionary dreams could whip him up into a state that was almost emotionally exalted. Thus his temperament and his will united to impose Young England convictions upon him, without his reason or conscience being engaged at all. In common experience, sincerity is often a matter of allowing one's temperament to dictate the acceptance of those ideas which are most in accord with it. And to this extent, Disraeli's character was certainly involved in his thinking, so that his political development should be seen as something more than calculated speculation for his own advantage. And the fact that the man and his writings are thus related gives more weight to them. The artificial constructions of a charlatan could hardly be taken seriously, but Disraeli's social novels have the interest and subjective truth of genuine expressions of his personality.

To the extent that he could feel the power of romantic reaction, Disraeli could believe in it. At the same time, his marvellous insight probed to the conservative instincts at the bottom of the English soul, and he was able to share in the feeling of national continuity. He grasped and expounded the native British belief in social stability and the wisdom of experience better than any writer since Burke. And his eloquent defence of the constitution and excellent account of the way in which viable social organisations develop were equally distinguished.[8] Finally, if historicism fascinated his imagination, he was also drawn to Young England by his antipathy to utilitarianism. From the outset of his career Disraeli made no secret of his hatred of rational and analytical social reorganisation.[9] The great intellectual movement which seemed to have triumphed around 1830, and to have ensured that, for the future, reason would dominate public and private life, was painful to Disraeli and moved him to an anger that has a genuine ring. He detested the rational, scientific doctrines of utilitarianism in every shape and form. He hated the dry, merciless analysis, bent on dissecting and dragging out into the light of day all the springs of action, however feeble or nervous. Disraeli was a man who had never really faced himself or determined to chase away any irrational fears from the corners of his life and well-being. He did not believe in deep introspection, but preferred comfortable lies to unpleasant truths. The advances of science and rationalism pained him deeply, and he obdurately opposed them. He defended time-honoured institutions, instinctive judgement, and spontaneous spiritual progress. His position is reminiscent of Dickens and Carlyle, but is tinged with questionable private motives in which one detects a personal anxiety which comes very close to being a fear of truth. But Disraeli turned on the same enemies as Dickens and Carlyle, and kept up the battle against a philosophy of life based on logic, preaching instead ethics, politics, and sociology grounded in instinct rather than reason.

Thus Disraeli's philosophy, the most profound expression of social Toryism, was originally drawn up for the negative purpose of opposing utilitarianism. Disraeli's personality permitted and encouraged this to be done by a positive assimilation of English conservative traditions. His natural bias was in favour of effective, plausible images which could evoke popular enthusiasm when they were presented in a traditional, nationalistic light.

Toryism looks to the past, and with its monarchical ideal and religious piety, it opposes radicalism like poetry confronting prose. Disraeli accepted it, but he transformed it. Popular Toryism had a reputation for stupidity: Disraeli claimed to have found weighty psychological and historical arguments in its favour. The *Vindication of the English Constitution* (1835) contains all the political ideas to be found in the later novels. It opens with a vehement attack upon utilitarianism as a false political system derived from false psychological premisses: 'Let the Utilitarian prove that the self-interest of man always leads him to be a tyrant, and I will grant that universal suffrage is a necessary and useful institution.'[10] Its abstract, analytical character made the new science of government a new scholasticism. 'The schoolmen are revived in the nineteenth century, and are going to settle the state with their withering definitions, their fruitless logomachia, and barren dialectics.'[11] This was totally unlike the procedure of political wisdom, which looked for the surviving elements of past glory, and set itself to cultivating these with love and respect. Wisdom put precedent before rules and reason. And then Disraeli outlined his own theory of history, with brilliant dash. The Glorious Revolution of 1688 was a mistake; it had cut down the power of the throne, and set up the Whig oligarchy. This had squeezed the king into a doge-like position in an essentially republican constitution on the

Venetian model. On the other side of the picture was the nation's glorious and illustrious past, and the great future of the Tory party, which alone could ensure the power of the throne and the liberty of the subject, and the prosperity of the nation. We shall come across the same ideas in *Coningsby*.

We still have not seen how Disraeli dealt with the new Toryism's social ideals. On the day in 1839 when the Chartists presented their petition to Parliament, Disraeli defended it in principle, if not in detail. On 9 May 1843 he uttered the following memorable words to his constituents in Shrewsbury: 'Let me next tell those gentlemen who are so fond of telling us that property has its duties as well as its rights, that labour also has its rights as well as its duties.'[12] *Sybil* puts forward a much more serious and well-stated case for feudal interventionism than Manners's poems had offered. Toryism had always contained an element of paternalism, deriving from the gentry's traditions and the inevitable component of organic social solidarity arising from the Romantic view of history. But Disraeli went beyond this. His own imagination suggested a return to the sovereign's authoritative protection of the subject, and he liked the idea of rural monasteries dispensing pious charity. But his views were too robust and decisive to have rested entirely on his imagination. His tough political intelligence went further, and grasped the needs of the times. Carlyle's writings had shown him the imminent dangers confronting England.[13] He saw Chartism as a powerful, dangerous force, but one which might yet save society, and make the fortune of the man, or party, who could control it and guide it wisely. The Oxford Movement, in spite of the opposition it had provoked, he saw as a triumph. The age of great causes and social upheaval seemed to have arrived: why, then, should not the people's hopes of political equality and justice be realised? As they were being pursued at the moment, these goals would prove destructive. But if they could be released from rationalist control, they might still make a great and glorious contribution to a peaceful social order based on benevolent authoritarianism. Here sincere patriotism and calculated self-interest pressed the same course on Disraeli: a fruitful line of development opened up before the ambitious politician, which would be equally valuable to the statesman with his devotion to his adopted country. And it is even possible that some genuine sympathy for the wretched touched his heart, and he really wished to render justice to the oppressed. He was, after all, always bitterly conscious of the persecutions suffered by his race. After he had conducted a personal investigation of the people's conditions he reached the conclusion that they were intolerable. This abstract conclusion, supported by theoretical indignation, may well have grown into a vital emotion, for there are some passages in *Sybil* which thrill with human feeling.

Disraeli used the social novel as a means of propaganda. For all its racy style, his pamphlet *Vindication of the English Constitution* had not reached a wide audience. Press reports of his speeches hardly put forward a serious, connected argument, and Young England still lacked a manifesto. The new Toryism had not enjoyed any great public success. In the Preface to the fifth edition of *Coningsby* we read:

> It was not originally the intention of the writer to adopt the form of fiction as the instrument to scatter his suggestions, but after reflection, he resolved to avail himself of a method which, in the temper of the times, offered the best chance of influencing opinion.

The novel, as a form, had already passed the test. Not to mention Bulwer or Miss Martineau, the popularity of Dickens proved it to be the most fashionable literary genre and, at the same time, the best vehicle for didacticism. And Disraeli would not be trying his hand at it for the first time: since *Vivian Grey* he had written several more novels, though none of them, it must be confessed, had been so successful.[14] All the signs were encouraging, and *Coningsby* (1844), *Sybil* (1845), and *Tancred* (1847) comprise a trilogy informed with the same spirit. These books have an original structure, unique among the social novels of the time. Disraeli created the 'political novel', and was its sole practitioner. He alone wanted a propaganda success for personal ends. But this is secondary. First and foremost, *Sybil* is the most eloquent outline of one of the main branches of reactionary interventionism.

'Coningsby'

The new Tory message came under three heads: political, social, and religious, set out in *Coningsby*, *Sybil*, and *Tancred* respectively. *Sybil* is the most interesting from our point of view, but our survey would be incomplete without a quick examination of *Coningsby* and *Tancred*. The author's ideas changed from novel to novel, so that it is best to consider them chronologically.

In *Coningsby, or The New Generation* Disraeli again takes the Reform Act as a vantage point from which to survey political conditions. The book concerns itself entirely with the ruling classes, so that the struggle for mastership of England rules out any real consideration of the proletarian struggle for justice. The new bourgeoisie is shown challenging the old aristocracy; the existence of an urban proletariat is glossed over, and the agricultural workers, romantically called 'the peasantry', are made to stand for the entire populace. Peasants and workers, it is suggested, comprise a unique historical class which was contented with feudal government, as it is naturally adapted to medieval forms. The danger to the nation lies in the rivalry of factory and manor-house. Public order has been seriously disturbed by the Reform Act. New upsets are feared, and the prevalent political theories do nothing but intensify the existing antagonism between the old ruling class and the new bourgeoisie. The problem is to reconcile the traditional rights of the one with the just expectations of the other. And the new Toryism puts forward a formula for just such a peaceful reconciliation. Of course it will restore the people's ancient rights as part of the procedure for settling society. And the order of barons, enlarged and enriched by the admission of the new aristocracy of industrialists, will dedicate itself to fostering the well-being of its vassals. The Church, recalled to its duty by the Oxford Movement, will dispense charity in the countryside. But above all, the expanding nation must be given a unifying moral vision: this will be the task of the 'new generation'.

Coningsby comes before *Sybil* logically as well as chronologically. Even its plot is dated earlier, running from the eve of the Reform Act of 1832 to the Tory electoral victory of 1841. The political vicissitudes of these nine years are examined exhaustively, while the depression, which reached its climax in 1842, is barely touched on. Chartism is left in the background. *Sybil* is quite different, opening as it does in 1837, and carrying the reader down to 1844.

The dedication of *Coningsby* to Henry Hope, a leading member of the Young England party, includes these words: 'In these pages I have endeavoured to picture something of that development of the new and, as I believe, better mind of England, that has often been the subject of our converse and speculation.' The leaders of the movement appear under different names. Coningsby, the hero of the book, is none other than George Smythe, and Lord John Manners is recognisable in his friend Henry Sydney. We follow a group of young men, all brilliant and ambitious, and nearly all of noble birth, from Eton, where their characters are formed and they become friends, to the threshold of their political careers and public lives. In the process we see them at university, where their studies have made them mature already, and in the metropolitan palaces or sumptuous country houses which are their family homes. The interest is focused on the hero's career. He is the orphaned scion of a rich, ancient family. By turns he is the favourite and the victim of the caprice of his grandfather, the Marquis of Monmouth. His early initiation into life's difficulties gives him the energy appropriate to a future party leader; and his exposure to the most generous side of the nobility, as well as its corruption, shows him both the advantages and disadvantages of oligarchy. A boyhood friendship, a journey to Manchester, and a romance with the daughter of Millbank the industrialist all serve to point out to him the existence, and inevitable future importance, of the industrial bourgeoisie. As he witnesses the merciless struggle between Monmouth, the typical old aristocrat, and Millbank, the representative of industrial greatness, Coningsby searches his heart and mind, and scrutinises history, to try and discover principles which will satisfy his personal and patriotic ambitions. His friends are troubled by the same uncertainties, and they arrive at the same conclusion as he does: the new Toryism appeals to the generous instincts of youth. It should also prove acceptable to men of superior intelligence when they have thought it over.

Meanwhile the mysterious Jew, Sidonia, whose birth, tastes, and enormous wealth all serve to keep him out of the centre of the world of affairs, has been helping the intellectual growth of Young England with his advice, his epigrams, and his profound and original ideas. This unique character unites the genius of a Disraeli with the wealth of a Rothschild. He is the outstanding figure, wherever he goes. He is the equal of kings, whom he supports or opposes with his personal diplomacy, and maintains on their thrones with his gold. He is the embodiment of modern high finance. Under a skilful yet transparent disguise, the author himself is represented in Sidonia in his unofficial role among the chiefs of the new Toryism.

'Young' England was dominated by the memory of olden days; the 'new' Toryism put itself forward as a return to the party's old, traditional principles. Not even Disraeli's art could enliven the political dissertations which make up a good part of the book. The arguments of the *Vindication of the English Constitution* appear again, though less rigorously and continuously put. After the Reformation, according to Disraeli, when the Church's property had been distributed among Henry VIII's favourites, a class of parvenus arose. These were the Whig nobility, and it was in their interest to destroy the monarch's absolute power, the equality of all faithful subjects before the throne, the prosperity of the nation, which had been ensured by wise paternalistic government, and the Church's welfare work. They strove for these dismal and unpatriotic objectives until the Revolution of 1688 brought them to power.[15]

The great object of the Whig leaders in England from the first movement under Hampden to the last most successful one in 1688, was to establish in England a high aristocratic republic on the model of the Venetian, then the study and admiration of all speculative politicians. . . . And they at length succeeded. . . . They brought in a new family on their own terms. George I. was a Doge; George II. was a Doge; . . . George III. tried not to be a Doge. . . . And a Venetian constitution did govern England from the accession of the House of Hanover until 1832.

Bolingbroke, Pitt, and Shelburne, in the eighteenth century, and Huskisson and Canning in the first years of the Liverpool administration had all tried to throw off the yoke of oligarchy. But their work had no lasting results, and the Reform Act enshrined the Whig triumph. The king had already been excluded from the cabinet, and the 'Seven Year Bill' emancipated Parliament. Now the reform of the electorate destroyed the internal balance of power in Parliament in favour of the Commons. Every source of division and discord in the nation – among which Disraeli even listed protective tariffs – was blamed onto the Whigs: 'The Whigs introduced sectarian religion, sectarian religion led to political exclusion, and political exclusion was soon accompanied by commercial restraint.'[16] By contrast, the Tory party was national, and stood for the instinctive aspirations of the whole people. In the past it had based the people's freedom and the nation's prosperity on the absolute power of the Crown:[17]

> Confidence in the loyalty of the nation, testified by munificent grants of rights and franchises, and favour to an expansive system of traffic, were distinctive qualities of the English sovereignty, until the House of Commons usurped the better part of its prerogatives.

Since then the party had degenerated, and in the hands of its present leadership its policy of loyalty to the Crown had become little more than a doctrine of self-denial. But the value of the old formula was not defunct: a return to the 'Pitt system' would restore England to health. The Tory ministers of Liverpool's Government were the only people who could have brought to a satisfactory conclusion the conflict which had been settled in so dangerous and revolutionary a manner by the Reform Act:[18]

> They might have adjusted the rights and properties of our national industries in a manner which would have prevented that fierce and fatal rivalry that is now disturbing every hearth of the United Kingdom.

Thus the political doctrine Disraeli wanted to introduce to England was a long way from the merely reflex Toryism of 1832. He put the character of Lord Fitz-Booby into *Coningsby* to represent 'stupid'

readers a recognition of existing conditions, for he understood the inadequacies of industrial society, even if he could not understand its spirit.

'Tancred'

Tancred, or The New Crusade (1847) was intended to illustrate the religious element in social Toryism. But the two years which had elapsed since the publication of *Sybil* had apparently changed some of Disraeli's ideas. The repeal of the Corn Laws in 1846 had tied him more closely to the landed aristocratic interest, and his open break with Peel had made him the effective leader of the opposition. Now that power was nearly in his grasp, he was more acutely aware of the chimeric nature of some of Young England's plans, and he saw that compromise would be necessary, even if it meant pruning his more ambitious schemes. Furthermore, the tone of this third novel is different. It is both mystical and self-mocking, and it openly uses implausible events and situations. Serious ideas are concealed under a mass of symbolism; scepticism peeps out of the most impassioned flights of declared faith. On the other hand, the union between industrialists and the nobility which *Coningsby* had proposed is no longer viewed as possible or even desirable. Disraeli is, at bottom, putting in a blow for reactionary politics in their bitter war with liberalism. He castigates the men and ideas of bourgeois civilisation immoderately, hurling diatribes at them which are as unremittingly violent and final as biblical curses.

As a matter of fact, an oriental flavour runs through the whole book. *Tancred* is first and foremost a plea for the Jewish race and spirit. Disraeli has moved away from the oppression of English working men to the persecution of his own race. The Victorian religious and sentimental reaction becomes the signal for a return to the Asiatic origins of Christianity. The divine element in human regeneration can no longer be represented adequately in the social role of the clergy or the philanthropic work of pious Catholic gentlemen. It will take a great mystical vision from the heart of Asia to revive decadent European society.

The French Revolution was a great Aryan apostasy. 'Half a century ago, Europe made a violent and apparently successful effort to disembarrass itself of its Asian faith.'[99] From this sprang the monstrous growth of industrial civilisation, and the secret evils endured by its victims. 'Enlightened Europe is not happy. Its existence is a fever, which it calls progress. Progress to what?'[100] Now impious doctrines denying the creation have been devised; philosophers question man's divine origin, and suggest that he evolved from an animal. '"I do not believe I ever was a fish," said Tancred.'[101] Only the reversal of all this, a revival of faith, will be of any help to the world. But where is salvation to come from? Catholicism cannot engender such a rebirth; it is itself derivative. Only the Holy Land can expect a new revelation; the God of Moses will speak from a second Sinai. The doctrine of 'theocratic equality' must come from Jerusalem, and then, when England has absorbed this ideal, it will find the faith and determination to carry out the grandiose schemes of social Toryism. But first, justice must be done to the persecuted children of the chosen race. England must recognise her inestimable debt to the descendants of the apostles, venerate the true cradle of Christianity, and take Jews all over the world under her protection.

The action begins in 1845. Tancred, son of the great Duke of Bellamont, belongs, yet again, to the highest nobility. But the promptings of his restless heart do not lead him directly to social work: several years of solitary meditation have made him the apostle of a new crusade. To destroy scepticism and materialism he must re-establish contact with God by visiting the holy places. The heroes of the two previous novels appear, and recognise a kindred spirit in him, while intellectuals, egoists, Whigs, and gilded youths see him as a dreamer. Sidonia encourages him, and promises his all-powerful financial support. Coningsby and Egremont sympathise with him, giving unity to the three novels.

Tancred, the passionate pilgrim, prostrates himself before the Holy Sepulchre. A daughter of Israel, Eva, becomes his guide and inspiration. He becomes involved in warlike adventures with the Maronites and Druses, and performs feats of valour in the desert. He is captured by Arabs who treat him courteously. He climbs to the top of Mount Sinai, and prays for inspiration from heaven:[102]

> 'Faith fades and duty dies. A profound melancholy has fallen on the spirit of man. The priest doubts, the monarch cannot rule, the multitude moans and toils, and calls in its frenzy upon unknown gods.'

And, as is only just, he does see a vision in which the divine message is delivered to him:[103]

> 'The equality of man can only be accomplished by the sovereignty of God. The longing for fraternity can never be satisfied but under the sway of a common father. . . . Announce the sublime and solacing doctrine of theocratic equality.'

And Tancred comes back down to earth, where failure, deception, gnawing doubts, and the slow decay of his cherished hopes await him. The book ends on a melancholy note:[104]

'Of all the strange incidents and feelings that we have been talking over this day,' said Eva, 'there seems to me but one result; and that is, sadness. . . .

'Perhaps, all this time, we have been dreaming over an unattainable end, and the only source of deception is our own imagination.'

The confession was unnecessary. *Tancred* is more of a brilliant fantasy than a social novel. The Eastern Question commanded a good deal of attention at this time, and the Jews had suffered persecution in Rhodes and Damascus around 1840. This was the origin of this remarkable novel, which opens in the only-too-real uncertainties of London during this difficult period, and then moves to a background of legend and dream in Palestine. The book's strength lies more in its defence of the Jewish people than in any exposition of practical philosophy. The Church of England is brought face to face with its own origins and doctrines, and effectively convicts itself of inconsistency. Its indifference to the cult of the Holy Sepulchre cannot be justified; it must recognise the chasm between medieval faith and modern disbelief. 'Persecute us!' cries Eva: 'Why, if you believed what you profess, you should kneel to us!'[105]

On the other hand, the plans for social reorganisation proposed in *Sybil* could have been damaged by their proximity to the extravagance of *Tancred*. But for Disraeli, serious ideas and imaginative dreams really were linked. The mystical basis of social Toryism was, as far as he was concerned, an experienced fact; only faith would bring about the alliance of Church, Crown, and People. In the most romantic pages of *Tancred* there is a sort of sincerity. The oriental themes, which seem to combine so strangely with the projects for feudal socialism, actually answer to logical and historical experience. At this point in time, the reaction against the eighteenth century associated itself with the spirit of national expansion. Utilitarian radicalism was, of its very nature, cosmopolitan. Historicism, in Britain as in Germany, was nationalist. Here again we find the seeds of imperialism. Fakredeen, a volatile young sheikh to whom Tancred has confided his beliefs, outlines a plan for British control over Asia:[106]

'Let the Queen of the English collect a great fleet, let her stow away all her treasure, bullion, gold plate, and precious arms; be accompanied by all her court and chief people, and transfer the seat of her empire from London to Delhi.'

Twenty-seven years later, Lord Beaconsfield had Queen Victoria proclaimed Empress of India.

Conclusion

We should like to leave Disraeli on this note. For the rest of his career his words and deeds were in harmony; he was able to be more straight-forward once he had gained power. When he became Prime Minister he was able to implement a large part of the social programme outlined in *Sybil*, and it was through no fault of his own that he could not carry out still more. As we take leave of this great man, whose abilities compel our admiration, however much he lacked charm, it is only fair to recall the fact that social Toryism really did do something for the people. But these belated fruits of the novelist's work are not our concern here. When we look at *Coningsby*, *Sybil*, and *Tancred* in the context of their own decade, they take on the worth of extremely valuable historical documents. They demonstrate the diffusion of certain attitudes and feelings throughout a particular section of society; attitudes which found expression in social Toryism.

After a long interval, Lord Beaconsfield returned to the novel in 1870 with *Lothair*, and followed this with *Endymion* in 1880. The first of these attacks the Church of Rome, which he had defended in *Sybil*.

In 1881, Lord Beaconsfield died.

Seven

Mrs Gaskell and Christian interventionism

Between 1840 and 1850 three lady novelists, Mrs Gaskell, Charlotte Brontë, and Charlotte Elizabeth, touched on the industrial question in a rather similar spirit. Mrs Gaskell's social novels are by far the most important of this group, although her rivals' books are also of some interest historically. They all met with public approval, and their similarity is evidence of the moral unanimity of the movement which was affecting the whole nation. One of the components of idealistic interventionism was exemplified better in the work of these lady novelists than anywhere else: this was the spontaneous repugnance felt by anyone of a religious disposition for an industrial system that violated scriptural teachings.

The manufacturing population of the North was predominantly Evangelical. Mill owners faithfully clung to their austere, Nonconformist sects until their fortunes brought them into elegant society and the Established Church.[1] At the time of the Oxford Movement, the factory was the stronghold of sober, conscientiously disciplined religion. Such a faith automatically appealed to men of rigid determination, rigorous energies, and well-ordered minds. It also offered divine sanction for the strict, narrow individualism of the industrial bourgeoisie. The mill-owners were fortified by their personal relations with God and their severe, narrow-minded morality. And they based their sturdy respect for the rights of property on the Ten Commandments: 'Thou shalt not covet thy neighbour's house, thou shalt not covet thy neighbour's wife, nor his manservant, nor his maidservant, nor his ox, nor his ass, nor any thing that is thy neighbour's.' Then they could get on with their implacable pursuit of profit, comfortably assured that their religion and conscience had nothing against it. They swept unseeing and unhearing past the silent evidence of misery around them, and the pleas of men for their charity; they were blind to any insight that had no practical use, and they braced themselves against all emotions, which they believed were dangerous. Only this radical inability to respond to any emotion, and a complete want of sympathy and understanding, can explain how men who were, in other respects, absolutely upright fought, tooth and nail against the introduction of industrial legislation.

But Evangelicalism and Bible Christianity carried within themselves the seeds of a revolt against individualist morality. The teaching of the Bible might be used to sanction enlightened self-interest, but it also forbade its excessive or cruel pursuit. Evangelicalism took as its daily bread precepts like 'Do unto others as you would that they should do to you;' 'Thou canst not serve God and Mammon;' the parable of Dives and Lazarus, and the oriental horror of the golden calf: all served to inhibit greed, and put a check to the advance of industrial self-interest. But imagination and sensitivity would have to be revived if pious eyes were to be opened; spiritual insight and physical observation would have to become more acute if the covert class struggle was to be brought out into the familiar open terrain of tradition-hallowed morality. We know that Dickens expected no such transformation in his businessmen; nor did Disraeli expect the miracle to take place with Lord Marney. It was left to women's gentler but more impulsive imaginations to mark the link between the charitable precepts of Christianity and the duty of social responsibility. Clergy wives and daughters, drawing their sentiments from a common source, demonstrated the nature and quantity of sincere religious belief which attacked middle-class individualism from its own ranks.

Mrs Gaskell's personality

We do not have a great deal of information about Mrs Gaskell's life. She knew from her own experience that biography was a delicate task – her life of Charlotte Brontë had offended many people – and wished that no one should write her own life. She was born in Chelsea in 1810. Her father, William Stevenson, tried his hand at preaching and farming before becoming a Treasury official. He also acquired some experience of journalism. Her mother, formerly a Miss Holland, died at the time of her birth. Elizabeth was adopted by her mother's sister, and brought up in Knutsford, Cheshire. She spent two years at a school in Stratford-upon-Avon, and then went to live with her father and continue her literary studies under his direction. He died in 1829, and she returned to Knutsford to live until her marriage in 1832. The man she married was the Reverend William Gaskell, pastor of the Cross Street Unitarian chapel in Manchester, and marrying him was the decisive event of her life. Although she was a busy housewife with seven children to bring up and a household to keep on very little money, she was fully alive to the busy world of the industrial city. Often she went to visit the sick and dying with her husband, and she took a personal part in his work during the long depression from 1839 to 1842. She was always ready to undertake charitable work, and became friendly with many leading philanthropists: Catherine Winkworth, Thomas Wright the prison reformer, and Thomas Madge, whom she helped in his campaign among the poor. She was a dedicated supporter of the Evangelical missions. She was particularly distressed by the neglect of working-class girls. Her good nature charmed them, and she started evening classes in her own home for them. She was on an intimate footing with many poor families, for even Chartists were won over by her sweetness. She was a pretty woman, with expressive eyes and a winning smile, and she might have been made for gentle, pacifying authority. During the famine of 1862 and 1863 caused by the American Civil War she came to the aid of weavers' wives and daughters by starting sewing circles, which did sterling service. She kept up a pattern of active, sincere, affectionate good works until her death in 1865. Her finest personal qualities contributed much to her literary work, as well as her philanthropic career.

Before 1844 she had sent contributions to several journals, and started a novel, *The Sexton's Hero*. But her inventive faculties were still dormant until private grief aroused them. Her only son died in infancy, and to distract her, William Gaskell advised her to write. So she began *Mary Barton*. It proved hard to find a publisher for the book at first, but at last Chapman & Hall bought it for £100, and on 14 October 1848 it came out. This was not long after the bitter political storm which ended Chartism, but the novel had been completed much earlier. It was an immediate resounding success. From then on Mrs Gaskell was famous. The leading social idealists were eager to welcome their new ally. Carlyle congratulated her. Dickens wanted to be introduced to her, and did actually meet her in 1849, subsequently taking contributions from her for his journal *Household Words*. She was received with acclaim in Paris as well as London; Guizot and Montalembert praised her. *Mary Barton* made so strong an impression that the public wanted nothing but working-class novels from her. *Ruth* (1853), for all its moral theme, disappointed their expectations. But *North and South* (1854–5), in which she returned to industrial problems, was a great success. Her other works are interesting, but not important from the social point of view. *Cranford* (1853) is a charming tableau of small-town life. The *Life of Charlotte Brontë* is admirably sympathetic, penetrating, and detached. *Wives and Daughters* (1864–6), the unfinished novel in which she put much of her finest writing, gives her an assured place after George Eliot in the first rank of women novelists. Nevertheless *North and South*, and even more *Mary*

Barton, remain her greatest achievements. The social problems she deftly and finely dealt with in these books give them more substantial interest than all her other novels.

'Mary Barton'

Mrs Gaskell wrote *Mary Barton* spontaneously.[2] It is evident that little artistic forethought went into its making. It is an overflow of sensitivity, prompted by the sort of life and experience described in the book. The kaleidoscope of familiar impressions, scenes, views, and recollected emotions keeps it going effortlessly. Mrs Gaskell instructs as painlessly as she writes. She puts down everything that Manchester has shown her in twelve years of daily life, only tinting it slightly with her own outlook. She contributes to social philosophy by giving an immediate, feminine, Christian interpretation of industrial questions. Although she read Adam Smith prior to writing *Mary Barton*, she was as little fitted as Dickens to construct an economic alternative to Ricardo. But, like Dickens, she knew how to evoke a passionate response to dismal and demanding conditions which would produce immediate action, and subsequently a new ideology.

John Barton is a cotton operative in Carson's mill in Manchester. His wife dies in childbirth, succumbing to the distress evoked by the departure of her sister, who has been tempted by big-city life to go on the streets. We see young Mary alone at home, where she has to keep house, and is already learning the ways of poverty. Her father is confused, exposed to bad influences, and prey to the class-hatred which rises in his breast. Times, having been good, are now getting progressively worse; it is the great depression of 1839 to 1842. The textile factories slow down or stop production, and dismiss their workers. John Barton suffers in silence, and ruminates for a long time on the injustices suffered by his class. He shivers by his cold fireplace, and takes opium to allay his hunger. But the country has one great hope. The people are suffering because the powers that be pay no attention to their distress. So Parliament and the Queen must be petitioned to put an end to unemployment. Barton is chosen as a Chartist delegate for the petition of 1839. He leaves full of hope, and returns downcast, with rage smouldering in his heart. The people's emissaries have been received with indifference and contempt. From now on Barton has no real hope, and the idea that oppression must be met with violence gains an obsessive hold on his mind. Carson has reduced his employees' wages; he feels he has no alternative, as there is a danger that he may lose his market altogether to continental manufacturers, who have taken orders as big as the Manchester industrialists' output in a final trial of strength. If Manchester cannot hold its prices down it will lose everything. But the employers are too arrogant to explain their conduct; they simply impose their will. Misunderstanding divides the classes, and hatred grows out of mutual ignorance. The workers strike. The masters meet together, and put forward a derisory offer to the men's delegation. Then negotiations are broken off, and all union members are dismissed. While the workers' representatives are awaiting the outcome of discussions Carson's son, a thoughtless young fool who has been paying attentions to Mary Barton, notices that their poverty has left them looking like scarecrows. He draws a caricature of their gaunt, haggard faces which he laughingly shows to his colleagues. But he has been observed, and after the meeting the paper is swept up by a striker. The strike leaders meet in a smoky inn to examine it, and are humiliated and outraged. They swear an oath to punish the man responsible, and Barton is chosen by lot to shoot young Carson dead. Here the specifically industrial drama ends: the rest of the book is concerned with the hunt for the murderer. Mary Barton's sweetheart, the young mill-hand Jem Wilson, is suspected and arrested, for was he not the dead man's rival in love? After a great deal of tension, in which fate intervenes and Mary acts like a heroine, the innocent young man is saved and Barton's crime is revealed. But misery and remorse have worn down this assassin, while suffering has softened old Carson's stubborn heart. The two come face to face as the young man's father comes to his murderer's deathbed to forgive him. Mary and Jem Wilson emigrate to Canada to start a family there, far from their unhappy memories.

A sub-plot, closely connected with the main action, runs through the book. It outlines the sufferings, temptations, and weaknesses which drive working-class girls to prostitution. With perfect delicacy of touch Mrs Gaskell interweaves the three stories of Mary, her father, and her aunt Esther. Barton succumbs to an appetite for violence which is explained, but not justified, by social injustice. Mary is pursued by her father's employer's son, and her economic situation brings her within a hair's breadth of ruin. Esther, like Barton, falls; and like him, she expiates her sin and is forgiven. In *Ruth*, Mrs Gaskell was to make a more extensive plea for the ruined women whom society punished with blind, implacable hatred. The argument is associated with a general belief in charity, which is also central to *Mary Barton*.

Acts of violence performed by hunger-maddened groups of workers deserve the same compassion as any other human errors. But what should be our moral attitude to industrial disputes? We should 'acknowledge the Spirit of Christ as the regulating law between both parties'.[3] Christian morality offers a policy for social peace, and shows the warring classes that they have common interests: 'Distrust each other as they may, the employers and the employed must rise or fall together. There may be some difference as to chronology, none as to fact.'[4] Classical economics had taught the same thing, but failed to add that nature, left to itself, will not bring complete order out of chaos. Man has a part to play in the full realisation of the divine order; the inadequacies of daily life must be corrected by love, justice, and charity. It is the duty of the rich to help the poor: 'When God gives a blessing to be enjoyed, He gives it with a duty to be done; and the duty of the happy is to help the suffering to bear their woe.'[5] *Mary Barton* proposes compassionate interventionism based on a religious ideal of human brotherhood.

Here again the case is illustrated rather than argued: graphic details bring abstract ideas to life. Mrs Gaskell created John Barton to exemplify the uncontrollable feelings of outrage which were driving workers to revolution. Barton is basically honest, with a Lancastrian's blunt candour, good sense, and native temper. He is deeply attached to his daughter Mary, and always ready to help his neighbours. He would give up his last crust to anyone worse off than himself. How does such a man become the enemy of an entire class, a would-be revolutionary, and a murderer? The answer is a complete indictment of society's indifference and neglect. Poverty sours Barton. He is unemployed and suffers want, while he sees his employers leading unchanged lives of luxury, with their carriages and choice food. While he is penniless and worn out with hunger, he watches the death of his young son, for whom the doctor has ordered a nourishing diet. And not a soul from among the rich holds out a helping hand to him.[6]

> 'Does the rich man share his plenty with me, as he ought to do, if his religion were not a humbug?...No, I tell you, it's the poor, and the poor only, as does such things for the poor. Don't think to come over me with the old tale, that the rich know nothing of the trials of the poor. I say, if they don't know, they ought to know. We are their slaves as long as we can work; we pile up their fortunes with the sweat of our brows; and yet we are to live as separate as if we were in two worlds; ay, as separate as Dives and Lazarus, with a great gulf betwixt us; but I know who was best off then,' and he wound up his speech with a low chuckle that had no mirth in it.

In this frame of mind he is sent to London with the petition that he hopes will bring about a reparation of injustice on a national scale. On the morning of the great day, breakfast is served to the delegates:[7]

'Many on our chaps though, I could see, could eat but little. Th' food stuck in their throats when they thought o' them at home, wives and little ones, as had, may be at that very time, nought to eat.'

Then they form a procession and march to the House of Commons, under the contemptuous stares of the middle classes. Policemen jostle them, and a stream of fine ladies going to Court in their carriages holds them up. But all this is trivial compared with the reception awaiting them:[8]

'It's not to be forgotten or forgiven by me or many another. . . . As long as I live, our rejection of that day will abide in my heart; and as long as I live I shall curse them as so cruelly refused to hear us.'

On top of this comes young Carson's gratuitous insult: his cruel cartoon, mocking the men's appearance. And the accumulated rancour explodes:[9]

'Well, we come before th' masters to state what we want, and what we must have, afore we'll set shoulder to their work; and they say, 'No.' One would think that would be enough of hard-heartedness, but it isn't. They go and make jesting pictures on us! I could laugh at mysel, as well as poor John Slater there; but then I must be easy in my mind to laugh. Now I only know that I would give the last drop of my blood to avenge us on yon chap, who had so little feeling in him as to make game on earnest, suffering men!'

John Barton becomes a Chartist, a communist, and a trade union member. For Mrs Gaskell these were all the same; at bottom they all implied social revolution. For her, as for Disraeli, the trade unions had the sinister, mysterious aura of secret societies. Mary Barton comes to dread looking out of the window at dusk,[10]

for there were not seldom seen sights which haunted her in her dreams. Strange faces of pale men, with dark glaring eyes, peered into the inner darkness, and seemed desirous to ascertain if her father were at home. Or a hand and arm (the body hidden) was put within the door, and beckoned him away. He always went. And once or twice, when Mary was in bed, she heard men's voices below, in earnest, whispered talk.

They were all desperate members of trades' unions, ready for anything; made ready by want.

When the leading strikers swear to avenge their class on young Carson, Mrs Gaskell's mind has run on syndicalist conspiracies. 'Then came one of those fierce terrible oaths which bind members of trades' unions to any given purpose.'[11] And we are told of their tyranny as well as their violence; the unreasoning solidarity which they seek to impose by force. Old Job Legh describes his experience as a working man:[12]

> 'I would work for low wages rather than sit idle and starve. But, comes the trades' union, and says, "Well, if you take the half-loaf, we'll worry you out of your life. Will you be clemmed, or will you be worried?" Now clemming is a quiet death, and worrying isn't, so I choose clemming, and come into th' union.'

We hear of atrocities committed against 'knobsticks', wretched scabs who have come forward to offer their labour, and had vitriol thrown at them by the infuriated strikers. Yet even as she condemns these crimes, Mrs Gaskell cannot help putting forward some excuse for them: they are the responsibility of the whole of society, which has done nothing to prevent them. The terrified bourgeoisie think of strikers as monsters, but they have feeling, human hearts under their fierce exterior. And who turned these lambs into wolves? Likewise, any one with eyes to see will realise that Chartism and communism are the noble delusions of sufferers in search of a remedy, not wild dreams of barbarism.[13]

> John Barton became a Chartist, a Communist, all that is commonly called wild and visionary. Ay! but being a visionary is something. It shows a soul, a being not altogether sensual; a creature who looks forward for others, if not for himself.

The faults of the ruling classes are shown in the manufacturer Carson. He too has solid, manly virtues. His wealth is of his own making: he was poor as a young man, but respectable poverty was a stimulus rather than a hindrance to ambition and industry. He is incapable of weakness, but devoted to his family: his eyes mist over as he opens the great gilded Bible where their births are entered, to record the death of his son. His luxuriously-furnished and tastefully-decorated house is outside the city, escaping the factory smoke. His pictures, flowers, and shrubs suggest a nobleman's castle, but he has none of the aristocrat's indolence. Mrs Gaskell was trying to be impartial, and the scene where Wilson, the working man, asks for a hospital ticket for his sick neighbour has the ring of truth about it: Carson does what is asked, but coldly:[14]

> 'Well, Wilson, and what do you want to-day, man?'
> 'Please, sir, Davenport's ill of the fever, and I'm come to know if you've got an infirmary order for him?'
> 'Davenport – Davenport; who is the fellow? I don't know the name.'

'He's worked in your factory better nor three years, sir.'

'Very likely, I don't pretend to know the names of the men I employ; that I leave to the overlooker.'

Carson has his pride; the pride of a more human Bounderby. 'No masters so stern, and regardless of the interests of their work-people, as those who have risen from such a station themselves.'[15] And his severity, lack of feeling, and want of sympathetic imagination can also make him unjust, egotistical, and cruel. When a fire burns down his mill he is in no hurry to rebuild it. His losses are covered by insurance, and besides, trade is going badly, so that it is to his advantage to delay: prices may rise, and in the meantime he saves himself having to pay wages. And he never gives a moment's thought to the men this policy throws out of work. Later, when the strike is threatening, he refuses to negotiate because 'It was the employers' will, and that should be enough for the employed.'[16] He stands out as the most intransigent of the assembled employers awaiting the men's deputation. Not that his colleagues wish to act any differently. Although a few are nervous, and suggest coming to terms, 'No one thought of treating the workmen as brethren and friends.'[17]

Classical economics ordained just such cold neutrality and systematic detachment; indeed it elevated it into a principle of right conduct. Carson's practice is based on theory. A final meeting brings him up against old Job Legh, whom the author takes as an exemplar of the good common sense which is better than logic:[18]

'We cannot regulate the demand for labour. No man or set of men can do it. It depends on events which God alone can control. When there is no market for our goods, we suffer just as much as you can do.'

'Not as much, I'm sure, sir; though I'm not given to political economy, I know that much. I'm wanting in learning, I'm aware; but I can use my eyes. I never seen the masters getting thin and haggard for want of food; I hardly ever see them making much change in their way of living, though I don't doubt they've got to do it in bad times. But it's in things for show they cut short; while for such as me, it's in things for life we've to stint. . . .'

'My good man, just listen to me. Two men live in solitude; one produces loaves of bread, the other coats, – or what you will. Now, would it not be hard if the bread-producer were forced to give bread for the coats, whether he wanted them or not, in order to furnish employment to the other: that is the simple form of the case; you've only to multiply the numbers.'

Job thinks for a little, and when he speaks, he offers no direct refutation.

Instead he moves the ground of the question, introducing the ideas of religion and charity into an argument which has hitherto excluded them:[19]

'I have lived long enough, too, to see that it is part of His plan to send suffering to bring out a higher good; but surely it's also part of His plan that as much of the burden of suffering as can should be lightened by those whom it is His pleasure to make happy and content in their own circumstances. . . .'

'Still, facts have proved, and are daily proving, how much better it is for every man to be independent of help, and self-reliant,' said Mr. Carson, thoughtfully.

'You can never work facts as you would fixed quantities, and say, given two facts, and the product is so and so. God has given men feelings and passions which cannot be worked into the problem, because they are for ever changing and uncertain. God has also made some weak; not in any one way, but in all. One is weak in body, another in mind, another in steadfastness of purpose, a fourth can't tell right from wrong, and so on; or if he can tell the right, he wants strength to hold by it. Now, to my thinking, them that is strong in any of God's gifts is meant to help the weak, – be hanged to the facts! I ask your pardon, sir: I can't rightly explain the meaning that is in me. . . . I'm not learned enough to argue. Thoughts come into my head that I'm sure are as true as Gospel, though may be they don't follow each other like the Q.E.D. of a proposition.'

And so Job Legh, who has read some geometry, shows in his own way the limitations of social mathematics, and attacks the inappropriate application of facts and figures with inarticulate perceptions from the heart. And so Mrs Gaskell denounces political economy in the same terms as Dickens and Carlyle: in the same terms, indeed, as the anonymous host whose illogical and sentimental revolt led to the establishment of the welfare and relief services of the time. Carson is shaken and softened by suffering, and gradually finds himself clinging to an inexplicable need for faith. He becomes a model employer and does all he can for his men's welfare, so that a bond of sympathy springs up between him and his workers as he carries out the duties he overlooked for so long. Mrs Gaskell hopes that an increase in sympathy in the national heart will improve social relations.

Mary Barton lays down irrefutable concrete evidence for thinking intervention to be necessary. In restrained yet moving language the book describes the worst years of distress in Manchester. There is no scene in any novel of the time which more powerfully evokes the conditions of social distress than that in which Barton and Wilson go to the aid of their comrade Davenport's family, when unemployment has reduced him to the last straits of poverty. The facts adduced by Adshead, Engels, and others take on life here, without the author resorting to any artistic exaggeration. We are shown a street littered with filth and ashes, and at the bottom of a flight of steps, six feet below street level, the cellar where the family lives. The area is too narrow for a man to stretch his arms out between the cellar window and the muddy wall opposite. The broken window-panes are stuffed with rags, and a fetid smell almost overpowers the visitors as they enter. Three or four children are rolling around the damp brick floor through which stagnant water oozes. The fireplace is empty, and the mother is crying alone in the gloom. Her husband has typhus, brought on by poverty, dirt, and physical and mental debilitation. It is infectious, but 'the poor are fatalists with regard to infection; and well for them it is so, for in their crowded dwellings no invalid can be isolated.'[20] There is no furniture in the cellar; only some scattered bricks. The husband is lying on a bed of mouldy straw, covered by a piece of sacking and all the clothes his wife and children can spare, but he is trembling with fever, and keeps uncovering himself. Wilson opens a door at the back:[21]

> it led into a back cellar, with a grating instead of a window, down which dropped the moisture from pigstyes, and worse abominations. It was not paved; the floor was one mass of bad-smelling mud. It had never been used, for there was not an article of furniture in it; nor could a human being, much less a pig, have lived there many days. Yet the 'back apartment' made a difference in the rent. The Davenports paid threepence more for having two rooms.

Now help has arrived, with food and medicine for the sick man, but it is too late:[22]

> At length he brought (with jerking convulsive effort) his two hands into the attitude of prayer. They saw his lips move, and bent to catch the words, which came in gasps, and not in tones.
> 'Oh Lord God! I thank thee, that the hard struggle of living is over.'

And so, only the poor have come to the deathbed. Like Dickens, Mrs Gaskell knew and described their charity to one another. But their kind actions are inadequate; even the rich would be helpless here. The law must step in. Briefly but eloquently Mrs Gaskell demands welfare legislation. The working day is too long: all the worst accidents happen in the last couple of hours. Girls start work too early: the factories warp them and make them unfit for housekeeping or motherhood.[23]

> 'I say it's Prince Albert as ought to be asked how he'd like his missis to be from home when he comes in, tired and worn, and wanting some one to cheer him; and may be, her to come in by and by, just as tired and down in th' mouth. ... So why can't he make a law again poor folks' wives working in factories?'

asks one old lady. Bearing in mind the Queen's popularity and affection for her husband, this indirect appeal was particularly shrewd.

Carson's conversion takes a practical form:[24]

> Many of the improvements now in practice in the system of employment in Manchester, owe their origin to short earnest sentences spoken by Mr. Carson. Many and many yet to be carried into execution, take their birth from that stern, thoughtful mind, which submitted to be taught by suffering.

In spite of the grim subject-matter, there is nothing melodramatic about the writing. The tone is grave and considered, and the general impression is of familiar reality. The realism is all the more convincing for being spontaneous rather than calculated. Even *Mary Barton*'s bitterest critics were forced to concede that it gave an accurate picture of conditions.[25] Mrs Gaskell's characters were more than generally representative symbolic types: they were recognisably of their local setting, with the mixture of simplicity and humour that is characteristic of Lancashire dialogue. Thus the hostile Greg said of the book's working-class conversations, 'We believe that they approach very nearly, both in tone and style, to the conversations actually carried on in the dingy cottages of Lancashire.'[26] Mrs Gaskell observed individual characteristics, and checked them in her daily life. She knew the stunted workers born in Manchester, offspring of local factory-hands. And she could distinguish them from the newly-arrived families, drawn to the city from farming counties by higher wages. These last were taller, and preserved something of the robust, healthy appearance of small farmers. She had heard the heart-rending comic songs in which poverty laughed at itself, and she wrote them down lovingly, for they spoke with the ring of truth. She used lines from them as epigraphs to several of her chapters. And she transcribed the whole of 'The Oldham Weaver' in her main text:[27]

> Oi'm a poor cotton-weyver, as mony a one knoowas,
> Oi've nowt for t' yeat, and oi've woorn eawt my clooas,
> Yo'ad hardly gi' tuppence for aw as oi've on,

My clogs are boath brosten, and stuckins oi've none,
    Yo'd think it wur hard,
    To be browt into th' warld,
To be – clemmed, an do th' best as yo con.

Owd Dicky o' Billy's kept telling me lung,
Wee s'd ha' better toimes if I'd but howd my tung,
Oi've howden my tung, till oi've near stopped my breath,
Oi think i' my heeart oi'se soon clem to deeath,
    Owd Dicky's weel crammed,
    He never wur clemmed,
An' he ne'er picked ower i' his loife.

We tow'rt on six week – thinking aitch day wur th' last,
We shifted, an' shifted, till neaw we're quoite fast;
We lived upo' nettles, whoile nettles wur good,
An' Waterloo porridge the best of eawr food,
    Oi'm tellin' yo' true,
    Oi can find folk enow,
As wur livin' na better nor me.

Owd Billy o' Dans sent th' baileys one day,
Fur a shop deebt oi eawd him, as oi could na pay,
But he wur too lat, fur owd Billy o' th' Bent,
Had sowd th' tit an' cart, an' ta'en goods fur th' rent.
    We'd neawt left bo' th' owd stoo',
    That wur seeats fur two,
An' on it ceawred Marget an' me.

Then t' baileys leuked reawnd as sloy as a meawse,
When they seed as aw t' goods were ta'en eawt o' t' heawse,
Says one chap to th' tother, 'Aws gone, theaw may see;'
Says oi, 'Ne'er freet, mon, yeaur welcome ta' me.'
    They made no moor ado
    But whopped up th' eawd stoo',
An' we booath leet, whack – upo' t' flags!

Then oi said to eawr Marget, as we lay upo' t' floor,
'We's never be lower i' this warld, oi'm sure,
If ever things awtern, oi'm sure they mun mend,
For oi think i' my heart we're booath at t' far eend;
    For meeat we ha' none;
    Nor looms t' weyve on, –
Edad! they're as good lost as fund.'

Eawr Marget declares had hoo cloo'as to put on,
Hoo'd goo up to Lunnon an' talk to th' greet mon;
An' if things were na awtered when there hoo had been,
Hoo's fully resolved t' sew up meawth an' eend;
    Hoo's neawt to say again t' king,
    But hoo loikes a fair thing,
An' hoo says hoo can tell when hoo's hurt.

Old Job Legh is a picturesque working-class philosopher and collector of biological specimens. He represents the educated working man, a class which, Mrs Gaskell suggests, is generally unknown. But she knew how keenly these men had educated themselves, reading Newton while working at their looms, and studying by candlelight at night.

One scene shows the neighbours gathering to celebrate John Barton's departure for London with the people's petition to Parliament. Each has his say. A widow, whose strapping son is under the legal age to work in a factory, demands that children be given back their freedom: a typical instance, this, of the way in which those who were protected by the first industrial laws were among their fiercest enemies. A pompous man, speaking in measured syllables, demands that Members of Parliament should wear calico shirts: ''twould make trade brisk, that would, wi' the power o' shirts they wear.' Job Legh is subtler: 'You take my advice, John Barton, and ask parliament to set trade free, so as workmen can earn a decent wage, and buy their own two, ay and three, shirts a year; that would make weaving brisk.'[28]

But nothing is more vivid than John Barton's account of his visit to the capital:[29]

'They're sadly puzzled how to build houses though in London; there'd be an opening for a good steady master-builder there, as know'd his business. For yo see the houses are many on 'em built without any proper shape for a body to live in; some on 'em they've after thought would fall down, so they've stuck great ugly pillars out before 'em. And some on 'em (we thought they must be th' tailor's sign) had gotten stone men and women as wanted clothes stuck on 'em.'

The road was crowded with carriages going to Court.[30]

'It were th' queen's drawing-room, they said, and th' carriages went bowling along toward her house, some wi' dressed up gentlemen like circus folk in 'em, and ruck o' ladies in others. Carriages themselves were great shakes too. Some o' th' gentlemen as couldn't get inside hung on behind, wi' nosegays to smell at, and sticks to keep folk off as might splash their silk stockings. I wondered why they didn't hire a cab rather than hang on like a whip-behind boy; but I suppose they wished to keep wi' their wives, Darby and Joan like.

For a moment, the splendour of the spectacle makes Barton forget the squalor he has left at home: 'I were like a child, I forgot a' my errand in looking about me.'[31]

This genuine simplicity adds to the charm of *Mary Barton*. In spite of its realistic subject and the vigour with which it propounded certain views, it was capable of entertaining the most squeamish reader. It was highly successful in dispelling social indifference. To the public congratulations of Dickens and Carlyle were to be added those of Miss Edgeworth, Walter Savage Landor, and Samuel Bamford, the radical writer, one of whose poems Mrs Gaskell had quoted. Manchester, however, was annoyed. The mill-owners objected to their role in *Mary Barton*. The *Manchester Guardian*,[32] the leading newspaper of the North, accused the author of calumny. W. R. Greg's criticism put the case against the novel. Greg belonged to a family of benevolent manufacturers whose praises were for ever being sung in the literature of the time. We have seen that he was probably the original of Trafford and Millbank. None the less he thought it was his duty to register a solemn protest. The general impression left by the book would be 'imperfect, partial, and erroneous',[33] owing to its 'false philosophy and the inaccurate descriptions'.[34] How could a sensible man like John Barton be so utterly ignorant of political economy? Inasmuch as he was an honest, intelligent man, why had he saved nothing when times were good? How could the author say that the masters suffered less than the men in bad times? Or if they did, was this not because they had providently put something aside in good times? In fact,[35]

> Not only is the employment of the factory population generally constant and regular, their wages also have long been, and doubtless will soon again be, comparatively very high. The wages of men in most such establishments vary from 10s. to 40s., and those of girls and women from 7s. to 15s. a week.

Thrift, on such wages, would be easy, but unfortunately it was uncommon. And finally, wasn't there as much poverty in the countryside as in Manchester? Why had Mrs Gaskell said nothing about the hospitals and infirmaries built out of middle-class charity? Passing over this in silence merely flattered the prejudices of the landed gentry, and inflamed the populace.

It would be hard to find a more complete misrepresentation of the sense, purport, and merits of *Mary Barton*. Greg's blindness is only explicable as a class instinct. His protest offers singular confirmation of the deep impression that contemporaries claimed the novel made upon them.

'North and South'

Six years separate the publication of *Mary Barton* and *North and South* (1854–5). In the interval the continental upheaval of 1848 had shaken the social order, and the resultant reaction had established it more firmly than ever. The tone of philanthropic literature after 1850 was different from what it had been before. A new timidity inhibited the most whole-hearted supporters of intervention. The revolution in Paris had impressed itself on people's minds; they felt vaguely that moderation was necessary since excesses had been committed, and their reforming intentions were directed towards prudent solutions by a more or less conscious fear of starting something that might get out of hand. Mrs Gaskell too shared this general tendency. Or perhaps it should be said that the development of her thought led her to correct what over the years she came to see, as did other idealists, as the intransigence of her earlier beliefs. In the end she was hurt by the accusations of bias her critics threw at her. Moreover *North and South*, structurally, is to *Mary Barton* as *Coningsby* is to *Sybil*: there is a similar change in the social basis: we are concerned with employers rather than workers, and from a vantage point among the middle classes, only see the proletariat from the outside. This changed point of view inevitably gave Mrs Gaskell a new perception of the problems. The tone of the book also led to a softening of *Mary Barton*'s impassioned eloquence. Nevertheless the new book, like the old one, demonstrates her familiarity with the workers. Some scenes take us into weavers' homes, and the general feeling is close to the interventionism recommended in *Mary Barton*.

In *North and South* the industrial question is no longer the whole of the novel. Manchester – renamed Milton in the book – stands for the industrialised, despoiled areas which, in turn, become one of the two poles on which England turns. The opposition is between the old and the new forms of civilisation, rather than merely capital and labour. The slow-moving agricultural South, pastorally idyllic, is contrasted with the feverish energy and tough austerity of the North. This profound contrast was, for the future, to be an essential part of English life and a fertile theme for moral, economic, and artistic consideration. It was quite an achievement on Mrs Gaskell's part to have grasped this clearly so soon, and to have characterised decisively some aspects, at least, of the question. Disraeli had gestured towards it in *Sybil*: the nation of the rich, by and large, live in the aristocratic South, and the reader is taken north to find the nation of the poor. But geography and economics did not tally precisely: the agricultural proletariat formed a 'Northern' enclave in Disraeli's South. He was, after all, primarily concerned with social opposition, to which he subordinated little picturesque effects. Mrs Gaskell, on the other hand, used her sensibilities to establish contrasts. Her imagination and senses could perceive the theoretical boundary dividing the green sunlit fields, where grey church towers rose behind aged oaks, and poets had idealised peasant poverty, from the noisy, smoky blackened cities, where the crowds moved gloomily between ugly little houses. Mrs Gaskell put a little of her own feeling into drawing the contrast. Her childhood and youth in Knutsford, and schooldays in Stratford, had given her a deep attachment to the splendid beauty of the English countryside. When she was abruptly uprooted she was only conscious of the full horror of Manchester, though as she became more accustomed to it she was won over by the affections and sympathy of the North. The personal note in *North and South* arises from this, as does the true feeling for modern England's economic dualism, which is so well conveyed.[36]

Industrial civilisation had a certain grandeur and beauty. It shared the solid merits of the men who had built it: dogged energy and initiative. If its environment was joyless, its capacity for human passion ran strong and deep. If the social setting seemed drab and utilitarian, the class struggle was savage, and there was room for huge improvement through education. It was a harsh, unyielding soil, but it might bring forth fruits of peace and justice when tilled by gentle intelligence and religious or humanitarian missions. The proud and worldly London merchants and southern squires who dismissed Northern manufacturers as 'tradesmen' were making a grave mistake, as were the cultivated university-educated humanists, like Mr Bell the tutor, who detested the iron qualities of the steam age. Manchester's barbarism should be seen as the birth-pangs of a new civilisation in which Northern energy and Southern grace would be harmoniously united.

Here, as in Disraeli, a marriage symbolises the social reconciliation. Margaret Hale is the daughter of an Anglican parson in Hampshire. She is a gentle, sensitive beauty, with aristocratic good looks, but also a proud spirit and headstrong will. (Mrs Gaskell had no wish to give the North exclusive rights to character.) From her childhood she has loved the simple poetry of country life. Her heart goes out to ruined cottages as she draws them. She has not escaped the prejudices of her background: she condemns the spirit of commerce without knowing anything about it, and dismisses the work of the industrial bourgeoisie as all being selfishly motivated. And then her father gives up his parish, from religious scruples. He goes to live in Milton, in the heart of the industrial area. At first Margaret is made utterly miserable by the move. The city is ugly; the populace crude; and the upper classes blunt, opinionated, and narrow-minded. A manufacturer called Thornton comes to know the family better and better. At first he affronts Margaret's delicacy with his harsh manner, but she is compelled to respect his vehement independence. And after their hostile meeting, the two end in unity, by a slow progress whose minute stages are traced by Mrs Gaskell. Each yields a little intransigence. Thornton's association with the Hales makes him more gracious and cultivated. Margaret penetrates the dry, abrasive surface of the North, and finds the deep affections underneath. When she has been orphaned and enriched by a legacy, she sends for Thornton, who is threatened with bankruptcy as his business has been going badly. Will he accept a loan? And as the manufacturer, trembling with emotion, wishes to kneel before her, she rests her lovely head on his strong shoulder.

That is the main plot of *North and South*. It casts an interesting light on the differences between Northerners and Southerners, and is even finer as a psychological study in contrasting personalities. The moral drama, too, has a severe, powerful beauty. Mrs Gaskell evinces great skill in handling her characters' interior lives, in the scenes where old Mr Hale announces his cruel decision to his family, or where Margaret, in the midst of her daily tasks, reflects on her capacity for self-denial.[37] But from our point of view, greater interest attaches to a sub-plot devoted to the problem of industry. The author found it easy to link the two narratives. The second, like the first, is built around the contrast between North and South, and Margaret Hale's influence converts Thornton to philanthropy. The manufacturer's faults, from the standpoint of that Christian kindness which ought to govern social relations, are similar to his cultural inadequacies, from the standpoint of superior cultivation. Once again the employer's failings are pride, severity, and want of feeling. His work-people look upon him as[38]

> what the Bible calls a 'hard man' – not so much unjust as unfeeling; clear in judgement, standing upon his 'rights' as no human being ought to stand, considering what we and all our petty rights are in the sight of the Almighty.

Like Carson, Thornton is a self-made man. His father died bankrupt, leaving him debts which he paid off by determined work. His mother, whose nature is as indefatigable and indomitable as his own, helped him along the road to success with stern affection. He has worked on, absorbed in his daily tasks, his attention directed to the ambition which had become the focal point of his life: to win and maintain an honourable place among Britain's industrialists. Wealth is not an end in itself for him; only a means of gaining authority and social standing. He is proud of his factory, where the latest machinery is in use: 'There is not such another factory in Milton. One room alone is two hundred and twenty square yards.'[39] But his struggle has cut him off from any understanding of hardship. He is hard on the weak, and is too strong-willed to make any allowance for their weakness. He generalises from his own experience, and puts unbounded faith in the power of hard work and individual independence. 'It is one of the great beauties of our system, that a working-man may raise himself into the power and position of a master by his own exertions and behaviour.'[40] He is implacably opposed to restrictive legislation, and refuses to interfere in the lives of his workers: his ideas of justice come into conflict with charity itself. He is a bitter enemy of trade unions: 'Upon my word, mother, I wish the old combination laws were in force.'[41] He is the epitome of individualism's finest virtues, and worst excesses.

The industrial drama is similar to that in *Mary Barton*. Misunderstandings between the classes lead to a strike, and all the violence associated with it. Under pressure of competition from America the owners cut wages, although their own prosperity seems undiminished. Mrs Gaskell argues that the action was justified, but they should at least have explained it. Thornton refuses arrogantly: 'Do you give your servants reasons for your expenditure, or your economy in the use of your own money? We, the owners of capital, have a right to choose what we will do with it.'[42] As the strike goes on, he brings in starving men from Ireland, ready to undertake any work whatsoever.[43] The workers immediately rise in protest. They have been worn down, and their morale is slipping as a result of their long patient strike. At home their wives and children are weeping with hunger, and now it seems that their last hope has been brutally overthrown, and the victory for which they have suffered so much will be taken from them. A maddened crowd storms the factory, breaks down the gates, and threatens to kill the Irish. Thornton defies them, standing on the steps of his house with folded arms while they hurl stones at him. His life is in danger, until Margaret throws herself before him to shield him with her body, and the rioters' hesitation is turned to flight when armed troops arrive. Soon the strike is over, and Thornton seems to have won outright. But he has been shaken by the challenge thrown at him by Margaret during the riot:[44]

> 'Mr. Thornton,' said Margaret, shaking all over with her passion, 'go down this instant, if you are not a coward. Go down and face them like a man. Save these poor strangers whom you have decoyed here. Speak to your workmen as if they were human beings. Speak to them kindly. Don't let the soldiers come in and cut down poor creatures who are driven mad.'

For a long time, he is troubled by the implications of this reproach. And his heart has been softened by love, so that he can accept the value of charity which he has never thought about before. He learns that one of the ringleaders of the strike has been turned away from work everywhere, and has drowned himself. So when old Higgins, the trade unionist, comes to ask for work, and meets his reproof with a resolute defence of working-class solidarity, he 'forgets entirely the mere reasonings of justice, and overleaps them by a diviner instinct.'[45] A man-to-man sympathy grows up between master and worker, and gradually Thornton becomes involved with the lives of fellow-creatures whom he previously chose to ignore. We see him, rather hesitantly, help them in organising a co-operative dining-room. And we hear him expounding new ideas which echo Carlyle:[46]

> 'My only wish is to have the opportunity of cultivating some intercourse with the hands beyond the mere 'cash nexus'. . . .
> 'I have arrived at the conviction that no mere institutions, however wise, and however much thought may have been required to organize and arrange them, can attach class to class as they should be attached, unless the working out of such institutions bring the individuals of the different classes into actual personal contact. Such intercourse is the very breath of life.'

Margaret has come to know Nicholas Higgins. We follow her to the bedside of his daughter Bessy, who has contracted consumption as a result of long hours in the factory:[47]

> 'I think I was well when mother died, but I have never been rightly strong sin' somewhere about that time. I began to work in a carding-room soon after, and the fluff got into my lungs and poisoned me.'
> 'Fluff?' said Margaret inquiringly.
> 'Fluff,' repeated Bessy. 'Little bits, as fly off fro' the cotton, when they're carding it, and fill the air till it looks all fine white dust. They

say it winds round the lungs, and tightens them up. Anyhow, there's many a one as works in a carding-room, that falls into a waste, coughing and spitting blood, because they're just poisoned by the fluff.'

'But can't it be helped?' asked Margaret.

'I dunno. Some folk have a great wheel at one end o' their carding-rooms to make a draught, and carry off th' dust; but that wheel costs a deal of money – five or six hundred pound, maybe, and brings in no profit: so it's but few of th' masters as will put 'em up: and I've heard tell o' men who didn't like working in places where there was a wheel, because they said as how it made 'em hungry, as after they'd been long used to swallowing fluff, to go without it, and that their wage ought to be raised if they were to work in such places. So between masters and men th' wheels fall through. I know I wish there'd been a wheel in our place, though.'

She has never seen the countryside:[48]

'When I have gone for an out, I've always wanted to get high up and see far away, and take a deep breath o' fullness in that air. I get smothered enough in Milton, and I think the sound yo' speak of among the trees, going on for ever and ever, would send me dazed; it's that made my head ache so in the mill.'

When Bessy dies, Margaret, on a kindly impulse, takes Higgins to meet her father, and the old pastor finds himself confronted with a working-class atheist. Higgins has the same blunt, sensible directness and simplicity as John Barton, with more good humour, and less bitterness. He tells the decent, honest, middle-class folk around him of his life and his feelings, and although Mrs Gaskell intends that their religious faith should emerge comfortably superior to his unbelief, she allows him some shrewd hits: 'If salvation, and life to come, and what not, was true – not in men's words, but in men's hearts' core – dun yo' think they'd din us wi' it as they do wi' political 'conomy?'[49]

Mrs Gaskell appealed to her readers with sober, truthful realism. Her characters were convincing, individual human beings. The reader was made to feel that he was meeting people from another class on an intimate footing. As he heard them he came to understand their joys and sorrows, and the justice of their inarticulate complaints was made crystal clear. *North and South*, moreover, was even more likely than *Mary Barton* to encourage every well-intentioned individual without affronting anyone. Its more cautious didacticism could only add to its effectiveness.[50]

Charlotte Brontë: 'Shirley'

In the sense in which we have been using the term, Charlotte Brontë never wrote a social novel. *Shirley* is not overtly intended to stimulate or resolve class tension. It is a lyrical love story, and a splendid study of finely-observed manners. Its only purpose, if indeed it has one at all, is to protest, as Jane Eyre had done, against the prudish hypocrisy of a society which forbade the free expression of passion. Nevertheless it is of interest to the historian. It describes scenes which make a valuable contribution to industrial history, and it is in itself a symptom of the moral movement of which *Mary Barton* was the most striking outcome.

We shall not attempt to outline Charlotte Brontë's life here: the recollection of one biographical source for *Shirley* will suffice. When Charlotte went to Roehead in 1831, she found that people there had vivid memories of the workers' riots against the introduction of steam in the textile industry. She was fifteen years old at the time – she was born in 1816 – and her lively imagination was strongly impressed by what she heard. She associated tragic incidents in the Luddite riots with the places where they had occurred, and created a faithful picture of both in *Shirley*. After the success of *Jane Eyre* she was famous, but in her new book she tried to follow G. H. Lewes's advice and eschew melodrama, taking Jane Austen's psychological realism as a model. In this frame of mind she wrote *Shirley*: her book was set in the West Riding in the years before Waterloo, and dealt with revolutionary workers smashing machinery because she wanted to write a realistic novel, and remembered Roehead.

It should be added that the social movement of the time, culminating n 1848, was not without influence. The industrial question had stirred men's hearts, and the new philanthropy had unsuspected friends in the depths of the countryside. Charlotte Brontë's life in the wild and desolate setting of Haworth, by the little church in whose cemetery her two sisters lay, was solitary. The only events to take place arose in her mind. And so she could share in the great wave of social conscience which was spreading out from the urban bourgeoisie to the most far-flung corners of society. The action of *Shirley* is set in the past, and it has only sporadic scenes of industrial life, but still it cannot be overlooked. It evinces an instinctive, almost unconscious, Christian concern, akin to the best feelings represented by the best of Mrs Gaskell. There is a social message of some power in *Shirley*.

This side of *Shirley* is strikingly similar to *North and South*: in each, a young girl's influence softens the harsh, driving energy of a manufac-turer.[51] Robert Moore bears a family resemblance to Carson and Thornton: he is related to the stern, hard-working industrialists to be found in Dickens, whose close similarity to each other is evidence of a decided opinion of the industrial personality in their creator's mind, and thus constitutes a psychological document of the first importance. Of course Charlotte Brontë has given a personal twist to the common model. There is something romantic about Moore: his pride and obstinacy just stray over the border from realism. And Charlotte Brontë gives her heroine, Caroline Helstone, more gentle, feminine grace than Margaret Hale. Otherwise the plot is the same. Robert only recognises his rights, and pursues his own interests. He is a bold, enterprising man, and rejects the old-fashioned installations in the mill he has just bought. He insists on improved power looms which increase output and cut down on labour. He is quite determined to have them, and dismisses the complaints of workers who are made redundant with disdainful confidence in the legality of his own indifference:[52]

> He did not sufficiently care when the new inventions threw the old workpeople out of employ: he never asked himself where those to whom he no longer paid weekly wages found daily bread; and in this negligence he only resembled thousands besides, on whom the starving poor of Yorkshire seemed to have a closer claim.

Here is how he answers a workers' deputation:[53]

> 'I'll make my cloth as I please, and according to the best lights I have. In its manufacture I will employ what means I choose. Whoever, after hearing this, shall dare to interfere with me, may just take the consequences. An example shall prove I'm in earnest.'

Moore comes up against resistance from the Yorkshire workers, who are themselves bigoted in their opposition to machinery. He is given a warning, and then the wagons bringing his long-awaited machines to the mill are ambushed. The machines are smashed, and a note pinned to a horse's harness tells Moore what has happened:[54]

> 'Your hellish machinery is shivered to smash on Stilbro' Moor, and your men are lying bound hand and foot in a ditch by the roadside. Take this as a warning from men that are starving, and have starving wives and children to go home to when they have done this deed. If you get new machines, or if you otherwise go on as you have done, you shall hear from us again. Beware!'

Moore is even more impervious to threats than he was to pleas. The damage is repaired, and the master's will carried out. But then the disturbances grow widespread. Armed bands roam across the industrial areas, pillaging and burning the mills. One spring night finds Caroline Helstone and her friend Shirley sitting up in the vicarage. They are listening, with their nerves on edge, until they hear the heavy tramp of marching feet. A few minutes later a volley of stones breaks the factory windows. The yard gates are forced, and the fiercest cry in the world goes up:[55]

> a rioters' yell – a North-of-England – a Yorkshire – a West-Riding – a West-Riding–clothing–district–of–Yorkshire rioters' yell. You never heard that sound, perhaps, reader? So much the better for your ears – perhaps for your heart; since, if it rends the air in hate to yourself, or to the men or principles you approve, the interests to which you wish well, Wrath wakens to the cry of Hate:...Caste stands up ireful against Caste; and the indignant, wronged spirit of the Middle Rank bears down in zeal and scorn on the famished and furious mass of the Operative class. It is difficult to be tolerant – difficult to be just – in such moments.

Moore is armed. He was prepared for the attack, and has sent for soldiers. A volley of musketry meets the rioters. After a moment of furious rage they scatter, leaving one of their number dead and several injured. Moore pursues the leaders of the conspiracy with determination, and has four of them arrested and sentenced to transportation. A few months later he is seriously injured by a pistol shot fired at him from behind a wall while he is travelling across country. Such incidents were common at the time; Charlotte Brontë had heard of several similar ones at Roehead.[56]

Suffering, and a long convalescence, break the hero's proud will. Every day Caroline Helstone's soft, gentle voice gains more power over him. For a long time she has been trying to humanise her 'Coriolanus', as she calls him:[57]

> 'You must not be proud to your workpeople; you must not neglect chances of soothing them, and you must not be of an inflexible nature, uttering a request as austerely as if it were a command. . . .
>
> 'I cannot help thinking it unjust to include all poor working people under the general and insulting name of "the mob", and continually to think of them and treat them haughtily.'

In the end, Moore is transformed. As he makes his plans for the future, and imagines what expanding industry may do for the fertile valley where his mill is situated, he envisages new towns and villages, busy roads, and heaps of ash and cinders; but also charitable works through which man can improve his environment. Moore will give work to the hungry and homeless, and let cottages to them cheaply. For their first week in his employ he will hand out food to them free of charge. There will be evening classes and a Sunday school to teach them, and every quarter the master will give his men a treat.

There is nothing more to say about Charlotte Brontë. She did not believe that the evils of industrialism were remediable:[58]

> As to the sufferers, whose sole inheritance was labour, and who had lost that inheritance – who could not get work, and consequently could not get wages, and consequently could not get bread – they were left to suffer on; perhaps inevitably left.

She was not in search of cheap literary effects, although she chose to write about a period when the very worst excesses of industrialism were unchecked; villainous characters were beyond her scope: 'Child-torturers, slave masters and drivers, I consign to the hands of jailers; the novelist may be excused from sullying his page with the record of their deeds.'[59] And so she makes no great declarations of principle, but seeks to ease the strained relations between the classes with a spirit of tenderness. Man does have a humane and religious duty to care for his brother's affairs. Christianity has not quite crystallised into social policy here, as it did in Mrs Gaskell. But Charlotte Brontë, the parson's daughter, is none the less a good example of the frame of mind from which Christian socialism developed.[60]

Mrs Trollope: 'Michael Armstrong'

In 1857 'Alfred' (Samuel Kydd) enumerated the works of literature which had served the cause in his *History of the Factory Movement* and remarked, 'Mrs. Trollope's novel *Michael Armstrong* has been much abused; it has, however, been useful, and so, also, has *Helen Fleetwood*, by Charlotte Elizabeth.'[61] That is almost the only reference made by any social historian to two books that were successful and influential in their day. Today they are completely forgotten, but the evidence of 'Alfred' testifies to their historical interest.

It is quite clear why *Michael Armstrong* came under attack; all Mrs Trollope's novels were abused in the same way. One contemporary critic lashed 'her constitutional coarseness' as the 'natural element of a low popularity', and said, 'We have heard it urged on behalf of Mrs. Trollope, that her novels are, at all events, drawn from life. So are sign-paintings.'[62] Yet the writer who underwent such heavy criticism was well known between 1830 and 1850. A few titles from her enormous output may surface in scholars' memories today,[63] but in her own time she was simply accepted as a follower of Dickens. *The Widow Barnaby* (1838), a comedy of domestic manners inspired by the *Sketches* and *Pickwick*, had a considerable success. Mrs Trollope made Dickens's acquaintance in the same year. In 1839 she announced her intention of writing an industrial novel.[64] It is evident that Dickens influenced her decision; *Oliver Twist* was then at the height of its vogue, and social feeling was focused on the martyred child as a representative of the working class. The hero of *Michael Armstrong* is another little boy.

On 20 February 1839 Mrs Trollope took a railway train for the second time in her life and, like Dickens, went to see Manchester for herself.[65] She took with her letters of introduction from Lord Ashley, who was interested in her project.[66]

> She spared no pains to acquaint herself with the real conditions of the people she intended writing about, and, with her son, visited many scenes of pitiable wretchedness and revolting squalor. Her investigations indeed needed a stout heart and a healthy frame to carry them out.

Michael Armstrong appeared in 1840. In spite of the humanitarian courage her biographer detected in it, Mrs Trollope seems anything but a likely moulder of public opinion. Not only did she observe nothing but the obvious faults on her visit to Manchester, but she described them in ways that made them unconvincing. The book is well-meaning, inflated, and bad. The story is a clumsy imitation of Dickens. Michael Armstrong, the little 'piecer', is adopted by the rich industrialist Sir Matthew Dowling when it suits his book to make a large gesture of public benevolence. Sir Matthew's behaviour and his upper-class associates have all the artificiality to be found in Dickens's aristocratic characters. The scenes of industrial life are made unconvincing by exaggeration.[67] The slum where Michael's widowed mother lives is described with calculated and self-conscious literary devices: the ultimate effect is to disgust the reader instead of evoking his pity. Sir Matthew is overtaken by melodramatic justice at the end when, ruined and delirious, he thinks he sees the bodies of all the victims who have died in his factories: 'There's a dead body walking about the room!...He is come for me! and I must go!...One? No!—it is not one, it is five hundred!—Take them!—take them away from me, I tell you!'[68] In keeping with this sort of morality and artistry, Michael Armstrong grows into a handsome young man, and marries an heiress.

The book is written in a spirit of vehement hostility to the industrial bourgeoisie, of which Sir Matthew, a parvenu whose title has only recently been granted, is a member. He and his friends Dr Crockley and Elgood Sharpton, the economist, cynically announce their villainous radicalism. The campaign against the Corn Laws is a gigantic hoax whose true aim is to lower wages. And the trio are carried away by visions of wealth. When Free Trade has been established, rivers of gold will flow into their coffers, and they will rule the world. France will become England's wine-cellar, and Russia her corn-bin. America will be one vast cotton plantation from east to west. 'England will become the paradise of manufacturers! – the great workshop of the world.'[69] It is a grotesque, demon-king caricature, following methods often used by Dickens, but without his poetic imagination, wit, or genius.

None the less, it is of some interest. *Michael Armstrong* shows the extremes to which some, at least, of the public were prepared to push the attack on the new bourgeoisie. It contains some curious evidence of the coarse manners of the period. Sir Matthew, for all his title and his pretensions to gentility, is as brutal as Bounderby. The scene at his family table, where he throws half a pigeon at little Michael's head, guffawing the while at his tasteless joke, gives one pause. That such behaviour could be accepted as feasible tells us a great deal about the culture of industrial society, or at least the general view of it.

If the book lacked persuasive power, how could it have had any influence? Mrs Trollope herself made a confession which throws light on the praise of 'Alfred': shortly after the book was published she wrote to a friend: 'The *Widow* continues to be in great favour. But between ourselves, I don't think any one cares much for *Michael Armstrong* – except the Chartists. A new kind of patrons for me!'[70] The book succeeded with people who already believed that industrial legislation was essential. But it had no influence with the great upper-middle-class reading public which most interests us. *Michael Armstrong* was without question one of the least effective social novels, as it was one of the worst.[71]

Charlotte Elizabeth: 'Helen Fleetwood'

The tone of *Helen Fleetwood* is utterly different. Mrs Trollope's empty flourishes and surface pathos give way to deeply sincere and weighty seriousness. The lady who wrote under the pseudonym of Charlotte Elizabeth was a second Miss Martineau, with the same polemical vigour and narrow Evangelicalism. But her inner passion was a matter of sentiment, rather than will and intellect. And she encouraged the opposite kind of social policy.

Charlotte Elizabeth was born in 1790, the daughter of the Reverend

Michael Browne, a Norwich clergyman.[72] Her family were strong Tories. In 1821, shortly after she had married unhappily, she left her husband, Captain Phelan. She led a retired life, first in Sandhurst, then in London, and occupied herself with literary and philanthropic work. Like Miss Martineau, she made her literary début in the field of religious controversy. She had been with her husband to Dublin, where she came to love the Irish character, but hate Roman Catholicism. Her first writings were directed against the Roman Catholic Church. She was something of a mystic, feeling herself to be perpetually in God's presence. In Ireland she underwent a conversion in which she felt that she was born again in Jesus Christ. Her philanthropy was first and foremost religious. She adopted a backward dumb boy whom she brought up with admirable kindliness. But she could never succeed in conveying a concrete image of God to him, until she hit on the stratagem of blowing a bellows over his face, and explaining that God was like the wind: always near, but invisible. The poverty and squalor of St Giles's, the notorious Irish colony in London, struck home to her. She proposed building an Anglican church as a remedy, and by steadfast patience succeeded in seeing this plan realised. She was still a devout churchwoman, albeit on the puritan and Evangelical wing of the Church of England: in 1841 she wrote a violent attack upon the Oxford Movement in the *Protestant Magazine*. She felt strongly about the persecution of the Jews, and when the Czar visited England in 1844 she sent him a memorandum on behalf of his Jewish subjects. According to her biographer, 'Her impulsive enthusiastic character would have been to her a great trial and temptation, if she had not been always in the habit of going to the Scriptures for direction.'[73]

This passionate puritan felt that she ought to write a plea for industrial legislation in the form of a work of fiction. Her ideas were far from revolutionary: we have seen her opinion of socialism.[74] She declared, according to Mrs Balfour, that it was essential to educate the least depressed section of the working classes, for the most dangerous agents of Chartism and other subversive beliefs were recruited from this group. *Helen Fleetwood* is written in this spirit.

The Greens – honest, pious, respectable folk – live in the country near the sea. They are part farmers, part fisherfolk, and they are happy and healthy. Little Helen Fleetwood, an orphan they have adopted, is equally edifying. But poverty comes to the home when the father dies. Cold, hard, middle-class public assistance inspectors pack them off to the city to get rid of them. They find there, as they have been promised, higher wages. But they also find the wretched poverty and degradation of industrial life. This is depicted conscientiously, accurately, and boringly.

The author assures us that she has invented nothing; all her facts are taken from official documents. It is easy to believe her. The book is a dissertation, not a work of art; a treatise in Christian apologetics, with Satan taking the shape of a manufacturer. Biblical and prophetic echoes abound:[75]

> On the system, the vile, the cruel, the body and soul-murdering system of factory labour, we cannot charge the innate depravity of the human heart; but we do denounce it as being in itself a foul fruit of that depravity under its hateful form of covetousness, and of being in turn the prolific root of every ill that can unhumanize man, and render an enlightened Christian country the mark of God's most just and holy indignation.

But we must not be misled by these violent words: the widow Green is forever mouthing the platitude 'We must do our duty in the station to which it has pleased God to call us.'

In the long run, however, *Helen Fleetwood* is moving and persuasive. The force of truth and genuine indignation compensate for the lack of artistic talent and save the book. The dogged determination of the attack produces the same final result as skill. The factual precision of the laborious minutiae described compels conviction. Cotton manufacture is described in detail, with careful accounts of the peculiar duties and strains of every kind of worker – spinner, piecer, or scavenger.[76] The loopholes in the Factory Act of 1834, and the measures used to evade it, are exhaustively exposed. One inspector, with a staff of four, is responsible for no less than five counties and half of Yorkshire, embracing a total of 1,800 mills. Their powers are too limited for effective control. A sub-inspector has to have permission from the owner to visit a mill. Any breach of the regulations must be brought to court within fourteen days, or the charge automatically lapses.[77]

Magistrates are shown as the natural allies of manufacturers, and impose derisory fines on any who actually are brought before them. The factory-owner lives in a parade of luxury: his home is ornamented with rare furniture and exotic plants in hothouses. But he is arrogant and severe with old Mrs Green, and bears an unmistakable likeness to Mrs Gaskell's more finely-observed specimens. And everywhere there is the all-pervasive power of Charlotte Elizabeth's narrow but decided religious conviction. Channelled into social paths, this sweeps away all obstacles and overcomes her natural middle-class caution, issuing in trumpet-toned denunciations. The 'free' contract of labour is sheer hypocrisy in Charlotte Elizabeth's eyes:[78]

Voluntarily! – No, it is not a voluntary act. You well know that the cravings of nature must be satisfied; and though your poverty-stricken brother asks no more than the dry morsel from which your pampered dog would turn away, still without that morsel he cannot exist.

It is the Bible which decrees brotherhood as a duty; the Bible, which the industrialist purports to read, but which still condemns him. The theme of 'white slaves' is eloquently developed.[79] Some passages are reminiscent of Engels at his most violent.[80]

Helen Fleetwood, with its mediocre literary quality, is significant. It shows the devout, Bible-reading, middle-class outlook which was the backbone of bourgeois England reacting against the works of its own class and its own practical genius. It is a book meant to be read slowly, so that it may lead to serious reflection culminating in lasting indignation. And this was exactly the way in which the bourgeoisie made up its worthy, weighty mind about things. The novel is addressed to a public accustomed to religious controversy and theological discussion; a public with a passion for accurate facts and concrete arguments. Such a public would most easily be won over by a novel evincing the minimum of artistry. Harriet Beecher Stowe, the author of *Uncle Tom's Cabin*, thought that Charlotte Elizabeth's pictures of industrial life were just what such scenes ought to be, and recognised that she knew remarkably well how to influence public opinion.[81] She taught without shocking, and described the horrors of evil without making the flesh creep. The pious, prudish, middle-class Englishwoman would have accepted this American judgement.

And so, once again, social conscience bounded on Christian intervention. It is of particular interest to note that the author wanted the Church to throw itself into the struggle, and believed that the clergy ought to wage war on industrial impiety: 'Any subject in which the glory of God and the welfare of the poor in the land were concerned, was perfectly and especially suited to the interest of a minister of the Gospel.'[82] The cautious indignation of a lady novelist conceived of the cleric as social reformer. Kingsley and his friends made clerical social work one of the main planks of the Christian socialist platform.

Eight

Kingsley: Christian socialism

Kingsley and his friends arrived at a final definition of Christian socialism around 1848. This group of clergymen and idealists extended social conscience to the point where it almost joined forces with revolutionary theory. Of course the unity was mainly a matter of words: their ideas never went as far as their rhetoric, and Kingsley at his boldest was always closer to philanthropic interventionism than Owenite socialism. Yet the combination of the words 'Christian' and 'socialist' was highly significant. It seemed the natural conclusion of all that had gone before, and led to an interesting sequence of events.

The novel had previously been used to expound Dickens's social sentiment, Disraeli's political romanticism, and Mrs Gaskell's protest against industrial *laissez-faire*. Now it was to be pressed into service as a propaganda vehicle again, on behalf of Christian socialism. *Yeast* and *Alton Locke* are the last and most informative of the books we are considering.[1] In them, a gifted writer gives a definitive view of the most vital aims and ideals of his time, under the guise of fiction.

The man

Charles Kingsley was born in 1819, at Holne Rectory in Devonshire, the son of a clergyman who was descended from an old country middle-class family.[2] His mother was the daughter of a Barbados magistrate, and had all the passion and imagination of a Caribbean upbringing. Heredity is often difficult to trace, but in Kingsley it is quite straightforward: he was an obvious mixture of squire and poet, from his father and mother respectively. In his plans for social reform the position of the 'gentry' was always carefully maintained, yet more than any other social novelist except Dickens, he was utterly remote from the rational cast of mind dominating intellectual circles. His supple, enthusiastic personality was permanently marked by every influence brought to bear upon it: not that he underwent any radical, traumatic experience: simply his parents and his upbringing remained reflected in his character. The biggest influence on him after them came from the places he lived in. He went with his father to Barnack in Northamptonshire, and came to love the melancholy, delicate charm of the fenlands, stretching out, flat and bare, to the north of Cambridge. Then, when his father became rector of Clovelly in 1830, he scrambled over the rocks, and loved the combination of grassy cliffs and sea, with the smell of seaweed. Before he knew anything about overwork and fatigue, he had acquired from fishermen an ideal of healthy, hardy manhood, such as he gave to the heroes of his books. He also learned from them how to get on with common people. He acquired an easy, sympathetic manner with simple folk, and learned how to adapt himself to others quickly. Later in life he was to be the most popular of all the Christian socialists when it came to addressing workers' meetings, and he had some personal influence over certain Chartists. In the end, Clovelly determined the principal features of his social thought. The rich outdoor life he led there ripened into a full enjoyment of sensory pleasure. His life and writings were always marked by exuberant, fiery animal vigour. He was keen on sports, and loved fresh air and running water. He went for long walks through sunshine and rain, and submitted to the buffeting of the elements happily. And so he was keenly alive to the physical horror of poverty. The sights and smells of urban life and the whole flavour of the proletariat's physical sufferings exercised a morbid fascination over him. The slum was, for him, the central social evil. His mission was to attack the insanitary living conditions of the poor: he was above all else a crusader for social hygiene.

He was remarkably precocious. At four he preached his first sermon. Before he was five he wrote his first poem. A religious upbringing, an instinct for poetry, a capacity for imitation, and a versatile temperament were thus early evinced. This last was to be a source of weakness as well as strength to him. From his earliest years he was attracted to the natural sciences, which he loved more as an artist than a scholar. At seventeen he came to London. His father was rector of Chelsea, and he followed the non-resident course at King's College. In 1838 he was placed on the books of Magdalene College, Cambridge. There he remained for the most fruitful four years of his youth. At this time he suffered from religious doubts; his intelligence revolted at the doctrine of the Trinity, and the Athanasian creed seemed to him 'bigotry, cruelty, and quibbling'.[3] Like Wordsworth, but more strongly, he felt the divine intuition he had gained from nature receding: the ecstasies of his childhood were being blotted out, and only the material world remained – striking and varied, but superficial.[4] Then another profound inner experience replaced the intoxication of pantheism in nature; in 1839 he met the young girl who was to become his wife. She introduced him to the idealist movement and the writings of Coleridge and Carlyle. Under their schooling his doubts disappeared. The gospel of work and intuitive religion swept away his mental uncertainties.

As we have seen, Cambridge, like Oxford, was a centre of religious revival. If from an early stage Kingsley was instinctively opposed to Catholic ideas, and declared his hostility to Newman and Pusey, he was profoundly influenced by their great rival, Frederick Denison Maurice.[5] This remarkable man was closely associated with Kingsley. His influence was general; he was better at throwing out ideas than examining any in detail. Like his master, Coleridge, Maurice did not put the best of himself into his books. Born in 1805, he was fourteen years older than Kingsley, and dominated him particularly because of his mature intellect. He spotted the incompatibility of classical economics with social ethics very early. His *Kingdom of Christ* (1842) carried on Coleridge's attempt to make religion rational, or rather, rationalism religious.[6] Kingsley accepted Maurice's theological ideas, which were based on the doctrine of the Incarnation. Jesus, the Logos of Greek philosophy, the Word of God, was made man. Thus he raised not only the human soul, but the whole body, to a new dignity. Human society and civilisation were of value in themselves, and their development was subject to the guidance of God. 'God has a plan for the world...it means that the policy of the cynic and the social agnostic is not only not true, but is a gross blasphemy against God's purpose for humanity...there *is* a Christian ideal for society.'[7]

Early in 1844 the two men established friendly relations. From then on their development was parallel. Kingsley's social ideas never went a step beyond Maurice's, although they were modified by the fire of his poetic temperament. He was well aware of his debt: 'I owe all that I am to Maurice....I aim only to teach to others what I get from him....I live to interpret him to the people of England.'[8]

He was overpoweringly drawn to work. In July 1842 he was ordained, and settled in Eversley in Hampshire. He stayed there for thirty-three years, first as curate, and then as rector from 1844, in which year he married. He was a model minister, and declared war on poverty and vice. With joyous, energetic fury he fought the local people's drunkenness and idleness and their habit of smuggling. At the same time he battled with Sir John Cope, the local old-fashioned fox-hunting squire, opposing his hostility and negligence, and total imperviousness to any notion of social duty.[9] He was always out travelling the countryside and visiting cottages, where he learned in detail the sufferings of the agricultural proletariat. He established the same friendly relations with his parishioners as he had known with the Cornish fishermen. His strength, good humour, and love of hearty exercise made him popular. And through experience he arrived at his social creed; his ideas grew out of the first instinctive steps he took in social work. They expressed his natural pugnacity (which had already been turned into religious zeal) in a new form. The burst of courage and optimism which replaced his vanished doubts made him an enthusiastic exponent of Anglicanism. He was later to engage Newman in a celebrated polemical battle.[10] The struggle with poverty was another aspect of the struggle with erroneous beliefs:[11]

> I will never believe that a man has a real love for the good and beautiful, except he attacks the evil and the disgusting the moment he sees it. Therefore you must make up your mind to see me, with God's help, a hunter out of abuses till the abuses cease – only till then. . . . I am deep in *The Perils of the Nation.*

We have already referred to this book, in which the as yet unknown voice of Christian socialism was anticipated by many years.[12] Kingsley found in it the possibility of carrying the Christian revival into social channels, which immediately appealed to him. His temperament and his situation were both pushing him in just such a direction. But although he had the will to act, missionary zeal, a sympathetic imaginative grasp of the problem and, indeed, all the characteristics of a great interventionist champion, what did he know about facts and theories?

His first experience of social strife had been unforgettable. He was at school near Bristol during the riots of 1831 which bathed the city in blood. From a distance he saw the skies lit up by fire. On that day, he said, he received his first lesson in what would later be known as social science. A few days later he saw the blackened walls of houses, and the charred remains of victims:[13]

> What I had seen made me for years the veriest aristocrat, full of hatred and contempt of these dangerous classes, whose existence I had for the first time discovered. It required many years – years, too, of personal intercourse with the poor – to explain to me the true meaning of what I saw here in October twenty-seven years ago.

The impression this made was ineradicable: at critical moments, Kingsley's horror of riot was always liable to boil up.

On the other hand, like Dickens, he had no experience of heavy industry. In London he caught glimpses of the social classes depicted in the *Sketches by Boz.* At Eversley he investigated the conditions of agricultural workers. Like everyone else he received a general impression of industrial evils from official reports, literature, and the press. Thus in 1844 he wrote, 'The refined man to me is he who cannot rest in peace with a coal mine or a factory, or a Dorsetshire peasant's house near him, in the state in which they are.'[14] But in these formative years he never came across mass production or a modern factory. Later, again in London from 1848 to 1850, he would associate with artisans in light industries, and the classes from which Chartists were recruited: tailors, shoemakers, printers, masons, cabinet-makers, and the like would be the normal audience for meetings arranged by the Christian socialists. And this explains the close similarity between Kingsley's social outlook and Dickens's. Although he was more self-aware, better educated, and more directly involved in the social struggle than his great rival, Kingsley, like Dickens, adapted his ideas to the needs of small workshop industries. Co-operation, as he saw it, would be the craftsman's defence against big employers. His policies differed from Owen's inasmuch as their starting point was different. His novels only dealt with the problems of light industry and small farmers.

He did, however, learn from books and life of alternative theories. Whether or not he read Ricardo and Malthus, he grasped the substance of their thought from pamphlets, journals, reviews, and the determined opposition to them in sentimental literature. He had seen the new Poor Law in operation for himself, and it gave him a concrete picture of the results of *laissez-faire*. He spoke in 1844 of 'the horrid effects of that New Poor Law. . . . You must be behind the scenes to see the truth, in places which Malthus's and ––'s know nothing of.'[15] In Carlyle, on the other hand, he had found a vigorous rebuttal of individualism. 'More and more I find that these writings of Carlyle's do not lead to gloomy discontent – that theirs is not a dark but a bright view of life.'[16] On one point, it is true, he broke with Carlyle. Democracy, for Kingsley, was not merely the political version of *laissez-faire*: and in any case, it was inevitable:[17]

> My whole heart is set, not on retrogression, outward or inward, but on progression. . . . The new element is democracy, in Church and State. Waiving the question of its evil or its good, we cannot stop it. Let us Christianize it instead.

Kingsley was not a conscious participant in the reactionary aspect of the idealist movement: his novels are generous to Chartist political aspirations, and 'on at least one occasion he publicly and deliberately declared himself a Chartist – a name which then meant a great deal.'[18] His ideal of co-operation was republican in spirit. But this difference could be misleading: Kingsley had aristocratic instincts and a conservative temperament. Like Dickens, he wavered between the egalitarian ideal and a deep feeling for benevolent hierarchies.

And so Kingsley's social philosophy, with all its complexity and limitations, came into existence. It was complete by about 1845. The influence of Carlyle and Maurice had brought him among the young leaders of the sentimental reaction. He stood out in the movement for his independent personality, and a certain assertiveness which, in a way, brought him close to individualism. Kingsley never insisted that the State should play a role; political subjection always seemed to him too high a price to pay for material well-being. And he was firmly cut off from Young England: he was as suspicious of feudal socialism as he was of the Oxford Movement. And yet his adversaries were the same as Carlyle's and Disraeli's: industrial self-interest, classical economics, the spirit of commerce, and competition. And he appealed to the same allies against these common foes: the Church, the gentry, and the traditional wisdom of the workers, who knew a social superior when they saw one. In 1852 he wrote,[19]

> I have never swerved from my one idea of the last seven years, that the real battle of the time is – if England is to be saved from anarchy and unbelief, and utter exhaustion caused by the competitive enslavement of the masses – not Radical or Whig against Peelite or Tory (let the dead bury their dead), but the Church, the gentleman, and the workman, against the shopkeepers and the Manchester School.

The Church would have to participate in the struggle. Disraeli had said this from the outside: now Kingsley the parson was saying it from the inside. As a minister he automatically enlarged the role of the clergy. His first book was already the work of a Christian socialist; theological argument is curiously mixed with social teaching in it. After a few years he had found the formula for his religious position: if Evangelicalism was on one side, and Rome on the other, with bourgeois 'Mammonite' unbelief in between, then the true position was on a pinnacle above impious unbelief. It was faith in the Church of England, pure and simple, with some of the philosophical expansiveness that was the mark of the 'Broad Church'.

The Saint's Tragedy, or the True Story of Elizabeth of Hungary (1848), a social drama, was intended to illustrate this thesis. Here the religious argument is dominant, but it is interesting to note that it is suffused with social aspirations. In the middle of the play, Elizabeth appears '*without cloak or shoes, carrying an empty basket.*'[20]

Elizabeth: We sit in a cloud, and sing, like pictured angels,
And say, the world runs smooth – while right below
Welters the black fermenting heap of life
On which our state is built: I saw this day
What we might be, and still be Christian women. . . .

I will taste somewhat this same poverty –
Try these temptations, grudges, gnawing shames,
For which 'tis blamed; how probe an unfelt evil?
Would'st be the poor man's friend? Must freeze with him –
Test sleepless hunger – let thy crippled back
Ache o'er the endless furrow; how was He,
The blessed One made perfect? Why, by grief –
The fellowship of voluntary grief.

A merchant ingenuously expounds his business morality:[21]

> I get my bread by buying corn that's cheap,
> And selling where 'tis dearest. Mass, you need it,
> And you must pay according to your need.

He draws down a crushing reply from Elizabeth. Walter of Vaila, who stands for 'the "healthy animalism" of the Teutonic mind',[22] defends the rights of the poor and preaches Christian interventionism to the orthodox Malthusian Count Hugo and the utilitarian individualist Abbot.

The Saint's Tragedy is a timid preliminary draft for the novels to come. It lacks the liveliness and fierce courage which stimulated Kingsley in 1848, and animated all he wrote for the next two years.

The Christian socialists of 1850

Kingsley expressed the common ideas of a group of men in his novels. The Christian socialists were, for a time, the principal representatives of social idealism. To make sense of *Yeast* and *Alton Locke* it is necessary to know at least the general outline of the movement.

There is no need to go right back to the origins of Christian socialism; we have already seen that certain profound national characteristics were in harmony with such a doctrine, and have glanced at some of the predecessors of Maurice and Kingsley. The name 'Christian socialism' itself did not emerge until 1850: it appeared for the first time in the title of *Tracts on Christian Socialism*, published by Maurice and his friends. In justification of the title, Maurice wrote to Ludlow,[23]

Tracts on Christian Socialism is, it seems to me, the only title which will define our object, and will commit us at once to the conflict we must engage in sooner or later with the unsocial Christians and the unchristian Socialists.

This shows clearly enough the twin preoccupations out of which Christian socialism emerged. According to Ludlow, the movement started in 1848 'because from that year grew up the conviction in the minds of those who became leaders in the movement that Socialism in its essence was in agreement with Christ's Gospel, and must be made Christian.'[24] The February Revolution in France produced an almost immediate backlash in England. On 10 April the final Chartist petition was presented to Parliament. No one doubted that this widely advertised and long awaited day would prove decisive. A battle, even perhaps a revolution, seemed imminent. Kingsley followed events with mounting excitement from his rectory in Eversley. Already he had made frequent visits to London, where Maurice, now chaplain to Lincoln's Inn, received him as a friend. On the eve of the crisis he hurried to the capital.[25] His opinions and his generous enthusiasm put him in the position of moderator, and he could not rest at a distance from the struggle when it looked as though such just complaints were going to collapse in overwhelming excesses. On 10 April he tried to go to Kennington Common, which O'Connor had settled on for his rallying-point. But the bridges were guarded, and he was unable to cross the Thames. In the anxieties of that day the men who were later to work together met at Maurice's house.[26] The disaster sustained by O'Connor freed their hands by removing all threat of revolution, and they were full of ideas, which were still important, for the underlying causes of unrest remained unaltered. England was still reeling from the crisis which had shaken it, as the Continent had been shaken that year, when these men joined together, resolving to pool their ideas and energy in concerted action.

Maurice was at the centre, by virtue of his intellect and his long commitment. Since 1846 he and Ludlow had been engaged in social work around Lincoln's Inn. Close to him, alongside Kingsley, stood Charles Mansfield, Thomas Hughes, Hare, Scott, Parker and, of course, Ludlow. They decided on a peaceful campaign in the press and from the platform. Chartism had collapsed, and this was no bad thing. Violence was absolutely rejected as a means towards progress. But there had been a core of truth in Chartism. Its grievances were real: its error had lain in the way it proposed dealing with the ills of society. The people were not yet politically educated. The success of the Oxford Movement's tracts was in everybody's mind, and Hare proposed that they start a new series of pamphlets putting their point of view. Maurice was chosen as editor of *Politics for the People*.

Seventeen numbers of this journal appeared; it ran from 6 May to the end of July. Maurice's Prospectus outlined the spirit in which it was written:[27]

> Politics have been separated from household ties and affections – from art, and science, and literature. . . . Politics have been separated from Religion. They must start from Atheism, or from the acknowledgement that a Living and Righteous God is ruling in human society not less than in the natural world.

The bulk of the collection was made up of articles on 'liberty, fraternity and equality', discussions of the new French republic, and extremely interesting political portraits which confirm the Christian socialists' instinctive preference for Tories and conservatives as against Whigs and radicals.[28] There were letters on events in France, and discussions of the Charter, the Game Laws, sanitary reform, and the universities. The last number contained a significant observation: 'We have not fairly entered upon the subject which we hoped would have been most prominent in our pages, the relation between capitalist and labourer.'[29]

The publication was wound up for lack of money; number 11, on 1 July, announced that the end was approaching. In spite of the number of readers, receipts were not covering expenses. According to the *Christian Socialist*, it had a faithful audience of something under 2,000 readers.[30]

Maurice and his friends did not lose heart. They had the idea of meeting to read the Bible and discuss its social implications, and they invited workers to these meetings. Thus in 1849 began the many meetings at which the Christian socialists met leading 'moral force' Chartists. The first of these meetings took place on 23 April 1849, and it is interesting to note that a Chartist tailor made a speech.[31] It was at these meetings that Kingsley met the men who were to influence *Alton Locke* profoundly. And it was at one of these meetings that Maurice made the significant pronouncement that the time had come for them to make it known that it was not true that competition was the law of the universe: they must answer this claim with a call for association – to work, and not to strike. For twenty years the conscientious objectors to individualism had been tentatively groping for just this formulation. Spokesmen for the idealist reaction had repeatedly attacked competition, but the idea of association, which Owen and his friends had drawn up and applied long ago, had not really impinged on the minds of the philanthropists. At last, in Maurice and Kingsley, co-operation appeared as the slowly-ripened fruit of social sentiment.

The first co-operative tailors' association was founded in 1849. Experience quickly showed that widespread general education was necessary before this new form of productive unit could be generally employed. In the autumn of 1849 the Society for the Promotion of Working Men's Associations was founded. Notable members were Maurice, Kingsley, Ludlow, Vansittart Neale, Hughes, and the French refugee Le Chevalier.[32] A new periodical, the *Christian Socialist*, was started in 1850 to further their cause.

Although the dynamic feeling behind the movement had been alive in England for a long time, and the idea of co-operation was indigenous, the decisive impetus at this point came from France. In the spring of 1849, when Maurice pronounced the declaration of war on competition, and faith in association, his friend Ludlow went to Paris, whence he returned full of enthusiasm for the *Associations Ouvrières*. He had found the answer they were looking for, and his friends were overjoyed.[33]

> 'I certainly thought,' said Mr. Hughes afterwards, 'and for that matter have never altered my opinion to this day, that we had found the solution of the great labour question; but I was also convinced that we had nothing to do but just announce it, and found one association or two, in order to convert all England, and usher in the millenium at once, so plain the whole thing seemed to me.'

Buchez had outlined his plans for co-operation in 1831. He urged skilled workers in certain trades to form fraternal industrial societies. Each society was to elect one comrade as director of labour and representative of the society. All profits made after members had received the going rate of pay should be divided into two equal halves: one to be put aside as inalienable capital, or to be used as a common fund; the other to be distributed among members according to the amount of work each had done, or set aside as educational or insurance funds for wives, widows, and children. Buchez's main concern was elimination of the entrepreneur; he wanted to establish the three republican virtues in industry: fraternity in labour, liberty to elect and depose the directors of labour, and absolute equality of rights among the associates. But he had limited his method to artisans whose capital was their technical skill, and who worked with tools, not machines, 'for, as a littérateur and a Parisian, he thought solely of artistic handicraftsmen, and he excluded from his consideration the novel facts of the new era of machinery.'[34] This was the idea that the Christian socialists took over. It suited their idealism and their ignorance of heavy industry. We shall see what kind of associations they formed, and how helpful their work was to the co-operative movement.

The *Christian Socialist*, 'a journal of Association, conducted by several of the promoters of the London working men's association. Price one penny', appeared on Saturday, 2 November 1850, and weekly thereafter. It ran until the end of 1851. The first number carried another manifesto, in which Ludlow, as 'John Townsend', explained the 'new idea' with his customary bluntness:[35]

> Socialism, the latest born of the forces now at work in modern society, and Christianity, the eldest born of those forces, are in their natures not hostile, but akin to each other, or rather...the one is but the development, the outgrowth, the manifestation of the other.

The tone was more aggressive and determined than that of *Politics for the People*. If the role of the State was not very prominent, the ideal of intervention was present. Railway workers were compared to officials: the public was entitled to exercise some control over them, to ensure that they were competent. One basic article examined 'The Aims of Political Economy':[36]

> We assert, and we have no doubt whatever that this view will ultimately obtain the suffrages of all – that the welfare of *man* is the end of political economy. . . .
> We assert that *the production of man*, and man in a continually higher condition, is the object, the end, the ultimatum of the science.

Some of the tenets of classical economics were printed opposite contrasting verses from the Bible.[37] The aesthetic element appeared plainly: some of Keats's poetry was quoted, and a passage from Ruskin's *Modern Painters*.[38] The opponents of Christian socialism were rebutted, and Kingsley's novels were praised. And of course there were reports on the workings of the first co-operatives, the movement's practical achievement.[39]

This brief account should give some impression of the nature of the journal carrying the common ideas of the Christian socialist movement. As can be seen, it was complex and indeterminate, with only two clearly established points: classical economics were rejected, and co-operation was to be substituted for competition. But the intellectual confusion of the movement is important; this was the intellectual air Kingsley breathed at the time when he was writing *Alton Locke*.

Kingsley's contributions to the *Christian Socialist*, like his writings in

Politics for the People, are interesting from this point of view. They evince all the passionate feeling about very moderate opinions which can be found underlying his novels. On 12 April 1848, two days after the fall of Chartism, he had a proclamation to the Workmen of England posted up, signed by 'A Working Parson': 'Workers of England, be wise, and then you *must* be free, for you will be *fit* to be free.'[40] His 'Letters to the Chartists'[41] in *Politics for the People* were in the same sort of language:[42]

> I think you have fallen into just the same mistake as the rich of whom you complain...the mistake of fancying that *legislative* reform is *social* reform, or that men's hearts can be changed by act of parliament.

Like his master Carlyle, Kingsley only believed in spiritual and moral revolution. The Charter was a shabby instrument for sacred work – 'trying to do God's work with the devil's tools'.[43] Two quotations bring out the violence of his antipathy to classical economics, and the timid conservatism of his politics. He wrote:[44]

> I expect nothing from the advocates of Laissez-faire; the pedants whose glory is in the shame of society; who arrogantly talk of political economy as of a science so completely perfected, so universal and all-important, that common humanity and morality, reason and religion, must be pooh-poohed down, if they seem to interfere with its infallible conclusions.

And a little later, in answer to those who accused him of preaching revolution, he said:[45]

> I believe that the Crown has now too little, and not too much power; that it is practically in commission, as the representation of the People is; that the ancient balance between King, Lords, and Commons, is destroyed; that the only element of English society now represented in either house, or by the Queen's ministry, is capital; that capital ought, like everything else, to be fully represented; but that where, as in England now, it monopolizes the whole representation, the state must end in the worst possible form of government, namely an oligarchy of wealth, which is contrary to the ancient spirit and fact of the British Constitution, as well as the abstract idea of a perfect government. . . .
>
> Finally, I believe that the modern French dogma, that the will of the People is the source of power, is Atheistic in theory, and impossible in practice, as the history of France for the last two years has sufficiently proved. I believe that there is no authority but of God, and that the authorities which exist are ordained by God.

These words are clear evidence of the unconscious affinity between *Politics for the People* and social Toryism. Disraeli himself might have said no less. We can also see the result of the events of June in France, and the fall of the Second Republic.

After 1848 Kingsley played an active role in the public eye. At workers' meetings his fiery and graphic speeches were very effective. 'The feeling among working men, when he addressed them, was always one of the heartiest admiration.'[46] Sanitary reform engaged most of his energies. Ludlow and Maurice were already busy with a campaign for public hygiene, and they had no difficulty in enlisting Kingsley's aid. During the cholera epidemic of 1849 he preached three widely-reported sermons in which he stood out against the fatalistic resignation that accepted sickness as a divine punishment. He was accused of preaching a theology of drains, just as, later, his passion for the moral and spiritual benefits of physical exercise would lead to his being dubbed a 'muscular Christian'. But his campaign was justified by Maurice's theology. Jesus had saved man: the whole of man. Nothing human was vile: the body was as dignified as the soul, which might guide it, but was still subject to its influence. Hygiene was a moral duty.

He was concerned about the spread of atheism among educated workers. Strauss's newly-translated work was very popular, and it seemed to him to be the great enemy of the Church and the poor, to whom he held up the hope of another life as their supreme consolation. In a letter to Ludlow written in August 1850, concerning the plan for the *Christian Socialist*, it is clear that his mind was bubbling over with projects and ideas.[47] Among them were the political, religious, and economic theories to be found in *Yeast* and *Alton Locke*.

For in these two busy years he did indeed write two novels. Why did he also select this particular vehicle for propaganda? The first number of *Politics for the People* noted an interesting parallel between literary and social history. During the Tory reaction at the beginning of the century, the novel had stressed class differences, and tended to deal with drawing-room manners. But after the Reform Act fiction became more democratic:[48]

> The fashionable novels, and the whole tribe that belonged to them, vanished from the stage, not without some hissing and laughter; their place was taken by Mr. Dickens, as the head of a company, which, whatever may be its merits or faults, has been most earnest and pertinaceous in asserting a common humanity with every dweller in St. Giles's.

Thus the attention of Christian socialists was drawn to the nature and importance of social novels. Like everybody else, Kingsley had read Dickens.[49] There is no need to go further than this in looking for the origins of *Yeast*. It is more of a tract than a novel: an extended and dramatised 'Letter to the Chartists'. *The Saint's Tragedy* had not been a great success. Kingsley had to look into his passionate heart for another form of expression; the novel was the most flexible, undefined form available, giving the maximum freedom to the imagination. And so *Yeast* came to be written, and after its success, *Alton Locke*.

'Yeast'

After the great excitement of April 1848, Kingsley went back to Eversley and wrote *Yeast* in a few months. It appeared as a serial in *Fraser's Magazine* that autumn, and was not issued in volume form until 1851. Logically and chronologically it is an earlier work than *Alton Locke*; less mature, less well-planned and, as a first attempt, something of a preliminary sketch:[50]

> Altogether, I am so dissatisfied with 'Yeast' that I shall lay it aside *pro tem*. It was finished, or rather cut short, to please Fraser, and now it may lie and ferment for a few years. You are right in your surmise that the finale is *mythic* and not *typic*. You will see why (please God...) when I finish it.

Something must be said about Kingsley's plan for bringing *Yeast* to perfection – a plan which he never fulfilled, as the additions and re-touching he gave the work did not alter its fundamental shape.[51] *Yeast* is clearly marked out as a product of the troubled times following the great scare of 1848. When Kingsley wrote it he would not yet have described himself as a Christian socialist; he knew nothing about the French co-operatives; and he had social aspirations, but no social policies to put forward. His politics still followed the lines laid down in *Politics for the People*: revolutionary Chartism was condemned, and a superior Chartism, integrated with the whole of life, including the spiritual, was proposed, in which political reform would fall back into its proper place. Social reform was of more importance, and social reform meant the new philanthropy. More important still was moral and spiritual reform, which alone was capable of revitalising the country. Kingsley did have a concrete basis on which to rest this vague idealism: he knew the agricultural proletariat, and had really understood their side of the problem. As a matter of course he turned to this material, and *Yeast* tries to use the

condition of agricultural labourers in the south of England to illustrate
the need for determined social work. But the substance of the book is
polemical rather than descriptive. It puts forward many different theories
and collocations of ideas, and shows the most diverse men with utterly
varying principles all urging the rebirth of idealism and the improvement
of the people's lot. Kingsley tries to differentiate between them and
bring out what is valuable in each, showing its proper place in moral and
social progress. 'In the following pages I have attempted to show what
some at least of the young in these days are really thinking and feeling,'
he wrote in the Preface of 1851. So the subject of *Yeast* is really young
England – the whole of young England, with a wider and more complex
range of ideas than was to be found among the mere party which had
adopted the name. Social Toryism has its place therein, but it is assessed
by an impartial critic who judges it by the standards of a higher ideal.
Yeast is the final proof of that essential identity we have ascribed to all the
manifestations of the idealist and interventionist reaction. It brings
together the Oxford Movement, the aesthetic revival, social Toryism,
and the new philanthropy; discriminates between them, and reconciles
them. Kingsley sensed that they all sprang from the same mental ferment.
Their policies and attitudes might be different, but this was because their
adherents came from different environments, and had different natures
and preoccupations. It was the combination of harmony and discord
between the movements which impressed Kingsley, and he tried to bring
them all together in one huge selection from which the reader might
eclectically choose the spiritual sustenance he needed. And he hoped that
his work of classification might make it easier for them to join forces and
direct the action of the spiritual yeast which was working all over the
country. Unfortunately his own thinking was not sufficiently precise
for him to accomplish this task, and his attempt at organising the idealist
movements failed. *Yeast* is valuable as a picture of the confused stirrings
of a critical period: it does not achieve a synthesis of them.

Like *Coningsby* and *Sybil*, *Yeast* relates the steps towards a man's
vocation. Instead of one hero it has two, and they are very unlike the
talented, elegant young noblemen who personified Disraeli's ideal.
Kingsley's heroes are like Carlyle's: they have the same boundless energy,
deep sincerity, rough exteriors, and contempt for convention. Their
spiritual masculinity verges on rudeness, and whenever possible goes
hand in hand with physical strength. Lancelot Smith, the son of a rich
merchant, and Tregarva the gamekeeper, a former Cornish miner, are
two athletic, muscular giants. Being respectively middle- and working-
class, they reflect Kingsley's democratic outlook. Their meeting, their

mutual friendship, and their agreement to work together stand for the Christian socialist dream of an association between the workers' movements and the intellectual aristocracy. But although they are spiritual equals, nature and upbringing have made one ineradicable difference between them: Lancelot is a gentleman. 'No man can take that from you. You may look the proudest duchess in the land in the face, and claim her as your equal.'[52] Tregarva can never cross the gulf separating him from the squire's daughter he loves, but in whose presence he seems only half civilised. 'Why should not the workman be a gentleman and a workman still? Why are they to be shut out from all that is beautiful, and delicate, and winning, and stately?'[53] Although Kingsley sympathises with the fury of the man whose poverty cuts him off from a cultivated life, he has not the slightest wish to see class distinctions abolished. By and large the old English nobility deserves its privileges, for it is physically and morally superior. The gentry rise naturally to the head of the people: there must be some classes to lead and others to follow. What is both feasible and desirable is that any career should be open to the gifted working man: the sons of the people must be free to develop their faculties so that their talents are not wasted.[54] 'What if the poor be raised above "their station"? What right have we to keep them down?... Are *we* to fix how far their minds may be developed?'[55]

Lancelot Smith has gone through the Romantic phase which all young people had to experience in the nineteenth century. Like his contemporaries, he has been influenced by Carlyle, and is now intoxicated with German philosophy, dedicated to natural science, and vaguely interested in finding something socially useful to do. He has energy, the essential heroic virtue. He will bring the courage of a martyr and the strength of a combatant to his life's work, whatever it may be. But he lacks the essentials for action: a faith to inspire it and beliefs to sustain it. He only believes in nature. 'My only Bible as yet is Bacon. I know that he is right, whoever is wrong.'[56] On the other hand he is profoundly ignorant of the people's distress: the 'condition of England question' is a closed book to him.

Another man makes up for these inadequacies. Lancelot recognises in Tregarva a mind which complements his own. A hunting accident keeps him immobilised with the Lavington family at Whitford Priory: after he has recovered he stays on, captivated by the beauty and noble, spiritual charm of the squire's daughter Argemone. Strolling along the fishing stream, and coming across a nocturnal engagement between poachers and gamekeepers, Lancelot becomes aware of the remarkably rich personality of Tregarva. He has deep but narrow Nonconformist religious beliefs: his Methodism has been intensified by a conversion, and he rejects the physical pleasures and cultivated life which Lancelot thinks the people ought to enjoy. Under Lancelot's influence his faith grows broader and more flexible; in return he gives his friend an example of sincere and manly Christianity. And above all he shows him the social wrongs he must fight to put right. Solitary meditation has made Tregarva socially conscious. He has visited the cottages of the poor, comforted the sick, and seen for himself the sufferings caused by the Game Laws. He is a natural poet, and has written some rough, powerful verses indicting the squire's cruelty and neglect:[57]

> There's blood on your new foreign shrubs, squire;
>   There's blood on your pointer's feet;
> There's blood on the game you sell, squire,
>   And there's blood on the game you eat.
>
> You have sold the labouring man, squire,
>   Body and soul to shame,
> To pay for your seat in the House, squire,
>   And to pay for the feed of your game.

Lancelot and Tregarva are united by mutual sympathy at first, and afterwards by a deep, reasoned friendship. Apart they are helpless, but together they make up a complete man – hero and prophet. They finally depart for the fabulous country where Kingsley places the dream – still a very tentative dream – of Christian socialism.

The book's other characters serve to influence Lancelot. Some of them inspire him directly; others are less closely involved with his life, and stand for some of the varying doctrines dividing young men of the day. Argemone Lavington is a direct inspiration. She loves Lancelot's strength and nobility, and confronted with his robust simplicity, drops the mystical excesses of her own piety which were leading her towards Rome. They influence each other, but happiness is denied them: she dies of fever contracted at the deathbed of a sick peasant, thus illustrating the theory of providential retribution, as her innocent being expiates her nation's crimes. But she has kindled a flame of social and religious idealism in her lover. By showing him God through nature she has paved the way for his conversion. Her noble spiritual beauty has elevated his pure, aesthetic fervour, and when she dies she leaves him a legacy of unfulfilled charity to carry out: 'You will do it! darling! Strong, wise, noble-hearted that you are!...You will be rich some day. You will own land, for you are worthy to own it.'[58] And falling back in her weakened state, she asks him to kneel down and pray. He obeys mechanically. 'No – not for me, for them – for them, and for yourself – that you may save them whom I never dreamt that I was bound to save.'[59]

Someone else intends Lancelot for this mission: Barnakill, a mysterious character who unmistakably reminds one of Sidonia. Kingsley affirmed that this was mere coincidence – 'Quite right; the Prophet is too like Sidonia; but I never read *Coningsby* till the other day, when the Prophet was months old'[60] – and there is no reason to doubt his word. The resemblance is none the less striking. Of course Barnakill is another Carlylean hero:[61]

> He was a huge, shaggy, toil-worn man, the deep melancholy earnestness of whose rugged features reminded him almost ludicrously of one of Landseer's bloodhounds. But withal there was a tenderness – a genial, though covert humour – playing about his massive features, which awakened in Lancelot at first sight a fantastic longing to open his whole heart to him.

This is a far remove from the strong but polished gentleman whom Coningsby accepted as prophet and mentor. But Barnakill plays the same role as Sidonia. No one knows where he comes from; his native country is the world, and his friends are kings. He knows the secret springs of human conduct, and providential fortune always leads him where he wants to go. Lancelot, shattered by the death of his beloved and ruined by the failure of his banker-uncle, gives way to temporary despair. Then Barnakill meets him three times. He amazes the young man, sweeps him off his feet, and brings him under his spell. He teaches him to see clearly into himself, strengthens his faith and courage, and shows him the path he must take: 'Here, or nowhere, must the solution be attempted of those social problems which are convulsing more and more all Christendom.'[62] The vague aspirations in which the young are embroiled can be reconciled:[63]

> Look at the enormous amount of practical benevolence which now struggles in vain against evil, only because it is as yet private, desultory, divided... but only waiting for the one inspiring Spirit to organise, and unite, and consecrate this chaos into the noblest polity the world ever saw realised.

This spirit is that of the Bible. Barnakill converts Lancelot: Maurice's theology, presented by Kingsley in impassioned argument, overcomes his sceptical doubts. His guide reveals to him the existence of a kingdom ruled by the word of God: 'You have heard tell of the country of Prester

John, that mysterious Christian empire, rarely visited by European eye?'[64]
Lancelot will go there to see for himself the example and laws which
may save England. He departs, and is swallowed up by the unknown – a
mysterious denouement indeed! Kingsley has wrapped up his vision of
Christian socialism in mystery rather than face the question of whether
it can, in practice, be attained. The strange novel, in which realism and
fantasy are mixed, ends on a note of allegory.

Barnakill did no more than sketch in the synthesis of Christianity and
human politics. The real interest of *Yeast* lies elsewhere, in the portrait
gallery of representative upper- and middle-class types. Which of the
contending movements should be accepted, and which should be rejected? Let us consider first those who are entirely bad. Lavington is the
traditional squire: a mighty huntsman and toper. He is reminiscent of Sir
John Cope, the squire of Eversley. His thick head has never held a notion
of any duty to his tenantry. His politics are Whig, but his conduct is
ferociously conservative, and he jealousy guards the unjust privileges the
Game Laws give him. He is impervious to feeling and spirituality, and
any new ideas. He is utterly opposed to social solidarity, and Kingsley has
no hope of any good coming from his direction.[65]

Colonel Bracebridge is another such man, whose value to the community is completely non-existent. He is a man of the world; Carlyle's
dilettante. He is witty, debauched, and cynical, and his natural talents
have been neutralised or destroyed by vice. He has seduced and abandoned a country girl, and he kills himself when he hears that she is in
prison for murdering his child.[66]

Next there is 'Mammonism' – that is, the financial bourgeoisie. Smith
the banker, Lancelot's uncle, is not a Dickensian grotesque. He is an
ordinary man, honest in his way, and capable of human feelings. But he
lives by business ethics and is surrounded by people who believe in them.
He has given up the idea of disinterested activity and has no wish for it.
The doctrine he professes and lives by is exposed as rotten when his
closest friends treat the occasion of his bankruptcy cynically, and when
he proves incapable of understanding Lancelot's enthusiasm. Individualism will not do as a basis for society:[67]

> Selfishness can collect, not unite, a herd of cowardly wild cattle, that
> they may feed together, breed together, keep off the wolf and bear
> together. But when one of your wild cattle falls sick, what becomes
> of the corporate feelings of the herd then?...Your Bible talks of
> society, not as a herd, but as a living tree, an organic individual body,
> a holy brotherhood and kingdom of God.

Here once again intuitive feeling has uncovered organic connections, and leads to social solidarity opposing rational social fragmentation.

The representatives of Puseyism are the last of the villains. As we have said, Kingsley was physically and morally repelled by the Oxford Movement. His robust, healthy fitness found asceticism and spiritual sensuality equally wounding, and as he saw it these were the two faces of Catholicism. The subtle finesse of casuistry looked to his direct mind like disguised lying. These are Lancelot's grievances against his cousin Luke, the Tractarian. The correspondence between the two gives the case for and against the pressures which were driving a number of Anglican priests over to Rome. Kingsley summed up all their arguments under one heading: weakness. Lack of moral courage and a capitulation of the will led Newman's followers into Catholicism. They found rest and repose there: they might equally well have found it in alcohol or opium. Says Luke,[68]

> 'We of the True Church have some one to keep our consciences for us. The padre settles all about what is right or wrong, and we slip on as easily as –'
> 'A frog or a butterfly!' said the vicar bitterly.
> 'Exactly,' answered Luke. 'And, on your own showing, are clean gainers of a happy life here, not to mention heaven hereafter. God bless you! We shall soon see you one of us.'

Kingsley is kinder to the aesthetic revival. He sees it as putting great truth alongside great error. It might become the fruitful source of art for the people; it might equally become the basis of a godless, unidealistic sensualism. Claude Mellot the painter lives for beauty. But he squanders his talents by painting Venus and her nymphs, creatures no one believes in. Art separated from faith is not of the highest. Here again, Barnakill pronounces the truth: 'Rather follow in the steps of your Turners, and Landseers, and Stanfields, and Creswicks, and add your contribution to the present noble school of naturalist painters.'[69] Landscape and portraiture are not only the genres best adapted to the English talent – they are also the fittest for the Protestant idea. What is this idea, asks Lancelot, and is told:[70]

> 'The universal symbolism and dignity of matter, whether in man or nature.'
> 'But the Puritans –'
> 'Were inconsistent with themselves and with Protestantism, and therefore God would not allow them to proceed.'

And so Kingsley draws his aesthetics from Maurice's theology. The Incarnation of Christ has made matter beautiful. The natural symbolism preached by Ruskin is a religious truth.[71] From this point on, Christian socialism is in harmony with the artistic revival. Indeed the restoration of the cult of the beautiful will be one of its tasks. Lancelot dreams of dedicating himself to it:[72]

> 'The beautiful?' he said to himself, 'they shall have it! At least they shall be awakened to feel their need of it, their right to it. What a high destiny, to be the artist of the people! to devote one's powers of painting, not to mimicking obsolete legends, Pagan or Popish, but to representing to the working men of England the triumphs of the Past and the yet greater triumphs of the Future.'

The political divisions of the day are also represented. Lord Minchampstead stands for the new Whig nobility, drawn from the ranks of the industrial bourgeoisie. He has many of the characteristics of Lord Everingham and Lord Marney, but Kingsley is less hostile to the type than Disraeli. Minchampstead's father was a wealthy commoner: he has pushed his fortunes further: 'From a mill-owner he grew to a coal-owner, ship-owner, banker, railway director to kings and princes; and last of all, as the summit of his own and his compeer's ambition, to land-owner.'[73] No sooner has he taken over the Minchampstead estate than he establishes a strictly rational régime that sets everyone at odds – squire, tenants, and labourers. There is to be no more hunting or shooting; every labourer is to have a new cottage, and every cottage shall have an allot-ment and a pig. The children are to have an industrial training school. But there is to be no more common land: no outdoor relief, and a rigid application of the new Poor Law. Why is Kingsley so indulgent to a man of this type, when so many social novelists would have cursed him roundly? The answer is that Minchampstead is industrious, and Carlyle's message had been the gospel of work.[74]

> He was always and in all things a strong man. Naturally keen, ready, and business-like, daring, he had carved out his own way through life, and opened his oyster – the world – neither with sword nor pen, but with steam and cotton.

Kingsley does not want to idealise the man: he describes his life as dry and narrow. He does harm, and his facile energy often produces un-happiness for those around him:[75]

> But of the harm which he did he was unconscious; in the good which he did he was consistent and indefatigable; infinitely superior, with

all his defects, to the ignorant, extravagant, do-nothing Squire Lavingtons around him. At heart, however Mammon-blinded, he was kindly and upright. A man of stately presence; a broad honest north-country face; a high square forehead, bland and unwrinkled.

Kingsley found much that was acceptable in Young England and social Toryism. Lord Vieuxbois is described as 'a quiet, truly highly-bred young man, with a sweet open countenance and an ample forehead, whose size would have vouched for great talents, had not the promise been contradicted by the weakness of the over-delicate mouth and chin.'[76] This was exactly how Young England appeared to Kingsley: its fair and generous opinions were vitiated by an excess of aristocratic refinement. Vieuxbois is sincerely concerned for the well-being of the people; we find him full of benevolent intentions, and anxious to estab-lish an art which reaches the masses, such as existed in the Middle Ages. His philanthropy has a religious basis, and he is not unsympathetic to Christian socialism. Kingsley cordially wishes him long life and pros-perity.[77] But he does question Vieuxbois's attempt to keep his depen-dants in a state of subjection, and suggests that he is wrong in never letting the people have their heads. His timid goodwill is too easily shocked by the mere verbiage of Chartism and trade unionism. One of the chapters added to *Yeast* in 1851 satirises the famous chapter in *Conings-by* where Eustace Lyle distributes alms to his tenants. And Kingsley cannot forget that social Toryism is a natural ally of the Oxford Move-ment. Vieuxbois has a lot to learn:[78]

> He has to learn that God is a living God now, as well as in the middle ages; to learn to trust not in antique precedents, but in eternal laws: to learn that his tenants, just because they are children of God, are not to be kept children, but developed and educated into sons.

Thus Young England offsets all that was modern and democratic in Kingsley's thought. Chartism, in *Alton Locke*, was to throw into relief its aristocratic and conservative foundation.

With Tregarva to guide him, Lancelot sets out to investigate agricul-tural poverty. The contrast between the distant prospect and interior reality of southern English villages is described in terms reminiscent of *Sybil*. The action of *Yeast* moves to Whitford, among the chalk downs which add so much beauty to the English countryside, and Kingsley gives a poetical account of the fresh charm of the landscape:[79]

> the perfect limpidity of the water, the gay and luxuriant vegetation of the banks and ditches, the masses of noble wood embosoming the

villages, the unique beauty of the water-meadows, living sheets of emerald and silver, tinkling and sparkling, cool under the blackest cloud.

But this appearance is deceptive: 'Those picturesque villages are generally the perennial hotbeds of fever and ague, of squalid penury, sottish profligacy, dull discontent too stale for words.'[80]

The fogs rising from the marshy river are not the only cause of disease. The squire and the parson are also blameworthy, both for what they have done and for what they have left undone. The villagers are badly housed and worse fed: the rubbish accumulating in their damp cottages is worse than that in the cellars of industrial cities. Is not the generosity of the rich, and the charity of the squire's daughters some relief? Not really, for they do not know the extent of the misery they are confronting:[81]

'But the oppression that goes on all the year round, and the want that goes on all the year round, and the filth, and the lying, and the swearing, and the profligacy that go on all the year round, and the sickening weight of debt, and the miserable grinding anxiety from rent-day to rent-day, and Saturday night to Saturday night, that crushes a man's soul down, and drives every thought out of his head but how he is to fill his stomach and warm his back, and keep a house over his head, till he daren't for his life take his thoughts one moment off the meat that perisheth – oh, sir, they never felt this; and therefore they never dream that there are thousands who pass them in their daily walks who feel this, and feel nothing else.'

Tregarva observes bitterly that the laws protecting game at the expense of crops are a piece of indefensible class legislation.

Disguised as a countryman, Lancelot goes to a village fair with Tregarva, hoping to meet the poor on an equal footing. This is the central chapter of *Yeast*; the convincing power of the book is drawn together in a wealth of vivid detail.

Kingsley's two predominant concerns were mental and physical hygiene. He felt and described the squalor of rural poverty both as a parson and as a spokesman for sanitary reform. When Lancelot finds fifty or so peasants living together in one tent, he particularly notices the evidence of vice and degradation. The men are stupefied with toil, and have an animal look: they seem incapable of rising above the level of beer and tobacco and the lewd songs they sing in slow, rough voices. And yet their robust frames show that they are proudly descended, and a few of their foreheads are grandly massive. This is a people who have degenerated, not an inherently inferior race. But the degeneracy shows signs of becoming congenital in the younger ones: they are smaller, slower, and weaker than their elders. The girls lack beauty, grace, and the bloom of health, and their language has grown coarse in the promiscuous association of field-workers. According to Tregarva, bastardy is common in the villages, and all too often the mothers allow their infants to die of neglect. Their very wretchedness, and the rumour that revolt is spreading from the North hardly elicits any response from them. Somebody mutters about Chartists; someone else mentions rick-burning, and an urchin sings a song celebrating the exploits of Captain Swing:[82]

> I zeed a vire o' Monday night,
>   A vire both great and high;
> But I wool not tell you where, my boys,
>   Nor wool not tell you why.
> The varmer he comes screeching out
>   To zave 'uns new brood mare;
> Zays I, 'You and your stock may roast,
>   Vor aught us poor chaps care.'
>
> Then here's a curse on varmers all
>   As rob and grind the poor:
> To re'p the fruit of all their works
>   In Hell for ever moor-r-r.

Their physical surroundings are corrupting the race as much as vice and overwork. Returning to Whitford, the two investigators pass through a hamlet struck down with fever. Dung hills reek outside the doors, and there is no water for washing or drinking. And so nature has retaliated against men who defiled her. Lancelot leaves just as Argemone slips into a cottage where she contracts her fatal fever.

Thus an indifferent society is menaced by ills it would rather not know about. Epidemic disease can pass at any moment from the slum to the mansion, and revolutionary anger, which may break out in blind violence and disorder, is brooding. Such is the implication of *Yeast*. A lesson in social solidarity emerges, illustrated both by Lancelot's experiences and his thoughts.

What sort of action should be taken? Kingsley did not say at this point, although he was later to outline a programme for agrarian reform.[83] His novel does no more than suggest the feelings and intentions which will be necessary as a starting-point for action. As far as can be seen, he is not recommending any policies that go further than the general interventionism developed by Dickens and Mrs Gaskell. He makes the same criticism as they do of political economy. At heart, Lancelot believes the arguments against indiscriminate alms-giving, but confronted by a fellow-creature in distress, an old poacher who has been caught red-handed, but pleads hunger and unemployment, he feels his dogmatic beliefs evaporating. 'In practice, one can't help feeling a little of that un-economic feeling called pity.'[84] His good sense shows him the gap between hypothetical Ricardian economic man and the abject, outcast, savage creatures actually produced by social indifference and individualism.

Kingsley affirms the right to life. 'If a country is so ill-constituted that it cannot find its own citizens in work, it is bound to find them in food.'[85] His belligerent nature and intimate acquaintance with the poor led him to favour hearty democratic charity. He did not want paternalistic philanthropy: he denounced 'that peculiar creed which allows everyone to feel for the poor except themselves, and considers that to plead the cause of working men is, in a gentleman, the perfection of virtue, but in a working man himself, sheer high treason.'[86] But all the same, the initiative was to come from the upper classes. Tregarva says that God made the gentry to preserve order in society: 'I say, sir, that God makes you gentlemen, gentlemen, that you may see into these things.'[87]

The book, as we have it, shows signs of being a stopgap. 'In *Yeast*,' Kingsley wrote to his friend Ludlow,[88]

> I have tried to show the feelings which are working in the age, in a fragmentary and turbid state. In the next part, *The Artists*, I shall try to unravel the tangled skein, by means of conversations on Art, connected as they will be necessarily with the deepest questions of science, anthropology, social life, and Christianity. And looking at the Art of a people as at once the very truest symbol of its faith, and a vast means for its further education, I think it is a good path in which to form my hero, the man of the coming age.

This book was to show that Argemone had not really died after all. She was to inherit Whitford, and try out schemes of social charity, eschewing everything that was not in keeping with the principles God had shown the present age. United at last, the two lovers were to find their field of action in Whitford; Lancelot would draw up theories and principles, and Argemone would provide the passionate enthusiasm needed to sustain altruistic energy in daily life. 'And so I think the two may become an ideal pair of pioneers towards the society of the future... which will be given in a third and last volume, to be written – when?'[89] This was

Kingsley's plan for a trilogy. It shows plainly how broad and ill-defined his social thinking was at the time when he wrote *Yeast*. All the ferment of the idealistic revival was working in his mind. When he re-issued the book in 1851 he had calmed down. Only a few points from the projected sequel were added to the revised edition.[90] *The Artists* never appeared. Kingsley was forced to concentrate his attention on economic problems in writing *Alton Locke*.

It is difficult to say how influential *Yeast* was. Kingsley wanted its effect to be widespread and general, but at the same time gentle and indefinable. The book was perfectly suited to this intention as it is extremely unsystematic, and relies heavily on suggestion. The novel went into its fourth edition in 1859, not counting the original serial publication in *Fraser's*. So it was being read. Of course establishment critics and the serious journals attacked it in the name of aesthetic laws and sound policy. The *Quarterly Review* condemned it as revolutionary, like all Kingsley's other publications: 'This, the crowning one, is entitled 'YEAST' – a suggestion that it is meant to *ferment* in the minds of the people and prepare them to *rise* under the heat of the Socialist oven.'[91] But common readers told Kingsley of the deep impression the book had made on them.[92] One of the letters was revealing: an old atheist said that he had been converted by *Yeast*, and he promised his wholehearted support to the system which had still not taken the name of Christian socialism:[93]

> I believe you have taken up the right ground in standing firmly by the spirit of Christianity, and the divineness of Christ's mission, and showing the people how they are their best friends and truest reformers.

Here indeed was the anonymous voice of religious feeling responding to the appeal of a man who had called upon it to save society.

From 'Yeast' to 'Alton Locke'

Kingsley learnt a lot between the publication of *Yeast* in 1848 and *Alton Locke* in August 1850. As Christian socialism became more self-aware it gave itself a name, which increased its self-understanding. The French co-operative movement had given it an example of how its nebulous idealism might be put into practice. Maurice and his friends came into contact with the real lives of the people at their meetings for workers, and their theories were strengthened and given greater precision through co-operative propaganda, and their struggle with upper- and lower-class enemies. In the autumn of 1849 Mayhew's *London Labour and the London*

Poor appeared as a series of letters in the *Morning Chronicle*, and this intensified the Christian socialists' social concern. Kingsley owed a lot to Mayhew's articles, which dealt in one of the most sensational numbers with working-class tailors victimised by the sweating system. This became the substance of *Alton Locke*. *Cheap Clothes and Nasty*, by 'Parson Lot', the polemical pamphlet which appeared in 1850 as the first in a series of *Tracts on Socialism*, makes Kingsley's debt to Mayhew even clearer. The cholera epidemic of 1849 had drawn attention to the insanitary conditions in which the poor lived, and in October Kingsley went to Bermondsey, the district most severely hit by the epidemic.[94] This gave him another chapter for his novel, and again it was the *Morning Chronicle* which had given him the idea of going there.

Kingsley's personal resources too must not be overlooked. He may not have known much about heavy industry, but he did know about the rural poor. And in a letter he denied that he owed anything to Mayhew: 'For fourteen years my father has been the rector of a very large metropolitan parish,' he wrote, 'and I speak what I know, and testify that which I have seen.'[95] He worked on the novel for a year and a half, from February 1849 to August 1850. And throughout that time it grew bigger and bigger, incorporating all the moral ideas and economic facts which came to the fore in Kingsley's assimilating mind.[96] But the original idea was his own – or at least, if it was suggested by an outside source, that source was not Mayhew.

We have seen that by the end of 1848 Maurice and his friends were organising workers' meetings to discuss their ideas. There Kingsley met many of the men who had controlled the Chartist movement in its final stages. He was struck by their strong characters and their intellectual and moral courage. *Alton Locke* bears witness to this: the author takes every opportunity to protest against the prejudice which dismisses the leaders of the workers' rising without having met them. At the same time, it is easy to imagine the state of mind these defeated men were in. After the complete overthrow of their hopes and plans they were ready for the sort of conversion which might renew a party's religious or political policies. Revolutionary Chartism had just failed: moral force had proved correct in its long dispute with physical force, and there was an important lesson to be learnt and reflected on in these events. Finally, nearly all these men of humble birth had educated themselves with dogged determination; some were even poets as well as men of action. All these real-life details guided Kingsley's imagination.[97]

As we have seen, he was not satisfied with *Yeast*, and was looking for a new way to express his ideas. The general plan for his first novel no longer held his attention; like Disraeli, he felt that the social novel ought to tell of a man's discovery of his calling. Now circumstances had combined to give him the material he needed to take up this theme in a new and expanded form. The fictional story of a Chartist leader would give him the opportunity to put his personal views on the great political movement that was still in everyone's mind. The choice of a working-class hero gave him a natural opportunity to go further into the urban and industrial side of the economic problem than had been possible in *Yeast*. By making the worker a poet, and describing his bitter struggle to educate himself in science and the arts, Kingsley would be able to outline his favourite policy – the need to bring truth and beauty within the workers' reach – without departing from his narrative. Kingsley was now well acquainted with Chartist atheism and revolutionary violence, and these could appear as errors from which the hero extricated himself as he learnt the better, peaceful religion of Christian socialism. His progress would thus have the accuracy of a historical example and a didactic power well adapted to the times. *Alton Locke* would put forward a policy by which hope might yet be recovered from the great delusion, and its message would reach not only the upper classes, as had been the case with *Yeast*, but even more, the people.

Alton Locke

Yeast described Lancelot Smith's young manhood in the third person. Alton Locke tells his own story. For the subject of the second novel is more psychological: it centres on the personality of a man who represents in himself the workers' revolt. Economic factors and political theories are only important in so far as they contribute to his development. Instead of a diary, written under the pressure of events as they take place, *Alton Locke* is a continuous retrospective narrative. Alton is writing his autobiography for the benefit of the public in general, and his own class in particular, aboard a boat which is taking him to Texas, a few months after 10 April 1848. Kingsley was far from being a dramatic writer sufficiently gifted to create the growth of a mind with which he disagreed, without constantly stepping in to set it right and put his own point of view. He may also have feared that it would endanger his pacificatory arguments to present the strife he wanted to heal with too much objectivity. In the event, we are offered a reformed Chartist retracing the story of Chartism for us. His whole narrative is dominated by the suggestion of a higher truth which appears obscurely in the early chapters and is clarified at the end. And so it is perfectly in keeping with the spirit of the book to disregard the chronological order of events, and to analyse them all together in the light of intentions which reflect equally upon them all.

The starting-point is the same as Carlyle's.[98] There were deep and urgent reasons for Chartism, which must be dealt with to root out the evil.

One of the principal causes of working-class rancour is the injustice which renders the intellectual gifts of the poor useless.[99] Alton Locke is the son of a small shopkeeper in the city. His father is a bad businessman, and dies leaving his family nothing. Mother and child only live by virtue of a rich uncle's niggardly generosity. The boy is sickly, stunted from an early age by foul air, constricted rooms, and a poor diet, 'a pale, consumptive, rickety, weakly boy, all forehead and no muscle.'[100] But he has a precocious intellect. Like the young Kingsley, he writes simple, affecting poetry. His growing curiosity is awakened by Bible stories and tales of other lands. When he is old enough to understand his need for education, he is apprenticed to a tailor. His day is now taken up with exhausting toil, but on his way to and from work he stops at a bookseller's, and devours a few pages. The bookseller notices his regular appearance, and lends him some books which Alton reads in his attic, without his mother's knowledge:[101]

> Before starting forth to walk two miles to the shop at six o' clock in the morning, I sat some three or four hours shivering on my bed, putting myself into cramped and painful postures, not daring even to cough, lest my mother should fancy me unwell, and come in to see me, poor dear soul! – my eyes aching over the page, my feet wrapped up in the bedclothes, to keep them from the miserable pain of the cold; longing, watching, dawn after dawn, for the kind summer mornings, when I should need no candlelight. . . . The lower classes uneducated! Perhaps you would be so too, if learning cost you the privation which it costs some of them.

At a cost to his health, Alton learns Latin and French, and reads English poetry to attune his metrical ear and refine his style. For all this, at every step he discovers 'the immense disadvantages of self-education.'[102] In Cambridge, where he goes to see his well-to-do cousin, he is humiliated by inadequacies he was never before aware of. Pride keeps him silent in the presence of the young men he meets there; their casual conversation, easy manners, and cultivated taste intimidate him, and fill him with deep and bitter rancour:[103]

The truth is, I did envy those men. I did not envy them their learning; for the majority of men who came into my cousin's room had no learning to envy, being rather brilliant and agreeable men than severe students; but I envied them their opportunites of learning; and envied them just as much their opportunities of play – their boating, their cricket, their football, their riding, and their gay confident carriage, which proceeds from physical health and strength, and which I mistook for the swagger of insolence.

In earlier times the universities had been democratic, but now they exclude the sons of the poor and have been taken over by the rich. When the Church of England excluded Nonconformists it was giving the upper classes a monopoly of education. 'No! the real reason for our exclusion, churchmen or not, is, because we are *poor*.'[104]

This accurate and dramatic account of a morbid state of mind is one of the great merits of *Alton Locke*. Self-educated workers existed – as witness Cooper and Lovett. And their very existence constituted a vital plea for the fair distribution of the right to knowledge.[105]

As well as truth, beauty ought to be widely distributed. The gloomy and degenerate people who struggled through the filthy city streets ought to be allowed the blessed experiences offered by art and nature. And here Kingsley associates the ugliness of working-class life with puritanism. Ascetic religion, be it Catholic or Evangelical, always aroused his hatred: he wanted his body and soul alike to be uplifted in religious exaltation.[106] Alton's mother is a Baptist:[107]

My mother moved by rule and method; by God's law, as she considered, and that only. She seldom smiled. Her word was absolute. She never commanded twice, without punishing. And yet there were abysses of unspoken tenderness in her. . . . But she thought herself as much bound to keep down all tenderness as if she had been some ascetic of the middle ages – so do extremes meet! It was 'carnal', she considered. She had as yet no right to have any 'spiritual affection' for us. We were still 'children of wrath and of the devil', – not yet 'convinced of sin', 'converted, born again'. . . .

So our god, or gods rather, till we were twelve years old, were hell, the rod, the ten commandments, and public opinion.

On Sundays they suffer sermons and constraint, and glance furtively from the windows at people shamelessly walking about. They are compelled to talk theology with men of God who are for ever raising the distressing question whether the soul is predestined to salvation or damnation. Under their inflexible guidance Alton is brought up with knowledge, books, poetry, secular painting, and all the innocent pleasures of childhood banned and damned.

Violated nature protests: Alton has a passion for life, and shuns religion like death. In Kingsley's eyes, narrow Nonconformists were primarily responsible for Chartist atheism. By contrast, Alton is enraptured when he finds a picture in the gallery at Dulwich wherein sublimity is expressed by beautiful forms and colours. He weeps before Guido's St Sebastian, and we can see that the tears represent a decisive turning-point in his life. And when the cockney, accustomed to the ugliness of London, sees the verdant beauty of the English countryside stretching away before him, he is overwhelmed by the sight:[108]

> I recollect lying on my face and fingering over the delicately cut leaves of the weeds, and wondering whether the people who lived in the country thought them as wonderful and beautiful as I did; – and then I recollected the thousands whom I had left behind, who, like me, had never seen the green face of God's earth; and the answer of the poor gamin in St. Giles's, who, when he was asked what the country was, answered, '*The yard where the gentlemen live when they go out of town*' . . . then I wondered whether the time would ever come when society would be far enough advanced to open to even such as he a glimpse, if it were only once a year, of the fresh, clean face of God's earth.

But to make a Chartist of Alton, it is necessary for him to encounter poverty too. Here, as in Dickens, there is no question of seeing the weavers or miners: Kingsley deliberately ignored heavy industry. Trade unions and the labour disputes of 1842 are likewise absent from his book. His life had only brought him into contact with the peasant and the small shopkeeper, and his social policies were adapted to their needs. Urban misery is represented in *Alton Locke* by tailors and sempstresses. Both, as we have seen, had already attracted the attention of the public.

Alton is apprenticed to a tailor in a fashionable district. Here he learns the conditions of 'honourable trade' as opposed to 'sweated labour'.[109] This then is a workshop where conditions are good:[110]

> A low lean-to room, stifling me with the combined odours of human breath and perspiration, stale beer, the sweet sickly smell of gin, and the sour and hardly less disgusting one of new cloth. On the floor, thick with dust and dirt, scraps of stuff and ends of thread, sat some dozen haggard, untidy, shoeless men, with a mingled look of care and reck-lessness that made me shudder. The windows were tightly closed to

keep out the cold winter air; and the condensed breath ran in streams down the panes, chequering the dreary outlook of chimney-tops and smoke.

For twelve hours a day the men cut and stitch and drink and swear. The newcomer is put among them, and learns why he is nearer heaven in this room than any other: he will die six months earlier than he would in any of the workrooms on lower floors. The cellar workshop is the rheumatic ward; the ground floor is the fever ward; the first floor is the asthmatics' ward; and the attic here is the consumptive hospital:[111]

> 'First you begins to cough, then you proceeds to expectorate... and then, when you've sufficiently covered the poor dear shivering bare backs of the hairystocracy –
>
> Die, die, die,
> Away you fly,
> Your soul is in the sky!
>
> as the hinspired Shakspeare wittily remarks.'

It is the owner who dies. His more practical and less scrupulous son changes the nature of the business. Why should not he do as everyone else does and grow rich by new methods? From now on the tailors will work at home; intermediaries will transmit orders to them, and pay them piece-rates. This decision sparks a revolt: Alton's companions know all too well that this means slavery at the hands of the sweater, starvation wages, a sixteen-hour day, unlimited competition from women and children, and a hopeless struggle against a murderous end. But what can they do? The Government sanctions the system. Domestic labour produces uniforms at rock-bottom prices for the army, post office, and police. A Member of Parliament to whom the tailors put their case shelters behind the law of supply and demand. 'He may have been a wise man. I only know that he was a rich one.'[112] Only Alton and his friend Crossthwaite prefer unemployment to exploitation. They are lucky. When, some months later, they break into the 'den' of their former comrade Jemmy Downes, who has become a sweater, they find a dozen almost naked creatures with their fingers worn to the bone by ceaseless toil. Their wages are taken from them to pay for their keep, and their bodily strength belongs to their masters, who squeeze every last drop of profit out of them.[113] Kingsley was neither inventing nor exaggerating. Workers were recruited by sweaters' wives who promised them fabulous pay. The shops were filthy. The middlemen massed capital by a system of fines and bonds. Workers would possess one communal coat, the 'reliever', which each man would wear in turn when allowed to go out. All these details were confirmed by the *Morning Chronicle*.[114]

Kingsley deals with sempstresses in an equally realistic episode. Like Dickens, he uses these unfortunates as his female representatives of the degradation brought about by competition and forced labour. Here again, misery leads inevitably to prostitution. In an attic an old woman shivers by a cold fireplace. She is obsessed by one idea: 'No workhouse, sir, for an officer's daughter!'[115] There are three young women in the room, one of whom is sick and bed-ridden. The other two ply their needles by day, and go on the streets at night. Why do they do this? Because they can only earn three shillings a week, out of which they have to pay for thread, coals, and candles, and support the sick girl, and feed the four of them. Ironically, they are working on a riding-habit that will adorn a fashionable beauty in Hyde Park.

Then we are shown the places where the poor live as they are killed off in their hundreds by cholera. Kingsley takes us to Bermondsey, and we are back at Dickens's sinister backwater in *Oliver Twist*, Jacob's Island. Some things have changed since 1837; there has been some attempt to improve the area, which means that a few tall middle-class houses have been built among the slums, and the deprived families driven out by them have been pushed into even more crowded conditions at the edge. But Folly Ditch is still there, and the same crazy, collapsing cottages hang out over the water. Downes, ruined in his turn, has fetched up in one of them. He shows Alton the bodies of his wife and children stretched out on the worm-eaten boards, with the miasma of the sewers floating around them. The rats have started to attack them, and the unhappy Downes, going mad, tries to force Alton to drink the ditch-water which was the only beverage of his family while they lived. But he slips, and falls into the water without a cry:[116]

> We rushed out on the balcony. The light of the policeman's lantern glared over the ghastly scene – along the double row of miserable house-backs, which lined the sides of the open tidal ditch – over strange rambling jetties, and balconies, and sleeping-sheds, which hung on rotting piles over the black waters, with phosphorescent scraps of rotten fish gleaming and twinkling out of the dark hollows, like devilish grave-lights – over bubbles of poisonous gas, and bloated carcasses of dogs, and lumps of offal, floating on the stagnant olive-green hell-broth – over the slow sullen rows of oily ripple which were dying away into the darkness far beyond, sending up, as they stirred, hot breaths of miasma – the only sign that a spark of humanity, after years of foul life, had quenched itself at last in that foul death.

The keen tone, physical horror, and sensitive repugnance of this have never been surpassed. Kingsley was realistic about hygiene. His imaginative fascination with the morbid ran ahead of scientific discoveries, and invested the death-giving fumes with strange animal life, as Downes, in his imagination, had seen swarms of insects passing down his children's throats and destroying them.[117]

Agricultural poverty has its place in *Alton Locke*, and the picture is grimmer than that in *Yeast*. Alton is deputed by the Chartist committee to attend a meeting in an eastern county. On the way he encounters nothing but hovels with sloping walls and leaky roofs. In a frozen field, two children are hoeing turnips with frozen hands. They are paid one shilling for a seven-day week. There is no school or church for them. Their feet are poking through their burst shoes, and they are shivering in tattered rags. Moreover fat healthy sheep are eating a swill of turnips and malt-dust beside them, protected against the cold by their thick fleece. Man is no longer the master of the beast; he has become his slave.[118]

On open downland, within the gloomy setting of an ancient earthwork, a crowd of labourers is milling round a block of stone. Their eyes are lacklustre, their lips droop, and they shuffle with heavy, dragging steps. The women among them look 'even more pinched and wan'.[119] Speakers take it in turns to climb upon the stone and give a dismal account of their common suffering, without any embellishments of eloquence or imagination.[120] Landowners lease cottages as well as farms to small tenants, to escape having to take any responsibility themselves. And so the labourer loses his natural protector, and is at the mercy of a middleman who will squeeze him to the last penny. Farmers are greedy and ignorant, and being poor themselves, refuse to undertake repairs, until the cottages collapse in ruins.

One man tells how his master has dismissed him at the end of harvesting, after he had worked for him for seven years. His son is growing up, and he has been replaced with younger, cheaper labour. The workhouse is closed to them, for they are able-bodied. What are they to do?

Another suggests that the remedy would be simple: every labourer should have an allotment. But the farmers are opposed to this at any price: they have no wish to see their wage-earners becoming independent.

When the price of corn falls, wages fall with it. But however high it rises, wages never rise. What does Free Trade or protection matter to the rural proletariat?

If only they could speak to the Queen, and take a petition to her. But no. Dragoons with drawn swords ride alongside her carriage, and would cut off the head of anyone who looked like approaching.

It is all the landowners' fault, says one man. Every misfortune comes from the farmers, according to another. In any case, says a third who has been to London and learnt something about politics, it is very simple. Landowners and farmers do well, and the labourers' sweat pays for the income of the first and the profits of the second.

It is a woman's turn. She does not want to go to the workhouse where her children will be taken away from her. But at home she has neither bread nor coal, and the children are crying with cold and hunger. If she breaks a branch for her fire, she will go to prison. When will the pack of cowardly men do something?

By contrast, we see an old blind man, resigned to his lot, who slowly turns his sightless eyes on the crowd around the stone:[121]

> 'It's all along of our sins, and our wickedness – because we forgot Him – it is. . . . He has turned His face from us, and that's why we're troubled. And so I don't see no use in this meeting. It won't do no good; nothing won't do us no good, unless we all repent of our wicked ways, our drinking, and our dirt, and our love-children, and our picking and stealing, and gets the Lord to turn our hearts and to come back again, and have mercy on us, and take us away speedily out of this wretched world, where there's nothing but misery and sorrow, into His everlasting glory. Amen!'

The last speaker puts his arms akimbo and laughs at that homily. What is the good of working? Stealing is more profitable. Prison is warmer than the workhouse, and the food is better. Hungry? The farmer has corn which might be taken from him. Then they may eat at his expense today and the Queen's tomorrow.

Alton tries to calm the crowd down, and wipe out the strong impact of the last speech. But the logic of the situation overrules him; the press of the crowd makes him feel giddy, and his speech, which began by being mollifying, turns into an incitement to riot.[122]

> 'Go, then,' I cried, losing my self possession... 'and get bread! After all, you have a right to it. No man is bound to starve. There are rights above all laws, and the right to live is one. Laws were made for man, not man for laws.'

The mob cascades down to a farm, where they rob the granary and fire the ricks, satisfying their twin appetites for food and violence, until the yeomanry arrive at a gallop with drawn swords, and take Alton prisoner, since against his will he has become the instigator of the riot.[123]

Then I first found out how large a portion of rascality shelters itself under the wing of every crowd; and at the moment, I almost excused the rich for overlooking the real sufferers, in indignation at the rascals.

This is the voice of the Kingsley who had seen the Bristol riots.

Thus personal and vicarious experience have turned Alton into a Chartist and a revolutionary. And this is Kingsley's first lesson for us. Class hatred, the seed of revolution, is instilled into Alton by resentment at the injustice to which he has been subjected, and the misery and degradation he has seen, all of which are tolerated and encouraged by society:[124]

> Yes, it was true. Society had not given me my rights. And woe unto the man on whom that idea, true or false, rises lurid, filling all his thoughts with stifling glare, as of the pit itself. Be it true, be it false, it is equally a woe to believe it; to have to live on a negation; to have to worship for our only idea, as hundreds of thousands of us have this day, the hatred of the things which are.

His religious faith has evanesced, leaving his mind distorted by envy and bitterness. 'How do you know, dearest man,' wrote Kingsley to Ludlow, 'that I was not right in making the Alton of the second volume different from the first? In showing the individuality of the man swamped and warped by the routine of misery and discontent?'[125] This is the moral of Alton's career. An indifferent society is committing suicide. It is breeding and nurturing very dangerous enemies to established order. And it is as guilty as they, for it first allows them to become hardened in crime, and then punishes them in the name of the law.

But Alton's career also suggests another, more individual message. Kingsley thought that there was a close connection between revolutionary violence and weakness of character and convictions. At the same time as Alton is succumbing to class hatred and the appeal of 'physical force' Chartism, he is losing the strength to resist the temptations of pride and sensuality. On the occasion when he wept before the St Sebastian, his emotional sincerity was observed by an ecclesiastical dignitary and his family. Their interest being aroused, they questioned him. At first sight, Alton became passionately infatuated with Dean Winnstay's daughter, and he sees in his new patron's kind words, goodwill, and hospitality, only occasions to be near her. This love, in which intelligence and true feeling play little part, causes the misfortunes of his life. Lillian Winnstay amuses herself with him, and drops him the instant society declares that he is a criminal. But she has already brought about his downfall, and caused him to betray his class and his social conscience for her. He has written some poems which, like those of Bethune, Cooper, and so many others, are resonant with the spontaneous eloquence of a man of the people. His rich friends offer to have his poems printed, but the publisher insists that they must be expurgated. The Dean advises Alton to agree, and he does so, denying his beliefs and playing the coward in the hope of seeing Lillian again. The poems are well received by the public, but from this point on Alton has lost faith in himself. And in this weak position he proceeds to face further trials. Lillian loves another – Alton's cousin – and he is reduced to a jealous observation of their happiness. Then his party denounces him as a traitor who has been bought by aristocratic flattery, and he sees men who used to acclaim him turn against him. Desperate to rehabilitate himself, he undertakes to spread Chartism in the country-side, with the result we have seen. He narrowly escapes the gallows, and spends three years in prison. By 10 April 1848 he has been released and he is present at the final collapse of his cause. The same day he contracts fever in Bermondsey. His body has already been weakened by privation and the stress of his unsettled life, and he has a long struggle with the disease. It is his final trial. He emerges from it purified, broken, and humble. He is ready for death, which he feels is coming soon, and ready for the religious and political conversion Kingsley has been leading him up to.

And, like Alton Locke, the noble-hearted, wrong-headed working men of England might find salvation in their defeat. Previously revolutionary Chartism had been a dire phenomenon, however understandable it might be. Yet it had some saving graces. Its demands were just. Its leaders were passionate, educated, idealistic men. Alton had left the Chartist meeting he attended overcome with admiration. Would anyone have believed working men to be capable of thinking and talking so well?[126]

> The only thing that did astonish me was to hear men of my own class – and lower still, perhaps some of them – speak with such fluency and eloquence. Such a fund of information – such excellent English – where did they get it all?

These were Chartists who had recommended temperance, chastity, self-respect, and moral education. Alton had previously found himself attracted to one of his companions on the shop-floor: Crossthwaite the Chartist, a sombre, taciturn man who exerted remarkable authority over those around him, and could stop blasphemy or lewdness with a look.[127]

> He was as I was – small, pale, and weakly. He might have been five-and-twenty; but his looks...were rather those of a man of forty. Wild gray eyes gleamed out from under huge knitted brows, and a

perpendicular wall of brain, too large for his puny body. He was not only, I soon discovered, a water-drinker, but a strict 'vegetarian' also.

He was a Carlylean hero to whom, for a long time, Alton dared not open his heart. But at last they are brought together in joint resistance to the sweater. Crossthwaite explains the mysterious word 'Chartism', the blood-shrouded terror of the bourgeoisie, to Alton:[128]

> 'Are the people represented? Are you represented? Do you feel like a man that's got any one to fight your battle in parliament, my young friend, eh?'
> 'I'm sure I don't know –'
> 'Why, what in the name of common sense – what interest or feeling of yours or mine, or any man's you ever spoke to, except the shop-keeper, do Alderman A––– or Lord C––– D––– represent? They represent property – and we have none. They represent rank – we have none. Vested interests – we have none. Large capitals – those are just what crush us. . . . They are chosen by the few, they represent the few, and they make laws for the many – and yet you don't know whether or not the people are represented!'

The Charter will be an instrument of social reform: let it be granted, and workers will sit in Parliament, and they will know how to deal with poverty, theft, and prostitution.

And can one, in the end, have too much of a good thing? Are not the Magna Charta and the Reform Act the pride of the bourgeoisie? Was it not said often enough in 1832 that the extension of the franchise was the universal panacea which would realise every dream? Why not take these promises and arguments to their logical conclusion?[129]

> From that night I was a Chartist, heart and soul – and so were a million and a half more of the best artisans in England – at least, I had no reason to be ashamed of my company. Yes; I too, like Crossthwaite, took the upper classes at their word; bowed down to the idol of political institutions, and pinned my hopes of salvation on 'the possession of one ten-thousandth part of a talker in the national palaver'.

Chartism may be a natural mistake; it is, none the less, deplorable. The means have become the end. The Charter is made an excuse for idleness, weakness and treachery. Individual moral reform is abandoned. For Kingsley, this political materialism is the ultimate impiety: his faith, like Carlyle's, revolts against making man the plaything of circumstances. The Chartists are heading for destruction, like Owen and the Bentham-ites, for they 'worship false gods'.

And in the end revolutionary Chartism is a wretched failure. From the start it has been doomed by internal rivalry, violence, and injustice. Its leader, O'Flynn (a portrait of O'Connor), is an eloquent, sincere, virulent, unscrupulous brute, capable of any heroics or crimes. His journal, the *Weekly Warwhoop*, probably intended for the *Northern Star*, is too often full of insults, personal abuse, and scurrility. It claims the freedom of the press, but itself tyrannises abominably over the freedom of thought of others. It denounces governmental corruption, and dirties its hands by publishing stories of bourgeois swindles. It is trying to regenerate England, and corrupts public morals by publishing French novels.

Could anything but confusion and disaster be the fruit of such seeds? 10 April provides an unforgettable day of shame, which English democracy must nevertheless do its best to forget. Human triviality, carrying the people's petition under the arches of Westminster, has aroused the laughter of the gods. 'We had arrayed against us, by our own folly, the very physical force to which we had appealed.'[130] The ruling classes have degraded themselves by having recourse to force, but they have won, and their dishonour is no consolation to their defeated adversaries.

But Kingsley's view of 'moral force' Chartism is quite different. It is represented by the lively and picturesque character of Sandy Mackaye, who stands for Carlyle's political ideas. If Lancelot Smith and Tregarva were Carlylean heroes, Mackaye is a simulacrum of Carlyle himself. The old Scotch bookseller is a patriarch of radicalism. He remembers the great days of the French Revolution, heard Cartwright speak, and fought alongside Cobbett and the Hunts. For sixty years of trials and tribulations, he has worked for freedom. His hair is white, and his spirit worn; hope and despair are inextricably intertwined within him. He is the product of a hard life, wise and benevolent. His dry humour is deliberately wrapped in some obscurity which is not made any easier by his Scotch accent and diction. His thought, speech, and conduct all combine profundity, comedy, and individuality. He has given up lofty ambitions, and selflessly undertakes the tasks that come to hand which can most certainly be accomplished. It was he who saw Alton's promise and lent him books. After the boy's mother has turned him out of his home for using his mind independently, Mackaye takes him into his own house. He is superbly tolerant of the ignorance and depravity of the poor. He sees that moral reform is urgently necessary, and knows that it can only be brought about by response to an accepted belief. Like Crossthwaite, he tries to make Alton the champion of his cause, but his method is different. He encourages the growth of a powerful, perceptive mind until it inevitably arrives at the complete vision of social justice. He has not given up the struggle himself. He mixes with Chartists and goes to their meetings. But their political superstition, their appeal to force, and O'Flynn's rousing rhetoric only excite his vein of pessimistic mockery. The downfall of the hopes he has placed in Alton seems to him all too sure a sign that the people's cause will collapse, and his strength begins to fail. He dies on the eve of 10 April, prophesying doom to his former comrades:[131]

> 'Tell 'em that they're the slaves o' warse than priests and kings – the slaves o' their ain lusts an' passions – the slaves o' every loud-tongued knave an' mountebank that'll pamper them in their self-conceit; and that the gude God'll smite 'em down, and bring 'em to nought, and scatter 'em abroad, till they repent, an' get clean hearts and a richt speerit within them, and learn His lesson that He's been trying to teach 'em this threescore years – that the cause o' the people is the cause o' Him that made the people; an' wae to them that tak' the deevil's tools to do His wark wi' !'

This is precisely the bitter tone of fierce idealism and scriptural denunciation that Carlyle adopted after 1848. Kingsley accepted without question all the critical side of Carlyle's teaching, though he did reproach him with being too negative. Christian socialism broke with Carlyle in that it held out some hope, and believed in some sort of democracy. According to Alton, 'Mackaye had nothing positive, after all, to advise or propound. His wisdom was one of apophthegms and maxims, utterly impracticable, too often merely negative, as was his creed.'[132]

Before outlining his programme, Kingsley prepared his readers to accept it. Christian socialism was naturally opposed to the commercial and industrial bourgeoisie as a class, and once again 'Mammonism' is vehemently denounced.[133] It is represented by Alton's cousin, whose career runs parallel to the hero's, forming a significant contrast. George is everything Alton is not. He is a worldly success, for he has worldly means, and it would be a miracle if he contrived to rush through his fortune in a hurry. His father is a rich grocer, as low-born as Alton, but a man who has used his driving, calculating ambition to attain power. Utilitarianism is his natural mode of thought; he never says, thinks, or does anything unless it pays. At Dulwich Gallery George also sees Lillian Winnstay, and sets out to inveigle himself into her father's good graces. We meet him again in Cambridge, where he has insinuated himself into the company of a noble friend, Lord Lynedale. Although he is an unbeliever at heart, he takes Holy orders because the Church is a career that offers equality of rank with the upper classes. When Chartism looks dangerous he pretends to sympathise with the workers, and sneaks into their secret meetings, where he hears what Alton has to say. Lillian gives him her affection: he is rich, handsome, and elegant, and has no difficulty in making her forget his weak and lowly rival. On 10 April he is enlisted on the side of law and order. He meets Alton, and the complete opposition of their ways finds expression in bitter words from Alton and contemptuous mockery from his cousin. 'Listen, cousin Alton! The strong and the weak have been matched for the same prize: and what wonder, if the strong man conquers?'[134] And indeed he enjoys the victory of competition. In the merciless warfare of desire his strength and cunning are uninhibited by scruples, and they overcome. But Kingsley wanted to replace such natural anarchy with a better order: his optimistic sense of justice ordained the downfall of the wicked. On the eve of his marriage to Lillian, George contracts typhus. His handsome new overcoat came from Downes's establishment in Bermondsey, where it had covered the fever-ridden bodies of the creatures who made it. George dies, and his death, like Argemone's, is a warning from Providence that society is interrelated. And with him the gospel of individualism, bourgeois self-interest, and liberal economics are condemned. For *Alton Locke* is just as much of a protracted protest against them as *Yeast*.

The aristocracy, on the other hand, deserves to survive. It is better than the Chartists think, and Alton has to learn respect for the merits of the ruling class. His aggressive, proletarian envy gives way when he comes into contact with natural superiors whose strength, grace, calm, and patiently unswerving goodwill give them the right to command. Dean Winnstay is an example of the good men to be found among the senior clergy. Lord Lynedale treats Alton with generous courtesy, and forgives his outburst of hatred. But he staunchly defends his own class against attack, although he evinces no personal pride.[135]

> They treated me as an equal; they welcomed me – the young viscount and the learned dean – on the broad ground of a common humanity; as I believe hundreds more of their class would do, if we did not ourselves take a pride in estranging them from us – telling them that fraternisation between our classes is impossible, and then cursing them for not fraternising with us.

And so the gulf separating the two nations is the work of the poor as much as the rich. Goodwill exists on both sides. Lord Lynedale represents Young England in *Alton Locke*. When he becomes Lord Ellerton he sells one of his estates in order to run the other properly. He is a model landlord, giving up his hounds, reducing rents, building schools and churches, repairing cottages, clearing and draining waste land, opening his picture gallery to labourers, receiving tenants at his table, and lending them books. He transforms an old manor into a co-operative farm and sets up a veritable little communist village. His wife Eleanor helps him enthusiastically with this work. Although she is a relative and friend of Lillian Winnstay, she is quite different from her. With her austere, dominating beauty and steadfast, thoughtful spirit, she exerts an unobtrusive, clearsighted influence over Alton Locke. She exemplifies the noblest ideal of authoritarian, aristocratic philanthropy. But Kingsley, as we have seen, did not accept that ideal unreservedly, and Eleanor and Lord Ellerton are by no means perfect. Like Lord Vieuxbois, they still have a lot to learn. Major misfortune prepares Eleanor for the mission Kingsley has up his sleeve for her. Her husband is taken from her in a riding accident, and grief breaks down her spirit of domineering authority and pride of caste. After three years of private charity among the workers and prostitutes of London she meets Alton, the day after 10 April. She calms him down, argues with him, and announces the doctrine towards which their lives have unconsciously led them.

After Mackaye's death, Kingsley wrote to his friend Ludlow, the book was 'intended to take a mythic and prophetic form...those dreams come in for the very purpose of taking the story off the ground of the actual into the deeper and wider one of the ideal.'[136] The last chapters of the book are, indeed, anything but dogmatic exposition. They instruct through symbols and an appeal to the imagination, as Kingsley intended. He said that he could not, and dared not, present actual realisations of Eleanor's sermons in practice:[137]

> How do you know that my idea of carrying out Eleanor's sermons in practice were just what I could not – and if I could, dared not give? That all I could do was to leave them as seed, to grow by itself in many forms, in many minds, instead of embodying them in some action which would have been both as narrow as my own idiosyncrasy, gain the reproach of insanity, and be simply answered by – 'If such things have been done, where are they?'

Kingsley was quite right. He was a poet, not a sociologist. The conclusion of *Alton Locke*, as it stands, is a fitting crown to his social writings. It sums up his generous idealism in striking images, and discloses the dream of Christian socialism which fired all that was best in the nation's religious life.

Disraeli's Tancred dismissed the theory of evolution with sarcastic contempt. Kingsley, on the contrary, accepted it. With his passion for natural history, he found in it a justification for his interest in lower forms of life. At the same time, his imagination was captivated by the grand and comprehensive view of unity in the chain of being. His mind associated the new theories with the Christian doctrines of the Fall and the Redemption. Socialism, the Bible, and the evolution of species came together in a sort of cosmogony which embraced the past and future of the human race. This is the explanation of the extraordinary chapter in which Kingsley tried to effect a switch from realism to symbolism.[138] The bizarre dreams which come to Alton in his delirium are organised by an interior pattern. Their starting-point is a sense of personal fall. Alton has failed: his Christian faith has given way to sensual paganism. He has sinned against religion, represented by his mother. He hears from Eleanor, the purifying spirit, of the punishment he must undergo: 'He who falls from the golden ladder must climb through ages to its top. He who tears himself in pieces by his lusts, ages only can make him one again.'[139] But science and the Bible show that the universe itself has followed just this course. The Fall came at the beginning of creation, and cosmic redemption took the form of evolution. Alton relives the history of the world, passing through every stage of life: 'The madrepore shall become a shell, and the shell a fish, and the fish a bird, and the bird a beast; and then he shall become a man again, and see the glory of the latter days.'[40] Alton feels himself living and dying through all the stages from protoplasm to rational man. And at every step the same drama is played out, involving three actors: the weak and defenceless hero, standing for the dignity and virtue which still remain in the fallen soul, and the foreshadowing of human nobility in earlier, animal forms of life; his strong, brutal cousin representing materialism and brutish appetites; and Lillian, the lure of the senses by which nature entraps the spirit. At every step evil seems to triumph, just as in real life Alton was beaten and watched his rival carry off Lillian. But then we come to the higher planes, where human consciousness appears, and the drama becomes social. Alton, purified by his sufferings, becomes a prophet, guiding the wanderings of a primitive people. The spirit of evil is no longer represented by a single creature: it is greed and pride, from which spring inequalities of wealth and class. When a mountain range bars the tribe from following their wandering course, they cultivate the valley in peace and plenty. Every man has an equal portion of land, and they all submit to the justice dispensed by heaven: they must work before they can cross the mountains. A time comes when this duty is forgotten: the strong oppress the weak and take their land from them. And from then on the tribe is decimated by wretchedness and famine. The prophet has gone up to the mountains to work and pray, and try to resist the temptations of the mysterious maiden,

Lillian, who is attempting to lure him into the voluptuous sloth of the plain. The poor revolt and drive out the rich, taking over their houses and lands. The prophet threatens them with divine retribution, and his words touch their hearts. The disorder is resolved in a mood of general penitence:[141]

> Then they all cried with one voice, 'We have sinned! We will go up and pierce the mountain, and fulfil the work which God set to our forefathers.'
>
> We went up, and the first stroke that I struck a crag fell out; and behold, the light of day! and far below us the good land and large, stretching away boundless towards the western sun.

At this climactic moment, Eleanor appears as a visionary prophetess from the promised land.[142]

> 'By selfishness you fell, and became beasts of prey. Each man coveted the universe for his own lusts, and not that he might fulfil in it God's command to people and subdue it. Long have you wandered – and long will you wander still. For here you have no abiding city. You shall build cities, and they shall crumble; you shall invent forms of society and religion, and they shall fail in the hour of need. You shall call the lands by your own names, and fresh waves of men shall sweep you forth, westward, westward ever, till you have travelled round the path of the sun, to the place from whence you came. For out of Paradise you went, and unto Paradise you shall return; you shall become once more as little children, and renew your youth like the eagle's. Feature by feature, and limb by limb, ye shall renew it; age after age, gradually and painfully, by hunger and pestilence, by superstitions and tyrannies, by need and blank despair, shall you be driven back to the All-Father's home, till you become as you were before you fell, and left the likeness of your father for the likeness of the beasts. Out of Paradise you came, from liberty, equality, and brotherhood, and unto them you shall return again. You went forth in unconscious infancy – you shall return in thoughtful manhood. You went forth in ignorance and need – you shall return in science and wealth, philosophy and art. You went forth with the world a wilderness before you – you shall return when it is a garden behind you. You went forth selfish savages – you shall return as the brothers of the Son of God.'

Alton wakes up, and finds Eleanor nursing him. She handles his bruised spirit as carefully as his broken body, as she explains the religious and social doctrine by which a new faith may be built upon the ruins of the old. Alton is already a socialist without knowing it; but he is not yet a Christian. Eleanor shows him living Christianity, and the cool arguments of Dean Winnstay's missionary colloquies add the force of philosophy. God's existence is proved by the logic of the heart: Jesus is 'the true demagogue'.[143] Eleanor 'spoke of him as the great Reformer; and yet as the true conservative.'[144] Christianity is the dream of the kingdom of God: historically it has been associated with every movement towards social justice. Look at the past, 'and say, when was there ever real union, co-operation, philanthropy, equality, brotherhood, among men, save in loyalty to Him – Jesus, who died upon the cross?'[145] But revolutionary ambitions have traditionally been allied with atheism; the people's champions have preached free thought. 'What gospel have they, or Strauss, or Emerson, for the poor, the suffering, the oppressed? The People's Friend? Where will you find him, but in Jesus of Nazareth?'[146] The gospel, and not man's abstract rights, must be the basis of the new movement. It is all very well to demand the Charter and the six points, but they must be sought from God. 'And therefore, before you attempt to obtain them, make yourselves worthy of them – perhaps by that process you will find some of them have become less needful.'[147]

And as a 'broad' churchman, the Dean answers Alton's rationalist doubts. Miracles appear to contradict the laws of nature? 'Who told you, my dear young friend, that to break the customs of Nature, is to break her laws?'[148] In the end Christ's miracles were miracles of healing, which did not contradict nature's laws, but restored them.

The purely social argument is sacrificed to Christian apologetics. The co-operative system is scarcely mentioned, appearing only as an economic version of Christian brotherhood. A discreet allusion calls to mind the recent establishment of a tailors' co-operative.[149] But Kingsley deliberately excluded economic propaganda from his artistic prophecy. He had just outlined the advantages of workers' associations in *Cheap Clothes and Nasty*: now he was trying to justify the social mission of the clergy.

Alton calls to mind the secular ties between the Church and the powers that be; the self-interested conduct of the Church, and its inert laxity over the past two centuries; its persistent opposition to the people's dream of freedom. In Catholic countries it has always exercised a sinister tyranny. Left to itself, would it not impose a new bondage on the people? No, is Eleanor's answer. Theocratic states are only experienced by weak nations, and priests only abuse their power when the will and beliefs of the faithful give way. And after all, what do past errors matter? Are there no signs of a great ecclesiastical revival?[150]

'Suppose that there were a rapidly-increasing class among the clergy, who were willing to help you to the uttermost – and you must feel that their help would be worth having – towards the attainment of social reform, if you would waive for a time merely political reform? ...They do not want to be dictators to the working men. They know that they have a message to the artisan, but they know, too, that the artisan has a message to them; and they are not afraid to hear it. They do not wish to make him a puppet for any system of their own; they only are willing, if he will take the hand they offer him, to devote themselves, body and soul, to the great end of enabling the artisan to govern himself; to produce in him the capacity of a free man, and not of a slave; to eat the food he earns, and wear the clothes he makes. Will your working brothers co-operate with these men?'

Nothing will be lost by acceptance, for the whole of society has lost faith in itself, and the victors were never closer to defeat: 'Believe me, that Tenth of April, which you fancied the death day of liberty, has awakened a spirit in high as well as in low life, which children yet unborn will bless.'[151]

Alton and Crossthwaite embark for Texas, the former to repair his shattered frame, and the latter to cultivate virgin soil, until the day when social harmony shall summon them back to England. Once again emigration, as preached by Carlyle, is the last resource of the proletariat. But Alton is fated to see neither the New World, nor the promised land of his dreams. He is to find liberty, equality, and brotherhood in death. His last poem is a triumphal marching song, mingling Chartist fervour with spiritual serenity:[152]

> Weep, weep, weep, and weep,
> For pauper, dolt, and slave;
> Hark! from wasted moor and fen,
> Feverous alley, workhouse den,
> Swells the wail of Englishmen:
> 'Work! or the grave!'
>
> Down, down, down, and down,
> With idler, knave, and tyrant;
> Why for sluggards stint and moil?
> He that will not live by toil
> Has no right on English soil;
> God's word's our warrant!

Up, up, up, and up,
Face your game, and play it!
The night is past – behold the sun! –
The cup is full, the web is spun,
The Judge is set, the doom begun;
Who shall stay it?

The press and the great reviews were hard on *Alton Locke*. The *Edinburgh Review*, in an article by Greg again, reproved Kingsley on three counts:[153] he had written a novel with a purpose; he had set up a wrong-headed protest against the supposed indifference of the upper classes; and, like so many others, he confused the nineteenth century with the fourteenth, and associated Chartism with the vagaries of feudal socialism.[154] Although Greg recognised that the novel contained passages of great beauty, he naturally denied that they were at all convincing. It was 'the absurd or violent language of a benevolent man whose understanding has been driven desperate by the sight of suffering which he cannot relieve.'[155]

The *Quarterly* preferred sterner charges. It found nothing in the book but exaggeration, prejudice, and injustice to the propertied classes and established order.[156] It goes without saying that neither review could see any difference between Christian socialism and revolutionary communism.

Nevertheless the book made a powerful and lasting impression. It sold reasonably well, reaching its third edition by 1852. 'I made £150 by *Alton Locke*,' wrote Kingsley, 'and...a name and a standing with many a one who would never have heard of me otherwise.'[157] The workers' leaders gave it an excellent reception, and recognised themselves in it. And it was enjoyed by men of all classes and all shades of opinion.[158]

I am quite astonished at the steady-going, respectable people who approve more or less of *Alton Locke*. It was but the other night, at the Speaker's, that Sir *** ***, considered one of the safest Whig traditionalists in England, gave in his adherence to the book in the kindest terms. Both the Marshals have done the same – so has Lord Ashburton. So have, strange to say, more than one ultra-respectable High-Tory squire – so goes the world. If you do anything above party, the true-hearted ones of all parties sympathize with you.

And Carlyle's opinion should be cited:[159]

Apart from your treatment of my own poor self...I found plenty to like, and be grateful for in the book: abundance, nay exuberance of generous zeal; headlong impetuosity of determination towards the manful side on all manner of questions;...everywhere a certain wild intensity, which holds the reader fast as by a spell.... At the same time, I am bound to say, the book is definable as *crude*; by no manner of means the best we expect of you – if you will resolutely temper your fire....

Of the grand social and moral questions we will say nothing whatever at present: any time within the next two centuries, it is like, there will be enough to say about them.

After 1850

After 1850, Kingsley's ideas were modified and his expression of them toned down by the general progress of social reconciliation and his own intellectual development. His temperament was enthusiastic and inconsistent, but profoundly moderate, and he could not sustain for long the tone of *Yeast* and *Alton Locke*. He felt the need of a respite from the violent abuse called down by his novels and the praise that had been heaped on them. Hostility made him fear that he had gone too far, while praise satisfied him that he had achieved his end.[160] After 1852 the change in his attitude became marked. In answer to an attack upon the Christian socialists, Kingsley wrote the pamphlet *Who are the Friends of Order?*, in which he claimed that they were the true guardians of social stability:[161]

> As to practical moral good, I cannot call it either a doubtful or a contingent one to make ardent and discontented spirits among the working-classes more patient and contented; more respectful to those institutions of which they have never been taught the value.... That this has been the moral effect, and the only moral effect of our labours, I distinctly assert.

At the same time, his social conscience was lulled by a tide of optimism. The economic and intellectual achievements of the interventionist reaction seemed to him good, important, and adequate. From then on, his writings were full of reassuring passages. The two Prefaces he wrote for *Alton Locke* in 1854 and 1861 acknowledge the progress achieved by the goodwill of the poor, and the even greater goodwill of the rich. Kingsley reproached the working men of England with having done so little to help themselves, and having failed to attend to the co-operative message as they should have done:[162]

> If you are better off than you were in 1848, you owe it principally to those laws of political economy (as they are called), which I call the

brute natural accidents of supply and demand, or to the exertions made by upright men of the very classes whom demogogues taught you to consider as your natural enemies.

The undergraduates of Cambridge, on the other hand, are congratulated upon the new interest that the upper classes take in the lives of their inferiors, and he extends his congratulations to the entire aristocracy:[163]

> How changed, thank God! is all this now. Before the influence of religion, both Evangelical and Anglican; before the spread of those liberal principles, founded on common humanity and justice, the triumph of which we owe to the courage and practical good sense of the Whig party; before the example of a Court, virtuous, humane, and beneficent; the attitude of the British upper classes has undergone a noble change.

His literary work was animated by the same spirit. After *Alton Locke* he wrote no more social novels. *Hypatia* (1853) distances the immediate religious problems it deals with by using a Roman historical setting. In fifth-century Alexandria Kingsley finds analogues and antecedents for the Oxford Movement, the Roman Church, celibacy of the clergy, and the monastic ideal. *Two Years Ago* (1857) was written under the immediate impact of the Crimean War. Certain characters from *Yeast* reappear, as if to mark the continuity between past and present.[164] The social problems briefly sketched in are now described as being dealt with:[165]

> I find, in every circle of every class, men and women asking to be taught their duty, that they may go and do it; I find everywhere schools, libraries, and mechanics' institutes springing up: and rich and poor meeting together more and more in the faith that God has made them all.

The novel deals with Anglo-Saxon imperialism, the theory of national efficiency, the glory of war, and the divine mission of the Germanic races.

Kingsley lived on until 1875, becoming Professor of Modern History at Cambridge, and a canon of Westminster Abbey. His output was large and varied, the product of a flexible, rather than a powerful intellect.[166] It is reasonable to consider *Alton Locke* as his masterpiece.

Meanwhile, theoretical and organised Christian socialism underwent a similar fortune. From 1850 until about 1854 the Christian socialists worked hard and effectively. They popularised their principles in a series of tracts, many of which improved upon their rather hazy notions of the co-operative ideal. They were directly responsible for founding twelve working men's associations: three of tailors, two of shoemakers, two of builders, one of piano-makers, one of smiths, and one of bakers.[167] All came from light industries and represented that section of the working class for which Kingsley wrote, and from which he drew his protagonists. Other associations in the South of England came into existence with their guidance and support. In the industrial North, which the Rochdale pioneers had opened up to the co-operative cause, Ludlow, Hughes, and Neale made a propaganda tour. Their enthusiasm and ability proved highly effective.[168] During the engineers' strike of 1852, the Christian socialists tried to act as intermediaries between employers and workers.[169] Finally, they took up the legal position of working men's associations. They drew up the Industrial Provident Society Bill, and saw it adopted by Parliament in 1852. The successive amendments to that Act by which co-operatives were enabled to participate in commercial and industrial life were also the work of Ludlow, Neale, and their friends.[170]

But on the whole, Christian socialism faded away after 1850. Kingsley and Maurice did not succeed in enlisting the bulk of the clergy: that 'rapidly-increasing class among them' promised by Eleanor remained an infinitesimal minority within the Church of England. And the material consequences of their activities were equally unsuccessful. All the co-operatives they had founded either collapsed, or turned into ordinary companies. At the outset they were organised along French lines, and hopelessly anarchic. Then they were nearly all rushed under the authority of a central committee. But they were past saving. The associations quarrelled incessantly with their elected directors, and they adopted an exclusive attitude to new members. Both factors tended towards their destruction. It is interesting to note that, for all their idealism, the Christian socialists had not rested their co-operative movement on a logical basis. They were themselves disinterested, but they were appealing to the workers' self-interest. Their idea of co-operation was not the elimination of profit, but profit-sharing. And so the sort of productive co-operative association they proposed was to be a closed shop, making its way in competition with the rest of society. Thus economic analysis revealed their dream of workers' organisations without management as nothing more than a roundabout form of individualism.[171] This ironical twist of fate was caused by the Christian socialists having only come across light industry, whether from accident or preference. If they had developed differently, and formed their opinions against a background of heavy industrial activity, they might have adapted their social concern better to the needs of the day.

Christian socialism was, nevertheless, to remain a force to be reckoned with in England. Its influence on English life after 1850 was diffuse, but decided. It survived in transformed and revitalised shapes, with theories from quite different sources added to it, and although only a few people professed themselves Christian socialists, it was always a potential influence on very many more. Kingsley and his friends had followers and successors.[172] Their idealism proved true and seminal, and they had shown the right spirit, even if conditions had proved against the practical activities they undertook. By indicating the moral sources of social change, and looking for the fundamentals of workers' associations in the spirit of collectivism they arrived, before their time, at the ultimate conclusion of later social research.[173]

> For co-operators have always been inspired by the ancient doctrine of human fellowship, by the new spirit of social service, by a firm faith that the day would come when each man and woman would work, not for personal subsistence or personal gain, but for the whole community.

By adopting an altruistic religious sentiment, Kingsley demonstrated one possible doctrine of human association. *Alton Locke*, which tentatively yet powerfully suggests that doctrine, is the culmination of the literary movement whose history we have traced.

Conclusion

The documentary value of the novel

We have tried to analyse the documentary value of social novels and examine their persuasive power. In Dickens we found an imaginative realism which threw specific abuses into strong relief, and cast a melancholy charm over the lesser sufferings of the lower middle classes. Disraeli's picture of agricultural and industrial poverty was highly externalised and unlifelike, but nevertheless extremely accurate. Mrs Gaskell, on the other hand, showed us the true faces of the people whose generally depressing lives were bound up with factory labour, together with the worst of urban poverty. In Kingsley there was no conflict between vitality and accuracy; and the condition of the peasantry, as well as a section of urban life, was more compellingly depicted than had ever been achieved before. From these relative, partial pictures an impression of the whole may be built up, and we can envisage the English people between 1830 and 1850. But we have not insisted on this possible generalisation, and drew on other sources for the brief outline of working-class conditions in chapter 3, '*Classes injured by individualism*'! For the novelists' description of poverty is incomplete, for all its historical and literary interest. It puts the most obvious and well-known features of poverty in the foreground, at the expense of factors that a scientific observer might have found more important. The social novel was dominated by small industries, although their hey-day was long over in society at large. The details of factory life and work were never imaginatively evoked, as happened in later novels. Writers described it timidly and externally, or else, like Dickens, as a monstrous fantasy, glimpsed though the terror it evoked. Neither novelists nor their audience yet had at their disposal habits of thought or points of reference which would permit an artistic exploitation of industry. And so delay in the novels is in keeping with delay in the minds of society at large.[2]

We have extracted the explicit and implicit arguments and intentions from the novels, in order to do justice to their persuasive force. After seeing how each writer arrived at his social philosophy, we have seen it in action in his books. We have defined his outlook as precisely as possible, and established the extent to which he was in sympathy with each of the three elements of the idealistic interventionist reaction. Except for Disraeli, whose positive thinking made up a genuine political platform, we found none of them putting forward a well-defined programme. The novelists, like all upper-class spokesmen for social compunction, were at their best in criticising the existing order. Their criticism fell into two distinct forms: vigorous denunciation of specific abuses, and satire on the sort of personalities and feelings associated with individualism.

Taken as a group, Dickens, Disraeli, Mrs Gaskell, and Kingsley had one common ideal: an efficient, paternalistic philanthropy, in which the State, or the great traditional estates of Church and nobility, carefully supervised social ills. Of course there were differences between their views. Dickens and Kingsley were, to differing extents, uneasy about Young England, which Disraeli led. Kingsley attacked the Oxford Movement, which had Disraeli's sympathy. Mrs Gaskell was sympathetic to Nonconformity, which Dickens and Kingsley ridiculed. But these differences were secondary. The same generosity and inadequacy attaches to the social ideals of all the novelists. We never find an ideal of progress which is both economic and democratic. (Kingsley is the sole exception here; at least, he is a partial exception.)[3] Conservatism is always present, alongside idealism and interventionism.

Finally, we have pointed out the novelists' influence, using contemporary evidence in every case. But this could never be defined precisely; it is impossible to produce exact documentary evidence of a book's moral and emotional impact. We have adduced such evidence as numbers of editions and contemporary reviews as far as possible, and these are important. But the essence of a book's influence lies in the impression it makes on unknown readers who give it power by sheer weight of numbers. And there is little or no written evidence on this; it is almost an imponderable, and may be very remote from the considered judgement of a professional critic. Therefore we have paid great attention to general observations in which contemporaries bore witness to a writer's influence on them. As they may sum up a whole host of casual remarks in daily life, such comments are almost as valuable as numbers of editions.

In 1861, in the final volume of his *Popular History of England*, Charles Knight glanced over the immediate past, and noticed the importance of the social element in its literature. He wrote the following assessment of the particular role of the novel:[4]

To understand, wherever possible, what are the habitual thoughts and feelings of the great mass of the people; to go to the root of that isolation which separates the receiver of wages from the capitalist; to see where the scientific laws which regulate Labour and Capital press unequally, and how their inevitable tendency to a segregation of classes can be modified; to ascertain what is the true nature of the popular prejudice which requires to be enlightened on political questions; to cast away all undue suspicion of democratic opinions and of religious dissent, and to open as wide as prudence may prescribe the doors of the Senate and of the Church; lastly, to trace crime to its dens, and finding out how much of it is identified with misery and with that barbarism which sits grim and dangerous by the side of civilization, to abate if possible the want, and to remove the ignorance before the dimness of the child becomes the total darkness of the adult; – such are the duties which it is the especial honour of many of the present race of our writers of prose fiction to have successfully inculcated. . . . All honour to those beguilers of life's dull hours who have laboured to bring us all to a knowledge of each other by repeated efforts, such as those of Charles Dickens; to the illustrious females, such as Elizabeth Gaskell, who have seen in this work an especial vocation; to a band of manly thinkers of whom Charles Kingsley is the type. They have their reward, though not a complete one, in seeing the great change which marks the difference between 1831 and 1861.

When one recalls the extent of the interventionist reaction and the wealth of social literature, of which the novel was only one section, this tribute may seem excessive. But the particular effectiveness of the novel as a means of literary communication should be borne in mind. Although there were a great many official reports and statistics and philanthropic treatises, these did not attempt to popularise understanding of social problems. As Charlotte Elizabeth made one of her characters say,[5]

'You see, the facts are brought before Parliament by having witnesses up to be examined on oath before the committee; these reports, as they are called, are printed, and sold too: but, Green, I don't think one lady in a thousand looks into them, to say nothing of other classes: and if they are not read, how can the statements be known?'

The rich and the poor, according to Disraeli, were[6]

Two nations; between whom there is no intercourse and no sympathy; who are as ignorant of each other's habits, thoughts, and feelings, as if they were dwellers in different zones, or inhabitants of different planets.

These passages were published in 1845, showing that at the very height of the crisis, as the new philanthropy was emerging, there was general ignorance about the state of affairs. And so we are shown again how useful *Sybil*, *Mary Barton*, and *Alton Locke* were in disseminating information.

Frederic Harrison, who read Kingsley as a young man of twenty, paid tribute to him later in the following terms:[7]

> It is possible that the 'genteeler' taste of our age may prevent the young of to-day from caring for *Alton Locke*. But I can assure them that five and forty years ago that book had a great effect and came home to the heart of many.

But this sort of praise was especially bestowed on Dickens. An enormous number of people declared with sincere gratitude that it was from him that they first learnt of the virtues and aspirations of humble life, and he had preserved them in their happier fortune from practising self-interest. The following representative verses by 'A Man of the Crowd', which appeared shortly after Dickens's death, voiced the general feeling:[8]

> I am but one of many; never saw
> Thy face, or heard the voice that now is stilled.... and yet
> My heart is heavy with a keen regret,
> Mine eyes with unaccustomed tears are filled....
>   That sense so sure, that wit so strong
> Did battle on our side against the oppressor's wrong....
>
> Thou, painter-poet as thou wert, did'st draw
> The hidden beauty meaner eyes ne'er saw;
> But which, set forth upon thy living page
> Drew all the eyes and hearts of an unthinking age.
> All inarticulate we; thou wert our voice....
>
> Therefore we loved thee, better than we knew
>   Old friend and true.
> Thy silent passing to an honoured tomb
> Has filled a people's heart with more than fleeting gloom.

Such comments suggest the true greatness and effectiveness of the social novel. It evoked feelings which restrained class-hatred by arousing compassion on the one hand and resignation on the other. It takes its place among the factors which saved England from revolution.[9]

Conclusion

The idealist reaction

We have examined the representative value of the social novel, and seen it as an index of the great movement which we have called the idealistic and interventionist reaction. We have tried to analyse its origins, nature and immediate effect.

We have seen social sentiment come to life, develop, and reach full flower in Christian socialism. The permanent interests of the landed gentry and the confused needs of the industrial and agricultural proletariat provided its economic support; the oscillation of the national spirit towards one of the two poles of its natural psychological rhythm gave it its inner shape. In spite of individual differences between men, and the divergencies of small parties, we found the reaction to be strikingly unified. Religious idealism, the aesthetic revival, and social altruism may not have had the same object, and the last of these may have been more decidedly reactionary among feudal socialists than Christian socialists; but in spite of the uneven strain between popular demands, and the aristocracy's superior sense of responsibility, the convergence of aims was remarkable. An ideal of personal conduct and social life grounded in the pursuit of collective emotion emerged in opposition to another ideal, comprising the precise analysis and methodical pursuit of private interests.

As a movement of the feelings, the idealistic reaction only expressed itself through emotional gestures. Properly speaking, it produced no theoretical intellectual results. It found its profoundest expression in Carlyle, in whose writings it took on the semblance of philosophy, only to declare that the highest reaches of intelligence were to be found in mystical intuition. But if it created no system of its own, it destroyed others. Its nature and consequences are a matter of historical interest.

Faced with depressions which showed that the economic system was unsatisfactory, upper-class England turned back on itself. Sensitivity was reawakened, and moved to spontaneous pity for suffering humanity. Religion put forward a case for condemning individualism in the name of Christianity. An instinct of national self-preservation suggested that remedial measures would have to be taken to mollify class-hatred. Of these three factors, it was religion which was the most important, in appearance at least. The average man's resistance to the cruelty of competition hardened around religious arguments, and the movement in its normal form took on the appearance of moderate conservative Christian interventionism.

From top to bottom of society people unanimously adopted this outlook. The movement was powerful, and although it was never universal, it embraced an influential section of the ruling class, and looked like a national transformation.

Its consequences were eminently practical. It issued in a series of measures which righted the most blatant wrongs of society. Industrial legislation, culminating triumphantly in the Ten Hours Bill of 1847, stepped in between capital and labour.[10] The State came to the defence of those who were too weak to look after themselves, and protected women and children from over-long hours, dangerous work, and unhealthy workshops. Men benefited indirectly from this protection. A great effort was made to clean up the congested centres of heavy industry: social sanitation became an upper-class obsession. The victims and outcasts of prejudice and neglect were treated with clear-sighted solicitude: criminals who were not responsible for their condition received humane severity. The criminal law was reformed; the press was set free; and education was brought nearer and nearer to the people's reach. By 1850 the blots defiling the England of 1830 had been wiped away.

Indirectly, the movement also had some theoretical consequences. After 1848 Mill introduced a note of change into economic dogmatism. Ruskin's impassioned diatribes found echoes even among the followers of Nassau Senior and McCulloch. Ethics was at last allowed to take its place in social science. And all this was unquestionably caused solely by the crisis of conscience between 1830 and 1850. Dickens and Carlyle did not obliterate intransigent individualism, any more than Ruskin who followed them and used the same strategy. They lacked the scientific arguments to put down an inadequately-grounded science for good.[11] But the idealist reaction made a powerful contribution to this work by attacking abstract beliefs at their psychological roots with emotional suggestions. And it used concrete examples to bring to light forgotten aspects of social life.

We have described this twofold action which was exemplified in the social novel. We have seen Dickens and his collaborators attacking the individualist personality, and drawing middle-class attention to disregarded areas of life. The novelists brought sensitivity to bear upon the ills of society, and by the emotions they evoked, revived all the mental activities that had been sacrificed to industrial discipline and economic arguments. Man became a sensitive being once more, responsive to all sorts of outside influences, instead of a plain, rational follower of enlightened self-interest. An exploration of the nebulous region between social life and emotional life led to the discovery that there was a natural basis for social solidarity. Enlarged self-awareness led to the discovery that others were to some extent like oneself. With the recognition that no man was an island, elementary sympathy and responsiveness to the promptings of conscience returned. And ideas were enriched and became more complex, until the original simply economic formulations could not withstand their opposition. Economic man disappeared, extinguished by the public conscience. The idealist reaction had laboriously broken the ground for a new ideology.

Social optimism after 1850

And so the reaction played its part in establishing the optimism which, after 1850, replaced the disturbances of the previous period. It collabora- ted with many other great forces, but was one of the formative influences of the mid-Victorian period. Economic prosperity revived around 1846. Free trade led to a general fall in prices.[12] Emigration relieved England of a good deal of its deprived population. Transport was improved by the construction of railways and the development of steam navigation, and this in turn led to a resurgence of industry.[13] The discovery of gold in California and Australia (1849 and 1851) had the same effect.[14] Between 1846 and 1852 taxes were cut, but revenue deriving from them increased. On 1 January 1852 only 800,000 people were registered as receiving public assistance in England and Wales.[15] A French traveller visiting the country was struck by the prosperity of English agriculture.[16] And the working class shared in the general prosperity. The trade unions moved decisively into the peaceful and orderly phase of their development, putting aside the politics of violence for patient and steady organisation.[17]

At the same time, a remarkable phenomenon appeared in the mental life of the nation. The two currents of thought which had diverged after 1832, and whose hostility had seemed implacable from 1840 to 1850, began to converge, partially at least. Bourgeois individualists gave up a little of their intransigence, and working-class leaders began to pay a little attention to liberal economics. The engineers' strike of 1852 was, without question, the last time that masters and men confronted each other from the old vantage points, with industrialists denying their employees the right to negotiate collectively.[18] But the time for heroics was over. For one thing, the whole of the middle class was vaguely aware that intervention was necessary. Moderate legislative reform was no longer controversial: it had been enacted, and could be judged by its results. And increasing numbers of men came to accept the need for legis- lation to control industry. In 1860 Roebuck, one of the last of the philo- sophical radicals, gave public support to Lord Ashley, whom he had always fought strenuously.[19] Gladstone and Sir James Graham followed suit: even Cobden wavered. Only Brougham and John Bright remained invincible.[20] On the other side of the fence, the trade unions moved further and further away from communism, and found a justification for their existence in the principle of free competition. The legitimacy of collective bargaining became their watchword, rather than the suspect demand for minimum subsistence earnings.[21] Around 1860 an enlarged, optimistic, flexible liberalism replaced the contradictory ideas of the preceding period, and temporarily reconciled individualism and socialism. It dominated politics until about 1880.

The social novel moved with these developments, and interpreted them. It became calm and sober in the hands of Charles Reade, Mrs Craik, and Mrs Balfour. It put forward a documented indictment of persistent flaws in the penal code[22] or a confident eulogy of the philanthropic bourgeois ideal.[23] As early as 1853, the anodyne sentiment of Miss Yonge's *Heir of Redclyffe* contrasted strikingly with *Alton Locke* and *Hard Times*. The novel no longer tackled the serious problem of class relations, or if it did deal with them, it employed the considered critical prudence of a George Eliot.[24] Her massive personality dominated the mid-Victorian novel. She exhibited intellectual compassion rather than the impassioned sympathy of a Dickens. She set out with patient affection to illuminate the complexity of dull lives, and give them some importance through her sympathetic understanding. English naturalism was a triumph of loving objectivity, and it seemed to be the natural development of social Romanticism as practised by Dickens and Kingsley. They had preserved the headlong impetuosity of Romanticism, but channelled it into a response to the experiences of others. Under the veneer of Byronic egoism, they had returned to Wordsworthian altruism. In their work English Romanticism made its final choice between the two conflicting tendencies from which it originated, and turned towards objectivity of feeling. When the scientific spirit of the new generation appeared in the novel after 1850, it preserved such romantic feelings as did not conflict with the tranquillity requisite for study. And this explains the easy transition from the romantic to the naturalist novel in England, and the difference in tone between George Eliot and Flaubert.

The practical work of social conscience

This does not mean that England had no more social problems. They had only become overshadowed by public prosperity, and swept from the surface of national life to fester out of sight. Beneath the optimism of commentators, hardship was as grievous as ever. Its most obvious and repulsive features had been done away with by the goodwill of the ruling class. But although so scrupulous a conscience as Kingsley's allowed him to retire from the fray feeling his work to be done, others surged forward, fired by the same sense of outrage and continuing the same battle. The rich, gleaming, thriving civilisation of the mid-Victorian period was no longer soiled by remnants of barbarism, but it still rested on the pursuit of material possessions and fundamental inequality between rich and poor. Some men attacked it with all the eloquence and idealism of the previous period. Matthew Arnold denounced the complacent mediocrity of the bourgeois ideal. At the beginning of 1857 Ruskin started his long campaign against the adversaries Kingsley had declared to be vanquished. Carlyle in his later years withdrew into himself and launched ferocious attacks upon the age. Karl Marx, a foreigner working in England, based his indictment of the capitalist organisation of industrial society on recent, scientifically-collected English data.[25] The main force of the interventionist reaction had not gone to the heart of the matter. It had adduced evidence which could not be overlooked by Christian charity and humane sensitivity, and had corrected the worst excesses of the evil overshadowing national life. But it had undertaken nothing by way of radical reform.

This was because it was always guided by an instinct for the necessary compromise. It seized on effective, but illogical, resolutions of conflicting demands. Like most of the answers England has found for its historical problems, this was only of relative value, and had limited implications. There was no clear and decisive replacement of rational individualism by emotional interventionism. The two intellectual movements which came together after 1850 were never systematically combined: they mingled confusedly. Neither social justice nor competition came firmly to the fore: they simply balanced each other out, and coexisted. And the logical inadequacy of this compromise solution only heightened its remarkable success. England found the formula for internal stability in the rejection of any formula whatsoever.

There was, then, an element of self-interest in the idealist reaction. How important was it? The evidence may be interpreted differently according to whether we are considering the leaders of the movement or the general public. Among the former, social self-preservation was always secondary. It is impossible to doubt their sincerity. Their feelings were true and uncalculating, without any ulterior motivation. Their social conscience was disinterested. They were primarily conscious of the moral and religious objections to social evils, and they invoked them before everything else. They tried to revive deadened sensitivity, put

indifference to shame, and shock Christian and humanitarian compunction into life. As they were ethically motivated, they assumed that others
were too. It would be false psychological reasoning to challenge the
sincerity of Ashley, Kingsley and Dickens, and argue that because their
charity served the long-term ends of their class it must have been hypocritical.

The case is different when we turn to the general public. Public wishes
have to conform with instinctive needs if they are to issue in corporate
action. And it is certain that the interventionist public was more or less
consciously guided by a wish for stability. We have seen that this utilitarian argument had its place among the idealists, and explicitly or
implicitly recurred in their social novels. 'What then? Look at France
and see,' wrote Kingsley at the end of *Cheap Clothes and Nasty* in 1850.
'Bide the end!' said Dickens's Spirit of Christmas Present to those who
obstinately closed their eyes to the evil around them. Disraeli ended *Sybil*
on the vision of a burning castle, pillaged by rioters. Behind them all
Carlyle had warned of the degeneration of the race, and the need to
refashion a healthy, contented people to attain the high destiny of
England. In Parliament, Lord Ashley announced that revolution was
imminent in the industrial areas.[26] These were the most effective tones
to take with the practical, materialistic politicians and men of affairs who
then, as always, dominated the administration and Government. The
new philanthropy swelled into a national movement under the influence
of fears generated by the riots of 1842.[27]

These were the needs of the time, considered for their own sake,
which compelled the nation to adopt rudimentary socialist measures.
'The "practical man",' according to Sidney Webb, 'oblivious or contemptuous of any theory of the Social Organism or general principles of
social organisation, has been forced by the necessities of the time, into an
ever deepening collectivist channel.'[28]

How did the average man reconcile these self-interested motives with
the altruistic impetus? This question confronts us with what is, perhaps,
the most difficult question one can ask about the Englishman's psychology. There is no simple answer. There were endless variations as different
individuals exhibited different proportions of sincerity and moral certainty. On the whole, though, it is fair to say that the problem was resolved because it was never put. Instinct dealt with a dilemma that would
have baffled reason, and thereby hampered the will to act. Instinct
suggested that there was a natural affinity between the prosperity of
nations or individuals, and their moral excellence. The concept was
nebulous, and held unconsciously, yet it could be relied upon as a basis

for the undertaking of useful, but contradictory, actions. And everyone could satisfy himself that the contradictions had been resolved by whatever formulation suited his temperament.

Charles Knight gave expression to this widespread, unshakeable bourgeois belief that the morally good and the socially useful were the same. After praising novelists for making known the submerged classes, he added:[29]

> It is a knowledge which promises safety to the great and to the rich; to the landowner and the merchant; to the lawyer and the divine; to all who serve the State in administrative functions; to the secular teacher, and even to the abstracted student who would 'let the world slip': – 'Blessed is he that considereth the poor; the Lord will deliver him in time of trouble.'

From this point of view, England exhibited a twofold restoration of balance between 1840 and 1850. On the one hand, the economic and social malaise created by the industrial revolution was settled. A larger share of governmental attention, public finances, and private charity was devoted to the hitherto neglected classes. The role of the State expanded, almost entirely for the benefit of its poorer citizens. Legislation and philanthropy disposed of a threat to social peace. Class-hatred was moderated and rendered harmless. The old balance of society which had been upset by the emergence of a new class was restored as far as possible. And at the same time, a similar compensatory movement was at work in the national spirit. The malaise caused by the undue predominance of a particular point of view was corrected by a psychological reaction. Idealistic notions rose up against the essentially English practicality and self-interest which had got out of hand in the systematic formulations of Benthamite utilitarianism and bourgeois materialism. Idealism succeeded because it went to work through practical efficacy and daily life to re-establish interior order.

And so the psychological and economic aspects of the movement were both directed to achieving balance in the face of excess. Does this mean that economic factors determined psychological changes? We have said that this seems an oversimplification. There were deeper reasons for the agreement between the two; they both appealed to aspects of the English character, and acted and reacted upon each other in harmony because they expressed a truth central to the life and being of the nation.

It was England's great good fortune that when its material growth demanded an unlimited expansion of practical skills, it was able to unearth the resources for an enormous leap forward in material inventions and industrial production. When it urgently needed restrictions on unfettered egoism, it again found the whole nation, led by an *élite*, drawing on deep resources of altruism, sympathetic imagination, and moral sentiment. In each case the response was sincere and spontaneous, as if in answer to the nation's destiny.

The reaction we have studied exhibits one other phenomenon. Utilitarianism, in the end, triumphed as well as idealism, but it was a better, expanded utilitarianism: a utilitarianism of life and instinct, not abstract ideology. Carlyle was more fully and profoundly utilitarian than Bentham. He was a better embodiment of the national passion for controlling things. The vague intuition of the race, yielding to the conditions of reality, perceived the dangers of systematic self-interest, and divined that religious, aesthetic, and moral sentiments held something that was essential to health and progress. Social intellectualism was overcome by the blind energy with which England reconciled the sincere pursuit of moral ends with the obstinate search for material betterment. It was a reconciliation achieved by action rather than thought.

The idealist reaction after 1850

It only remains to enumerate the ways in which the results of the idealist reaction were prolonged beyond 1850. They constitute a large part of English history down to the turn of the century.

Industrial legislation increased, moving into new areas of heavy industry and adapting itself to conditions that differed from small sweatshops. State and municipal controls grew stronger all the time. Public and private philanthropy carried on its good work. Interventionist ideas spread imperceptibly until they affected even the most prejudiced, and influenced governmental practice. Official thinking may not have followed social data to their logical conclusion, but it was steadily affected by the new spirit. And we find the imprint of the original upheaval we have examined on many subsequent ideas and activities.

Christian socialism remained a lively unobtrusive force to be reckoned with. At every crisis in the nation's affairs it was ready to spring up again. Social Toryism was even more brilliantly successful: it came to power with its creator, Disraeli, and found expression in a series of measures enacted between 1870 and 1880 which partially carried out the programme of *Sybil*. From then on it had traditional standing. Freed from any connection with purely democratic ideas, the notion that the law ought to protect the weak in the interests of social stability became an implicit tenet of Toryism. The monarch's prestige was heightened, and the position of the Established Church confirmed, while a jealous regard for aristocratic authority neutralised the effect of the Reform Acts. In association with imperialism, social Toryism gained strength by assuming patriotic appeal.

Imperialism itself, as a matter of fact, originated in the idealist reaction. Carlyle was its true creator. Disraeli predicted it in rudimentary form in *Sybil* and *Tancred*. Kingsley's belligerent temperament and belief in the mission of the Germanic races combined to produce a bellicose nationalism which was hardly perceptible in *Alton Locke*, but inescapable in *Two Years Ago*.

The social novel casts light on the link between these two very different philosophies – altruistic philanthropy and militant nationalism. Men allowed their feelings to have free play, became aware of their emotions and approved of them, and were enabled to sympathise with their fellow beings to the extent that they could communicate from those troubled depths where feeling borders on social experience, and the remotest impulses of other people's existence can be felt in the blood. At the same time racial feelings grew up alongside social compassion. A new sense of kinship with fellow-nationals was experienced, and a hostility to men of other nations. And at the same time these national feelings expunged men's plain recognition of logical distinctions. The demands of justice, like all other rational demands, are impersonal, and so they were obscured. The rejection of calm and lucid deliberation predisposed men to an almost willing acceptance of the stupidities of inflamed feelings. We find that men who felt strongly and spoke out against rationalists and the error of social mathematics in the early part of the century were still speaking out against rationalists in the latter half. Only now they were speaking out against the oppressed as well. Only intellectuals of the old rationalist school protested about the Governor Eyre affair. Carlyle, Ruskin, and Kingsley saw nothing wrong; it needed a conscience stiffened by an understanding of abstract ethics to see where justice lay on that occasion. British imperialism and socialism alike were inextricably rooted in the reaction which gave the instincts a place among the sources of national strength.

Finally, aesthetic and religious idealism flourished, closely linked to each other, and to the other offshoots of the movement. Ruskin's artistic work is inseparable from his social campaign. Ritualism in the Church answered the same needs as the quest for aesthetic beauty in secular life. The authority of ecclesiastical powers followed the same upward trend as the authority of civil powers. And it seemed more and more as though public splendour and the prestige of the established order had become the ultimate goals to which logical truth and abstract justice were to be sacrificed.

One thing however must not be forgotten. Social conscience was born in England around 1840. It never died. From then on there was always vague awareness, or positive certainty, that something would have to be done. Consciences would not be stilled, or Englishmen could not be at peace with themselves. However crude or timid it might be in practice, that feeling redeemed a society which would otherwise be detestable. It was reflected in literature, as the novel again became the favourite form of expression between 1880 and 1900. It had enormous consequences which were to be felt for a very long time.

In the end, when we look at the idealist reaction in the context of the history of ideas, it takes on a more general importance. It marks a turning point in philosophy. At one and the same time it contributed to knowledge, and hindered the progress of learning. This can best be tested and proved in the career of the contemporary who gave the best summary of the movement. When John Stuart Mill came into contact with Germano-Coleridgean philosophy, the perfectly constructed system of ideas in which he had put his faith was both enriched and shattered. He had discovered the existence of other realities in nature and the soul. Around 1850 his social philosophy became more flexible and complex: it accepted new ideas along with the old formulations, and gained in truth and justice. But it lost its cohesiveness. From then on Mill oscillated between the two poles, strongly attracted to each, but unable to bring them together and reconcile them. As a mystical logician, a utilitarian humanitarian, and a Ricardian socialist, he exemplifies the imperfect reconciliation of clear thought and intuitive feeling, and the reciprocal corrective influence they exerted over each other.

By 1850 the rationalist attempt to place society on a logical basis had been overthrown by a spontaneous national reaction. And so traditional rationalism, a beaten force, was driven out from political economy, its last citadel. Economics, the youngest of the sciences, saw its prematurely ambitious ideal of dogmatic abstract accuracy slipping from its grasp. Popular resistance forced it to accommodate a vital element of political humanity; for without this, economic laws meant physical and mental suffering. The victorious idealists took over economics, but refused to bow down before material facts, so that the logical unity of classical economics could not be maintained. From then on monolithic political economy was shattered, torn apart by the rival schools of thought. It swung between the poles of scientific rigour and social justice, trying in vain to reconcile the impassive study of cause and effect with the dedicated pursuit of moral social goals.

And so the transitional phase of the social sciences at the end of the century was ushered in. From then on the problem was to appear in familiar terms in all the social sciences. Any revival of rationalism had to accommodate emotion. This placed it on the knife-edge between two dangers: either intellectual abstraction might choke human sympathy; or a tide of emotion might sweep away the framework of reason. But there was no other way of avoiding a defeat which would drag down with it the dignity of the intellect, and the hopes placed in learning. Such a failure would debar mankind from that reasonable control over the will which offers the only hope of freedom from the tyrannous caprice of emotion and instinct. There was no other way of taking in experience, and overcoming the limits nature seems to have set on philosophy. It was a difficult task, which particularly exercised sociological theorising, for this attempted to comprehend the fullness of man's utilitarian and emotional life, and his ideals. And all this could only be explained by a theory resting securely on laws and precepts.

Practice was driven by the same urgent necessity as theory. Stable society can only be achieved in a psychological climate which reconciles clear intellectual decisions with instinct and feeling. Of course, perfection is a long way off, and may never be attained. But we may conclude that the idealist reaction brought England a little closer to it. It did nothing to hasten the advent of perfect abstract justice, and may even have hindered it. But it permitted that poor, provisional justice which is indispensable to life, and is one of the first conditions of life. From this point of view it did more good than harm. The historic role of the early-Victorian novel was to contribute to the reaffirmation of social order and the re-establishment of a just balance of opinion in the mind of the nation.

Notes

Introduction

1 See Sidney Webb, *A History of Trade Unionism*, 1890, p. 360 et seq., for an account of this.

2 Certain detached writers, e.g. Ruskin and Matthew Arnold, vigorously criticised this optimism. However, they received little attention.

3 George Eliot's work dominated this period.

4 One particular incident, the engineers' strike of 1852, prolonged the occurrence of industrial strife as a topic in fiction. We shall indicate its influence below.

5 From 1816 to 1851 an average of 100 new novels each year was published, the total number over the 35-year period being 3,500. It is interesting to compare this with the 10,300 theological works published over the same period. As there were also 3,400 dramatic and poetic works and 2,500 scientific books, the novel only bowed to the very strong lead maintained by theology (Charles Knight, *Popular History of England*, vol. VIII, ch. XXVI).

6 Carlyle, in 1839, insisted on the need for concrete, personal observation. 'The condition of the working-man in this country, what it is and has been, whether it is improving or retrograding, is a question to which from statistics hitherto no solution can be got. Hitherto, after many tables and statements, one is still left mainly to what he can ascertain by his own eyes, looking at the concrete phenomenon for himself' (*Chartism*, ch. II).

7 In *It is Never too Late to Mend* (1856) Reade criticises the prison system in the spirit of Dickens, but he gives no general background of social protest.

8 Thackeray's major works appeared between 1848 (*Vanity Fair*) and 1855 (*The Newcomes*), and belong to the transition between the two periods. Their emotional restraint links them mainly to the second. Their psychological analysis and mistrust of sentimentality distance them from Dickens and associate them more with George Eliot. For Thackeray's opinion of social sentimentalism, see *Pendennis*, vol. I, ch. XXIX. But the decisive reason for excluding Thackeray is that he did not write 'social novels' in the sense in which we are using the words. He hoped to achieve his effects and exert a democratic influence by *moral* satire (cf. *The Book of Snobs*, esp. 'Great City Snobs'; 'Snobs and Marriage';

'Concluding Observations on Snobs'). Thackeray jeered mercilessly at the social novels of Bulwer and Disraeli (cf. 'Novels by Eminent Hands: *George de Barnwell*' and '*Codlingsby*', which are parodies of *Paul Clifford* and *Coningsby*). Thackeray's aesthetic temperament revolted against the social novel, cf. 'A Plan for a Prize Novel': 'Unless he writes with a purpose, you know, a novelist in our days is good for nothing. This one writes with a socialist purpose; that with a conservative purpose.'

9 In spite of its enormous popularity in England, *Uncle Tom's Cabin* (1852) is excluded from this study as American. Likewise the social novels of William Carleton (e.g. *Black Prophet*, 1847) are disregarded as the problems they deal with are exclusively Irish. Ireland and its miseries form a chapter apart in the literature of the period. English idealists for the most part ignored the sufferings of Ireland, which cannot be said to have played a part in the development of interventionism, although they produced some political reaction in England.

10 Even so, such a study would be inevitably incomplete. The social novelists described some aspects of social life, but missed others. It would be more sensible to use the novel as a contributory source of information in a general picture leaning heavily on the more accurate documents which exist in large numbers for this period.

11 Except for one brief account which is taken as an example of his artistic methods as it contains the clearest expression of his ideas.

12 In all work which presents a detailed selection as well as the overall picture it is difficult to harmonise the general and the particular. This is particularly true of social investigations, where a large number of phenomena linked by many points of contact have to be borne in mind. *A priori*, three orders of presentation are possible: the general information may precede the particular; or it may follow it; or the two may be offered together. The second plan is the most scientific, but it could not be applied here, as some knowledge of the setting is essential to an understanding of the novels. The third, and most artistic, plan would involve insuperable difficulties: every novel, to a greater or less extent, deals with many of the social and moral problems of its time, yet there is no such thing as a novel which does them all equal justice. Interesting parts of novels, then, would constantly be pushed out of sight while other books were brought out to clarify the general historical pattern. The plan we have chosen is systematic, but artificial and quite unlike research procedure. It minimises the effectiveness of any particular factual data investigated by predisposing the reader's mind towards the conclusion before showing how it was obtained. But the advantages seem to outweigh the drawbacks.

13 References for quotations from novels give volume (where such a division exists) and chapter. The lack of authoritative editions makes page reference impracticable: the multiplication of paragraphs by dialogue rules out paragraph references.

One   *The rise of individualism*

1 We can only give a brief account of the results of the industrial revolution here. See the Bibliography for further reading.

2 The great inventions were made between 1770 and 1790. See Arnold Toynbee, *The Industrial Revolution*, ch. VIII, and H. de B. Gibbins, *The Industrial History of England*, 2nd ed., ch. II.

3 The population of Great Britain rose from 19 million in 1816 to 24 million in 1831 (Spencer Walpole, *A History of England from the Conclusion of the Great War in 1815*, 2nd ed., vol. III, p. 247).

4 Cotton imports stood at 3,870,392 lb. in 1764. By 1841 they reached 489,900,000 lb. (Charles Beard, *The Industrial Revolution*, 2nd ed., p. 39). Iron production rose from 61,300 tons in 1788 to 1,347,790 tons in 1839 (ibid., p. 40). There were 2,400 steam-driven looms in 1813, and more than 100,000 in 1833 (ibid., p. 28). In 1832 there were 3,000 factories in England; in 1838, 4,000 (Gibbins, op. cit., in p. 184). Between 1800 and 1821 the populations of Liverpool, Manchester, Glasgow, and Bradford rose by 75 per cent (G. T. Warner, *Landmarks in English Industrial History*, p. 281). In 1833, 1,500,000 workers were employed by the cotton industry alone (ibid., p. 308).

5 The first steamship was launched in 1812, and the first crossing of the Atlantic by steam was made in 1837.

6 On these roads and canals, see Warner, op. cit., pp. 278–80.

7 On the effect of these measures, see Gibbins, op. cit., p. 178.

8 Between 1760 and 1843 more than 7 million acres were enclosed (Toynbee, op. cit., ch. VIII, p. 89).

9 See Toynbee, op. cit., ch. VIII, p. 88. Cf. Harriet Martineau, *History of England during the Thirty Years' Peace*, vol. II, ch. VI, pp. 344–5: 'The increase of agricultural families was only $2\frac{1}{2}$ per cent of the whole in the 20 years from 1811 to 1831, while that of the manufacturing and trading families was nearly $31\frac{1}{2}$ per cent.'

10 'In 1760 the economic, political, religious, and social organisation in England was essentially mediaeval, presenting the two chief and all-pervading characteristics: rigidity of structure and immutability of function' (Beard, op. cit., p. 19).

11 For the restrictions on commercial and industrial freedom, see Toynbee, op. cit., ch. VII. On the Act of Settlement, see Walpole, op. cit., vol. I, pp. 161–2.

12 Andrew Ure, *The Philosophy of the Factory System*, p. 407. (Cazamian *sic*, but the passage cannot be traced in Ure, M.F.)

13 Ibid., Preface, p. vii.

14 Ibid.

15 Ibid., p. 278.

16 J. S. Mill defined it thus: 'a combination of Bentham's point of view

with that of the modern political economy, and with the Hartleian metaphysics' (*Autobiography*, 2nd ed., p. 105).

17 We are considering theoretical individualism from a psychological standpoint. For further information, see the Bibliography.

18 The *avant-garde Westminster Review*, established by the radicals in 1823, exemplifies the connection between radical philosophy and middle-class interests. See, especially, the article 'The State of the Nation' in the number for October 1826: 'The value of the middle classes of this country, their growing numbers and importance, are acknowledged by all. These classes have long been spoken of and not grudgingly by their superiors themselves, as the glory of England, and that which alone has given us our eminence among nations; as that portion of our people to whom everything that is good among us may be traced' (p. 269).

19 On all this, see É. Halévy, *La formation du radicalisme philosophique*, vol. I, pp. 88–92.

20 On utilitarian politics, see Leslie Stephen, *The English Utilitarians*, vol. II, pp. 74–136.

21 Ricardo was no better than his predecessors at presenting his work systematically. They all based their thought on an algebraic conception of society, which they never disentangled from their developments on it. For Ricardo's scientific interest in chemistry and the decomposition of organic matter, see M. Fonteyrand's biographical note in *Œuvres Complètes de Ricardo*, Paris, 1882, p. xvii.

22 The main tenets of Ricardian economics are concisely expressed in the following: 'The theory is based on the assumption of competition. . . . It assumes that landlord and tenant respectively are actuated by competitive considerations alone; that the landlord endeavours to obtain the highest rent he can, and the tenant the lowest; that both are independent intelligent agents, able and willing to carry their wares and services to the best market; that the landlord will not be influenced by kindly feeling, or political obligation, or long connection; and that the tenant produces with a single view to the sale of his produce, and, knowing all the advantages of different soils, and places, and trades, is able and willing to move, taking with him his improvements or their value, to any soil, or place, or trade, where he will be more favourably situated' (L. L. Price, *A Short History of Political Economy in England*, 3rd ed., p. 80).

23 W. R. Greg, a typical rationalist individualist philanthropist, contrasted the two types of social awareness between 1830 and 1850 thus, in his review of *Alton Locke*: 'There are two classes of philanthropists – the feelers and the thinkers – the impulsive and the systematic' (*Edinburgh Review*, vol. XCIII (1851), pp. 3–4).

24 Sir James Mackintosh recommended criminal law reform in the following words: 'The main part of the reform which I would propose

would be, to transfer to the statute book the improvements which the wisdom of modern times has introduced into the practice of the law. . . . My object is, to bring the letter of the law more near to its practice – to make the execution of the law form the rule, and the remission of its penalties the exception' (Speech on moving for a Committee to enquire into the state of the Criminal Law, 1819, in *Miscellaneous Works*, vol. III, p. 370).

25 *Principles of Political Economy and Taxation.*

26 Brougham, *Speeches*, 1838, vol. II, pp. 287–486.

27 See Stephen, op. cit., vol. II, pp. 51–7.

28 Ibid., vol. II, pp. 61–2.

29 The Bristol riots of 9–10 October were the most notorious. See Walpole, op. cit., vol. III, pp. 225–30.

30 Thus the first Chartist petition in 1839 said: 'It was the fond expectation of the friends of the people that a remedy for the greater part, if not the whole of their grievances, would be found in the Reform Act of 1832' (G. C. Lee, *Leading Documents of English History*, p. 531). See also J. Holland Rose, *The Rise of Democracy*, pp. 44–5.

31 *Dissertations and Discussions*, vol. II, p. 21.

32 On all this see Charles Seignobos, *Histoire politique de l'Europe contemporaine*, 2nd ed., pp. 41–4; and Walpole, op. cit., vol. IV, ch. XIV.

33 On the old and new Poor Laws, see Walpole, op. cit., vol. III, pp. 442–8.

34 e.g. by Ebenezer Elliott in *Corn-law Rhymes* (1838), a volume dedicated to the memory of Bentham.

35 For the repeal of the Corn Laws and the circumstances surrounding it, see Walpole, op. cit., vol. V, ch. XIX.

36 John Morley, *Life of Cobden*, ch. VI, p. 141.

37 Thomas Cooper recalls the following words of a Chartist orator in Leicester in 1840: 'Don't be deceived by the middle classes again. You helped them to get their votes – you swelled their cry of "the bill, the whole bill, nothing but the bill!" But where are the fine promises they made you? Gone to the winds! . . . And now they want to get the Corn-Laws repealed – not for your benefit, but for their own. "Cheap Bread!" they cry, but they mean: "Low Wages!" Do not listen to their cant and humbug. Stick to your Charter' (*Life of Thomas Cooper, written by himself*, pp. 135–7).

38 Cf. A. Held, *Zwei Bücher zur sozialen Geschichte Englands*, book II, p. 322: 'It was only after 1830 that theories and policies emerged which were exclusively based on the structure of society.'

39 *Journal of the Reign of Queen Victoria*, vol. II, p. 236 (31 March 1844).

40 Until 1820 the word carried the definite implication of revolutionary tendencies. But Bentham and his followers weakened this implication when they described themselves as radicals. Cf. Halévy, op. cit., vol. II, p. 212.

41 Cf. Mrs Grote, *The Philosophical Radicals of 1832*; Samuel Bamford,

Passages in the Life of a Radical; R. G. Gammage's reference to the early Chartists as the 'Radical party' in his *History of Chartism*, new ed., 1894, p. 8. Carlyle wrote on 11 February 1843: 'The people are beginning to discover that I am not a Tory . . . but one of the deepest, though perhaps the quietest, of all the Radicals now extant in the world' (Froude, *Carlyle's Life in London*, new ed., 1890, vol. I, p. 186). Stephens, the passionate advocate of industrial legislation, was a convinced Tory: his biographer, Holyoake, calls him a 'Tory-Radical' (*Life of J. R. Stephens*, p. 134). For the rest of the century the word was to oscillate between individualists and socialists. Cf. Sidney Webb, *Socialism in England*, pp. 124–5.

42 Quoted in *The Life of Lord Lytton* by his son, vol. II, p. 309.

43 See Rose, op. cit., p. 83.

44 See G. Howell, *Labour Legislation, Labour Movements, Labour Leaders*, pp. 78–85.

45 Ibid., pp. 67–76.

46 *The Factory Controversy, a warning against meddling legislation*, p. 6.

47 Ure, op. cit., p. 291.

48 Quoted in Graham Wallas, *Life of Francis Place*, p. 174. In fact, Place was already willing to accept minimal legislation (Wallas, p. 173). Cf. Hume, the philosophical radical who told Parliament he was 'perfectly satisfied that all legislation of this nature is pernicious and injurious to those whom it is intended to protect' (Toynbee, op. cit., p. 18).

49 Wallas, op. cit., p. 174.

50 Ibid.

51 See H. M. Hyndman, *Commercial Crises of the Nineteenth Century*, ch. III, and Walpole, op. cit., vol. IV, p. 356.

52 On all this, see Rose, op. cit., pp. 39–49.

53 M. Fouillée writes: 'If the English have developed the first of the two Germanic characteristics "realism" and "idealism" to the highest degree, this does not mean that the other has disappeared. They could not co-exist equally, but have withdrawn to separate domains. In practical affairs, and the realm of pure intelligence, the English remain realistic: in poetry we can see how they preserve the old Germanic idealism, without losing their grasp on the real' (*Esquisse psychologique des peuples européens*, 2nd ed., 1903, book IV, p. 195).

54 For a psychological examination of Whiggism, see A. Chevrillon, *Sydney Smith et la renaissance des idées libérales en Angleterre*, p. 211 et seq.

55 On Smith's philanthropy, see Chevrillon, op. cit., pp. 56–7. Macaulay's is exemplified in his speech on the Ten Hours Bill of 1846, *Miscellaneous Writings and Speeches*, new ed., 1871, p. 718 et seq.

56 On the origins of utilitarianism, see E. Albee, *A History of English Utilitarianism*, chs I–VII.

57 *Dissertations and Discussions*, vol. I, p. 336.

58 Ibid., p. 346.

59 Ibid., pp. 339–40.

60 Ibid., p. 386.

61 *Autobiography*, p. 50.

62 'The science which . . . most fascinated and interested [Molesworth], was that of pure Mathematics' (Mrs Grote, op. cit., p. 3).

63 J. S. Mill, *Dissertations and Discussions*, vol. I, p. 332.

64 ' "Jug" (short for Juggernaut) with its derivations, "juggist", "anti-jug", etc., were constantly used in the Bentham circle as a conveniently unintelligible synonym for orthodox Christianity' (Wallas, op. cit., p. 82n).

65 J. H. Overton, *The Anglican Revival*, p. 96.

66 *Dissertations and Discussions*, vol. I, p. 178.

67 Ure, op. cit., p. 417.

68 *Edinburgh Review*, vol. XLIX (June 1829), pp. 440–4.

69 A story related by Greville (op. cit., vol. III, ch. XXIV, pp. 141–2 (25 September 1834)) demonstrates the instinctive Whig distaste for Benthamites. Greville had dined with Lord Melbourne, and the conversation turned to a utilitarian called Bickersteth. 'Melbourne said, he was a Benthamite, and they were all fools. (He said a doctrinaire was a fool, but an honest man.) I said, the Austins were not fools. – "Austin? Oh, a damned fool. Did you ever read his book on Jurisprudence?" I said I had read a great part of it, and that it did not appear to be the work of a fool. He said he had read it all, and that it was the dullest book he ever read, and full of truisms elaborately set forth.' Bearing in mind that Lord Melbourne was the finished type of the Whig statesman, we can see how the conventional English mind regarded all dialectic and purely logical argument as 'truisms elaborately set forth'.

Two *The utilitarian novel*

1 See E. Dowden, *The French Revolution and English Literature*, and E. Legouis, *La Jeunesse de Wordsworth*.

2 Quoted by W. L. Cross, *Development of the English Novel*, p. 88. Cf. also Godwin's Preface to *Caleb Williams*: 'This is a truth highly worthy to be communicated to persons whom books of philosophy and science are never likely to reach. . . .'

3 The heroine of *Anna St. Ives* writes to a suitor: 'There are many leading principles in which we differ; and concerning which till we agree, to proceed to marriage would be culpable. . . . You think no doubt that the lover ought to yield, and the husband to command; both of which I deny. Husband, wife, or lover, should all be under the command of reason; other commands are tyranny. . . . You think that the claims of birth to superiority are legitimate; I hold them to be usurpations. I deem society, and yourself to be the first of claimants. Duels with you are

duties, with me crimes. . . . You maintain that what you possess is your own; I affirm it is the property of him who wants it most. Nor are these all, but perhaps they are more than sufficient to end the alliance we were seeking' (vol. IV, letter 79).

4 See *The Prelude*, book IX.

5 Godwin went on writing, but *Mandeville* (1817), *Cloudesly* (1830), and *Deloraine* (1837) contain little but character studies and psychological arguments. Nonetheless these works are of interest, as they represent a link between the revolutionary novel and the utilitarian novel which is usually obscured by Walter Scott's career as a historical novelist. They reveal direct connections between Godwin and Bulwer; a prominent character in *Mandeville*, for example, is called Clifford, like Bulwer's hero. For the theory of the psychological novel, see the Preface to *Cloudesly*.

6 This aspect of *Oroonoko* is secondary: the book is first and foremost a witty comedy in the Restoration style. Certain episodes have, nonetheless, a practical realism.

7 '*The Fortunes and Misfortunes of the Famous Moll Flanders*; Who was Born in Newgate and during a Life of continu'd Variety for Threescore Years, besides her Childhood, was Twelve Year a whore, five times a Wife (whereof once to her own Brother), Twelve Year a Thief, Eight Year a Transported Felon in Virginia, at last grew Rich, liv'd Honest and died a Penitent, written from her own memorandums.' For the didactic intention of all this, see Defoe's Preface.

8 e.g. *Roderick Random*, chs XXII–XXV. See Y. Péronne, *Englische Zustände im XVIII Jahrhundert, nach den Romanen von Fielding und Smollett*.

9 See *The Vicar of Wakefield*, ch. XXVI: 'A reformation in the gaol. To make laws compleat they should reward as well as punish', and ch. XVII: 'The same subject continued'.

10 Cf. Lloyd's Preface: 'The following pages were written with the design of counter-acting that generalising spirit, which seems so much to have insinuated itself among modern philosophers. . . . That indefinite benevolence which would respect the mass of existence without addressing its operations patiently to the parts of that mass. . . .' Thus Lloyd attacks the abstract and generalising character of Godwin's philosophy.

11 It is worth noting that Miss Edgeworth's Irish novel *Castle Rackrent* is also a philanthropic novel.

12 By L. Maigron, *Le roman historique à l'époque romantique*, p. 91.

13 On all this, see H. A. Beers, *A History of English Romanticism in the Nineteenth Century*, ch. VII, and Sir Leslie Stephen, op. cit., vol. II, pp. 365–8.

14 Cf. *Ivanhoe*, ch. I and *Past and Present*, book I, ch. III: 'Gurth, a mere swineherd, born thrall of Cedric the Saxon, tended his pigs in the wood and did get some parings of the pork.'

15 The leading 'Silver Fork' writer was Theodore Hook. Charles Knight (*Popular History of England*, vol. VIII, ch. XXVI) attributes Hook's success to aristocratic aloofness from the middle class, whose vulgarity is satirised in the novels. On the other hand, the *Edinburgh Review* (vol. LV (Jan.–June 1832), p. 209) insists on bourgeois curiosity as the main cause of the same success. The two views are not necessarily mutually exclusive.

16 The phrase is taken from the *Quarterly Review*, vol. LXIV (June 1839), article IV (on *Oliver Twist*), p. 86.

17 In 1843 Greville wrote, 'Then the condition of the people, moral and physical, is uppermost in everybody's mind; the state and management of workhouses and prisons, and the great question of education. The newspapers are full of letters and complaints on these subjects, and people think, talk, and care about them very much' (*Journal*, vol. V, ch. XIV, p. 138).

18 The name of Charles Knight is associated with this work. See article in *Dictionary of National Biography*, and Miss Martineau's Preface to Knight's *History of England*. In addition to the *Penny Cyclopædia* and *Penny Magazine*, intended for the propagation of useful knowledge, he published *The British Almanac and Companion* and the *Library of Entertaining Knowledge*. The *Penny Magazine* reached a circulation of 200,000 (Cf. Walpole, op. cit., vol. IV, p. 75).

19 In 1836 after a long struggle the radicals succeeded in reducing the tax on each copy of a publication from 4*d*. to 1*d*. Cf. Walpole, op. cit., vol. IV, pp. 76–9, and Rose, op. cit., ch. IV: 'The Fight for a Free Press'.

20 Dickens claimed credit for this invention: 'That I hold the advantages of the mode of publication to outweigh its disadvantages, may be easily believed of one who revived it in the *Pickwick Papers* after long disuse, and has pursued it ever since' (Postscript in lieu of Preface to *Our Mutual Friend*). On the original plan for *Pickwick*, and the reasons for its form of publication, see F. G. Kitton, *The Novels of Charles Dickens: a Bibliography and Sketch*, article on *Pickwick*.

21 'There is this difference between the present times and all former times; that, in former times, governments made and fashioned the opinions of their people nearly as much as they made their laws; at present, the people throughout Europe, and especially in England, form opinions to a great degree for themselves, and are every day allowing government less and less of a share in settling what they shall think on any subject. This is a novelty in the state of the times, the force of which existing governments might be expected to undervalue'(*Westminster Review*, Oct. 1826, pp. 265–6).

22 He took the name Bulwer-Lytton on his mother's death in 1843.

23 Mill, *Autobiography*, ch. III, 'Last Stage of Education and First of Self-Education'.

24 Ibid.

25 Ibid., ch. IV, 'Youthful Propagandism. The *Westminster Review*'.
26 The Preface to the first edition of *Paul Clifford* denies that Pelham is a self-portrait, but in spite of literary flourishes, the likeness is not really in doubt.
27 *Pelham*, ch. XXXVII. The pamphlet in question is James Mill's article on government in the 1820 edition of the *Encyclopædia Britannica*.
28 Ibid., ch. XXXVII.
29 Ibid.
30 Ibid., ch. XXXVIII.
31 John Stuart Mill experienced this excitement, and gave a representative account of it. *Autobiography*, ch. III.
32 *Pelham*, ch. XXXVII.
33 Bulwer criticises the educational system at Eton (ch. II). His hero passes through the depressed parts of London, and his curiosity is aroused by those who live there (ch. XLIX). The Game Laws are criticised from a utilitarian standpoint (ch. LXII). A passing reference is made to the barbarous régime obtaining in lunatic asylums (ch. LXXIV), etc.
34 *The Disowned* (1828) and *Devereux* (1829) are Godwinian character analyses.
35 *Life of Edward Bulwer* by his grandson, vol. I, book III, ch. III.
36 Ibid.
37 *Paul Clifford*, 1835, Dedicatory Epistle, p. vii.
38 Ibid., p. viii.
39 Ibid., pp. viii–ix.
40 Ibid., p. ix.
41 Ibid., p. xii.
42 Cf. *The Philanthropist*, New Series, vol. II (March 1830), article on 'Punishment of Death': 'We are glad to find that this disgrace to our national character is increasingly attracting public notice, as appears by the petitions lately sent and now sending up to both Houses of Parliament.'
43 *Paul Clifford*, ch. VII.
44 Ibid., ch. VIII.
45 Ibid., ch. IX.
46 Ibid., ch. XV.
47 Ibid., chs. XXII–XXV.
48 Ibid., ch. XXXVI.
49 *Life of Edward Bulwer* by his grandson, vol. I, book III, ch. I.
50 Ibid. The account follows the *Newgate Calendar*, vol. XIII. See also, *The Lindfield Reporter, or Philanthropic Magazine*, 1835, p. 40: 'Number of persons condemned to death, and the number executed, in the 4 years ending 1831, for crimes which, by Act passed in 1832 and 1833, cease to be any longer capital: Condemned, 3,786; Executed, 66.' The age of the victims was another scandal: in 1814, 5 children were condemned to death for theft, of whom the youngest was 8 and the

eldest 12. Sentence was usually commuted in such cases, but the children still suffered transportation (cf. *The Philanthropist*, vol. IV (1814), p. 190).

51 Bulwer claimed that he had personally measured the cell in which Paul Clifford was confined with two companions (*Paul Clifford*, ch. VIII).

52 Cf. Joseph Adshead, *Our Present Gaol System*, p. 16.

53 Adshead, op. cit., p. 25.

54 *Paul Clifford*, ch. XXXV.

55 Ibid., ch. VIII.

56 Ibid., ch. XXXV.

57 A key to these characters may be found in *The Life of Lord Lytton* by his son, vol. II, pp. 248–9.

58 '*Tomlinsoniana*; or the posthumous writings of the celebrated Augustus Tomlinson, professor of moral philosophy in the university. Addressed to his pupils, and comprising: I. Maxims on the popular art of cheating. . . . II. Brachylogia; or, essays, critical, sentimental, moral, and original.' Bulwer explained, 'I add them as a fitting Appendix to a Novel that may not be inappropriately termed a treatise on Social Frauds' (Introduction).

59 Cf. *Paul Clifford*, chs. I–IV.

60 Bulwer offered the following apology for his failure to carry out in detail the development of Paul Clifford's character: 'We do not intend, reader, to indicate, by broad colours and in long detail, the moral deterioration of our hero; because we have found by experience that such pains on our part do little more than make thee blame our stupidity instead of lauding our invention' (ch. VIII).

61 The novel seems to have been very popular: 'In our early days the name of Bulwer, not Lytton, was already a household word. His *Paul Clifford* and *Eugene Aram* had, unlike his previous works, by means of cheap pirated editions found their way into the homes of the poorest, and were there read with avidity' (B. Jowett, *Lord Lytton, man and author*, p. 11).

62 *Life of Edward Bulwer* by his grandson, vol. I, book III, ch. I.

63 *Contributions to 'Punch'*: 'Novels by eminent hands: *George de Barnwell*, by Sir E. L. B. Bt.'

64 *Life of Lord Lytton* by his son, vol. II, pp. 258–9.

65 'Le beau et philosophique roman de Sir Edward Bulwer Lytton' (*Le Temps*, 5 February 1864).

66 R. H. Horne, *A New Spirit of the Age*.

67 Bulwer was well aware that this was an innovation. Cf. Dedicatory Epistle to *Paul Clifford*: 'I am willing to risk an experiment, tried successfully in Scotland and Ireland – though not in the present day attempted in England. . . .'

68 *Life of Lord Lytton* by his son, vol. II, p. 244. The *Edinburgh Review*, however, in its review of *Paul Clifford* seems to pay little attention to the argument. Cf. vol. LV (Jan.–July 1832), pp. 211–12.

69 On all this, cf. H. D. Traill, *Social England*, vol. VI, pp. 230–4.

70 *Eugene Aram*, Preface, datelined Brussels, to ed. of 1840.

71 It is interesting to note that Bulwer's appearances on the platform at
    Cambridge before his conversion to Benthamism were as a champion of
    monarchy and aristocracy. He attracted such attention that the
    conservative party offered him a seat in Parliament when he reached
    his majority (cf. J. C. Watt, *Great Novelists*, p. 230). Similarly, in the
    autobiographical fragments Bulwer wrote many years later, and which
    his son used in writing his *Life*, Bulwer skated quickly over his Cambridge
    days, and made no mention of his utilitarian phase (cf. *Life of Lord Lytton*
    by his son, vol. I, book III, chs. I–III).

72 Bulwer's principal plays were *The Lady of Lyons* (1838) and *Richelieu*
    (1839). His principal novels were *The Last Days of Pompeii* (1834),
    Rienzi (1835), *Day and Night* (1841), *The Last of the Barons* (1844), and
    The Caxtons (1850). All of these enjoyed great success.

73 Nassau Senior was Professor of Political Economics at Oxford from
    1825 to 1830. A few years later McCulloch was elected by the new
    University of London.

74 We find among Disraeli's creations the characters of Lord Everingham
    and Lord Marney; Kingsley created Lord Minchampstead. All three are
    keen on economics.

75 Cf. the preceding chapter. The Society for the Diffusion of Useful
    Knowledge took a particular interest in this work, and encouraged Miss
    Martineau. Mrs Marcet's *Conversations on Political Economy*, a simple
    guide to the subject, prepared the way for Miss Martineau. Mrs
    Marcet's book was intended for 'young persons'; it adopted a tone of
    scientific authority and almost irreproachable Ricardian orthodoxy.

76 On all this, see Sidney Webb, *A History of Trade Unionism*, pp. 102–20.

77 For what follows, see Harriet Martineau's *Autobiography*, esp. vol. I:
    first period (up to nine years old) and second period (up to seventeen).

78 *Autobiography*, vol. I, p. 19.

79 Ibid., p. 11.

80 Ibid., p. 35.

81 Ibid., pp. 160–1.

82 Ibid., pp. 189–90.

83 Ibid., p. 193.

84 Ibid.

85 Ibid., p. 194.

86 Ibid.

87 Ibid., p. 195.

88 Ibid.

89 Ibid.

90 *Illustrations of Political Economy* (1832–4) in 25 numbers. *Illustrations
    of Taxation* (1834) in 5 numbers. *Poor Law and Paupers Illustrated* (1833–4)

in 3 numbers. Each number was a story in itself, but the subject under discussion was carried on from one part to the next.

91 *Illustrations of Political Economy*, vol. I, no. I, Preface.
92 Ibid.
93 Ibid.
94 Ibid.
95 See *Illustrations of Political Economy*, vol. II, 'Ella of Garveloch'.
96 *Illustrations of Political Economy*, vol. I, no. I, 'Life in the Wilds', ch. II.
97 Ibid., ch. VI.
98 Ibid., ch. IX.
99 *Illustrations of Political Economy*, vol. I, no. 2, 'The Hill and the Valley', ch. III.
100 Ibid., ch. VI.
101 Ibid.
102 Ibid.
103 Ibid., Ch. VIII.
104 *Illustrations of Political Economy*, vol. III.
105 *Illustrations of Political Economy*, vol. II.
106 *Autobiography*, vol. I, pp. 178–9.
107 *Quarterly Review*, vol. XLIX (Apr.–July 1833), p. 151.
108 *Edinburgh Review*, vol. LVII (Jan.–July 1833), p. 26.
109 Charles Knight, *Popular History of England*, vol. VIII, ch. XXVI.
110 Ibid.
111 *Autobiography*, vol. II, pp. 244–5.
112 In 1841 Miss Martineau published *The Playfellow*, a series of tales (4 vols), and in 1852 *Forest and Game-Law Tales* (3 vols). For the two sides of her personality, see the interesting portrait of her left by Charlotte Brontë (in Mrs Gaskell's *Life of Charlotte Brontë*, vol. II, ch. IX): 'She is both hard and warm-hearted, abrupt and affectionate, liberal and despotic'. It seems that already, by 1857, her philanthropy was active rather than theoretical: 'She seems to me the benefactress of Ambleside.'

Three   *Idealism and the interventionist reaction*

1 In 1831 the Game Laws were amended for the first time. Cf. Walpole, op. cit., vol. III, pp. 301–2.
2 On the great landowners' loss of social standing, see Walpole, op. cit., vol. III, pp. 302–3.
3 The agrarian revolution was actually more complicated than this simple summary suggests. For one thing, capital was needed for the application of the new improved methods of farming. When small farmers had been put out of business by the enclosure of the old open fields, their lands, too, would go to swell the better-equipped holdings. At the same time, *nouveau riche* industrialists were buying up the huge estates which

had come into being at the expense of smallholdings, and transforming
them into parks and meadows. And finally, the collapse of home
loom-weaving and the concentration of the cloth industry into
factories took away a valuable economic standby from the smallholders.
The total effect of these factors was the dispersal of an entire class.
'While at the beginning of the 18th century, King estimated there were
180,000 freeholders in England, Arthur Young, writing after the wars
against Napoleon, speaks of the small freeholder as practically extinct'
(G. T. Warner, *Landmarks in English Industrial History*, p. 298).

4 On the causes of agricultural depression, cf. Walpole, op. cit., vol. III,
pp. 318–21.

5 See Engels on rural poverty, in *The Condition of the Working-Class in
England in 1844*, ch. x, 'The Agricultural Proletariat'.

6 *Rural Rides*, 1830.

7 'In 1832 more than £7,000,000 was expended on the relief of the poor
in England and Wales alone. The maintenance of the poor threw an
annual charge of 10 shillings on every man, woman and child of the
population.' Walpole, op. cit., vol. III, p. 322.

8 E. G. Wakefield, in *Swing Unmasked; or, The Cause of Rural Incendiarism*,
cited by Engels, loc. cit.

9 See the Bibliography. We make extensive use of Engels, whose
conclusions may be controversial, but whose summaries of parliamentary
reports and special studies, like those of Gaskell, Kay, and Rashleigh, are
precise and confident. Gaskell mistakes factory workers for the entire
working class; otherwise his book is useful, especially as evidence of
his state of mind. We do not attempt to describe working-class life
from Blue book evidence: rather we turn to the Blue books for
confirmation of the picture drawn in the novels.

10 *Reports of Commissioners and Assistant Commissioners on the conditions
of the hand-loom weavers*, 7 parts, 1837–41.

11 *Reports from Assistant Hand-Loom Weavers' Commissioners*, part II, J.
Mitchell on the East of England, p. 232.

12 Ibid.

13 Ibid., p. 238.

14 Ibid.

15 Ibid., p. 243.

16 *Report of the Commissioners*, parts IV and V.

17 In 1844, when Engels was writing, this particular exploitation of
tailors was not generally known. But by 1850 it had grown, to become
one of the main themes in Kingsley's *Alton Locke*.

18 On the causes of the great depression of 1839–42, see Walpole, op. cit.,
vol. IV, pp. 356–67.

19 On the first attempts at industrial legislation before 1830, see W.
Cooke Taylor, *The Factory System and the Factory Acts*, ch. III.

20 J. Fielden, *The Curse of the Factory System*, p. 2.

21 *Report of the Select Committee on the Bill to regulate the labour of children In Mills and Factories; with Evidence and index.* This is the famous Sadler report, named after the Committee's chairman.
22 Cited Fielden, op. cit., p. 18.
23 Cited ibid., p. 19.
24 *Minutes of Evidence taken before the select committee on the factories bill,* 1832, pp. 157–8.
25 P. Gaskell, *Artisans and Machinery,* reprinted 1968, p. 164.
26 Engels, op. cit., ch. VI, 'Single Branches of Industry: Factory Hands'.
27 Gaskell, op. cit., p. 229.
28 Engels, loc. cit.
29 Ibid.
30 On the truck system, cf. Walpole, op. cit., vol. IV, pp. 364–73.
31 *Royal Commission on the employment and conditions of children and young persons – First Report; Mines and Colleries,* 3 parts, 1842.
32 Joseph Adshead, *Distress in Manchester,* p. 16.
33 J. P. Kay, *The Moral and Physical Condition of the Working Class,* pp. 12–26.
34 Adshead, op. cit., pp. 14 et seq.
35 Ibid., p. 27.
36 P. Gaskell, op. cit., p. 82.
37 Engels, op. cit., ch. II, 'The Great Towns'.
38 Eugène Buret, *La misère des classes laborieuses en France et en Angleterre,* vol. I, p. 136.
39 Engels, op. cit., ch. V, 'Results'.
40 Walpole, op. cit., vol. IV, p. 405.
41 Engels, op. cit., ch. V, 'Results'.
42 Ibid.
43 Ibid.
44 Walpole, op. cit., vol. IV, p. 358.
45 Buret, op. cit., vol. II, p. 475.
46 Engels, op. cit., ch. XI, 'The Attitude of the Bourgeoisie Towards the Proletariat'.
47 *Notes of a Tour in the Manufacturing Districts of Lancashire,* pp. 90, 84.
48 Cited by A. Toynbee, *The Industrial Revolution in England,* 1884, p. 193.
49 *Coningsby,* 1844, book V, ch. VIII.
50 *Report of the Commissioners on Hand-Loom Weavers,* p. 124.
51 Greville, *Journal,* vol. IV, ch. I, (August 1837).
52 *A History of the Factory Movement,* by 'Alfred' [S. Kydd], vol. II, pp. 294–5.
53 Cited by J. H. Rose, *The Rise of Democracy,* p. 61.
54 Cf. *The Philanthropist; or Repositary for hints and suggestions calculated to promote the comfort and happiness of man,* vol. I (1811), pp. 66, 143; vol. II (1812), p. 227.
55 Carlyle, *Past and Present,* book IV, ch. V.
56 *The Excursion,* 1814, esp. book VIII, 'The Parsonage'.

57 *The Statesman's Manual; or the Bible the best guide to political skill and foresight. A Lay Sermon addressed to the highest classes of society*, 1816; and *A Lay Sermon addressed to the higher and middle classes on the existing distresses and discontents*, 1817.

58 *Colloquies on Society*, 1829.

59 C. Andler, *Les Origines du socialisme d'État en Allemagne*, p. 166.

60 For Carlyle's youth, see J. A. Froude, *Thomas Carlyle: History of the first forty years of his life*.

61 *Edinburgh Review*, vol. XLIX (1829).

62 Ibid., pp. 448–9.

63 *Chartism*, December 1839.

64 Carlyle's philosophy is exceptionally unsystematic in form and presentation. It has proved necessary to disregard the chronological order of publication of his social writings in the summary that follows.

65 *Chronica Jocelini de Brakelonda, de rebus gestis Samsonis Abbatis Monasterii Sancti Edmundi; nunc primum typis mandata*, London, 1840. Publication was by the Camden Society, on which see below, p. 193.

66 *Past and Present*, book II, 'The ancient monk'.

67 Ibid., book I, ch. I, ch. IV.

68 Ibid., book IV, ch. V.

69 Ibid., book III, ch. II.

70 *Chartism*, ch. IV.

71 *Past and Present*, book III, ch. II.

72 Ibid.

73 Ibid., book III, ch. I.

74 Ibid., book III, ch. X.

75 Ibid., book III, ch. XI.

76 *Chartism*, ch. VIII.

77 *Past and Present*, book III, ch. XIII.

78 Ibid.

79 Ibid., book IV, ch. III.

80 Ibid.

81 Ibid.

82 Ibid.

83 Ibid., book I, ch. IV.

84 Ibid., book IV, ch. VIII.

85 Greville, *Journal*, vol. III, ch. XXIII, (1834).

86 Cf. Augustin Filon, *La caricature en Angleterre*.

87 W. G. Ward, *The Ideal of a Christian Church*, p. 32. The Oxford Movement exerted its social influence in a peculiarly indirect manner. It held back from Kingsley's Christian socialism on account of theological differences.

88 Cf. J. W. Mackail, *Life of William Morris*, pp. 39, 41, 50. Morris was also influenced by Charlotte Yonge, whose novel *The Heir of*

Redclyffe (1852) would merit attention if its theme were not more religious than social.

89 The first novels of Bulwer and Disraeli, *Pelham* and *Vivian Grey*, were Byronic.

90 An astonishingly small section, in the light of Byron's importance historically and on the Continent.

91 *Corn-law Rhymes*, 1827. Mrs Norton, a poor but well-intentioned poet, deserves mention. Her two collections, *A Voice from the Factories; in serious verse; dedicated to the right honourable Lord Ashley* (1836), and *The Child of the Islands* (1845), are gushing pleas for industry's child victims as described in official reports.

92 e.g., Bramwich and Ernest Jones, cited by R. G. Gammage, *History of the Chartist Movement*, pp. 214–15. And James Montgomery of Sheffield is named by 'Alfred' as a poet who furthered the cause of industrial legislation.

93 See below, pp. 1107–8.

94 *Études sur la littérature et les mœurs de l'Angleterre au dix-neuvième siècle*, p. 448.

95 Cf. *Punch*, vol. VI (1844), p. 240; vol. VII (1844), pp. 233, 248; vol. VIII (1845), p. 252.

96 *England's Trust, and Other Poems*.

97 'England's Trust, III', *England's Trust, and Other Poems*, p. 16.

98 'Christmas', *England's Trust, and Other Poems*, pp. 95–7.

99 Sidney Webb, op. cit., p. 165.

100 This happened in the winter of 1832. Cf. Edwin Hodder, *The Life and Work of the Seventh Earl of Shaftesbury*, vol. I, p. 148.

101 From an Address to the Crown delivered in 1843, cited by E. Hodder, *The Seventh Earl of Shaftesbury as a Social Reformer*, p. 123.

102 *Quarterly Review*, vol. LXVII (Dec. 1840), p. 181. See also Mill's essay 'The Claims of Labour', 1845 (in *Dissertations and Discussions*, vol. II). Discussing a book published under the same title, Mill lucidly describes the new philanthropy: 'But it is not in this spirit that the new schemes of benevolence are conceived. They are propounded as instalments of a great social reform. They are celebrated as the beginning of a new moral order or an old order revived, in which the possessors of property are to resume their place as the paternal guardians of those less fortunate.'

103 The phrase is Sidney Webb's, but it is applicable to a feeling that emerged around 1840.

104 *Chartism*, 1839, ch. I.

105 e.g. *Physical and Moral Condition of the Children and Young Persons employed in Mines and Manufactures, Illustrated by extracts from the Debates of the Commissioners*, J. Parker, 1843.

106 For an account of Blincoe, see R. W. Cooke-Taylor, *The Modern Factory System*, pp. 189–98.

107 Cf., e.g., *Punch*, vol. II (1842), p. 205, 'Philanthropy and Coals'.

108 *The Perils of the Nation*, [R. B. Seeley], London, 1843. The tone of the work might have led readers to believe that the author was a clergyman. For the effect it produced, cf. W. G. Ward, *Ideal of a Christian Church*, ch. II, section v.

109 *The Perils of the Nation*, 'Preliminary Observations'.

110 Ibid.

111 Mill, *Principles of Political Economy*, book IV, ch. VII.

112 'The Claims of Labour', *Dissertations and Discussions*, vol. II.

113 Sir Theodore Martin's *Life of the Prince Consort*, gives details of Prince Albert's philanthropic work. See, esp., vol. II, chs. XXV, XXXV, and vol. IV, ch. LXXIV.

114 Walpole, op. cit., vol. IV, p. 375.

115 Cooke Taylor, *Notes of a Tour in the Manufacturing Districts of Lancashire*, pp. 22–3.

116 'Model Prisons', *Latter-Day Pamphlets*, 1850.

117 *Helen Fleetwood*, ch. xx.

118 *Quarterly Review*, vol. LXV (1840), pp. 484–5.

119 'The Claims of Labour', *Dissertations and Discussions*, vol. II.

120 'Coleridge', *Dissertations and Discussions*, vol. I, p. 397.

121 Ibid., p. 398.

122 Ibid., p. 403.

123 H. de B. Gibbins, *English Social Reformers*, chs I–IV, gives a psychological interpretation of the principal social movements of England.

124 Newman, *The Idea of a University Defined*, 1873, Discourse IV, paragraph xi.

125 'The Christian Socialists of 1848', J. M. Ludlow, *The Economic Review*, vol. III, no. 4 (Oct. 1893), p. 486.

126 Rose, *The Rise of Democracy*, p. 45.

127 On these men, see Rose, op. cit., chs IV–VI, and Lovett's memoirs (*The Life and Struggles of William Lovett, in his Pursuit of Bread, Knowledge, and Freedom*).

128 See Cooper's *Life written by Himself*, and Holyoake's hostile portrait, *Thomas Cooper Delineated as Convert and Controversialist*, 1861.

129 R. G. Gammage, *History of the Chartist Movement*, p. 196. Cf. pp. 195–7, and also, on pp. 214–15, a Chartist poet's funeral hymn to be sung for a comrade who died in prison.

130 Gammage, op. cit., p. 55.

131 Ibid., p. 57. The speech was delivered in Glasgow on 1 January 1838. The *Life of Stephens* by Holyoake (1881) is interesting, especially for the definition of social Toryism given in ch. IX, 'The two kinds of Conservatism'.

132 Gammage, op. cit., pp. 69–70.

133 Rose, op. cit., pp. 119–20.

134 Cf. Gibbins, *English Social Reformers*, ch. IV, 'The factory reformers'.

135 See Bibliography.

136 Gaskell, *The Manufacturing Population of England*, p. 215.
137 This was apparent by 1725, according to W. Thomas, *Le Poète Edward Young*, Paris, 1901.
138 *Autobiography*, ch. v.
139 Ibid.
140 Ibid., ch. vii.
141 Ibid., ch. vi.

Four   *Dickens: the philosophy of Christmas*

1 John Forster, *The Life of Charles Dickens*, vol. i, ch. i.
2 Ibid.
3 Ibid., ch. ii.
4 Ibid.
5 Cf., e.g., Oliver Twist, David Copperfield, Florence Dombey, Louisa Bounderby (*Hard Times*), and the young Scrooge (*A Christmas Carol*).
6 Cf. *Sketches by Boz*, 'Shabby-genteel People', etc.
7 Forster, op. cit., vol. i, ch. xvii.
8 Dickens carried a tendency to set his novels in the near past over into the latter part of his career. Cf., e.g., *Great Expectations*, whose action takes place around 1825 or 1830.
9 Gissing, *Charles Dickens, A Critical Study*, p. 196.
10 The two men met for the first time in 1840. The impression Dickens made on Carlyle is described in Froude, *Carlyle's Life in London*, vol. i, p. 389. Their relations soon became friendly: Carlyle was present at Dickens's private reading of the manuscript of *The Chimes* in 1844. A. W. Ward examines Carlyle's influence on Dickens in the 'English Men of Letters' *Dickens*. According to Weber, *Charles Dickens als sozialer Schriftsteller*, Dickens derived all his social ideas from Carlyle, especially his antipathy to political economy. But this overstates the case: chapters vii and xix of *Oliver Twist* excoriated economic dogmatism before Dickens had met Carlyle and, moreover, before Carlyle had published his social thought. Carlyle's influence served to intensify attitudes Dickens already held, and sometimes gave them coherent form.
11 In 1855 he wrote: 'I really am serious in thinking…that representative government is become altogether a failure with us' (Forster, op. cit., vol. iii, ch. xix). And his public utterance, 'My faith in the people governing is, on the whole, infinitesimal; my faith in the People governed is, on the whole, illimitable,' was ambiguous: it could be taken as a democratic or a paternalistic statement. When challenged, Dickens declared it was the former, but the second was clearly possible. See Gissing's *Charles Dickens, A Critical Study*, pp. 197–8, for a discussion of this point.
12 The following is an attempt to sketch in the salient traits of Dickens's

personality without trying to convey its total complexity. A more detailed study is to be found in Kitton's *Charles Dickens – his Life, Writings and Personality*. The man had his faults, described thus by Gissing: 'They were strictly, *les défauts de ses qualités*, and might be summed in the statement that a vigorous will sometimes, though rarely, got the better of his large humanity and fine discretion' (*Forster's Life of Dickens, abridged and revised*, p. 325). For Carlyle's laudatory and penetrating observations on Dickens's character, see Kitton, op. cit., p. 127, and Forster, op. cit., vol. III, ch. XIX: 'A most cordial, sincere, clear-sighted, quietly decisive, just and loving man.'

13 In the Preface he wrote for the 1867 edition of *Oliver Twist*, Dickens himself referred to 'Sir Edward Bulwer's admirable and powerful novel' as one which handled a similar theme in a different spirit.

14 'Indeed, Dickens had a special affection for the *Vicar of Wakefield*. When thinking of his first Christmas Book...he says that he wishes to write a story of about the same length as the *Vicar*' (Gissing, op. cit., p. 29).

15 Cf. 'The Broker's Man', 'The Drunkard's Death', 'Gin-Shops', etc.

16 Forster, *The Life of Charles Dickens*, vol. I, ch. VI.

17 For the relations between Dickens and Ashley, see Hodder's *Life* of the latter, vol. I, p. 227 et seq.

18 *Household Words*, from 1850 to 1859, and *All the Year Round* from 1859 until his death. Writing to Mrs Gaskell to ask her to contribute to *Household Words*, Dickens described its purpose thus: 'the raising up of those that are down, and the general improvement of our social condition' (*Letters*, 1882, vol. I, pp. 233–4).

19 He died on 9 June 1870. His novels were, in chronological order: *Pickwick Papers*, 1837; *Oliver Twist*, 1838; *Nicholas Nickleby*, 1839; *The Old Curiosity Shop*, 1840; *Barnaby Rudge*, 1841; *A Christmas Carol*, 1843; *Martin Chuzzlewit* and *The Chimes*, 1844; *The Cricket on the Hearth*, 1845; *The Battle of Life*, 1846; *Dombey and Son* and *The Haunted Man*, 1848; *David Copperfield*, 1850; *Bleak House*, 1853; *Hard Times*, 1854; *Little Dorrit*, 1857; *A Tale of Two Cities*, 1859; *Great Expectations*, 1861; *Our Mutual Friend*, 1865; *Edwin Drood* (unfinished), 1870. All these books were hugely successful, and Dickens's sales figures were the highest of the period. In two years, 30,000 copies of *Pickwick* were sold (*Edinburgh Review*, vol. LXVIII, p. 77). The monthly parts in which the novels appeared were looked forward to with impatience: the Christmas books would sell out their first editions within a few days. In 1846 Dickens wrote, on 19 December, '*Christmas Book* published today; twenty-three thousand copies already gone!!!' (*Letters*, 1880, vol. I, p. 175). This truly vast popularity was to be his until he died. The great majority of thinking and reading people in the English-speaking world were acquainted with them.

20 Forster, op. cit., vol. II, ch. VI; and Kitton, op. cit., p. 133.

21 *Letters*, 1882, vol. I, p. 139, cf. ibid., p. 136.
22 Ibid., p. 145.
23 *The Chimes*, 'First Quarter'.
24 Ibid.
25 Ibid.
26 Ibid.
27 Ibid.
28 Ibid.
29 Ibid.
30 Ibid.
31 Ibid.
32 Dickens was portraying a real man, Sir Peter Laurie, who spoke of having 'put down' suicide by firm magisterial action when there was a great deal of it among the poor at the worst of the great depression, 1839–42.
33 *The Chimes*, 'First Quarter'.
34 Ibid.
35 Ibid.
36 Ibid., 'Second Quarter'.
37 Ibid.
38 Ibid.
39 Ibid.
40 Ibid., 'Third Quarter'.
41 Ibid.
42 Ibid.
43 Ibid.
44 Ibid.
45 Ibid., 'Fourth Quarter'.
46 Ibid.
47 Ibid.
48 Ibid.
49 Ibid.
50 Dickens hoped it would have a great success and wield some influence over society: 'I believe I have written a tremendous book, and knocked the *Carol* out of the field. It will make a great uproar, I have no doubt' (Kitton, op. cit., p. 136). The success was unquestionably considerable – Dickens gained £1,500 from the sale of the first 20,000 copies – but it did not live up to his expectations. 'It must be confessed that *The Chimes*, when published, hardly created the excitement which the author anticipated' (ibid., p. 138). The *Edinburgh Review*, noticing the book favourably, predicted reservations on the part of the public, which it thought would be a consequence of the book's aggressive tone. Moreover, said the reviewer, 'questions are here brought to view which cannot be dismissed when the book is laid aside' (vol. LXXXI (Jan. 1845), p. 181). The representative overwhelming, universal success was achieved by the first of the Christmas books, *A Christmas Carol*, which is

a finer work of art than *The Chimes*, and more convincing, but a less clear examination of society. Thackeray said of it, 'It seems to me a national benefit, and to every man or woman who reads it a personal kindness.' Lord Jeffrey wrote to the author, 'You should be happy yourself, for you may be sure you have done more good by this little publication, fostered more kindly feelings, and prompted more positive acts of benevolence, than can be traced to all the pulpits and confessionals in Christendom since Christmas 1842' (Kitton, op. cit., pp. 120–1). The *Gentleman's Magazine* confirmed that its influence had been immediate and practical: 'Nor have his benevolent intentions been unavailing, as we have reason to believe that more extensive kindness has been dispensed to those who are in want at the present season than at any preceding one' (New Series, vol. XXI (Jan.–July 1844), p. 170).

51 On all this, cf. *A Christmas Carol*, esp. 'Stave Three: the second of the three spirits'.

52 See the anecdote related by Forster, *Life*, vol. II, ch. I.

53 'Lilian Fern whose mother died in Dorsetshire...' (*The Chimes*, 'Fourth Quarter').

54 *A Tale of Two Cities* markedly exhibits the direct influence of Carlyle.

55 There is no doubt that Dickens originally intended to have an explicit representative of Young England in *The Chimes* – cf. Forster, *Life*, vol. II, ch. VI. The rough plan of the book is supported by Dickens's letter to Forster: 'As you dislike the Young England gentleman, I shall knock him out, and replace him by a man...who recognises no virtue in anything, but the good old times.' Thus the man with shiny buttons is the successor of 'the Young England gentleman'.

56 This is, of course, connected with Dickens's preference for pre-1832 England. His views on the Corn Laws are known from editorials in the *Daily News* on 9, 13, and 16 March 1846 during his short-lived editorship. It is still significant that this part of the social struggle was of so little interest to him.

57 The novels contain numerous attacks upon economic orthodoxy, but they are of a kind to be found in all interventionist writings. They simply set the results of economic practices alongside the emotions they evoke, to make an emotional point about the nature of economics. Cf., e.g., *Oliver Twist*, ch. XII; *A Christmas Carol*, 'Stave Three'; *Hard Times*, book I, ch. IX; book II, ch. I; book III, ch. VIII.

58 Forster, *The Life of Charles Dickens*, vol. II, ch. VI. We have noted that his education was disrupted, and he was never really a well-educated man.

59 Cf. M. Langlois's article in *Revue de Paris*, 1 April 1903.

60 Preface to *Nicholas Nickleby*, ed. of 1867.

61 For the public effect, cf. A. S. G. Canning, *The Philosophy of Charles Dickens*, p. 102 et seq.

62 Cf. Langlois, loc. cit.

63 Preface to *Nicholas Nickleby*, ed. of 1867.
64 *Dickens as an Educator*, Editor's Preface, p. v.
65 *Barnaby Rudge*, ch. XXXVII.
66 Cf. *Nicholas Nickleby*, ch. XLVI.
67 *Hard Times*, book I, ch. IX.
68 *Dombey and Son*, ch. XXXIV.
69 *Pickwick Papers*, ch. XLII.
70 Cf. Frank Lockwood, *The Law and Lawyers of Pickwick*: 'The public, to my mind, owe a deeper debt of gratitude to the man who, by his wit, courage, and industry, has brought about reforms in our legal administration, for which all litigants and honourable practitioners should all alike be grateful' (p. 104).
71 Cf. *Quarterly Review*, vol. LXV (1839–40), p. 272 et seq. for a contemporary examination of the question.
72 Forster, *The Life of Charles Dickens*, vol. III, ch. I.
73 *Judge Lynch of America: His Two Letters to Charles Dickens*, Letter I.
74 *Oliver Twist*, ch. L.
75 Cf. *The Old Curiosity Shop*, chs XXXVIII and LXXXIII; *A Christmas Carol*, 'Stave Four'; *Dombey and Son*, ch. XLVII; *Bleak House*, ch. XVI; *Little Dorrit*, book I, chs IX and XII.
76 *Dombey and Son*, ch. XLVII.
77 *The Old Curiosity Shop*, ch. XV.
78 Cf. *Nicholas Nickleby*, chs XXII and L; *Bleak House*, ch. XXXI; *Little Dorrit*, book I, ch. III; *Oliver Twist*, ch. XXXII.
79 *Pickwick Papers*, ch. VII; *Hard Times*, book II, ch. I.
80 See, esp., *Oliver Twist*, ch. III.
81 Cf. *Nicholas Nickleby*, ch. L; *The Old Curiosity Shop*, ch. XXXI.
82 *A Christmas Carol*, 'Stave Three'.
83 Kitton, *The Novels of Charles Dickens: a Bibliography and Sketch*, pp. 38–9, gives an example of the novel's influence on 'the formation of institutions for the benefit of waifs and strays like poor Oliver.'
84 See, esp., *Bleak House*, chs XI, XXI, XLVII.
85 *American Notes*, ch. III, 'Boston'.
86 *Bleak House*, ch. IV, 'Telescopic Philanthropy'.
87 *Oliver Twist*, ch. II. The immediate reference is to one board, but it seems to apply to the whole law.
88 Cf. also *The Chimes*, 'Second Quarter'; *Little Dorrit*, book I, ch. XXXI; *Our Mutual Friend*, book I, chs XI and XVI; book II, ch. IX.
89 *The Factory Controversy; a Warning against Meddling Legislation*, pp. 35–6.
90 Cf., e.g., *Punch*, vol. IV (1843), p. 46: 'The Milk of Poor law kindness'.
91 Walpole, op. cit., vol. IV, p. 365.
92 Ibid.
93 *Workhouses and Pauperism*, 1898, p. 22.
94 *Prisons and Prisoners*, ch. II, 'The fictions of Dickens upon Solitary Confinement'.

95 *American Notes*, ch. vii, 'Philadelphia, and its solitary Prison'.
96 *Prisons and Prisoners*, ch. ii.
97 Garraud, *Traité de droit pénal français*, 1898, vol. ii, p. 40.

Five *Implicit social comment in Dickens's novels*

1 A. S. G. Canning (*The Philosophy of Charles Dickens*, p. 13) says the
novels were 'sought for, read, mentally devoured by the British public,
with an eager delight never surpassed if equalled.'

2 Cf. 'Horatio Sparkins'; 'The Tuggs's at Ramsgate'; 'Mrs Joseph Porter';
'The Steam Excursion'; etc.

3 Cf. 'The Broker's Man'; 'Miss Evans and the Eagle'; 'Shops and their
Tenants'; 'Thoughts About People'; 'Greenwich Fair'; 'Shabby-Genteel
People'; 'Making a Night of it'; etc.

4 *Nicholas Nickleby*, ch. i.

5 Ibid.

6 Ibid., ch. ii.

7 For the 'Railway Mania' cf. Walpole, op. cit., vol. v, pp. 58–9: 'Less
than 2,000 miles of railway had been constructed in 1843, and more
than 5,000 miles had been constructed in 1848.' Cf. also Greville, *Journal*,
vol. v, ch. xix, pp. 306–7 (16 Nov. 1845).

8 *Nicholas Nickleby*, ch. ii.

9 Ibid.

10 Ibid., ch. xliv: 'Stern, unyielding, dogged and impenetrable, Ralph cared
for nothing in life, or beyond it, save the gratification of two passions:
avarice, the first and prominent part of his nature, and hatred the second.'

11 Ibid., chs lvi and lxii.

12 Ibid., ch. x.

13 Ibid., ch. xix.

14 *A Christmas Carol*, 'Stave one'.

15 *Martin Chuzzlewit*, ch. viii.

16 *Dombey and Son*, ch. i.

17 Ibid.

18 *Hard Times*, book i, ch. vi.

19 Ibid., book i, ch. ii.

20 *Martin Chuzzlewit*, ch. lii.

21 *Nicholas Nickleby*, ch. xxi.

22 *Old Curiosity Shop*, ch. xxxi.

23 *Dombey and Son*, ch. xxxvi.

24 *Hard Times,* book i, ch. vii; book ii, chs x, xi, xii.

25 *Little Dorrit*.

26 *Our Mutual Friend*, book i, chs ii, x, xi. Cf. also the Hunters and
Nupkinses in *Pickwick* (chs xv, xxv) and the Waterbrooks in *David
Copperfield* (ch. xxv).

27 *Bleak House*, ch. LV.

28 Ibid., ch. LIV.

29 It should be observed that there was some public reaction against the portrayal of aristocratic elegance in the 'Silver Fork' school of novels. Dickens recognised his own opposition to this school, and exploited it in *Nicholas Nickleby* (ch. XXVIII), where Mrs Wititterley has the three-volume novel *The Lady Flabella* read to her, and a long burlesque quotation reveals Dickens's opinion of such writing.

30 *Quarterly Review*, vol. LXIV (June–Oct. 1839), article IV, p. 86.

31 Ibid., pp. 86–7.

32 R. H. Horne, *A New Spirit of the Age*, vol. I, p. 93.

33 *A Christmas Carol*, 'Stave Three: the second of the three spirits'.

34 Ibid.

35 Ibid.

36 Ibid.

37 Ibid., 'Stave Four: the last of the spirits'.

38 Cf. also the protagonists of 'Mrs. Lirriper's Lodgings', 'Doctor Marigold', and other Christmas stories.

39 *Nicholas Nickleby*, ch. XXXV.

40 *A Christmas Carol*, 'Stave Two: the first of the three spirits'.

41 Taine, *Littérature anglaise*, vol. V, p. 63.

42 For the 'Marchioness', see *The Old Curiosity Shop*, chs XXXIV, XXXVI. Cf. also *Bleak House*, ch. X, for the portrait of Guster.

43 *Sketches by Boz*, 'Scotland Yard'; *Nicholas Nickleby*, chs XXXVII and LII.

44 The *Quarterly Review* upbraided Dickens for having portrayed in Tony Weller an earlier type of coachman than existed by 1837 (vol. LIX, p. 500). Here again we may note Dickens's archaising tendency.

45 *The Old Curiosity Shop*, ch. XLIII.

46 *Bleak House*, chs VIII and LVII. Cf. Karl Marx, *Das Kapital*, English translation, vol. II, p. 467.

47 Cf. *Pickwick*, ch. XVI; *Oliver Twist*, ch. XXXII; *Nicholas Nickleby*, ch. XXII; *The Old Curiosity Shop*, ch. XV.

48 Hodder, *Life and Work of the Seventh Earl of Shaftesbury*, vol. I, p. 227.

49 Hodder (loc. cit.) cites a letter to Edward Fitzgerald in which Dickens said, 'With that nobleman's [Ashley's] most benevolent and excellent exertions, and with the evidence which he was the means of bringing forward, I am well acquainted.'

50 Cited Hodder, loc. cit.

51 *The Old Curiosity Shop*, ch. XLV.

52 Ibid., ch. XLVI.

53 Ibid., ch. XLIV.

54 *Fraser's Magazine*, vol. XXXVII (Jan.–June 1848), p. 15, article on 'The manufacturing poor'.

55 *American Notes*, ch. IV.

56 *Dombey and Son*, ch. IV.

57 *Bleak House*, ch. XI.
58 Cf. 'Mugby Junction', 1866.
59 *A History of Trade Unionism*, pp. 196–7.
60 Forster, *The Life of Charles Dickens*, vol. III, ch. II.
61 *Hard Times*, book I, ch. X.
62 *Unto This Last*, 1860, essay I, par. 10 n.
63 Possibly, over and above the inadequacy of his material, Dickens wished not to injure Mrs Gaskell's *North and South*, which was being written at the time. He wrote to her in April 1854, 'I am not going to strike, so don't be afraid of me. But I wish you would look at the story yourself, and judge – where and how near I seem to be approaching what you have in your mind' (*Letters*, 1882, vol. I, p. 355).
64 *Hard Times*, book II, ch. IV.
65 Ibid., book II, ch. I.
66 Ibid., book II, ch. I.
67 Ibid., book I, ch. I.
68 Ibid, book I, ch. III.
69 Ibid., book I, ch. II.
70 *Letters*, vol. I, p. 351.
71 *Hard Times*, book I, ch. XI.
72 Ibid., book I, ch. IX.
73 Ibid., book II, ch. VI. Cf. also book III, ch. IX.
74 *Unto This Last*, 1860, essay I, par. 10n.
75 Kitton, *Dickensiana: a Bibliography*, Introduction.
76 An analysis of this popularity would involve a lengthy aesthetic study of Dickens's novels. The social and psychological factor is the most important, but it is not the only one. In England, and even in America, Dickens was constantly being stopped in the streets by workers and lower-middle-class readers of his books who wanted to shake hands with him, and thank him from the bottom of their hearts (cf. Kitton, *Charles Dickens, his Life, Writings and Personality*, pp. 380–1, and *Letters*, vol. I, p. 66: letter to Mitton from Baltimore, 22 March 1842).
77 See the Conclusion.

Six   *Disraeli: social Toryism*

1 *Vivian Grey*, book I, ch. II.
2 Ibid., book III, ch. VI.
3 Ibid., book I, ch. VIII.
4 Cf. *Punch*, vol. VIII (1845), pp. 127, 168, 252, etc.
5 See above, pp. 98–9.
6 There is no obvious reason why Disraeli should not have been assimilated, but in fact he never felt like an Englishman. 'He had none of the hereditary prepossessions of a native Englishman' (J. A. Froude,

Lord Beaconsfield, a Biography, p. 68). 'No Englishman could approach Disraeli without some immediate consciousness that he was in the presence of a foreigner' (F. Greenwood, *Encyclopaedia Britannica* entry: 'Beaconsfield').

7 For the hostile reading of Disraeli's character, see T. P. O'Connor's *Life of Lord Beaconsfield*. The book is partisan and emotional, but it has the merit of bringing together between two covers all the unfavourable interpretations of Disraeli's actions that can be made. Many are plausible.

8 See his *Vindication of the English Constitution*, 1835.

9 Cf. *Popanilla* (1828) which contrasts 'the greatest good of the greatest number' with progress.

10 *Vindication of the English Constitution*, new edition, 1895, p. 88.

11 Ibid., p. 90.

12 *Selected Speeches of the Late Rt. Hon. the Earl of Beaconsfield*, ed. T. E. Kebbel, vol. I, pp. 51–2.

13 For Carlyle's influence on Disraeli, and his opinion of Disraeli, see Froude, *Lord Beaconsfield, a Biography*, ch. VI, 'Disraeli's brief, political and religious'. Traces of the influence will be observed in the novels.

14 Apart from *Popanilla* and his political pamphlets, Disraeli published, among other novels, *Contarini Fleming* in 1832, and *Henrietta Temple* in 1837.

15 *Coningsby*, book V, ch. II.

16 Ibid., book II, ch. I.

17 Ibid.

18 Ibid.

19 It was shortly after this time that the names 'Liberal' and 'Conservative' replaced 'Whig' and 'Tory'.

20 *Coningsby*, book II, ch. V.

21 Ibid.

22 Ibid., book VII, ch. II.

23 Ibid., book III, ch. III.

24 Ibid., book III, ch. II.

25 Ibid., book VII, ch. II.

26 Ibid., book II, ch. VII.

27 Ibid., book IV, ch. XIII.

28 Ibid., book III, ch. I.

29 Ibid., book IV, ch. III.

30 Ibid.

31 Ibid., book IV, ch. III. Disraeli is probably describing the Greg factory, near Manchester, which he had either seen, or read about in the social literature of the period, where it was frequently described. 'Millbank' is reminiscent of 'Quarrybank', which was the name of the Gregs's establishment. On the Gregs and their philanthropy, see Ure, op. cit., p. 346 et seq., and Engels, op. cit., pp. 186–7.

32 *Coningsby*, book IV, ch. IV.

33 Ibid., book IV, ch. IV.

34 Ibid., book II, ch. I.

35 Ibid., book III, ch. III.

36 Ibid.

37 Ibid., book III, ch. III.

38 Ibid., book IV, ch. XIII.

39 Ibid.

40 Ibid., book IX, ch. I.

41 Cf. Greville, op. cit., vol. IV, ch. I (4 January 1838), the account of the celebrations at Belvoir Castle for the Duke of Rutland's birthday, and his lavish generosity to his guests and tenants.

42 Belvoir Castle, the home of the Dukes of Rutland, can be recognised in Beaumanoir. Yet Disraeli's description, in *Coningsby*, book II, ch. II, differs remarkably from Greville's in vol. III of his *Journal*. Greville found the interior 'full of enormous faults, and wholly irretrievable'. The key to the mystery lies in one of Disraeli's letters to his sister, dated from Belvoir Castle, 10 August 1846: 'I thought you would like to have a line from Beaumanoir, though it is not in the least like Beaumanoir, but Coningsby Castle to the very life.' Now in book IV, ch. V Coningsby Castle is said to be built 'in a faulty and incongruous style of architecture'. Disraeli did not, however, wish to decry the Rutlands' taste publicly; they were his friend Manners's family.

43 The *Correspondence of Lord Beaconsfield with his Sister, 1832–52*, passim shows the preparation for this study of manners. Disraeli moved in aristocratic circles, and in 1842 visited Paris (where the king received him), and noted down his impressions.

44 *Sybil*, book VI, ch. XIII.

45 *Correspondence of Lord Beaconsfield with his Sister*, 30 August 1844.

46 *Sybil*, 'Advertisement', 1845.

47 Ibid., book I, ch. V.

48 Ibid., book II, ch. I.

49 Ibid., book III, ch. VIII. The final sentence is a reference to Carlyle's famous phrase: 'Cash-nexus the sole link between man and man'.

50 Ibid., book III, ch. VIII.

51 Ibid., book II, ch. XII. Disraeli is drawing on Cobbett's *The Protestant Reformation* here. For a critique of this historical theory, see W. J. Ashley's *English Economic History and Theory*, 1888, vol. II, ch. V.

52 *Sybil*, book II, ch. XII.

53 Ibid.

54 Ibid.

55 Such torchlight meetings were a common feature of the labour movement at the time. Cf. Walpole, op. cit., vol. IV, p. 384; Gammage, op. cit., p. 95, gives an account of a celebrated meeting at Hyde in 1838 which might have been Disraeli's model.

56 *Sybil*, book IV, ch. IV.

57 The Chartists did in fact add a sixth point to the five Disraeli
enumerates: the equalisation of parliamentary electoral constituencies.

58 On the Birmingham riots, cf. Walpole, op. cit., vol. IV, pp. 386–7.

59 On the arrest of the Chartist leaders, cf. Walpole, op. cit., vol. IV, p. 388;
and Lovett, *Autobiography*, pp. 227–41. Disraeli follows the main lines of
these recent events, but idealises and dramatises in detail to please his
fancy.

60 *Sybil*, book V, ch. I.

61 Ibid., book IV, ch. XV.

62 Ibid., book III, ch. I. The principal tenet of Owenism was indeed that
there should be self-supporting communities organised along
co-operative lines. But the co-operative sketched in here by Disraeli,
whose object is to create new capitalists, is quite unlike Owen's dream
villages. 'The keystone of Robert Owen's Co-operative system of
industry was the elimination of profit, and the extinction of the
profit-maker': B. Potter, *The Co-operative Movement in Great Britain*,
p. 21. Disraeli, like the other reactionary interventionist leaders, seems
to have accepted the popular view of Owenism.

63 *Sybil*, book V, ch. IV.

64 Ibid., book V, ch. III.

65 Ibid., book II, ch. III.

66 Ibid., book II, ch. III.

67 Ibid., book III, ch. II.

68 Ibid., book II, ch. III.

69 Ibid., book II, ch. IX.

70 Ibid., book II, ch. IX. If we are to believe W. R. Greg, who knew the
industrial population well, Disraeli's picture was 'singularly unreal and
untrue....His costume too (to speak technically) is almost uniformly
incorrect' (*Westminster Review*, vol. XLIV, p. 143).

71 *Sybil*, book II, ch. XIII.

72 Ibid., book III, ch. I. Disraeli almost quotes the text of the 1842 Report
word for word: 'In this mode of labour the leather girdle passes round the
body, and the chain is between the legs, attached to the cart, and the
lad drags on all-fours, as in figure 20' (*Children's Employment
Commission, First Report*, p. 98). The Report was illustrated with figures
showing the various attitudes assumed in work, and these did much to
affect readers' feelings.

73 Ibid. Cf. *Children's Employment Commission, First Report*, p. 81, for an
engraving of a trapper, squatting by the door he has to open to let
waggons through. 'Their occupation is one of the most pitiable in a
coal-pit, from its extreme monotony....Their whole time is spent in
sitting in the dark for twelve hours' (*Report*, p. 61).

74 Disraeli draws the subsequent information from the *Report of the
Select Committee on Payment of Wages* (Truck Report), 1843.

75 *Sybil*, book III, ch. I.

76 Disraeli stayed close to the official Report, but exaggerated certain
details. Waistcoats were never mentioned in the inquiry, only pieces
of cloth (p. 2, q. 2). Disraeli made particular use of the first
deposition, made by Squire Autey. There he found: the threat of
dismissal for recalcitrant workers; the general increase of prices;
foodstuffs distributed as wages (tea, sugar, bacon, etc.); and the great
distance to be travelled to the shop each morning (pp. 2–4). Nevertheless,
the scene is unconvincing; it seems as though Disraeli had no idea how
to make working-class people speak. According to Greg, the dialect
he puts into their mouths is artificial and false (*Westminster Review*,
vol. XLIV, p. 143).

77 On the unique character of Willenhall, see *Children's Employment
Commission*, Appendix to the *Second Report*, part II, pp. 368–9.

78 *Sybil*, book III, ch. IV.

79 According to Horne, the population had grown from 5,834 in 1831 to
8,695 at the last census (loc. cit.).

80 *Sybil*, book III, ch. IV.

81 The depositions taken by Horne are full of analogous cases.

82 'I have it in evidence, corroborated by a private letter, that a master,
wishing to get rid of an apprentice, sold him' (Horne Report, no. 484,
q. 46).

83 Here again Horne provides abundant evidence from life: 'They have no
morals; moral feelings and sentiments do not exist among the children
and young persons of Willenhall' (no. 542, q. 49). 'Does not know the
Queen's name' – these words recur frequently in Horne's examination
of witnesses: cf. no. 155, q. 35; no. 160, q. 36; no. 163, q. 37.

84 For the malformation produced by working with files, see Horne,
no. 402, q. 41. Another witness showed Horne a scar on his forehead:
no. 148, q. 34.

85 *Sybil*, book III, ch. IV. Cf. Horne's witness no. 140, q. 32: 'His master
has cut his head open five times – once with a key, and twice with a
lock; knocked the corner of a lock into his head twice – once with an
iron bolt, and once with an iron shut – a thing that runs into the staple.'
Other parallels can be found.

86 Many of Horne's witnesses could not spell their names: some did not
even know them. Cf. no. 133, q. 30; no. 140, q. 32.

87 *Sybil*, book III, ch. IV. There is no support in Horne for this ceremony;
Disraeli has either invented it, or attributed a popular superstition from
some other source to Willenhall. The pagan and barbaric customs
described in the report might have suggested it, and Horne does say that
the inhabitants of Willenhall did not marry outsiders.

88 Ibid. This is well supported by Horne's witnesses. Cf. pp. 561–2, q. 52.
And consider no. 136, q. 31: 'Never heard of Moses; never heard of St.
Paul. Has heard of Christ; knows who Jesus Christ was: he was Adam.'

89 The workers called the linty cotton waste that flew around the mills

'devil's dust'; it was also a cheap cloth they used for their clothes.

90 'Laudanum and treacle, administered in the shape of some popular elixir, affords these innocents a brief taste of the sweets of existence' (*Sybil*, book II, ch. x). It was sold under the name of 'Godfrey's Cordial', and used to soothe infants. On its effects, cf. Engels, op. cit., ch. v, 'Results'.

91 *Sybil*, book IV, ch. IV. Disraeli is exaggerating and dramatising at this point. The ritual described by Sidney Webb, *A History of Trade Unionism*, (p. 114) is far less complicated. Moreover, such practices were not universal. Disraeli had no parliamentary inquiry on union practices to refer to; he was reduced to newspapers and rumour. Note that he uses the word 'lodge' later in the scene; clearly he has drawn on freemasonry for his setting.

92 *Sybil*, book IV, ch. IV.

93 *Westminster Review*, vol. XLIV, p. 141.

94 *Punch*, cf. nos. for 26 June 1847, 7 July 1849, etc.

95 *Correspondence of Lord Beaconsfield with his Sister*, letter of 17 September 1845.

96 He was well aware that he was doing this. Thomas Cooper tells how he went to see Disraeli shortly after the publication of *Sybil* to ask for his help with the publication of his own *Purgatory of Suicides*. Disraeli said to him, 'I wish I had seen you before I finished my last novel. My heroine, Sybil, is a Chartist' (Cooper's *Autobiography*, p. 264).

97 For the publicity given to parliamentary reports, and its limitations, see the Conclusion.

98 *Sybil*, book I, ch. v.

99 *Tancred*, book III, ch. I.

100 Ibid., book III, ch. VII.

101 Ibid., book II, ch. IX.

102 Ibid., book IV, ch. VII.

103 Ibid.

104 Ibid., book VI, ch. XII.

105 Ibid., book III, ch. IV.

106 Ibid., book IV, ch. III.

Seven *Mrs Gaskell and Christian interventionism*

1 'His father was Mr Obadiah Newbroom, of the well-known manufacturing firm of Newbroom, Stag, and Playforall. A staunch dissenter himself, he saw with a slight pang his son Thomas turn Churchman, as soon as the young man had worked his way up to be the real head of the firm' (Kingsley, *Yeast*, ch. VI).

2 Professor Minto's conjecture that *Mary Barton* was suggested by Disraeli's social novels does not seem plausible. Mrs Gaskell's novel was

started in the same year as *Coningsby* (1844), and shows no sign of having been influenced by it. The two writers share a certain common spirit, but it is only that of the interventionist reaction, which was in the air at the time. *Mary Barton* and *Sybil* are alike products of the emotional needs which turned the novel to the social predicament (cf. *Fortnightly Review*, New Series, vol. XXIV (1878)). Nor does Mrs Gaskell ever seem to have owed anything to Dickens; on the contrary, Dickens was indebted to her; many of the characters and incidents in *Hard Times* (1854) were suggested by *Ruth*.

3 *Mary Barton*, ch. XXXVII.
4 Ibid., ch. XVI.
5 Ibid., ch. XXXVII.
6 Ibid., ch. I.
7 Ibid., ch. IX.
8 Ibid.
9 Ibid., ch. XVI.
10 Ibid., ch. X. Mrs Gaskell's frequent use of the form 'trades' union' shows that she still confused unions of men in one craft or occupation with a general league of all workers. Cf. Sidney Webb, *A History of Trade Unionism*, p. 102.
11 *Mary Barton*, ch. XVI.
12 Ibid., ch. XVII.
13 Ibid., ch. XV.
14 Ibid., ch. VI.
15 Ibid., ch. XV.
16 Ibid.
17 Ibid., ch. XVI.
18 Ibid., ch. XXXVII.
19 Ibid.
20 Ibid., ch. VI.
21 Ibid.
22 Ibid.
23 Ibid., ch. X.
24 Ibid., ch. XXXVII.
25 Cf. W. R. Greg, 'Mary Barton', *Edinburgh Review*, vol. LXXXIX, p. 402 et seq., reprinted in *Essays on Political and Social Science, contributed chiefly to the Edinburgh Review* (1853), p. 346 et seq.
26 *Essays on Political and Social Science*, p. 347.
27 *Mary Barton*, ch. IV.
28 Ibid., ch. VIII.
29 Ibid., ch. IX.
30 Ibid.
31 Ibid.
32 *Manchester Guardian*, 28 February and 7 March 1849.
33 *Edinburgh Review*, vol. LXXXIX, p. 402 eq seq., reprinted in *Essays on*

Political and Social Science, contributed chiefly to the Edinburgh Review, p. 346.

34 *Essays on Political and Social Science,* p. 347.

35 Ibid., pp. 362–3.

36 For the picturesque contrast between North and South, cf. *North and South,* ch. VII, 'New scenes and faces'.

37 *North and South,* chs IV, XVI.

38 Ibid., ch. XXI.

39 Ibid., ch. XX.

40 Ibid., ch. X.

41 Ibid., ch. XVIII.

42 Ibid., ch. XV.

43 The importation of Irish labour played an important part in the social history of the period. The temptation to use this cheap and docile work-force was particularly strong for the Lancashire industrialists who were close to Liverpool and could communicate with Ireland easily.

44 *North and South,* ch. XXII.

45 Ibid., ch. XXXIX.

46 Ibid., ch. LI.

47 Ibid., ch. XIII. See Ure, op. cit., pp. 380–1, on the workers' complaints about ventilators.

48 *North and South,* ch. XIII.

49 Ibid., ch. XXVIII.

50 Dickens warmly congratulated the author (A. W. Ward, loc. cit.). The book went into three editions before the end of 1855.

51 It is quite possible that Mrs Gaskell's novel owed something to *Shirley,* which was published first. The two writers were friends, and wrote to each other about their literary projects.

52 *Shirley,* ch. II.

53 Ibid., ch. VIII.

54 Ibid., ch. II.

55 Ibid., ch. XIX.

56 Cf. *Life of Charlotte Brontë,* by Mrs Gaskell, vol. I, ch. VI.

57 *Shirley,* ch. VI.

58 Ibid., ch. II.

59 Ibid., ch. V.

60 It should be added that the working-class characters in *Shirley,* like Joe Scott the overlooker (ch. V) and William Farren the weaver (ch. VIII), are picturesque and convincing. Although Charlotte Brontë knew nothing about the urban industrial populace, she knew the Yorkshire peasantry intimately. And the mill-workers in the uncultivated valleys where mills began to appear at the time of the action of *Shirley* were almost unchanged peasants.

61 *A History of the Factory Movement,* vol. II, p. 259.

62 R. H. Horne, *A New Spirit of the Age*, vol. I, pp. 239–41. As editor, Horne furnished a corrective note to his contributor's strident criticism, submitting 'that the critic does not admit enough on the other side. We think that Mrs. Trollope is clever, shrewd, and strong.'

63 *Domestic Manners of the Americans*, 1832: *The Vicar of Wrexhill*, 1837.

64 *A Memoir of Frances Trollope*, by her daughter-in-law, Frances Eleanor Trollope, vol. I, pp. 295–300.

65 Ibid., vol. I, pp. 300–2.

66 Ibid., vol. I, p. 301.

67 See especially the scenes at the Deep Valley Factory.

68 *Michael Armstrong*, book III, ch. IX.

69 Ibid., book II, ch. XI.

70 *Memoir of Frances Trollope*, vol. I, p. 301.

71 In 1844 Mrs Trollope published another novel dealing with social problems: *Jessie Phillips*, which protested against the cruelties of the new Poor Law. It was as weak and unconvincing as *Michael Armstrong*, and is not worth consideration here, as it does not consider the industrial question.

72 See Mrs C. L. Balfour, *A Sketch of Charlotte Elizabeth*.

73 Ibid., p. 43.

74 See above, pp. 106–7.

75 *Helen Fleetwood*, ch. X.

76 The spinners were the principal workers, superintending the frames. 'Piecers', or 'pieceners', were workers – often children – who joined up the thread whenever it broke. 'Scavengers' were usually children, who had to crawl under the machines while they were working, to pick up the cotton waste.

77 The author is quoting from parliamentary reports.

78 *Helen Fleetwood*, ch. XIX.

79 Ibid., ch. XI.

80 See, e.g., the rhetorical tirade, packed with factual evidence on child labour in factories, in ch. X.

81 Charlotte Elizabeth, *Works*, American edition, Introduction by Mrs Harriet Beecher Stowe.

82 *Helen Fleetwood*, ch. XVII.

Eight   Kingsley: Christian socialism

1 *North and South* and *Hard Times* were written after *Alton Locke*, but Kingsley was still the latest arrival on the scene of interventionist novel-writing.

2 The following account of his life is taken from *Charles Kingsley. His Letters and Memories of his Life*, by his widow, Fanny Kingsley; 3rd ed., 1877.

3 F. Kingsley, *Charles Kingsley. His letters and Memories of his Life*, vol. I, p.48.

4 Most of the young men entering upon literary life between 1830 and 1840 underwent some such crisis: cf. Browning's *Pauline* (1833) and *Paracelsus* (1835). Kingsley came to hate pantheism, and Shelley, who had given him the greatest pleasure: cf. *Yeast*, ch. I. Nevertheless it left him with an instinctive imaginative preference for a theory of divine immanence, against which his reason protested in vain. Rigg, in *Modern Anglican Theology* (1857) charged him with pantheism, and substantiated his case.

5 On Maurice, see *Life and Letters*, by his son.

6 For the influence of this book on Kingsley, cf. *Charles Kingsley. His Letters and Memories of his Life*, vol. I, p. 84 et seq.

7 C. W. Stubbs, *Charles Kingsley and the Christian Social Movement*, p. 21.

8 Quoted by Ellis Yarnall in 'Charles Kingsley: a reminiscence', in *Wordsworth and the Coleridges with other memories*, 1899, p. 190.

9 J. M. Ludlow (in *The Economic Review*, 1893, p. 497) says that Kingsley incurred the squire's ill-will by refusing to sit up and drink with him: he was a 'five-bottle man' of the old school. Also Kingsley asked him for money to build schools with, and dared to tell him that 'some of his cottages were not fit to live in'.

10 It was in the course of this that Newman wrote his *Apologia pro vita sua* (1864).

11 *Charles Kingsley. His Letters and Memories of his Life*, vol. I, p. 121.

12 See above, pp. 101–2.

13 'Great Cities and their influences on good and evil', in *Sanitary and Social Essays*.

14 *Charles Kingsley. His Letters and Memories of his Life*, vol. I, p. 121.

15 Ibid.

16 Ibid., p. 119.

17 Ibid., p. 141.

18 Ibid., p. 306.

19 Ibid., pp. 314–15.

20 *The Saint's Tragedy*, act II, sc. iv.

21 Ibid., act II, sc. vii.

22 Ibid., Introduction.

23 *Life of F. D. Maurice*, vol. II, p. 35.

24 J. M. Ludlow, loc. cit., p. 486.

25 The following is drawn from Ludlow, loc. cit.; Stubbs, op. cit.; and Brentano, *Die Christliche-soziale Bewegung in England*, 2nd ed., 1883.

26 It was here that Maurice introduced Kingsley to Ludlow (*Life of F. D. Maurice*, vol. I, p. 460). It is significant that Maurice went to the recruiting office to try and register as a special constable against the Chartists (ibid., vol. I, p. 472).

27 *Politics for the People*, 'Prospectus', no. 1.

28 Ibid., 'Party Portraits, by John Townsend' [Ludlow]: 'The Tory', no. 4; 'The Conservative', no. 7; 'The Whig', no. 12; 'The Radical', no. 13.

29 Ibid., 'More Last Words', no. 17.

30 *Christian Socialist*, no. 10.

31 *Life of F. D. Maurice*, vol. I, pp. 536–8.

32 Cabet, who came to London at this time, may have exchanged ideas with them: see a letter describing him as 'Cabet the Icarian', in the *Christian Socialist*, no. 35. On the 'Union Shop movement', from 1828 to 1832, see Beatrice Webb, *The Co-operative Movement in Great Britain*, 2nd ed., p. 44 et seq.

33 Beatrice Webb, op. cit., p. 119.

34 Ibid., p. 120.

35 *Christian Socialist*, no. 1.

36 Ibid., no. 12. Ruskin's famous phrase 'There is no wealth but life' amounts to the same thing.

37 Ibid., no. 4.

38 Ibid., nos 31 and 32.

39 e.g., ibid., no. 2.

40 *Charles Kingsley. His Letters and Memories of his Life*, vol. I, p. 156.

41 These letters were signed 'Parson Lot'. Kingsley took this name at a meeting at Maurice's one night when he found himself alone in his opinion, and subsequently used it for several pamphlets.

42 *Politics for the People*, no. 2, p. 28.

43 Ibid., p. 29.

44 'Thoughts on the Frimley Murder' by Parson Lot, contd. (*Christian Socialist*, no. 3).

45 'My Political Creed', by Parson Lot (*Christian Socialist*, no. 7).

46 J. M. Ludlow, loc. cit., p. 500.

47 *Charles Kingsley. His Letters and Memories of his Life*, vol. I, p. 236.

48 *Politics for the People*, no. 1, p. 3.

49 *Yeast* contains several allusions to Dickens's books, e.g. in chs VI and VII. We should have assumed that he had read Disraeli, like everybody else, if he had not told John Conington in a letter dated 18 December 1848 that this was not so; he had read *Coningsby*, but only after the publication of *Yeast*. Later in life he recalled that he had read Mrs Gaskell's novels, but there is nothing to indicate whether he knew *Mary Barton* when he started on *Yeast*. There is a gap of some months between the two novels. Cf. Edna Lyall, 'Mrs. Gaskell' in *Women Novelists of Queen Victoria's Reign*, by Mrs Oliphant et al., pp. 121–2.

50 *Charles Kingsley. His Letters and Memories of his Life*, vol. I, p. 191.

51 In all, he added three chapters (*Yeast*, chs V, VIII and XV) and an Epilogue. The differences between the texts of 1848 and 1851 are interesting in detail, but not of great importance. In his additions Kingsley expanded the aesthetic theme more than anything else, and heightened the attack on the Oxford Movement.

52 *Yeast*, ch. XV.

53 Ibid.

54 Kingsley speaks of 'the capacities of each man' in ch. VI. Whether he
   had read him or not, Kingsley had some acquaintance with Fourier: cf.
   Yeast, ch. III, ' "Fourierist!" cried Lancelot,' etc. And in *Charles Kingsley.*
   His Letters and Memories of his Life, vol. I, p. 219, there is a reference to
   'Fourierism', which Kingsley sees as a pagan doctrine. (Cazamian, *sic.*)
55 *Yeast*, ch. XIII.
56 Ibid., ch. X.
57 Ibid., ch. XI.
58 Ibid., ch. XVI.
59 Ibid.
60 *Charles Kingsley. His Letters and Memories of his Life*, vol. I, p. 191.
61 *Yeast*, ch. XV.
62 Ibid.
63 Ibid., ch. XVII.
64 Ibid.
65 Ibid., Epilogue.
66 Ibid., ch. XVI.
67 Ibid., ch. XIV.
68 Ibid., ch. XII.
69 Ibid., ch. XV.
70 Ibid.
71 Kingsley knew Ruskin's early work, although he seems not to have
   read him until after *Yeast* had been written. Cf. *Charles Kingsley. His*
   Letters and Memories of his Life, vol. I, p. 211: 'Read, by way of a nice
   mixture, Rabelais, Pierre Leroux and Ruskin.... The third, a noble,
   manful, godly book, a blessed dawn too' (letter dated 17 August
   1849).
72 *Yeast*, ch. XV.
73 Ibid., ch. VI.
74 Ibid. This is scoring a point off Disraeli, who had put at the head of
   Vivian Grey the Shakespearean epigraph, 'Why then the world's mine
   oyster, Which I with sword will open.'
75 *Yeast*, ch. VI.
76 Ibid.
77 Ibid., Epilogue.
78 Ibid.
79 Ibid., ch. III.
80 Ibid.
81 Ibid.
82 Ibid., ch. XIII.
83 *The Application of Associative Principles and Method to Agriculture; a*
   lecture, etc., 1851. Cf. Stubbs, op. cit., ch. IV.
84 *Yeast*, ch. VIII.
85 Ibid., ch. XIII.
86 Ibid., ch. XI.

87 Ibid., ch. IV. Cf. *Charles Kingsley. His Letters and Memories of his Life*, vol. I, pp. 314–15.

88 Ibid., pp. 219–20.

89 Ibid., p. 220.

90 e.g. Claude Mellot's aesthetic argument, carried over from the plan of *The Artists* (ch. xv).

91 *Quarterly Review*, vol. LXXXIX (1851), p. 531.

92 *Charles Kingsley. His Letters and Memories of his Life*, vol. I, pp. 285–7.

93 Ibid., p. 285.

94 Cf. *Charles Kingsley. His Letters and Memories of his Life*, vol. I, pp. 216–17, and the *Morning Chronicle* for 24 September 1849.

95 *Charles Kingsley. His Letters and Memories of his Life*, vol. I, p. 249. Kingsley was sensitive to the charges of plagiarism insinuated about *Alton Locke*, as may be seen from the passage in ch. VIII of the revised version of *Yeast* where he denies having learnt about agricultural distress from the *Morning Chronicle*. Chronology bears him out: ch. XIII of *Yeast* appeared in 1848, and the inquiry on *London Labour and the London Poor* in 1849.

96 Ibid., vol. I, p. 205.

97 See, e.g., *Kingsley et Thomas Cooper; Étude sur une source d'Alton Locke*, by L. Cazamian, Paris, 1903.

98 Carlyle's influence is to be found throughout *Yeast* and *Alton Locke*. Kingsley venerated him, and cited him constantly, especially in *Alton Locke*. He adopted his phrases – 'The Infinities', the 'Upper Powers', etc. – and imitated his general style, with coined words, contorted phrases, and apostrophes.

99 'I have tried to express in this book what I know were, 20 years ago, the feelings of clever working men looking upon the superior educational advantages of our class' (*Alton Locke*, 'Preface to the Undergraduates of Cambridge', 1861).

100 *Alton Locke*, ch. II.

101 Ibid., ch. III.

102 Ibid., ch. XIII.

103 Ibid.

104 Ibid.

105 Phrenology crept into this argument: head for head, the working class was as good as any other, if not better! (ch. IV).

106 Emersonian transcendentalism was equally distasteful to 'muscular Christianity'. Cf. *Alton Locke*, ch. IV, 'An Emersonian Sermon'.

107 *Alton Locke*, ch. I.

108 Ibid., ch. XI.

109 Kingsley took both phrases from Mayhew: cf. *Morning Chronicle*, 14 December 1849, letter XVII on *London Labour and the London Poor*.

110 *Alton Locke*, ch. II.

111 Ibid.

112 Ibid., ch. x. The details are repeated in *Cheap Clothes and Nasty*.
113 *Alton Locke*, ch. XXI. Kingsley was a natural anti-Semite, and stressed the part played by Jews in running the London sweat-shops.
114 Cf., e.g., *Morning Chronicle*, the issue of 18 December 1849, where a workshop is described with most of the technical details Kingsley puts forward. The role of the artist is reduced to a minimum in this writing, but remains, nonetheless, considerable.
115 *Alton Locke*, ch. VIII.
116 Ibid., ch. XXXV. Cf. Kingsley's account of his visit to cholera-ridden Bermondsey in 1849, in *Charles Kingsley. His Letters and Memories of his Life*, vol. I, pp. 216–17.
117 A pupil who knew him closely said of Kingsley, 'His senses were acute to an almost painful degree' (ibid., vol. I, p. 299).
118 *Alton Locke*, ch. XXVIII.
119 Ibid.
120 Here again the novel is following reality. Such meetings of farm labourers were common. Perhaps Kingsley had in mind the meeting at Goatacre in Wiltshire described by Léon Faucher in *Études sur l'Angleterre*, 1844, 2nd ed., 1856, vol. II, pp. 175–7. There are striking similarities between the general feeling of the two narratives, and some of the speeches reported. Faucher was drawing on contemporary newspaper reports which may have been known to Kingsley.
121 *Alton Locke*, ch. XXVIII.
122 Ibid.
123 Ibid.
124 Ibid., ch. IV.
125 Hughes, 'Prefatory Memoir to *Alton Locke*'.
126 *Alton Locke*, ch. X.
127 Ibid., ch. II.
128 Ibid., ch. X.
129 Ibid. Kingsley was quoting from memory: Carlyle had written of the 'twenty-thousandth part.'
130 Ibid., ch. XXXIV.
131 Ibid., ch. XXXIII. Kingsley has reverted to his own phrase from the 'Letter to the Chartists' in *Politics for the People*, no. 2.
132 *Alton Locke*, ch. XX. For a comparison of Kingsley and Carlyle as social thinkers, cf. M. Kauffmann, *Charles Kingsley, Christian Socialist and Social Reformer*, p. 181 et seq., and W. R. Greg, 'Kingsley and Carlyle' in *Literary and Social Judgements*.
133 The *Quarterly Review* listed twenty-two occurrences of the name 'Mammon' in *Alton Locke*, and objected to Kingsley's misuse of 'that misrepresented and misapplied Scriptural expression' (vol. LXXXIX (1851), p. 528).
134 *Alton Locke*, ch. XXXV.
135 Ibid., ch. XIV.

136 Hughes, 'Prefatory Memoir to *Alton Locke*'. Ludlow's query was only natural; the ending of *Alton Locke* is obscure and formless.

137 Ibid.

138 *Alton Locke*, ch. xxxvi, 'Dreamland'. Such writing was not uncommon in English Romanticism. Kingsley might have remembered Byron's *Heaven and Earth* without turning back to Lamartine's *Chute d'un ange*.

139 Ibid.

140 Ibid. This is clearly influenced by Robert Chambers's *Vestiges of Creation* (1844) and Darwin's work on coral reefs (1842).

141 Ibid., ch. xxxvi.

142 Ibid.

143 Ibid., ch. xxxvii.

144 Ibid.

145 Ibid.

146 Ibid.

147 Ibid.

148 Ibid., ch. xxxviii.

149 Ibid., ch. xl.

150 Ibid.

151 Ibid.

152 Ibid., ch. xli.

153 *Edinburgh Review*, vol. xciii (1851), reprinted in W. R. Greg, *English Socialism*.

154 Kingsley was highly sensitive about this charge. The Christian socialists, he complained, as true moderates, were doomed 'to hear Edinburgh Reviewers complaining of them for wishing to return to feudalism and medieval bigotry while Quarterly Reviewers are reviling them for sedition and communism' (*Who are the Friends of Order?*, p. 4). When he sent a copy of *The Saint's Tragedy* to Thomas Cooper, he wrote: 'At first sight it may seem to hanker after feudalism and the middle ages; I trust to you to see a deeper and somewhat more democratic moral in it' (*Charles Kingsley. His Letters and Memories of his Life*, vol. i, p. 184). The fact remains that, for all his objections, Kingsley's contemporaries thought they saw something of the idealistic revival's reactionary tendency about him.

155 Loc. cit., p. 9.

156 *Quarterly Review*, vol. lxxxix (1851), pp. 527–9.

157 *Charles Kingsley. His Letters and Memories of his Life*, vol. I, p. 277.

158 Ibid., p. 268.

159 Ibid., pp. 244–5.

160 For the attacks and abuse heaped on Kingsley, see *Charles Kingsley. His Letters and Memories of his Life*, vol. i, pp. 282–5. His sermon 'The message of the church to the labouring man' was attacked by the incumbent of the parish where it was delivered (ibid., vol. i, p. 289 et seq.).

161 *Who are the Friends of Order?*, p. 7.
162 *Alton Locke*, 'Preface to the Working Men of Great Britain', 1854.
163 *Alton Locke*, 'Preface to the Undergraduates of Cambridge', 1861.
164 e.g. Lord Vieuxbois, Lord Minchampstead, Claude Mellot, Miss Lavington.
165 *Two Years Ago*, 'Introductory'.
166 His principal works, other than those cited, were *Westward Ho!* (1855), *The Water Babies* (1863), and *Hereward the Wake* (1865). He was professor at Cambridge from 1860 to 1869.
167 Beatrice Webb, *The Co-operative Movement in Great Britain*, 2nd ed., p. 122.
168 Ibid., ch. v.
169 Kingsley was opposed to their interfering: cf. his letter to Hughes cited in the 'Prefatory Memoir to *Alton Locke*'. Its tone is already significant.
170 Beatrice Webb, op. cit., p. 171.
171 Ibid., pp. 154–6.
172 A. Métin, *Le socialisme en Angleterre*, ch. IV.
173 Beatrice Webb, op. cit., p. 221

Conclusion

1 This outline was intended as a brief, objective framework, presented once and for all, as a common measure of the information put forward in each novel. If the reader has held it in mind as a control, each novelist's personal addition or approach to social realities should have become apparent.
2 'It is a singular circumstance that at this day the factory system and its influence on society should be so little known in England; and that it should be possible for persons to advance the most contradictory opinions on the working of that system, and the morals and conduct of the people employed under it. Grafted as it now is in our political and social existence, its real character is yet to be learned by the people at large' W. Cooke Taylor, *Notes of a Tour in the Manufacturing Districts of Lancashire*. These words were written in 1842 (Cazamian *sic*, but the passage cannot be traced in Cooke Taylor's book; M. F.).
3 Kingsley's democratic instincts were closely connected with his pugnacity. But the influence of his personality and ideas did nothing to prevent Christian socialism from being only minimally democratic in 1850. Maurice, for example, was far more timid and conservative than Kingsley. He was alarmed by the outspokenness of *Alton Locke* (*Life of F. D. Maurice*, vol. II, p. 54), and appealed to the views of Southey and 'other eminent conservatives' (ibid., vol. II, p. 92). He disapproved of a pamphlet by Lord Goderich which described democracy as the great fact of the age (ibid., vol. II, p. 126 et seq.).

4 *Popular History of England*, vol. VIII, p. 478.

5 *Helen Fleetwood*, ch. XVIII.

6 *Sybil*, book II, ch. V.

7 *Kingsley's Place in Literature*, reprinted from *The Forum* (1895), p. 570.

8 E. J. Milliken, 'A Man of the Crowd to Charles Dickens', *Gentleman's Magazine* (1870), pp. 277–9.

9 Fragments at least of other testimony ought to be cited. On learning of Dickens's death, Lovett wrote, 'In his own inimitable way he has perhaps done more to expose wrong and injustice and to improve society socially and politically than any other worker or writer of the present century' (*Autobiography*, p. 416). The *Spectator* of 2 June 1870, pp. 716–17, said: 'he has given a greater impulse than any man of his generation to that righteous hatred of caste-feeling and class-cruelty which more and more distinguishes modern society.' Cf. also the *Graphic*, Christmas number, 1870, p. 19. In a sermon preached after Dickens's death, Dean Stanley summed him up as follows: 'By him that veil was rent asunder, which parts the various classes of society. Through his genius the rich man, faring sumptuously every day, was made to see and feel the presence of Lazarus at his gate....If by any such means he has brought the rich and poor nearer together, and made Englishmen feel more nearly as one family, he will not assuredly have lived in vain' (*A Sermon Preached in Westminster Abbey, the Sunday following the funeral of Dickens*, pp. 12, 14). Lord Ashley wrote in his journal on 20 December 1871: 'Forster has sent me his Life of Dickens. The man was a phenomenon, an exception, a special production.... He was sent, I doubt not, to rouse attention to many evils and many woes' (*Life*, book III, ch. XXXI, p. 298).

10 The first historian of industrial legislation attributed this triumph to a transformation of public feeling: 'Many who, in 1830, were startled at the novelty and extreme nature of a remedial measure, regulating the hours of labour in all factories to ten per day...were, in 1847, astonished that opposition should have been offered, to a proposition so reasonable and humane' ('Alfred', op. cit., vol. II, p. 289).

11 On all this see J. K. Ingram, *History of Political Economy*, p. 221 et seq.

12 Walpole, op. cit., vol. V, p. 205.

13 Ibid., pp. 58–60.

14 Rose, op. cit., p. 148.

15 Walpole, op. cit., vol. V, p. 458.

16 Leonce de Lavergne, *Essai sur l'Économie rurale de l'Angleterre*, 1854, pp. 15, 104, etc.

17 Sidney Webb, *A History of Trade Unionism*, ch. IV, 'The New Spirit and the New Model'.

18 Ibid., p. 183.

19 *The Times*, 22 March 1860.

20 Hodder, *The Seventh Earl of Shaftesbury as a Social Reformer*, pp. 46–7.

21 Sidney Webb, op. cit., pp. 161, 171, 221–2, 282.

22 Reade, *It is Never too Late to Mend*, 1856.

23 Mrs Craik, *John Halifax, Gentleman*, 1857.

24 *Felix Holt*, 1866. George Eliot defined the *roman-à-thèse* in the following account of her work: 'My function is that of the aesthetic, not the doctrinal teacher – the rousing of the nobler emotions that make mankind desire the social right, not the prescribing of special measures, concerning which the artistic mind, however strongly moved by social sympathy, is often not the best judge' (*Life*, by J. W. Cross, vol. III, p. 330).

25 *Das Kapital*, 1867. See esp. vol. II. The great majority of observations, statistics, reports, etc. cited by Marx were published after Engels's book (1844), and most of them later than 1860. Marx was studying an England that had been transformed by 'social compunction'.

26 Speech on 20 July 1838, *Hansard*, series 3, vol. XLIV.

27 Kingsley said that the Bristol riots of 1831 had a similar effect: 'From the sad catastrophe I date the rise of that interest in Social Science; that desire for some nobler, more methodic, more permanent benevolence' ('Great Cities and their influences on good and evil', *Sanitary and Social Lectures and Essays*.)

28 *Socialism in England*, p. 116.

29 *Popular History of England*, vol. VIII, ch. XXVI.

Bibliography

This bibliography is necessarily short. More extensive bibliographies are contained in the works on social history listed here. We have not mentioned purely literary studies of the novel. (See also p. xi.)

I   The social background

1   General English history, 1830–1850

Gardiner, S. R., *A Student's History of England*, vol. III, new ed., 1894.
Knight, Charles, *Popular History of England*, vol. VIII, *1856–62*, 1868.
Lee, G. C., *Leading Documents of English History*, 1900.
MacCarthy, J., *History of Our Own Times*, 1897.
Martineau, Harriet, *History of England during the Thirty Years' Peace*, 2 vols, 1849.
Seignobos, Charles, *Histoire politique de l'Europe contemporaine*, Paris, 2nd ed., 1899.
Walpole, Spencer, *A History of England from the Conclusion of the Great War in 1815*, 6 vols, 2nd ed., 1890.

Seignobos's book contains a bibliography of the principal source material.

2   Heavy industry around 1830

Babbage, Charles, *On the Economy of Machinery and Manufactures*, 3rd ed., 1832.
Baines, Sir E., *History of the Cotton Manufacture in Great Britain*, 1835.
Beard, Charles, *The Industrial Revolution*, 2nd ed., 1902.
Cunningham, W., *The Growth of English Industry and Commerce*, vol. II ('Modern Times'), 1892.
Gibbins, H. de B., *The Industrial History of England*, 2nd ed., 1891.
Hobson, J. S., *The Evolution of Modern Capitalism*, 1894.
Hyndman, H. M., *Commercial Crises of the Nineteenth Century*, 1892.
Macrosty, H. W., *Trusts and the State*, 1901.
Toynbee, Arnold, *The Industrial Revolution*, 1887.
Warner, G. T., *Landmarks in English Industrial History*, 1899.

Cunningham's work carries a bibliography. M. P. Mantoux's study of the origins of British industry carries a detailed bibliography.

3   Poverty around 1840

Adshead, Joseph, *Distress in Manchester*, 1842.

Buret, A. Eugène, *De la misère des classes laborieuses en Angleterre et en France*, 2 vols, Paris, 1840.

Cooke Taylor, W., *Notes of a Tour in the Manufacturing Districts of Lancashire*, 1842.

Engels, Frederick, *The Condition of the Working-Class in England in 1844*, English translation 1892.

Faucher, Léon, *Études sur l'Angleterre*, Paris, 1845.

Gaskell, P., *The Manufacturing Population of England*, 1833.

Gibbins, H. de B., *The Economic and Industrial Progress of the Century*, 1902.

Giffen, Sir Robert, *The Progress of the Working-Class in the Last Half Century*, 1884.

Kay, J. P., *The Moral and Physical Condition of the Working Class*, etc., 1832.

Mayhew, Henry, *London Labour and the London Poor*, 1851, etc.

Porter, G. R., *The Progress of the Nation*, 1851.

Rashleigh, W., *Stubborn Facts from the Factories*, 1844.

Torrens, R., *Letter on the Condition of England*, 1843.

Tuckett, J. D., *A History of the Past and Present State of the Labouring Population*, 1846.

It is impossible to give a full bibliography of the Parliamentary Reports relating to labour and the conditions of the poor here. The full list may be found in the *Catalogue of Parliamentary Reports, Papers, etc., Relating to Labour* published by King and Son, 3rd ed., 1894. The following were the reports which had the greatest effect on public opinion between 1830 and 1850:

Report of Select Committee on the Bill to Regulate the Labour of Children in Mills and Factories (Sadler Report), 1832.

Reports of Commissioners and Assistant Commissioners on the Condition of the Handloom Weavers, 1839–41.

Report of the Select Committee on the Operation of the Law which Prohibits the Payment of Wages in Goods, etc. (Truck Report), 1842.

Royal Commission on the Employment and Conditions of Children and Young Persons:
    First Report: Mines and Collieries, 1842.
    Second Report: Trade and Manufacture, 1842–5.

Karl Marx's *Das Kapital*, 1867, gives a complete bibliography relating to poverty around 1860, parts of which are relevant to the earlier period.

4   Industrial legislation

'Alfred' [Samuel Kydd], *A History of the Factory Movement from the Year 1802, to the Enactment of the Ten Hours' Bill in 1847*, 1857.

Cooke-Taylor, R. W., *The Modern Factory System*, 1891.

——, *Introduction to a History of the Factory System*, 1886.

——, *The Factory System and the Factory Acts*, 1894.

Fielden, J., *The Curse of the Factory System*, 1836.

Bibliography

Plener, Ernst von, *English Factory Legislation*, tr. F. L. Weinmann, 1873.
Weyer, O. W., *Die englische Fabrikinspection*, Tübingen, 1888.

There is a detailed bibliography in B. L. Hutchins and A. Harrison, *History of Factory Legislation*, 1903.

5   The labour movement

Bamford, Samuel, *Passages in the Life of a Radical*, new ed., 2 vols, 1894.
Cooper, Thomas, *Life, Written by Himself*, 1872.
Gammage, R. G., *History of the Chartist Movement*, new ed., 1894.
Halévy, Elie, *Thomas Hodgskin*, Paris, 1903.
Holyoake, R. G., *Life of Stephens*, 1881.
Howell, G., *The Conflicts of Capital and Labour Historically and Economically Considered*, etc., 2nd ed., 1890.
——, *Labour Legislation, Labour Movements, Labour Leaders*, 1902.
Lovett, William, *The Life and Struggles of William Lovett, in his Pursuit of Bread, Knowledge, and Freedom*, 1876.
Rose, J. Holland, *The Rise of Democracy*, 1897.
Schulze-Gaevernitz, Gerhart von, *Zum socialen Frieden*, 2 vols, Leipzig, 1890.
Webb, Sidney and Beatrice, *A History of Trade Unionism*, 1894.

The Webbs' book contains a bibliography of the union movement. The *Life of Francis Place* by Graham Wallas contains a lot of useful incidental information on Chartism.

6   Society and manners

Filon, Augustin, *La caricature en Angleterre*, Paris, 1902.
Greville, G. C., *Journal of the Reign of Queen Victoria, 1837–1852*, 8 vols, new ed., 1888.
Hart, A. B., *How our Grandfathers Lived*, 1903.
Hodder, Edwin, *The Life of a Century*, 1901.
Horne, Richard H., *New Spirit of the Age*, 2 vols, 1844.
Jameson, Mrs, *Memoirs and Essays, Illustrative of Art, Literature, and Social Morals*, 1846.
Lee, Sidney, *Queen Victoria, a Biography*, 2nd ed., 1903.
Martin, Sir Theodore, *Life of the Prince Consort*, 5 vols, 1875–80.
Punch; or the London Charivari, vols I–X, 1841–6.
Smith, Albert, *Gavarni in London*, 1849.
Traill, H. D., *Social England*, vols V and VI, 1896–7.

II   The intellectual climate

1   Individualism

(a) *Utilitarianism, radicalism, and liberal reform*

Albee, Ernest, *The History of Utilitarianism*, 1902.

352

Armitage-Smith, G., *The Free-Trade Movement*, 1898.
Chevrillon, André L., *Sydney Smith et la renaissance des idées libérales en Angleterre*, Paris, 1894.
Grote, Mrs Harriet, *The Philosophical Radicals of 1832*, 1866.
Halévy, Elie, *La formation du radicalisme philosophique*, 2 vols, Paris, 1901.
Held, A., *Zwei Bücher zur sozialen Geschichte Englands*, Leipzig, 1881.
Mackintosh, Sir James, *Miscellaneous Works*, 3 vols, 1846.
Morley, John, *Life of Cobden*, 2 vols, 1881.
Nicholls, Sir George, *History of the English Poor Law*, 2 vols, new ed., 1898.
Stephen, Sir Leslie, *The English Utilitarians*, 3 vols, 1900.
Ure, Andrew, *The Philosophy of the Factory System*, 1835.
Wallas, Graham, *Life of Francis Place*, 1898.

Held's book, tracing the individualist movement down to 1830, contains numerous bibliographical details.

(b) *Political economy*

Ingram, J. K., *History of Political Economy*, 1888.
McCulloch, J. R., *Principles of Political Economy*, 1825.
Malthus, T. R., *Essay on the Principle of Population*, new ed., 1803.
Marcet, Mrs, *Conversations on Political Economy*, 1816.
Mill, John Stuart, *Principles of Political Economy*, 1848.
Price, L. L., *A Short History of Political Economy in England*, 3rd ed., 1900.
Ricardo, David, *Principles of Political Economy and Taxation*, 1817.
Smith, Adam, *The Wealth of Nations*, Thorold Rogers edition, 1880.

McCulloch's *Literature of Political Economy*, 1845, is a bibliography of classical economics. The *Dictionary of Political Economy*, ed. J. Palgrave, gives separate bibliographies of each economist.

2   *The idealist and interventionist reaction*

(a) *The religious revival*

Caldecott, Alfred, *The Philosophy of Religion in England and America*, 1901.
Lecky, W. E. H., *History of England in the Eighteenth Century*, 12 vols, 1892.
Overton, J. H., *The Anglican Revival*, 1897.
Pike, G. H., *Wesley and his Preachers*, etc., 1903.
Thureau-Dangin, P., *La Renaissance catholique en Angleterre au dix-neuvième siècle*, parts 1 and 2, Paris, 1903.
Ward, W. G., *The Ideal of a Christian Church*, 1844.
Wesley, John, *The Journal of*, etc., popular ed., 2 volumes, 1903.
Withrow, W. H., *Makers of Methodism*, 1903.

A complete bibliography of the Oxford Movement would run to considerable length. None as yet exists.

(b) *Philanthropy*

Adshead, Joseph, *Prisons and Prisoners*, 1845.
——, *Our Present Gaol System*, etc., London, 1847.
Hodder, Edwin, *Life and Work of the Seventh Earl of Shaftesbury*, 1886.
——, *The Seventh Earl of Shaftesbury as a Social Reformer*, 1897.
Low, Sampson, *The Charities of London*, 1850.
Philanthropist, The, (quarterly journal), 1811–19.
Philanthropist, The, New Series, 1829–30.

The *Dictionary of National Biography* contains useful entries on the
philanthropists: Wilberforce, Wright, Buxton, Mrs Fry, etc.

(c) *Aesthetic and literary idealism*

Bardoux, J., *John Ruskin*, Paris, 1900.
Beers, H. A., *History of Romanticism in the Nineteenth Century*, 1902.
Brandes, G. M. C., *Die Haupströmungen der Literatur des neunzehnten
    Jahrhunderts*, vol. IV: *Der Naturalismus in England*, tr. A. Strodtmann,
    5th ed., Berlin, 1897.
Brooke, Stopford A., *The Poetry of Robert Browning*, 1902.
Browning, Elizabeth Barrett, *Poetical Works*, 6 vols, 1900.
Brunhes, J., *Ruskin et la Bible*, Paris, 1901.
Mackail, J. W., *Life of William Morris*, 2 vols, 1899.
Norton, Mrs C. E. S., *A Voice from the Factories*, 1836.
Tennyson, Alfred, Lord, *Poetical Works*, 1898.

Bardoux's book contains a bibliography of Ruskin. There is no list of social
poetry between 1830 and 1850. For the works of Cooper, Bethune,
Elliott, etc., consult the *Dictionary of National Biography*. For literature in
general, see V. Scudder, *Social Ideals in English Letters*, 1898.

(d) *Carlyle*

Flugel, E., *Carlyles religiöse und sittliche Entwicklung*, Leipzig, 1887.
Froude, J. A., *Thomas Carlyle; a History of the First 40 Years of his Life*, new
    ed., 1890.
——, *Thomas Carlyle; a History of his Life in London*, 1884.
Garnett, Richard, *Carlyle* (Great Writers series), 1887.
Hensel, Paul, *Thomas Carlyle*, Stuttgart, 1900.

Garnett's book gives a bibliography of Carlyle by J. P. Anderson.

(e) *English interventionism*

Andler, Charles, *Les origines du socialisme d'État en Allemagne*, Paris, 1897.
Boutmy, E. G., *Essai d'une psychologie politique du peuple anglais*, Paris, 1901.
Chasles, Philarette, *Études sur la littérature et les mœurs de l'Angleterre au
    dix-neuvième siecle*, Paris, 1850.

Bibliography

Coleridge, S. T., *Lay Sermons*, etc., 1845.
Gibbins, H. de B., *English Social Reformers*, 1892.
Helps, Sir Arthur, *The Claims of Labour*, etc., 1845.
Lalor, J., *Money and Morals*, 1852.
Landor, Walter Savage, *Imaginary Conversations*, 6 vols, new ed., 1891–3.
Manners, Lord John James Robert, *England's Trust, and Other Poems*, 1841.
Métin, A., *Le socialisme en Angleterre*, Paris, 1897.
Mill, John Stuart, *Autobiography*, 2nd ed., 1873.
——, *Dissertations and Discussions*, 3 vols, 1875.
Seeley, R. B. (published anonymously), *The Perils of the Nation*, 1843.
Smythe, G. S., *Historic Fancies*, 1844.
Southey, Robert, *Colloquies on Society*, 1829.
Verhaegen, P., *Socialistes anglais*, Louvain, 1898.
Webb, Sidney, *Socialism in England*, 3rd ed., 1901.

The Fabian pamphlet *What to Read*, etc., (4th edition: Fabian Pamphlets No. 29) gives a bibliography of the best works on interventionism in England.

III The social novel

1 Novels with a purpose, before 1830

Behn, Mrs Aphra, *Oroonoko*, reprinted from the original edition, 1886.
Brooke, Henry, *The Fool of Quality*, 4 vols, 1766.
Cross, Wilbur L., *Development of the English Novel*, 1899.
Defoe, Daniel, *Moll Flanders*, 1722.
Dowden, Edward, *The French Revolution and English Literature*, 1897.
Godwin, William, *Things as they Are*, etc. (*Caleb Williams*), 3 vols, 1796.
——, *St Leon* 3 vols, 1800.
——, *Mandeville*, 1817.
——, *Cloudesly*, 1830.
Holcroft, Thomas, *Anna St. Ives*, 7 vols, 1792.
Lloyd, Charles, *Edmund Oliver*, 2 vols, 1798.
Maigron, Louis, *Le roman historique à l'époque romantique*, Paris, 1898.
Opie, Mrs Amelia, *Adeline Mowbray*, 1805.
Péronne, J., *Englische Zustände im XVIII Jahrhundert, nach den Romanen von Fielding und Smollett*, Berlin, 1890.
Raleigh, Sir Walter, *The English Novel*, popular edition, 1903.
Stoddard, F. H., *The Evolution of the English Novel*, 1900.

Cross's book contains bibliographical information on the history of the English novel.

2 Bulwer

Bulwer, Edward, *England and the English*, 1833.
Cooper, Thomson, *Lord Lytton, a Biography*, 1873.

Jowett, B., *Lord Lytton*, 1873.
Life of Lord Lytton, by his son, 2 vols, 1874.
Watt, J. C., *Great Novelists*, 1885.

3   *Harriet Martineau*

Martineau, Harriet, *Autobiography*, 3 vols, 1877.
——, *The Factory Controversy; a Warning against Meddling Legislation*, 1855.
Miller, Mrs Fenwick, *Harriet Martineau*, 1884.
Morley, John, *Miscellanies*, vol. 3: 'Miss Martineau'.
Stephen, Leslie, 'Harriet Martineau' (*Dictionary of National Biography*).

4   *Dickens*

Canning, A. S. G., *The Philosophy of Charles Dickens*, 1880.
Dickens, Charles, *The Letters of Charles Dickens*, 2 vols, 1882.
——, *Speeches (Literary and Social)*, 1879.
Forster, John, *The Life of Charles Dickens*, 3 vols, 1872–4.
Gerschmann, Hans, *Studien über der modernen Roman*, Königsberg, 1894.
Gissing, George, *Forster's Life of Dickens, abridged and revised*, 1902.
——, *Charles Dickens; a Critical Study*, 1898.
Harrison, Frederic, *Dickens's Place in Literature*, 1894.
Hughes, J. L., *Dickens as an Educator*, 1900.
Joubert, André, *Charles Dickens, sa vie et ses œuvres*, Paris, 1872.
Judge Lynch of America; his Two Letters to Charles Dickens, 1859.
Kitton, F. G., *Charles Dickens, his Life, Writings and Personality*, 1901.
——, *The Novels of Charles Dickens: a Bibliography and Sketch*, 1897.
——, *Dickensiana: a Bibliography*, 1886.
Langton, Robert, *Dickens's Childhood and Youth*, 1883.
Lockwood, Sir Francis, *The Law and Lawyers of Pickwick*, 1896.
Marzials, F. T., *Life of Charles Dickens*, 1887.
Pierce, G. A., *The Dickens Dictionary*, etc., 1872.
Schmidt, Julian, *Charles Dickens. Eine Charakteristik*, Leipzig, 1852.
Taine, H. A., *Histoire de la Littérature anglaise*, vol. v, Paris, 1863.
Trumble, A., *In Jail with Charles Dickens*, 1896.
Ward, A. W., *Dickens*, 1882.
Weber, Ludwig, *Charles Dickens als sozialer Schriftsteller*, Müllheim, 1895.

Marzials's book contains a bibliography by J. P. Anderson, complete to 1895.
See also R. H. Shepherd, *The Bibliography of Dickens*, etc., 1880.

5   *Disraeli*

Bauer, B., *Disraelis romantischer und Bismarcks sozialistischer Imperialismus*,
    Chemnitz, 1882.
Beaconsfield, Lord, *Letters, a New Edition*, 1887.
Brandes, G., *Lord Beaconsfield, a Study*. tr. G. Sturge, 1880.

Bibliography

Bryce, James, *Studies in Contemporary Biography*, 1903.
Courcelle, Maurice, *Disraeli*, Paris, 1902.
Mr. Disraeli's Opinions, Political and Religious, etc., 1852.
B. Disraeli in a Series of 113 Cartoons from Punch, 1881.
Disraeli, B., *Selected Speeches of the Late Rt. Hon. the Earl of Beaconsfield*,
    2 vols, ed. T. E. Kebbel, 1882.
——, *Vindication of the English Constitution*, new ed., 1895.
——, *Correspondence with his Sister, 1832–52*, 1886.
Ewald, A. C., *The Rt. Hon. Benjamin Disraeli,…and his Times*, 2 vols, 1883.
Fraser, J. A. L., *Disraeli*, 1901.
Froude, J. A., *Lord Beaconsfield, a Biography*, 1890.
Gorst, H. E., *The Earl of Beaconsfield*, 1900.
Harrison, Frederic, *Disraeli's Place in Literature*, 1894.
Kebbel, T. E., *Life of Lord Beaconsfield*, 1888.
Meynell, W., *Benjamin Disraeli*, 2 vols, 1903.
O'Connor, T. P., *Life of Lord Beaconsfield*, 1879.
Traill, H. D., *Introduction to Sybil*, 1895.
Valmont, V., *La jeunesse de Lord Beaconsfield*, Paris, 1878.
Vogüé, E. M. de, 'Les Romans de Disraeli', *Revue des Deux Mondes*, 1 May
    1901.

6 Mrs Gaskell, etc.

Axon, W. E. A. and E., *Gaskell Bibliography*, 1895.
Balfour, Mrs C. L., *A Sketch of Charlotte Elizabeth*, 1854.
Bayly, Mrs A. E., *Mrs. Gaskell*, 1897.
Charlotte Elizabeth, *Helen Fleetwood*, 1841.
——, *Works, with an Introduction by Mrs. H. B. Stowe*, 2 vols, 1849.
Greg, W. R., *Mistaken Aims and Attainable Ideals of the Artizan Class*, 1876.
Lyall, Edna, *Mrs. Gaskell* (*Women Novelists of Queen Victoria's Reign*), 1897.
Montégut, E., *Écrivains modernes de l'Angleterre*, 2nd series, Paris, 1889.
Trollope, Mrs Frances, *Life and Adventures of Michael Armstrong, the Factory
    Boy*, 1840.
——, *Jessie Phillips*, 1844.
Trollope, Frances Eleanor, *Frances Trollope; her Life and Work*, 1895.

7 Kingsley

Brentano, L., *Die christliche-soziale Bewegung in England*, Leipzig, 1883.
Christian Socialism (*Tracts on*), *and Tracts by Christian Socialists*, 1850–1.
Christian Socialist, 1850–1.
Greg, W. R., *Literary and Social Judgements*, 1869.
Groth, E., *Charles Kingsley als Dichter und Sozialreformer*, Leipzig, 1893.
Harrison, Frederic, *Charles Kingsley's Place in Literature*, 1895.
Kauffmann, Revd M., *Charles Kingsley, Christian Socialist and Social Reformer*,
    1892.

Bibliography

Kingsley, Charles, *The Saint's Tragedy*, 1848.

——, *Sanitary and Social Lectures and Essays*, 1880.

——, *His Letters and Memories of his Life*, by his wife, 2 vols, 1877.

——, *The Message of the Church to the Labouring Man*, 5th ed., 1851.

——, *Alton Locke*, new ed. with a Memoir by T. Hughes, 1876.

——, *Who are the Friends of Order?* etc., 1852.

Marriott, J. A. R., *Charles Kingsley: Novelist*, 1892.

Maurice, F. D., *Life and Letters*, by his son, 2 vols, 1884.

——, *Politics for the People*, 1848.

Potter, Beatrice (Mrs Sidney Webb), *The Co-operative Movement in Great Britain*, 2nd ed., 1893.

Rigg, J. H., *Modern Anglican Theology*, 1857.

Stubbs, C. W., *Charles Kingsley and the Christian Social Movement*, 1899.

Brentano's book contains an excellent bibliography of Christian socialism after 1850.

Index

Index